cruz

P9-AOV-660

Smart
Kids
with
School
Problems

PRISCILLA L. VAIL

Smart Kids with School Problems

Things to Know and Ways to Help

E. P. DUTTON　　NEW YORK

Published in the United States by E. P. Dutton,
a division of NAL Penguin Inc.,
2 Park Avenue, New York, N.Y. 10016.

Published simultaneously in Canada by
Fitzhenry and Whiteside Limited, Toronto.

Library of Congress Cataloging-in-Publication Data

Vail, Priscilla L.
Smart kids with school problems.

Bibliography: p.
1. Gifted Children—Education—United States.
2. Learning disabilities—United States.   I. Title.
LC3993.9.V35   1987   371.95   87-502
ISBN: 0-525-24557-x

COBE

DESIGNED BY EARL TIDWELL

3 5 7 9 10 8 6 4

Grateful acknowledgment is made for permission to reprint excerpts from
the following works:

"Coaching for the SATs: What the Colleges Think," by William C. Hiss.
Reprinted by permission from *Independent School* (October 1984), copyright © 1984 by the National Association of Independent Schools.

Book review of *Frames of Mind: The Theory of Multiple Intelligences* by
Howard Gardner, by Priscilla L. Vail. Reprinted by permission from *In-*

TO
DONALD VAIL,
WHO GIVES ME
CARE, CRITICISM, AND COURAGE

CONTENTS

x   *Contents*

ACKNOWLEDGMENTS

To my lodestars, mentors, and companions, thank you.

Jean Anderson Luke, her colleagues Margaret Lawrence and Helen Ross, Katrina de Hirsch, Rita Rudel, Louise Bates Ames, and Leah Levinger opened windows on human development.

My colleagues in The Orton Dyslexia Society and the National Association of Independent Schools, particularly on the Academic Committee, have taught me a great deal. Through their national and regional conferences these organizations make research and practical educational techniques available to teachers and parents. But speakers finish speaking, and seminar planners fold up their easels; the printed word remains. To Blair McElroy, champion of wombats and editor of *Independent School*, and to Rosemary Bowler, meticulous, droll editor of *Annals of Dyslexia*, thanks on behalf of the millions of smart kids with school problems who benefit from the knowledge you make available.

The Fisher-Landau Foundation focuses on gifted children with learning disabilities. To Emily Fisher Landau, thanks for your great generosity, and for beaming in on this population. I appreciate the privilege of sitting on the Advisory Board and working alongside such distinguished colleagues.

Thanks to the Rippowam-Cisqua students, and others I have worked with, for sparking ideas, being willing to take risks, hanging in when the going was rough, and chanting that beautiful phrase "Oh, now I get it!"

To my colleagues in our profession, which, though beleaguered, is surely the most exciting in the world, thank you for all you give, daily, to students, parents, and one another. To parents of conundrum kids, thank you for trusting educators with your children. We shall try to be deserving.

Unending thanks to those companions who have test-driven this manuscript; left me alone when I needed to work, and been there when I emerged; offered suggestions, made me laugh, and kept me going. Particular thanks to Waldo, Margaret and Bill, Anne and Johnny, Gordon, Buzz, Soulsister Jane, and Betty.

To my family: Donald, Melissa, Norman, Luke, Thomas, Lucia, Jesse, Polly, Mark, and Angus, thanks for moral support, for enduring burned or tepid dinners, and understanding "sure, after the book is done." To those yet unborn, warm welcome when you arrive. To those no longer here, thank you for knowledge I sometimes fought against receiving.

To Ida Genovesi in Bedford and Gail Woodrow in Stonington, thank you for the comfort of your patient practical help.

Paula Diamond, new but valued friend; Margot Marek, teacher and author; Dick Marek, editor and publisher: what a wonderful team you are. I am proud to work with you.

Thanks.

PRISCILLA L. VAIL

Bedford, New York

PREFACE

Anger, fear, self-doubt, frustration, and pressure are typical of the reactions that intensify when an intelligent student has a school problem. Negative responses contaminate the classroom, invade the home, and squeeze the spirit and intelligence of smart kids. In their confusion, parents, teachers, and students themselves may be quick to lay blame. This book offers ways to find the roots of academic problems and suggests specific ways to circumvent or surmount them.

Smart kids with school problems often shine in the arts, athletics, or interpersonal skills or show great promise in mathematics, engineering, or science. But many are turning away from education because their school problems are misunderstood.

What are these kids like? They may be young people who welcome challenge outside school, but avoid it in the classroom. They may be students who relish thinking and problem solving but have poor organizational skills. Some are imaginative, verbal students whose written work is poor. Others remember their experiences, people, and emotions but can't seem to memorize schoolwork.

Some have trouble listening and following directions. Others don't seem to harness their intelligence. Often, for reasons we shall explore, they do not get high scores on standardized tests. This increases their vulnerability to pressure because many current cries for educational reform are really calls for higher test scores. These students need recognition, understanding, and help from concerned adults because their bright promise is at risk, and because there are many of them.

How many? Probably between 20 and 30 percent of any school population. Among the obvious learning disabled there are those with high though hidden intellectual potential. Among the gifted there are those with subtle learning disabilities. Among the "average" students are those in whom giftedness and disability mask one another, pulling academic performance into the middle range. Thus these students may be found in the top, middle, or low groups of any grade.

How should we describe them? We might call them gifted and learning disabled, learning disabled and gifted, academic ugly ducklings, street smart and school dumb, atypical learners, or smart kids with school problems. Because each one is a glorious though challenging puzzle, I name them after a type of puzzle: I call them *conundrum kids*.

The long-term implications of being a conundrum kid are exhilarating whenever talent and self-respect are kept alive. The student who is understood and helped faces short-term periods of discomfort and hard work as well as times of great satisfaction. But the student who is not diagnosed and helped faces short-term academic discomfort snowballing into long-term self-doubt, a poor education, diminished professional opportunities, and, often, an unfulfilled life.

In spite of the difficulties, the message of this book is optimistic. As a learning specialist, diagnostician, teacher of children, leader of teacher training workshops, and parent, I have puzzled over—and taught—smart kids with school problems. By following the research, trying different methods and materials, watching master teachers, and noticing what strategies work in which circumstances, I have learned some things to know and ways to help.

This book is laid out in ten chapters.

Chapter 1 describes traits and emotional needs frequently found in bright or gifted students, discusses different learning styles, and cites school problems conundrum kids may meet at particular grade levels.

Chapter 2 discusses the young child's developmental readiness for schoolwork and offers guidelines for grade placement in the early years.

Each of the next five chapters explores one learning system. Just as the health of a human body depends on separate but inter-related systems, active learning relies on its own discrete but interdependent systems. Healthy people and successful students needn't bother teasing them apart, but in times of trouble it is important to see which systems are functioning smoothly and which are causing trouble. We shall look at strengths and weaknesses in visual learning, motor function, auditory learning, language and learning, and psychological availabililty for schoolwork.

Chapter 8, "Testing Demystified," explores testing and interpretation of test scores in general and gives examples of constructive ways to use test results to help conundrum kids.

Chapter 9 looks at maturation and higher education for smart kids with school problems.

Chapter 10 tells the stories of three gifted people who survived schooling and have realized their true potential.

P.L.V.

1

RECOGNIZING, UNDERSTANDING, AND HELPING CONUNDRUM KIDS

The jagged learning profile of a conundrum kid looks like a cross section of the Alps. One student may have high conceptual power and low ability to read, write, and spell. Another may be strong with words and weak with numbers. Another may have great artistic talent but flounder in formal academics. The discrepancy between the highs and the lows is uncomfortable, even painful, for the student. The greater the discrepancy the more intense the discomfort: unexercised talents itch, unsupported weaknesses ache.

Because failure is easy to see, unenlightened adults may ignore the student's talent, fostering a negative self-concept by focusing on what he can*not* do. (To avoid the cumbersome use of double pronouns, I have arbitrarily settled on the general use of *he* for students and *she* for teachers.) Many kids with high potential face discouragement every time they walk in the school door. Smart kids with school problems need the advocacy of informed adults to help them acquire necessary skills and, equally important, to protect the talent, originality, and power they offer.

For example, Charlie, an eighth grader, built a tree house with a cantilevered deck and sold five of his paintings at the community art show. He made the drawings for the poster but couldn't do the lettering because each time he tried to copy the words *Community Historical Association* he made a different mistake. Although he understands advanced mathematical concepts and has a natural interest in science, he scores poorly on standardized tests, his written work is weak, and he is failing history

Looking at Charlie's test scores, his spelling, and his history exam, it would be easy to think him stupid. In his case, as is true with many other students we shall meet throughout the book, specific talents are often the flip side of specific disabilities.

Although talent and trouble are intertwined in every conundrum kid, by looking at giftedness and other atypical learning styles separately, we have a better chance of understanding the child who carries both. Let's look first at giftedness.

GIFTEDNESS

The criteria for giftedness are numerous, often nit-picking, and they differ widely from place to place or from test to test. They often identify good test takers or high scorers who may or may not be original thinkers, and they frequently eliminate gifted kids who do not excel in traditional ways. Therefore, in this book I use *gifted* to describe those who happen to meet the criteria and also those who are highly intelligent, talented, or just plain smart. Trying to distinguish among these categories takes time that could be better used by meeting the students' needs.

Gifted people frequently have clusters of the following ten traits: rapid grasp of concepts, awareness of patterns, energy, curiosity, concentration, exceptional memory, empathy, vulnerability, heightened perceptions, and divergent thinking. While these traits invigorate learning, they may also create friction in the classroom or in the home. In fairness to the students we are trying to understand, we need to acknowledge that singly, or in combination, they can be both blessings and burdens.

RAPID GRASP OF CONCEPTS

Gifted people grasp concepts so quickly it seems as if the knowledge has been inside them all along, waiting to be awakened simply by being mentioned. While such *instant learning* can be stimulating, it can also be unsettling to classmates, teachers, and the student himself.

Classmates may resent a peer who learns without apparent effort, and teachers may resent students who learn without explanations. Students themselves are often perplexed by their instant learning, enjoying the excitement but wondering whether it is dishonest—a sort of intellectual shoplifting—and worrying whether knowledge that arrives without effort might vanish without warning. Some gifted students who learn quickly think easy learning doesn't count, and they develop a cynical attitude toward schooling in general.

AWARENESS OF PATTERNS

Gifted people are unusually alert to patterns. They recognize symmetry in nature, in seashells or leaves, and in such man-made creations as architecture and art. They notice patterns of interval and repetition in mathematics and music, frequently relating the one to the other. They understand the abstract conceptual patterns that may connect such seemingly different disciplines as science and art, and, through language, they recognize the psychological patterns in literature that parallel those in daily living. Thinking in patterns is a way of thinking by analogy, the foundation of much higher level academic work. But it is not always easy for others to understand the patterns the gifted student sees. Adults or peers may think he is being purposely obscure, just as he may become annoyed by their apparent slow-wittedness.

ENERGY

Intellectual and psychological energy levels may exceed a gifted person's level of physical energy. Although physical energy is more evident to the casual observer than the other two, these energies of the mind are the fuel for abstract exploration and discovery. Unfortunately, an uncertain or weary adult may misinterpret a student's high intellectual energy as personal challenge instead of recognizing it as the urge to pursue a problem longer and more deeply than other people. The student who persists with "but have you stopped to think about . . ." or "I know something else about that that no one else thought of" is sometimes an unwelcome challenge.

CURIOSITY

Curiosity spurs vigorous investigation of physical, intellectual, or psychological realms. It is as natural a force to gifted thinkers as physiological hunger and thirst. Questions like Why? How come . . . ? Where did . . . ? When was the first . . . ? What is . . . made of? have led to great discoveries, but such questions are not always welcome in school. They may take time from the matter at hand, and they are seen as diversions. Sadly, too, teachers who are uncomfortable not knowing an answer resent students with wide, deep curiosity. When a student of any age finds his curiosity unwelcome in school, he often saves it for extracurricular endeavors.

CONCENTRATION

Many gifted people can focus their intellectual energies for long periods of time. While the ability to concentrate is admirable and deserves exercise, it is often at odds with academic schedules and family living. Big ideas need generous pieces of time if they are not to be lost, but school schedules are built of forty- or fifty-minute class periods, and the clock governs such family activities as car pools, soccer practices, music lessons, and dentist appointments, not to mention mealtimes. The gifted need large unstructured pieces of time.

EXCEPTIONAL MEMORY

The gifted person may have an encyclopedic memory for people, events, and emotions, both in his experience and from his reading. He may have a vivid recollection of the blue front door to his grandmother's house, which he hasn't seen since the age of four. Paradoxically, this same student may forget last week's spelling rule, the multiplication tables, or the capital of North Dakota. This discrepancy between a powerful experiential memory and a weak memory for specific factual information may create an incorrect impression of a kid who "doesn't care," "hasn't studied," or "only learns what he feels like learning."

EMPATHY

The gifted person is often highly sensitive to the feelings of others. If he feels welcome in school, he will use his empathetic skills positively, enhancing the quality of everyone's life in the classroom, on the athletic field, in the lunchroom and halls, or wherever he happens to be. But the unwelcome gifted thinker whose traits create friction in conventional academic settings may choose to use his empathy negatively, knowing just how to gain attention or make trouble.

VULNERABILITY

While a young poet creating new patterns or metaphor may trust his own sense of innovation and be invulnerable to the criticisms of an unimaginative teacher, this same individual is often socially and emotionally more vulnerable than his peers, particularly to loneliness and the kind of self-doubt that comes from perceptive self-scrutiny and the knowledge of being different. A look at real children shows that intellectual strength confers no immunity to emotional pain.

HEIGHTENED PERCEPTIONS

Like the other traits, heightened perceptions complicate life for gifted people. They focus on beauty and also on ugliness, on joy and also on pain, on the attainable and on the unattainable. These perceptions cast a mercilessly bright light on the discrepancies between reality and the ideal, sometimes throwing the perceiver off balance. For example, young children with heightened perceptions often become intellectually aware of the idea of death before knowing how to make emotional peace with its inevitability. The knowledge arrives spontaneously, pushing the child into a period of distress aroused by his heightened perceptions but not alleviated by them.

DIVERGENT THINKING

Divergent thinkers who enjoy open-ended questions see problems and situations from unusual angles, and can tolerate the ambiguity of seeing things from several different points of view. They are willing to wrestle with "What if . . ." and are happiest exploring questions that have no verifiable answers in the back of the book. Their ability to recognize patterns, combined with their heightened perceptions, often lead them to insights that are bewildering to the rest of us, or seem "off the track" or "beside the point." This kind of originality can create friction between a gifted student and a teacher who wants everyone in the class to use identical procedures.

Students with clusters of these traits have high intellectual potential, but keeping this promise alive is no easy task. Although these characteristics are precursors of discovery and innovation, many of them are inconvenient or disruptive in routine academic settings.

It is important to remember that high grades are not always evidence of gifted thinking: precocity may accompany giftedness but does not certify it, and the ability to memorize does not guarantee the ability to think. Many intellectually powerful students do poorly on rote exercises, and are uninterested in filling in workbook blanks or selecting answers from multiple-choice options. For reasons we shall explore in detail in Chapter 8, "Testing Demystified," test scores alone are unreliable indicators of the presence or absence of gifted thinking.

LEARNING STYLES

An individual's learning style is his intellectual fingerprint, unique and permanent. The term *learning style* refers to the way a student learns: aptitudes, compensations, and weaknesses. The math student who learns easily with *manipulatives* (blocks, chips, or rods) may struggle with worksheets. The failing reader may be unable to remember sight words but catch on quickly with phonics. One student may learn as quickly from a demonstration as another may from a verbal explanation. Current neurological research indicates that learning styles reflect individual brain development and architecture.[1]

According to Geschwind, Galaburda, Masland, and Behan, to name but four outstanding contributors to this field, the mother's level of testosterone (the male sex hormone) influences the migration of cells to certain parts of the fetal heart and brain between the sixteenth and twentieth weeks of gestation. Stimuli that cross the placenta prompt a response in the brain that, in turn, accounts for reorganization of brain architecture. This reorganization may predispose a person both to particular types of talents and aptitudes and to "a climate inhospitable to language," which could account for many school problems in highly intelligent kids.

These patterns of brain architecture underlie such seemingly unrelated conditions as left-handedness, learning disorders, autoimmune disease, allergies, migraine, some types of ulcerative colitis, and specific types of epilepsy. Left-handedness does not cause a learning disorder any more than allergies cause epilepsy; they are manifestations of a common set of circumstances.

Of note is the frequent coincidence of people with remarkable talent in three-dimensional work—architects, mathematicians, engineers, scientists, and surgeons—who are also left-handed or ambidextrous, who are vulnerable to the previously cited conditions, and who have or had school problems.

These patterns of brain architecture occur in a 4 to 1 male/female ratio. Trying to explain why, scientific researchers now hypothesize that female fetuses affected by the agent causing brain reorganization do not survive gestation as often as males. This hypothesis reverses previously held ideas that the male is more vulnerable to learning disorders and also provides a neuroanatomical explanation for male aptitude for such disciplines as math, reducing the impact of cultural influences.

Teachers and parents need to understand that there are neuroanatomical reasons for learning styles; that a student who learns one way but not another isn't being purposely uncooperative. In teaching we also need to remember that, while individual preferences remain, students who are skillfully taught can develop alternative or compensatory ways of learning.

Often a smart kid's school problem arises from a mismatch between his learning style and the methods and materials used in the curriculum. When this happens, it is the student who is diagnosed as learning disabled, instead of the material's being labeled inappropriate.

Learning disabilities can be created as well as inherited. Some should properly be called *pedagenic*: they spring from inappropriate schooling. They may be *chronogenic*, caused by a poor match between the age of the child and the concepts being introduced, or they may be *sociogenic*, springing from an inhospitable or even hostile setting. Others, to be sure, are truly *genetic*, springing from being "just like Uncle Charlie."

The term *learning disability* may be appropriate or it may have lost its precision through overuse. *Learning disability*, translated literally, means being not able to learn, but although learning disabled (LD) kids have trouble learning in some situations, many learn rapidly in others.

The term *learning disability* has an air of finality that promotes pessimistic thinking at home and at school: "He has a learning disability so there's nothing I can do. He needs a specialist." An alternative term, *learning difference*, has the optimistic ring conundrum kids deserve. They can learn, and often, with some adjustments in materials and methods of presentation, they can learn in the regular classroom.

Learning differences can account for the discrepancies between one learning system and another and also for highs and lows within a single learning system. Here are some examples:

In the visual learning system, a student who is highly talented in the visual arts may have trouble learning to recognize letters or sight words.

In the motor system, the highly skilled athlete with exquisite coordination may have barely legible handwriting.

In the auditory learning system, the student with perfectly good hearing may not remember oral instructions.

In the language system, the talkative student may have trouble understanding what he reads or organizing his written work.

In psychological availablity for schoolwork, the imaginative thinker may have trouble focusing his attention.

As we investigate these learning systems in the ensuing chapters we shall see some reasons for such discrepancies and examples of ways smart kids can be helped.

Learning differences are lifelong, and although they may create embarrassment or failure during school years, later on they may be part of personal charm.

For example, I have a friend, an extremely successful administrator, who can't sing on key or cut tidily with scissors. She was embarrassed by these "disabilities" in her elementary school years but they don't matter now. In fact they are considered humorous idiosyncrasies. One of my favorite authors was considered a weak student because she was a slow reader. Now that she is a successful author, her enjoyment of individual words invigorates her writing and is no longer a weakness. A distinguished lawyer whose agile mind can go directly to the center of a complicated issue sometimes has trouble with rote memory. Telephone numbers don't stick in his head, and when he is tired or under stress he spells incorrectly. As a student he disguised his spelling with sloppy handwriting. As a professional adult, he dictates to a secretary in the office, uses a word processor with an automatic spelling corrector at home, or ducks the whole question by making a telephone call instead of writing a letter. School problems may cease to matter after graduation. They are what they are called: school problems.

PERSONAL NEEDS

To help smart kids overcome their school problems concerned adults must recognize their personal as well as curricular needs. The combination of intellectual power and school problems intensifies these students' needs for belonging, care giving, output as well as intake, three-way development, adult leadership, and humor.

THE NEED TO BELONG

Conundrum kids are particularly vulnerable to loneliness and isolation, and often seek what Frankie, in Carson McCullers's *The Member of the Wedding,* called "the we of me." Ninth grader Julie, a talented young dancer who is failing algebra and Latin, said, "I guess I'm a different species. I mean, giraffes can find other giraffes, porcupines have other porcupines, adults have adults, even kids have other kids . . . and then there's me."

Common-interest groups, being read to, and appropriate grade placement all foster a sense of belonging. Weekend or vacation groups that offer activities in the student's area of strength can help him find others with similar interests. In addition to traditional opportunities for athletes to join local teams, many associations for the gifted and talented sponsor Saturday Clubs with topics ranging from electronics to chess to magic. Increasing numbers of colleges cooperate with parent groups and local schools in programs for the gifted in story writing, computers, drama, drawing, and sculpture. Science museums, art museums, and libraries often provide exciting opportunities for hands-on learning. The number of mentors, adults with an interest or skill they are willing to share with young people, is growing, particularly in large cities where people are actively seeking ways to meet others with similar interests. Although some programs for the gifted require the student to submit an IQ score, many will waive that requirement if the student is genuinely interested in the topic.

Another way to reinforce a sense of belonging is for adults to read aloud *to* kids in school and at home. Students who feel different are profoundly reassured to find that other people enjoy the same stories they do, catching their breath, laughing, crying, and shuddering at the same episodes. The selections need not be lengthy; it is hearing a story as part of a group that builds a sense of community. Because of their universal themes, myths, folk tales, and fairy tales are particularly well suited to these students' needs.

Like myths and folk tales, fairy tales deal in a permissible way with the emotional forces our students feel but often fear. The triumph of the seemingly weak over the seemingly strong is a welcome theme to the smart kid with school problems, as are the explorations of jealousy, revenge, and power these tales offer.

Discovering that people in other times and cultures have puzzled over the questions about creation that appear in mythology and folk tales is heartwarming to the student who enjoys open-ended exploration and has clusters of the traits mentioned earlier.

Appropriate grade placement is another way to help a student belong. Putting a child with others who are at a different developmental level isolates him immediately. Some parents hesitate to place an intellectually advanced child with his chronological, social-emotional peers, fearing their child will be bored. They need to meet Michael, whose story I heard from Leah Levinger, child psychologist and professor at Bank Street College of Education in New York.

Michael was a four-year-old who understood the concept of time. Not only could he call out the hour and minute on demand, but he really understood what the numbers meant. He had a solid grasp of present, future, and past tenses and could even anticipate elapsing time. For example, if his mother said, "We'll be going in half an hour," he would appear at her side twenty-nine minutes later, without looking at his watch or being reminded.

To celebrate his ability to tell time, his parents gave him a watch. Although its round face was bigger than the width of his four-year-old wrist, he strapped on his timepiece proudly and wore it everywhere. His classmates would ask him what time it was and he would call out joyfully "10:22" or "9:55." They didn't know whether that was correct, nor did they really care; it was just a companionable litany they called back and forth.

One day when it was time for the group to go to Rhythms class, Michael seemed nervous about his beloved watch and asked his teacher to hold it for him. In passing it from his hand to hers, he dropped it on the cement floor. Seeing it was broken, he sobbed while she tried in vain to console him: "It was an accident." His tears continued to flow. "No one will be angry with you . . . it was an accident." His shoulders were shaking with his crying. "Your parents will get you a new watch." By now he was trembling all over. "I'll get you a new watch." Nothing soothed his distress until the teacher's aide came from the other side of the room. "Here, Michael, do you want to borrow my watch?" Instantly the crying stopped. He fastened the replacement, snuffed up the last of his tears, and, holding his hand tightly over the watch face, said with relief, "Good. Now my mother will know when it's the right time to pick me up."

Michael's powerful intellect had absorbed the invisible concept of time, but emotionally he was a four-year-old magical thinker who equated the loss of his timepiece with the risk of abandonment. His feelings told him that if time weren't firmly anchored to his body, he might not get his mother there to collect him. His watch was more than a recorder—it was the creator of time. Michael didn't need to learn letters and numerals ahead of schedule. He would get those in due course and make good use of them. He needed to be four with other fours and be cared for by those who understood the needs of a four-year-old's heart as well as mind.

THE NEED TO GIVE CARE

Many of the traits of gifted thinkers make it difficult for them to make friends, and many students with learning differences feel both unloved and unlovable. The conundrum kid who carries both burdens may need extra help with relationships. In being responsible for another living creature, the growing child finds the confirmation of being needed, which shows him he can give as well as receive.

An eighteen-year-old girl won a prestigious literary award for her poem about grief and mourning. When asked how she knew about such things, she gave the credit to her hamster. She said that as a child she had been sharp-tongued and lonely. Because she was a voracious reader who enjoyed doing her homework, she was usually quick to answer the teacher's questions. With her ready tongue and book learning, she squelched the other kids in class, and they avenged themselves on the playground.

She was unhappy in school, but at home she had a hamster who seemed to love her as much as she loved him. She played with him, confided in him, made him Valentines, and even gave him a birthday party. Her affection poured out. One day the hamster discovered how to open his cage, and began a series of daily escapes, finding his way to the closet, into the hall, and finally to the bathroom, where he learned how to scale the towel rack and go from there to the toilet seat, which he ran like a racecourse. One Friday, he fell into the toilet and drowned. Margaret found him when she got home from school. She said, "I sobbed and grieved for the whole weekend and my mother didn't interfere. She didn't try to tell me everything would be all right, and she didn't buy me another hamster. I touched the bottom of sadness. Then we had a funeral, and I could deal with life again, but I never forgot."

THE NEED FOR OUTPUT AS WELL AS INTAKE

The ten traits of giftedness mentioned earlier act as wide-diameter pipes for the intake of information, ideas, and experiences. Students with vast capacity for intake need equally generous outlets to regulate the flow. But a word of caution: Because we know gifted thinkers are capable of high achievement, we sometimes overlook their need to be allowed the error half of trial and error, forgetting that a project-gone-wrong can be the seedbed of discovery. If we encourage output while insisting on perfection, we jeopardize students' willingness to take risks. By thwarting exploration, we condemn gifted thinkers to living in other men's discoveries.

Output needn't always be academic. Something as simple as making up a batch of cookies is the type of output that allows a conundrum kid to extend a friendly hand to a world that often misinterprets his actions. Making cookies with another child may be a way of making a friend, and offering to share them may show a generosity other people don't recognize.

THE NEED FOR THREE-WAY DEVELOPMENT

True education encourages the development of the student's aesthetic and moral values as well as academic progress.[2] But a culture that rewards high test scores and verifiable answers frequently shortchanges exploration of ambiguities and time-consuming enigmas. The student whose education emphasizes rational-scientific factual work at the expense of aesthetic and moral development is being prepared to function as a machine rather than a human being.

Aesthetic nourishment is essential for students with heightened perceptions, awareness of patterns, and delight in divergent thinking. In addition to traditional art, music, or dance classes, interdisciplinary projects that encourage students to join poetry with paintings, to illustrate stories, to combine words and art with music, or to find patterns in their surroundings are exercises in aesthetic development that enrich the entire educational atmosphere. Most smart kids with school problems excel at this kind of endeavor, but, ironically, such opportunities are often considered "enrichment," reserved for high-scoring students, and offered in the same time block as the remedial training conundrum kids need.

Students need opportunities to probe moral and ethical questions, to learn what Abraham Tannenbaum of Columbia University calls "the moral consequences of having a very good idea." A glance at history provides examples of brilliant ideas that caused deep human suffering: the scholarly writings of Karl Marx, the invention of DDT, or the splitting of the atom. Today's students are going into uncharted moral, ethical worlds in which even death and life are being redefined. With their capacity for original insight, intellectual power, and barrier-breaking work, our students need to develop their ethical and moral codes before being asked to rely on them.

THE NEED FOR ADULT LEADERSHIP

Gifted students need adult leaders to help them make choices, take chances, and accept themselves when they fall short of perfection. Adult leaders can help young people avoid unnecessary disappointment by helping them choose potential projects according to degree of difficulty and likelihood of success.

Some high-scoring students need adult leadership to liberate them from the prison of their own accomplishments. Early and continual academic success can make a student so dependent on perfect papers and correct answers that he relinquishes an original idea because it might earn a *C* instead of an *A*. Conundrum kids under pressure to improve their grades may also limit their work to what they think will please the teacher. When parents or teachers praise high grades extravagantly, they impoverish both the weak and the strong students' innovative capacities.

Effective adult leadership can promote creativity and liberate a student who is imprisoned in a grid of grades by offering projects and exercises that honor originality over conformity.

Gifted thinkers resent failure and blame themselves when they cannot meet their own expectations. The gifted thinker with a learning difference hates failure as much as his unencumbered peers but meets it twice as often. Warm adult leadership can remove some obstacles, help him over others, and reassure him he is understood.

THE NEED FOR HUMOR

Sometimes adults take school and school problems so seriously that they overlook the nature of children and the importance of laughter. Humor is a dowser's wand to the pools of affect and energy that characterize real learning. If we can locate these pools through humor and tap them through the academic exercises we offer in school, we encourage the student to join his natural energy to academic requirements.

Cartoons, skits, articles or stories in the student newspaper, satire, dramatic productions, and verse are but a few of the many appropriate vehicles for student humor that encourage the abstract thinking underlying funny things.

As part of a schoolwide cleanup and antilitter campaign, students in kindergarten through grade twelve read (or heard) Shel Silverstein's poem about the girl who refused to do her household chore: "Sarah Cynthia Sylvia Stout Would Not Take the Garbage Out."[3] Each verse gives vivid descriptions of rotting refuse. As their literary contribution to the campaign my fourth-grade language arts class made a poster of a garbage can labeled "Great Garbage," to which they attached their own garbage poems, and invited other classes to contribute. Here are three gourmet selections.

Eyeballs bulging out of frogs
Coffee cans and catalogues
Bread crusts soaked in soup from tortoise
Two dead mice with rigor mortis.

Crushed-up mushed-up lollipops
Rusty broken bottle tops
Purple spotted old band-aids
Ripped-up dirty window shades
Mystery mushrooms, sour cider
Kitty litter, squished-up spider.

Dribbling, drooling purple eggnog
Slimy leg and skin of frog
Snouty mouty old fish heads
Cookie crumbs from unmade beds.

The authors of these verses were conundrum kids, two years ahead
of their classmates in math and two years behind them in reading
and spelling.

We can encourage humor in school in the tasks we give students
to do, the selections we give them to read, and, above all, in the
example we set through our perceptions of ourselves.

PRINCIPLES OF GOOD PRACTICE

The smart kid with school problems needs coordination of support,
evaluation of strengths and weaknesses, anticipation of curriculum
demands, and accommodation of learning style.

COORDINATION OF SUPPORT

Conundrum kids need coordinated support from the professionals and nonprofessionals in their lives. From the educational
field they need sympathetic administrators who understand their
needs and are willing to bend some of the institutional machinery.
They need classroom teachers who accept atypical learning styles

and are willing to use a variety of materials and teaching techniques. Although they need specialists to help lay out the particulars of their programs, they do not always need to be taught by specialists. They need one person to plan and oversee their total educational program, a person I call the *overseer.*

This overseer must be available for consultation with the student's teachers, for conferences with the student's family, and for planning with the student himself. Whether this overseer is a learning specialist, an administrator, a counselor, a school psychologist, a guidance counselor, or a seasoned senior teacher acting as an academic adviser doesn't matter. But the student needs a continuing advocate whose job it is to offer encouragement and smooth the way, to make educational recommendations on the basis of diagnosis and clinical observations, and to interpret test results to the family and the school. The overseer should be able to deflect, yet understand, parental anxiety or rage at slow progress and be tactful enough to make suggestions to teachers without putting them on the defensive. The job requires a combination of gentleness and strength.

In coordinating their support and working with the overseer, teachers and parents need to recognize one another's vulnerabilities. Teachers need to understand that parents suffer vicarious pain when their children struggle. Pain brings fear and often fatigue. Confused and apprehensive parents may blame themselves, find fault with the school, or lose faith in the student. Teachers who make themselves available for conferences, and who sympathize with a student's dilemma, can help parents grow as they increase their understanding of academic problems.

Parents need to understand that teachers want their students to succeed and suffer self-doubt when they don't. When personal uncertainty turns inward, it causes discouragement; turned outward, it causes defensiveness. Parental support of teacher efforts can bring out the best in the situation; blame worsens it.

True coordination requires the educators and parents to compare notes. The high-achieving student who takes three hours an evening on homework other students complete in an hour is sending an important signal. His parents need to know how long the assignments are meant to take; the teacher needs to know how much effort is going into the task. The student who seems pulled together in school but is temperamental at home may be functioning under too much pressure. Parents and teachers need to be aware of both kinds of behavior. The student who is passive in school but active outside it is leading the kind of double life that drains psychological energy. Bed-wetting, nail-biting, stomachaches, and headaches are the kinds of symptoms teachers and parents need to share.

Other nonprofessional adults in the student's life, be they grandparents, coaches, aunts, uncles, family friends, or mentors, have important support to give. In order to believe in himself, the struggling student needs acceptance, love, and optimism to counteract the message of inadequacy school problems convey.

EVALUATION OF STRENGTHS AND WEAKNESSES

A master file is vital to the evaluation and education of a conundrum kid. Ideally the parents and overseer maintain the file together. If this is not possible, the parents should assume the primary responsibility, either on their own initiative or at the suggestion of the educators. Evaluation should begin the minute a teacher or parent thinks, "There's something different about this kid."

The master file should begin with the first dated notes listing concerns, questions, traits, indications of learning differences, and the student's personal needs. (The earlier part of this chapter provides a useful framework.) The more specific the notes the better. "Tom has trouble concentrating when people are moving around, but noise doesn't seem to bother him" tells more than "Sometimes Tom gets distracted." The format can be informal, but good evaluation is a cumulative process, which depends on a flow of written records.

The master file should contain test scores and report cards as well as a few samples of the student's work demonstrating both strengths and weaknesses.

Each year's work samples, report cards, and any anecdotal materials should be clipped together, and at least twice a year the adults in charge of the student's schooling should use the master file for review and planning. They need to return to the original dated paper to note consistency or change in patterns, to judge the efficacy of remedial measures, and to be sure talent is being kept alive. Once again, they should write down their comments. Written notes from these twice-yearly sessions should be clipped to the other papers from that year.

Understanding the root of the problem is the basis for on-target remediation. Putting a runner with a sprained ankle in a sling or offering crutches as a headache remedy doesn't help any more than giving academic support that doesn't match the need. But it is a sorry truth that many conundrum kids are getting general tutoring— a diffuse combination of pep talks and homework help—rather than the specific training they need. Chapters 2 through 8 are designed to help educators and parents focus their efforts precisely.

An individual psychoeducational evaluation makes an important contribution and belongs in the master file. We shall explore the when, why, and how in detail in Chapter 8, "Testing Demystified."

A careful review of the student's learning history and samples of work can distinguish the true conundrum kid from the student who is simply the victim of unrealistically high parental expectations. Sometimes a parent will label an average learner LD because he is not at the top of the class. It is easier for some parents to say "My kid is LD" than it is to say "My kid is average." The contents of the master file may give the overseer material to help the family set realistic expectations.

The master file should be shared by teachers, parents, the overseer, and the student himself as soon as the adults agree he is mature enough to understand its contents.

ANTICIPATION OF CURRICULUM DEMANDS

Educators and parents who understand a conundrum kid's learning style can often prevent trouble by anticipating the demands of the curriculum and giving early help.

Here is a general sequence of curriculum showing different types of thinking required at successive grade levels, and tied to Piaget's learning stages: *preoperational,* approximately ages two to seven or eight; *concrete operations,* approximately ages seven to eight to eleven to twelve; and *formal operations,* eleven to twelve continuing through life. Teachers accustomed to working with one particular age group or subject matter may find this overview helpful. So may parents who remember their own schooling but haven't studied learning.

Kindergarten and first-grade students are in the *preoperational stage* in which behavior and thinking are still egocentric. The student grows ready for mental symbols and symbolic play and learns through simple trial and error rather than logic.

In kindergarten the conundrum kid who is very quick at some tasks and slow or disabled in others has trouble fitting in with a standardized curriculum. Because early school experiences color the student's view of himself as a learner, it is easy for the smart kid to decide he is either omnipotent or inadequate.

In first grade most children learn to read, write, spell, and do paper-and-pencil arithmetic, and the child who is unready or unable to learn these skills usually feels different and scared. The next chapter, "The Young Child: Developmental Levels and Academic Requirements," explores some specifics of kindergarten and first-grade readiness.

Students from roughly the second through sixth grades are in Piaget's stage of *concrete operations*. The student learns to make groupings of classes and relations and begins to develop logic, which is initially bound to the manipulation of objects. The student develops the concept of *conservation*, understanding that four ounces of water is four ounces of water even though one four-ounce pouring barely covers the bottom of a big pot and another fills a juice glass.

In second grade, students consolidate their basic language arts and math skills. The conundrum kid who missed them is likely to be overwhwelmed by the double burden of trying to grasp and consolidate simultaneously. The student who has not developed the concept of conservation doesn't really know the "fourness" of four and will have trouble understanding math.

In third grade, those reading, writing, spelling, and math skills, which had previously been goals in themselves, now become the foundations of reading comprehension, creative writing, and the solving of practical problems in arithmetic. The student with inadequate reading, writing, language, or math skills is in the precarious position of trying to build a structure with a half-full tool box. Chapters 3, 5, and 6, "Visual Learning," "Auditory Learning,"

and "Language and Learning," demonstrate the connections between these systems and the three *R*s.

In fourth grade, students are expected to increase the fluency
of their written expression. Because writing competence traditionally lags behind reading facility, the shaky reader will have trouble
meeting this requirement, as will the poor speller or student with
handwriting difficulties. We shall explore the far-reaching effects of
early handwriting problems in Chapter 4, "Motor Function and
School Achievement."

Fifth and sixth graders are expected to acquire information and
organize their thoughts. The student with a weak language base will
have trouble with both. Former problems with reading may seem
to bloom anew as the volume and complexity of assignments increase. Handwriting problems will undercut conceptually good work.

Around seventh grade, the student enters the age of *formal
operations*, which brings the ability to think abstractly without working with physical objects, the ability to coordinate several variables
in thought or action, and a refinement of the ability to hypothesize,
predict consequences, and consider implications in new situations.

In seventh and eighth grades, the intelligent student is expected to integrate the skills from the earlier years, using them to
absorb and express concepts, orally and in written work, on increasingly abstract levels with reliable mechanical skills. The conundrum kid who is still collecting those skills falls further and
further behind.

In high school the successful student relies on a good memory,
organization, well-developed concepts, reasonable psychological
stability, and solid mechanical skills. Students with ragged development may have trouble with the transitions these years encom-
pass: from childhood to adulthood, from one subject matter to another,
and from enjoyment of the activities they're good at to struggles
with subjects that are difficult. Intelligent or brilliant young people
who feel unsuccessful in school during this period may reject the
idea of any further education. They may drop out, turn against
society, or harm themselves.

College is a time for exploring new disciplines, or old disciplines
at new levels. The atypical student may need help assembling his
credentials for admission, and must anticipate his needs for special

support once he starts college. Otherwise, he risks being turned down or flunking out. There are specific suggestions for help in Chapter 9, "Maturation and Higher Education."

If there are so many hurdles and perils, what makes the process worthwhile? Theodore Sizer, former dean of the Harvard Graduate School of Education and author of *Horace's Compromise, The Dilemma of the American High School* (see Annotated Bibliography), says that a true education confers these three: *power, agency,* and *joy.*

Smart kids with school problems need the *power* of basic skills to support their ideas. And they need psychological power to keep their dreams alive during the years when school problems bring discouragement.

Agency refers to the opportunity to exercise and display that power. Good students have easy access to agency; they can write for the school newspaper, be on the debating team, or enter Olympics of the Mind contests. Conundrum kids often have trouble finding appropriate places or ways of displaying their power in school and need adult help in finding a showcase.

Joy, the outgrowth of power and agency, is what makes learning worthwhile. The smart kid with school problems has as great a capacity for joy as his unencumbered classmates but needs help to keep it alive.

Anticipation of curriculum demands and perils particular to conundrum kids at successive grade levels can help head off difficulty. Prevention can build power, provide for agency, and protect joy.

ACCOMMODATION OF LEARNING STYLE

To accommodate the atypical learner's needs, adults in charge of his program need to budget time for the nurture of talent, for remedial help, and for steady progress with regular schoolwork.

Talent withers without nurture. Because it is talent that will bring joy long after the legal requirement for schooling is satisfied, ample time must be allocated for the student's particular interest.

Remedial help may come from several sources. In some instances, classroom teachers can provide it themselves without relying on specialists. In more serious situations, a specialist may need to prescribe the materials or provide remedial training. It is fortunate when sufficient help is available through the school system. When it is not, the parents must pick up the slack, either hiring a tutor or trying to provide the help themselves, using materials suggested by the overseer or teacher. Although trying to combine the roles of parent and teacher is difficult, and can have negative results, sometimes it is the only available option.

Remedial help can be given as prevention as well as cure. This is the best type of accommodation. Unfortunately, some smart kids don't get the help they need until they are failing.

A thoughtful, worried parent called me last fall. She and her husband had just moved to our area with their sixth grader son. When the boy was in first and second grades, he had needed extra help with reading and writing, which the school had provided. They predicted he might need help again later on, but all went well in third and fourth grades, where his interest in science really bloomed. His reading problem began to surface again in fifth grade when the pace picked up: he had a different teacher for each subject, and more work was required. Because this boy had good early training, he is not in real trouble; his A in science pulls his overall average up, but nevertheless he is discouraged and scared. He wants to get to the top but realizes he is only just getting by. He is caught in a school policy that says a student must be two years below grade level in reading before receiving extra help. "Where can we turn?" his mother asked. "He's too strong to qualify for help and too weak to manage without it."

Accommodation sometimes means lifting a requirement. A sophomore at a competitive New England college was failing French. When she received a letter from the academic dean, she was certain it was a notice of academic probation and was astonished at the message: "In view of your persistent difficulty with languages, evident in your high school transcript and college record, we suspect you may have the kind of learning disability which will exempt you from the foreign language requirement. Please make an appointment through this office to have the appropriate testing." She passed the test by failing it, the foreign language requirement was lifted, and she traded French for a course in engineering.

Learning styles must be accommodated in the regular classroom as well as in special situations. The classroom teacher can help the atypical learner do regular schoolwork through careful grouping. Conundrum kids need to work alone, as well as in small groups, and with the whole class.

Because they need to work at their own level and pace (which may be faster or slower than their peers', depending on the subject), they need opportunities for independent study.

They also need to work in small groups where talents can combine; the artist who spells poorly, working with an accomplished writer, can create a work more powerful than either could achieve alone.

Most regular schoolwork is done with the whole class, and the conundrum kid can often hold his own if given appropriate remedial support and such alternative teaching strategies as we shall explore in the ensuing chapters.

To accommodate divergent thinking, heightened perceptions, awareness of patterns, and other traits of giftedness, the wise adult, either teacher or parent, will offer exercises that honor originality over conformity. Children of all ages can create folk tales describing the origins of such natural phenomena as fire or thunder. They can write about and illustrate their own imaginary creatures. They can listen to three-fourths of a story and then try to write an ending different from the one they think the author has used. Just as there is no such thing as a wrong poem, there is no wrong fable, wrong imaginary animal, or wrong origin of the first rainbow. Gifted students are often interested in future studies. They can design means of transportation, new foods, or games for the future.

Mathematics offers brainteasers and mind-benders with infinite numbers of different, yet correct answers. I watched a group of seven-year-olds deciding "How many ways can you add and subtract to get seven?" In a very short time, the group had brainstormed over forty! Moving quickly beyond $3 + 4 = 7$, and its companion $4 + 3 = 7$, they went on to such elaborations as $2 + 1 + 1 + 1 + 2 = 7$ and $9 - 6 + 4 = 7$ and $100 - 90 - 3 = 7$.

Later in the day I watched some ninth graders use the "four

fours" trying to build every number from zero to fifty. The rules require the use of all four fours, along with any mathematical sign or process, to reach a specific number. For example, twenty could be $4/4 + 4 \times 4 = 20$. Sixteen might be $4 + 4 - 4 \times 4 = 16$, or, equally correctly, it could be: $4 \times 4 \div 4/4 = 16$. The combinations are endlessly fascinating to those who enjoy playing with numbers, and there is a wide variety of equally correct answers.

Even though it takes time and care to accommodate conundrum kids' learning styles, teachers become better teachers by increasing their repertoires of styles and materials, schools are richer for the contributions these kids make to the fabric of school life, and our society needs their power, agency, and joy. Many great intellectual, artistic, and scientific contributions have come from those who had severe academic problems, or would have, had they been required to attend school. From Leonardo da Vinci to Albert Einstein the list is long and the intellectual power great. It includes the geniuses, the highly accomplished, and the just plain competent.

A CASE HISTORY: BART

Angry, curious, and *gentle* were the three words Bart's mother chose to describe her eighth grader son. His father said, "He's all contradictions. He's smart in thinking but dumb in school; he remembers the hard things and forgets the simple ones. He's always gotten along with us and our friends but can't get along with his teachers." Bart said of himself "I always mess up," "Max is the smart one in our family," and "I used to be smart when I was little."

Bart was an early stairclimber, walker, tricycle rider, and block builder, but a late talker. Although he understood everything, he said little, and his speech was difficult to understand. His father was proud of Bart's physical prowess and overlooked his verbal difficulties, but Max mimicked him and often reduced him to tears. His mother arranged for a course of speech therapy when Bart was three, which proved successful. Although some minor misarticulations linger (he says *vis* for *this* and *Mattasusetts* for *Massachusetts*), these, like his unusual combination of blue eyes and dark hair, simply contribute to his individuality.

When he started first grade, his speech sounds were clear but his conversation came in pauses and spurts. He had trouble associating letters with sounds, didn't learn his sight words, and frequently tangled letter sequence in spelling. Max would never let him forget the time he signed his paper "B-r-a-t."

Although Bart could create intricate structures with blocks, sugar cubes, tongue depressors, or whatever was at hand, his pencil control was poor. By the end of second grade, his letters and numerals were still large and awkwardly formed. He struggled with reading and the pencil-paper aspects of school but enjoyed classroom discussion and taking care of the guinea pig.

Using phonics in third, fourth, and fifth grades, he consolidated his reading skills, but his spelling contained such errors as: *pepul, wus, thay, sed,* and *on perpis,* and his handwriting problems persisted.

By sixth grade Bart's silent reading and comprehension were strong, but his oral reading was jerky and rushed. His written work was untidy, disorganized, and littered with incorrect spelling. As his ideas increased in pace and complexity, his hand lagged further and further behind. His speech rhythms of pause and spurt continued, and he didn't use punctuation for either phrasing or logic. In one exercise, omitting a vital comma and question mark, he wrote "when are we going to eat Max."

He had a different teacher for each subject, and his performance varied widely. On the athletic field, in the science lab, in the art room, on the stage, or in independent reading, Bart was competent and confident. In math class he understood the concepts but his papers were sloppy. He frequently "forgot" his homework, and he did poorly on tests because, in his haste to write the problems and the answers, his columns would drift or he would transpose the numbers, writing 17 for 71, or 256 for 265. Although he handled lab materials skillfully, he was so ashamed of his science notebook, and so afraid his mother (or Max) would see it, that he threw it away, pretending he had lost it on the bus.

In social studies he enjoyed immersing himself in other cultures, but his written work was helter-skelter. He would jump from one topic to another, and couldn't seem to use a topic sentence and a paragraph to organize his thoughts.

The comment on his sixth-grade report card was "Bart nearly failed language arts. He will be taken out of art and physical education if he doesn't improve next term."

He entered seventh grade angry with himself and the system. His teachers considered him a troublemaker. His father thought Bart wasn't trying, Max thought Bart was dumb, and his mother hoped he was simply going through a bad time.

This tall, strong, angry boy who enjoyed problem solving in math, art, and the out-of-doors had very poor rote memory, handwriting, and spelling. He was misunderstood while being exhorted to try harder and do better.

When Bart was in eighth grade, his parents decided to take him to a psychologist for testing. Combining Bart's parents' descriptions, quoted earlier, with a review of his school history and the results of the testing, the psychologist found recurrent patterns of wide discrepancies in Bart's learning style. This jagged profile accounted for many of his academic highs and lows.

The psychologist felt Bart's anger came from the frustration of feeling smart and dumb simultaneously, and offered several suggestions. The first was to share the test results with Bart himself. Seeing his high scores should boost the boy's self-confidence, and identifying the weak areas would help him see them as specific difficulties instead of symptoms of overall stupidity.

The next suggestion was to find a tutor to work with Bart five times a week in hourly sessions for the remainder of the academic year and over the summer. The goals would be to improve his handwriting, work on his spelling, combine the spelling and handwriting training with one another, and develop organizational skills for written work. In addition, the psychologist suggested that Bart's parents buy a computer with a word processor and have him learn both touch-typing and the use of the word-processing program as soon as school let out in June. With such training under his belt, Bart could return to school in September with brighter prospects for success.

At first, Bart did not want to talk to the psychologist or review his test results, but when he agreed to go he was enormously relieved by what he heard. Although he is not delighted to sacrifice his summer freedom to remedial work, he has agreed and is particularly looking forward to having a computer. His parents feel able to plan intelligently now that they understand the specifics of Bart's difficulties. They will stay in touch with the psychologist, who will act as an overseer in coordinating Bart's education. They have begun a master file. Because Bart is understood, he and his family have traded fear and frustration for "things to know and ways to help."

2

THE YOUNG CHILD

DEVELOPMENTAL LEVELS
AND
ACADEMIC REQUIREMENTS

A good fit between the student's developmental levels and the academic requirements of the school promotes joyful, solid learning. Mismatches can create learning disabilities, distort personal relationships, cap creativity, and impoverish the overall quality of a human life. Talented, intelligent children are not simply a national resource, they are a universal treasure. To dull the glow of their promise through inappropriate placement is a form of child abuse.

This chapter is designed to help educators and parents ward off unnecessary school problems by exploring developmental readiness for kindergarten and first grade, and appropriate grade placement in the early years of schooling. It is so much easier to start out at the right level than to try to undo the harm of a poor placement decision by later retention or acceleration. Since the child's view of himself as a learner—as a worthwhile human being—is heavily influenced by his first experiences in school, the initial placement decision has lifelong impact.

FACTORS IN A STUDENT'S DEVELOPMENTAL LEVEL

A student's developmental level is a combination of his age, social-emotional maturity, and intellectual development. Let's explore them one by one.

AGE

Turning five doesn't automatically make a child ready for school. Chronological level may be the least important of the three developmental components, yet it is often the major determinant of school placement.

Birth date frequently controls the decision about who should enter school and in which grade. For example, in six public school districts in or adjoining the town of Bedford, New York, policies variously state that a child who is going to turn five during the school year by either December 1, December 15, or December 31 should enter kindergarten in September of that school year. When the child's birthday is near the cutoff date, or in cases of unusual psychological, intellectual, or developmental function, the school may recommend, or parents may request, a departure from standard procedure. Although the parent has the option to request accelerated or delayed entry, the school retains the authority to make the final decision, and, increasingly, in public, parochial, and independent schools (which some people call private), schools recommend waiting. This is particularly true as more and more kindergartens step up the curriculum with formal academic training.

Instead of, or in addition to, using birth dates, some schools encourage a "three before first" policy. They want their students to have three years of preschool, including kindergarten, before first grade. These can be two of nursery school and one of kindergarten; one of nursery school, one of kindergarten, and one in a transitional kindergarten–first grade program; or one of nursery school and two of kindergarten.

Traditionally, independent schools throughout the country have used earlier birth-date requirements, selecting September or June as the cutoff date rather than December. In addition, many are pleased with the results of using different cutoff dates for boys and girls: to be eligible for kindergarten in the fall, a girl must turn five by September 1, and a boy must have turned five by the previous June 1. This policy is born of many years of observing the relative readiness of male and female children.

"Three before first" and birth-date cutoff policies can be shifted if necessary, but they may buy the child the extra time he needs for developmental growth, at the same time helping anxious parents save face. It's easy to say, "He missed the kindergarten deadline, so he'll go a year later."

Research, such as that done by Jeannette J. Jansky at Columbia University, shows that prematurely born children, particularly males and particularly left-handed males, are often developmentally delayed in their readiness for schoolwork. This lag may mask high intellectual potential, creating an incorrect impression of average or low intelligence. In spite of its impact, parents often forget to mention premature birth, and educators often overlook it in school placement.

Given a choice of sending a student into school several months younger or several months older than the average age in the class, both common sense and current research indicate a greater chance of overall readiness in the chronologically older child. Time alone will not immunize against school problems, but the readier the child, the greater his chance of success.

SOCIAL-EMOTIONAL MATURITY

Social-emotional maturity allows the child to approach learning with the expectation of success and provides resilience in times of stress. An observant adult can make a useful estimate of a student's social-emotional level by noting how easily he makes friends with others his age. The child who likes himself finds it easy to like others, and if his level of social-emotional development matches his classmates', friendships will come automatically.

It is important to assess the child's social-emotional maturity in large group activities as well as with one or two other children. Some young children can seem socially well developed in an intimate setting, but become silly, babyish, or wild when more children are involved. Others, intelligent and emotionally well developed, need time to watch before participating. The enlightened observer sees social-emotional maturity in the restraint of "look before you leap," distinguishing it from the self-doubt of the child who always seeks safety on the sidelines.

INTELLECTUAL LEVEL

We can assess a child's intellectual level by using direct observation and formal and informal screening instruments.

In direct observation we need to watch for the child's understanding of concepts and not be fooled by mere facility in rote recitation. For example, five-year-old Marnie can say the numbers from one to one hundred. She sits on her grandfather's knee and entertains him by counting to one hundred, but when she looks at the buttons on her sweater she sometimes tallies up six, sometimes nine, or ten. Marnie is not a budding mathematical genius. She is a sociable little girl who memorizes easily and likes to recite.

Ella, another five-year-old, enjoys playing with attribute blocks and making patterns with colored beads. She likes to see whether her older brother can continue her patterns. Her most recent was three red beads, four blue beads, five red beads, six blue ones. Ella is not a particularly good memorizer, but she obviously enjoys thinking.

Formal and informal screening highlight children who may be at risk for formal academics, illustrating some reasons for their potential difficulty and, by inference, indicating the specifics of preventive or remedial help. The section Principles of Good Practice, later in this chapter, gives examples of tasks included in well-known, reliable screening tests.

READINESS FOR FIRST GRADE

The ready child starts first grade with four abilities. He can postpone gratification, sit still and concentrate, manage symbols (with a pencil as well as verbally), and separate reality and fantasy.

These four abilities unfold as part of the developmental process; they are to be encouraged, not forced. If they are superimposed prematurely, they are like splints and crutches instead of skeletal structure.

The child who can *postpone gratification* can tolerate the inevitably slow pace and methodical nature of introductory learning, accepting preliminary drudgery for the sake of future enjoyment.

The child who is able to *sit still* can be physically at peace while learning, and being able to *concentrate* allows him to practice his newly acquired skills. A short concentration span will disrupt the practice he needs for consolidation.

The child who can *manage symbols* is ready to learn the abstractions of letters, numerals, and printed language. The child whose pencil is a saboteur instead of an ally has trouble writing symbols and is at risk for problems in handwriting, spelling, and pencil-paper math.

The child who can separate fantasy and reality, and has established a firm boundary between the two, can sort himself out from the creatures of his own imagination and deliver himself to the tasks at hand. Separating reality and fantasy helps the child distinguish between the probable and the improbable, sharpening his perceptions of cause and effect and helping him predict the consequences of his own actions.

Ironically, smart kids may develop these abilities later than other children; clusters of the ten traits of giftedness discussed in Chapter 1 may get in the way. Postponing gratification may seem a waste of time to the instant learner who "just knows things." Sitting at a desk may be confining to the child who wants to explore mathematical patterns. Printed symbols may be an annoying hindrance to the high-energy hands-on learner. Heightened perceptions and divergent thinking make it hard for the highly imaginative child to establish the boundary between fantasy and reality; he has a greater supply to manage. Katrina de Hirsch, a pioneer in theories of child development and learning, calls such children *superior immatures*.

The advanced verbal skills of superior immatures can often camouflage unreadiness. The child who can talk a good game at an early age deserves our skepticism of his readiness for schooling ahead of schedule. When adults push children into formal academic situations prematurely, they are behaving as if schooling were a train about to pull out of the station with not another one in sight.

To prevent unnecessary school problems, many superior immatures profit from taking an extra year before going to first grade. They need what Louise Bates Ames, of the Gesell Institute for Human Development, calls "the gift of time."

What happens if the school finds a child developmentally unready and wants to give him more time, but the parents want to move him ahead? The educators involved should use their strongest powers of persuasion, while also recognizing that parental endorsement of the decision is critical to its success.

GRADE PLACEMENT

Grade-placement questions may involve an unready child, a child who is ready in some ways and not in others, a ready child in a restrictive curriculum, an underestimated or an overestimated student, or a different learner in a standard curriculum. See the effect of grade placement decisions on these smart kids.

EMMETT

Emmett was a classic superior immature, whose aggressive father thought it would "grow the boy up" to be the youngest in first grade rather than waiting for the following year to be among the oldest. Emmett was a street-smart, wiggly little boy with a streak of sweetness that didn't show in the classroom. He couldn't sit still in first grade, and he used his pencil as a pretend gun or rocket instead of an instrument of communication. He was often sent out into the hall and frequently asked to be excused to go to the bathroom.

In second grade Emmett started having stomachaches in the morning before coming to school, where his teacher frequently kept him in from recess for uncompleted work. The resource-room teacher diagnosed him as learning disabled, having both "an attentional deficit and a weak visual memory." But Emmett was just a seven-year-old trying to do eight-year-old work.

In third grade Emmett was placed in the remedial reading track, which, because of scheduling, automatically placed him in the slow math group. This boy who had scored at the top of the class in the quantitative section of the Metropolitan Readiness Test at the end of kindergarten, who had loved numbers since he was three and had understood complicated math concepts easily, was confused at feeling smart and being placed dumb.

In fourth grade, he was disciplined for decorating the boy's bathroom with graffiti and is now considered a disciplinary as well as academic problem. Academic frustration fuels increasingly rebellious behavior. The mismatch between his developmental level and academic demand began in first grade and continues to cause trouble. Emmett has a school-created learning disability.

DAVEY

Davey seemed ready in some ways and unready in others. His parents asked a colleague of mine to evaluate his readiness for first grade. Davey had squeaked into kindergarten just under the cutoff date, and seemed doubly young for his class because, when there had been a question, most parents of his classmates had chosen to give their children extra time rather than starting them off early.

By midkindergarten, Davey still hadn't decided which hand to use for writing. He ate with his right, threw a ball with his left, and used both for block building and digging in the sandpile. At home he was a self-reliant, contented child who could amuse himself for hours. He played the piano by ear extraordinarily well for a child his age and was fascinated by the natural world. He carefully mounted his leaf collection and made constant, ambidextrous use of the junior microscope he got for his birthday. Whereas his self-reliance seemed adult at home, it was considered an indication of immaturity at school.

On the playground, Davey was shy and likely to play by himself. He was afraid of some of the bigger boys and cried easily if one of them took a plaything from him.

In spite of his obvious intelligence, Davey reverted to baby talk when formal reading readiness instruction was introduced. And, although he continued to be conversationally fluent, he frequently misunderstood such linguistic subtleties as dependent clauses and passive constructions when he heard them in conversation.

Because learning differences frequently run in families, my colleague was interested to learn that Davey's grandfather and two uncles are successful businessmen who had trouble with reading in school, and, as adults, seldom read for pleasure.

She recommended that Davey take an additional year in kindergarten. Although his musical ability, his interest in animals, and his general level of thinking indicated high intelligence, his language skills were weak, there was a family history of reading problems, and he responded negatively to formal classroom instruction. Both school and parents agreed he needed more time.

For his second year in kindergarten, the school planned a strong multisensory reading readiness program to help him learn his letters and sounds. This approach emphasizes the reliable relationship between sounds and letters. Students use their eyes, ears, and hands as they see a letter and make its sound, hear a sound and write the letter. Multisensory training, originally designed for dyslexic students, benefits all beginning readers and writers. Regular classrooms that use this technique show a significant drop (as much as 30 percent) in the number of students requiring remedial help. It is called by various names: *Orton-Gillingham, Slingerland, Alphabet Phonics, Project Read,* and *Recipe for Reading* to name a few.

Davey's teachers emphasized social development and gave him the opportunities for cooperative play he so clearly needed. Being at the older end of the class gave him a better shot at the success his family expected of him.

During that second kindergarten year Davey made friends, really learned to enjoy stories, and even developed a certain facility in telling them. He entertained at the year-end school fair as a magician in cloak, top hat, and spectacles. He delighted his audience with the "Step right up, ladies and gentlemen, and . . ." patter and the simple tricks he had learned in the Saturday morning Young Magicians' Workshop sponsored by the community college. As my colleague watched him exercising his power, she thought, "Yes in-

deed, magic." But a main part of his magic was the invisible magic
of time.

ISABELLA

Isabella was a ready child in a restrictive curriculum. "I'm going
to be a space settler and a doctor," said Isabella confidently, "and
when I get there I'm going to grow the first vegetables and flowers
they have. Where I live in Space is going to be really pretty. Do
you want to see a picture?" Five-year-old Isabella held out her
drawing. There, indeed, was a rendering of a domed space station,
complete with a house for Isabella and her family, a lush garden of
multicolored flowers and vegetables, a sign reading NO WEEDS IN
SPAC, and Isabella herself, surveying the scene, smiling broadly,
stethoscope slung casually from her neck.

Isabella goes to the local kindergarten. She has a math workbook, a reading workbook, and a workbook for something called
concept development in which she does such exercises as drawing
lines from pictures of objects to the rooms in which they belong.
Each day the teacher and the teacher's aide correct the workbook
pages during the morning, and any errors must be corrected at
recess. Last Thursday Isabella spent recess at her desk wondering
what she needed to fix on page 37. The teacher had said, "You have
made a thinking mistake. Stay at your desk until you find it." By
the end of recess, she was still puzzling. "Look," said the teacher,
"you've drawn a line from the piano to the bedroom." "But that's
where it is in our house," Isabella replied. "No," said the teacher,
"that's not the correct answer. The piano belongs in the living room.
Don't be stubborn, Isabella."

During art period Isabella and her classmates color predrawn
figures on ditto sheets, and once a week children who wish to may
copy a short poem from the blackboard, mount it on colored con-
struction paper, and hang it on the bulletin board.

Attempting to balance out the negatives, Isabella's parents have
found an afternoon modern dance class at the Y, and her mother is
showing her how to play simple melodies on the piano—in the
bedroom. Her parents keep plenty of paper, pencils, crayons, felt-

tip pens, and clay on hand, and they give her time to use them. They have resisted the temptation to overprogram her every moment with formal enrichment programs. Isabella goes to Children's Story Hour at the library every Saturday morning. Her parents read aloud to her and her little brother every day without fail. Her father lets her wear his stethoscope and has shown her how to use it.

Isabella is as ready for intellectual exploration as she is eager to go into space. She is a smart kid with a school problem because her imagination and originality are cramped in her present setting. Acceleration by skipping a grade would only intensify the mismatch; Isabella would be separated from her peers while facing increased amounts of paper-pencil work. Isabella's wise parents will continue to encourage the intellectual and aesthetic exploration missing, to date, in her formal schooling.

AURORA AND ANDY

Meet an underestimated and an overestimated child. Some highly intelligent first and second graders, often male, are ready to learn concepts but are uninterested in the mechanics of the three Rs. Because they appear to be at the bottom of the class, their academic potential is frequently underestimated; they are the *pseudo-limited*. First and second graders whose mechanical skills develop rapidly may be placed in the top group, and their conceptual abilities overestimated. They might be called the *pseudo-gifted*.

Aurora, a tidy little girl with well-kept workbooks, disdained Andy both in the classroom and on the playground. Her socks were always clean and pulled up; his were rumpled and sometimes even disappeared into his shoes. While he was dropping his pencils; she was sharpening hers. Her hair was groomed and shiny. His was unruly and sometimes clumped in sweaty spears by the end of recess. They were in the same class for three years of mutual revulsion. She tattled on him whenever she could. He ignored her to the best of his ability. In first and second grades, Aurora was at the top of the class. She seemed to be a smart kid with no school problems; whereas Andy was in the bottom reading group and his papers were never displayed on the bulletin board.

Imagine her chagrin and Andy's amazement when he passed

her in third grade on his way to the very top of the class! He who, pockets full of Lego, had made boats, written about boats, drawn boats, and spent his recesses pretending to cross the Atlantic or fend off pirates—in short "that DUMB boy"—was the one who solved the math stumpers and the mind-benders. His poem about storms and his short story about fog were chosen for the school magazine.

In spite of some early reading and spelling difficulties, Andy's first- and second-grade teachers kept his spirits up. His first-grade teacher put Andy in charge of a three-ring notebook titled "Important Boats," which she kept on a shelf at the front of the classroom. Whenever Andy finished his required work, he was allowed to go and work in "the boat book." The teacher encouraged him to invite a friend to work with him on particular pages. Often the friend would write the words while Andy labored over the illustration. When Andy got discouraged about spelling or handwriting lessons, his teacher would say, "You'll be able to use this in the boat book. It's going to look fine!" She honored Andy's interest while acknowledging his difficulty. She brought his passion right into the schoolroom and found a way to integrate it with the required mechanical work.

In second grade, Andy's teacher wisely encouraged the continuation of his previous interest, but also required him to branch out. When the class studied American Indians, she designated him the resident expert on trapping, tanning, and leather. He learned thoroughly and eagerly.

Meanwhile in third grade, Aurora grew increasingly impatient with open-ended questions, yearned nostalgically for her flash cards, and asked to be the keeper of the class calendar. She recorded daily weather and each month filled in the class birthdays, trips, and holidays.

It was important for the educators to readjust their estimates of these two students' abilities and to recognize the influence of developmental patterns on academic achievement. They needed to convince Andy's parents that their son's slow start had been no indication of his scholastic potential. Andy's parents were initially skeptical of the good news, but relieved and joyful. Aurora's parents needed several conferences before they really understood why their daughter was no longer the star student. Their first impulse was to hire a tutor, their next was to blame the teacher, but finally they were able to adjust their expectations and accept her as she is, a competent, but not creative student.

THOMAS

Thomas is a different learner in a standard curriculum. One February day in kindergarten he dashed off a hillside snow scene, complete with evergreen trees, shadows, children on sleds with their scarves flying, dogs romping, and a father blowing on his hands to keep them warm. It was chosen for the permanent collection of children's art at a major museum.

Yet on that same day he could not recognize one single sight word or give the name of any letter. He could produce whole shapes with his pencil, but he could not read words by their overall design. He could draw fine details, but could not remember letters. Socially, emotionally, and conceptually he was ready for formal academics, but he had trouble with all the verbal symbols of our language. His different learning style masks his developmental readiness.

It is hard to create a comfortable setting for the developmentally ready student with a learning difference. Extra time can help if it is used for preventive training. Educators can recognize learning differences through screening instruments such as those we shall investigate in the Principles of Good Practice section. Using this understanding, they can anticipate mismatches and head off trouble for the developmentally ready, intellectually curious different learner.

PRINCIPLES OF GOOD PRACTICE

OBSERVATION AND SCREENING

Understanding developmental criteria, recognizing readiness for first grade, and making appropriate grade placement depend on observation and screening. The first part of this chapter explored observation. Following are examples of subtests and tasks culled from screening instruments that have proved trustworthy over the years. They may be helpful as foundations for observation or for developing informal tests within a school. A skillfully constructed, administered, and interpreted screening often reveals the patterns of academic talents and limits that underlie the paradox of smart kids with school problems.

Caution! A parent who is tempted to try testing his or her own child runs the serious risk of getting inaccurate information, making a child inappropriately familiar with material that could otherwise be used for accurate evaluation, and giving the child the unspoken message that something is wrong with him. If the parent weren't worried, he or she wouldn't test. The wise parent will want accurate evaluation from a professional and will do nothing to cloud the clarity of the picture that the parents, the child, and the school deserve.

Pencil-and-paper work. Most three-year-olds can make a single circle, most four-year-olds can copy a square, most five-year-olds can make a recognizable copy of a triangle. Students who are comfortable with these tasks will probably be adept in forming letters and numerals and spacing them appropriately on the paper.

Visual match. Most five-year-olds can find (not read) the two matching words in a group of four. Children who are skillful at matching overall visual configurations are frequently nimble sight readers. Children who can match accurately by analyzing letter sequence are often careful readers and orderly spellers.

Visual memory. Most five-year-olds can remember the names of some letters of the alphabet. They can look at an unfamiliar geometrical shape and, when shown four alternatives, can select from memory the one that matches the one they saw. Children with a strong visual memory are quick to recognize letters and sight words.

Auditory discrimination. Most five-year-olds can listen to a pair of words and tell whether the two are the same or different. They can discriminate between similar initial consonants, vowels, and final consonants (examples: *bit/lit, sat/sit, cap/cab*). Students with keen auditory discrimination usually perceive the sounds of words accurately and learn consonant and vowel sounds with relative ease.

Auditory memory.   Most five-year-olds can remember and re-peat word for word a simple sentence such as "Sam wants to eat a big hamburger at the picnic." Students with good auditory memory remember verbal instructions and explanations well.

Auditory analysis.   Most five-year-olds can hear and mimic a compound or two-syllable word and then repeat it again, omitting one of the two parts. Example: "Say *sandbox*; say it again but leave out *box*"; or "Say *magnet*; say it again and leave out *mag*"; or "Say it again and leave out *net*."[1] Students with a strong capacity for auditory analysis will probably use phonics successfully for both reading and spelling.

Naming (both letters and pictures).   Most five-year-olds can name many letters of the alphabet and can give the specific names of such common objects as keys, telephones, pocketbooks, combs, toolboxes and tools, or flashlights. Students with a good supply of labels have precise expressive tools, and also a good linguistic supply on which to draw when trying to match printed symbols to words in their own vocabularies. This ability to match visual and verbal symbols underlies competent reading, as we shall see in greater detail in Chapters 3 and 6.

Verbal reasoning.   Most five-year-olds can complete a simple verbal analogy involving such concepts as opposites: "Fire is hot, ice is . . ." They can explain why people do things: "People wear shoes because . . ." Students who are skillful in verbal reasoning have the capacity to enjoy abstract academic work.

Nonverbal reasoning (puzzle assembly).   Most five-year-olds can complete a simple ten-piece jigsaw puzzle. Students who enjoy nonverbal spatial reasoning frequently have the capacity to excel in mathematics and science.

Sequence.   Most five-year-olds can put three to five picture cards in the correct order to tell a story. Students who can establish a sequence show an understanding of the temporal relationships that govern narrative, history, and some kinds of mathematics.

Story recall.   Most five-year-olds can hear, remember, and retell a simple ten- or twelve-sentence story. Students who can hear and retell a story have the capacity to understand conversation and narrative and are usually strong in reading comprehension.

Math (counting and patterns).   Most five-year-olds can tell you how many pencils you are holding in your hand if you are holding five or fewer, and can tell you what would happen if you took two away. They can also analyze and continue a colored-cube or colored-bead pattern involving three colors. The student who can count and subtract is showing the ability to understand what a number represents. The student who can analyze and continue a pattern is showing an awareness of repetition and interval that augurs well for understanding mathematics, music, and some kinds of science.

Screening results can be used in deciding grade placement and in recommending specific help for individual children. Often some extra training in kindergarten can shore up minor weaknesses and prevent the growth of subsequent problems. A student whose scores are high across the board is ready for formal academic work. A student who is low in all the subtests has either low intellectual endowment or a low developmental level (or both), or he may have been coming down with chicken pox the day of the testing. A child with a low or erratic screening profile needs further evaluation. A student who is high in some areas and low in others is showing the kind of discrepant function associated with learning differences. The next five chapters are designed to shed light and offer ways to help.

Whether learning differences are tolerable or grow into disabilities depends on the *degree* of the discrepancy, the *flexibility* of teaching methods and materials offered by the school, and the student's *ability* to develop *alternative* learning strategies.

A CASE HISTORY: IAN

Ian is the youngest of four children in a family with a tradition of high academic standards. He grew up around books, paper, pencils, and school paraphernalia.

Ian was a sociable child who missed his brother and sisters when they were in school. Although he has an October birthday, he seemed so eager for playmates that his parents enrolled him in a nursery school program for three-year-olds even though he was only two when school began.

The following year he entered the program for four-year-olds and, although he was eager to set off for school in the morning, he was often weepy by lunchtime. His teacher said he particularly enjoyed the story hours and preferred playing with one or two children to playing in larger groups. She complimented his imaginative use of a large and varied supply of general information and said he was proud of learning to write his name.

Approaching his fifth birthday, Ian entered kindergarten at his siblings' school. He felt very grown-up to be a student in the building where he had previously been a visitor. During that year, he learned his letters and sounds and even discovered how to decode and encode simple words and to recognize some words by sight. He also started wetting his bed.

At the November parent-teacher conference, his teacher reported that although intelligent Ian was keeping up, the effort to keep up was taking its toll. He hated making errors and didn't want to have his workbook corrected. He was happiest in art projects, the costume corner, and drama. Socially, he had two close friends in the group, but he liked to play with them away from the other children. If they joined the group on the playground, Ian watched them from the sidelines.

In January, the learning specialist gave each kindergarten child a screening test, and Ian's parents were called in for a conference. They were told he had done well on all the screening subtests. His overall performance put him at the high middle of the class. Why the meeting?

The learning specialist said that Ian had been very tense and apprehensive throughout the testing, constantly asking, "Am I right?" and "Did the other kids do this?" During one difficult subtest the tears had welled up in his eyes, and when a few spilled down his cheeks, the examiner had given him a tissue, saying, "Don't worry, you're doing fine." Ian had bluffed, "I have a cold . . . a new cold . . . my Daddy says it's a cold."

When the educators said they wanted to give Ian another year in kindergarten, his parents were appalled. "We've never had anything like this in our family," they said. "Our kids are all good students and smart kids. Ian is too." "He'd die if he got left back," and "He's kind of spoiled being the youngest. School will toughen him up."

As the conference progressed, the educational team tried to emphasize the positive aspects of Ian's taking another year. They reiterated that he was putting enormous pressure on himself to live up to his own expectations. They pointed out examples of his intelligence but also his increasing reluctance to take risks. They described his timidity on the playground and in the gym. Ian's father, who had been very quiet throughout the meeting, said, "I was the youngest all the way through school, college, and medical school, and I always felt as if I were there by somebody else's patronage instead of by my own merits. I was near the top of the class, but I was always scared, and I never felt part of the group. I think we ought to give this idea a lot of consideration."

Ian's mother asked to help out with the forthcoming class trip. Afterward she said, "I saw things that help me with this decision. I noticed the way the other kids walk; they stride right along; Ian still kind of hops up and down. The other kids have lost the baby fat on their cheeks and hands; Ian still has his. Next to them, he looks really little."

At the second conference everyone agreed that Ian was an intelligent, inquisitive, sensitive superior immature who needed another year in kindergarten. They planned ways to keep him from being bored, agreed that if he were eager to read he would be given instruction, and that no ceiling of any kind would be put on his intellectual development.

Although Ian was initially embarrassed at the prospect of "staying back," his parents explained to him that they had started him in school too early, and that this was the time to put him with people his own age. They explained he was not "being left back"; he was "being given a whole year." He and his siblings took their cues from the parents, who were confident about the decision. Ian bloomed.

The next year Ian was screened again. His approach was joyful and carefree; his performance was superior. He made a minor error, said, "Oops, I goofed," wrote a correct answer over the mistake, and said, "Well, it looks a little messy, but that's okay." Willing to take chances and content with himself, Ian began a journey through formal education that proved stimulating and successful. Is there a doctor in the house? There soon will be. Ian has just been admitted to a combined program in liberal and medical education at a prestigious university.

3

VISUAL
LEARNING

Through the visual learning system, the child or adult recognizes objects, distinguishes sizes and shapes, perceives depth, notes color, and uses visual spatial awareness to estimate where he is. His visual system helps him organize the concrete realities of daily living and also to understand their symbolic representations; he recognizes his grandmother when she comes to his house and also recognizes her in a snapshot. When the child starts school (if not before), he will learn to see, interpret, and remember such printed symbols as letters, words, and numerals.

THE COMPONENTS OF VISUAL LEARNING

In school, visual learning underlies such varied disciplines as reading, mathematics, science, art, and athletics, but in this chapter we shall concentrate on the connections among visual learning, reading, and writing. To understand the paradox of a visually strong smart kid with a reading or reading-related school problem, let us consider three components of visual learning: vision, visual perception, and visual memory.

VISION

The ability to see ranges from blindness to perfect acuity. Someone with normal eyesight can see clearly at different ranges and is able to maintain or shift focus. If there is any question about a student's visual acuity, his eyes should be checked. Parents, teachers, and the students themselves, hoping for quick solutions, often pin high hopes on a trip to the eye doctor. Sometimes a pair of glasses does the trick, but more frequently than not, trouble persists.

Although good eyesight is handy, it is not a prerequisite to reading. I once taught a second grader with two weak eyes, each of which needed different and powerful corrective lenses, whose favorite pastimes were reading and baseball. Arnold Gold, M.D., pediatric neurologist at Columbia Presbyterian Medical Center, makes this distinction: "You see with your eyes, but you read with your brain."

VISUAL PERCEPTION

Accurate visual perception allows human beings to organize and understand what we see in the following ways:

Recognize visual images, remember their connotations, and distinguish the familiar from the unfamiliar. In daily living we probably recognize and understand such visual images as traffic signals and know whether a particular trademark is familiar. In reading we recognize the letters and words we have been taught and we know whether or not we have seen such symbols as abbreviations.

Discriminate among similar visual images. We can tell Fred, Jim, and Robert apart even though all three are six foot tall nineteen-year-old boys with brown hair and brown eyes. In reading we can distinguish *b* from *d* and *could* from *cloud.*

Understand the relationship of parts to wholes. We probably realize that single bricks combine to make a wall, and we see how they are arranged to form the complete structure. In reading, we understand that the word *do* is contained in the word *undoing*.

Distinguish between figures and their backgrounds.   Looking over a harbor we know which images are boats and which are water or sky. We can read black letters on white paper, white letters on a blackboard, green letters on yellow paper, generously spaced or dense print.

Maintain object constancy.   We recognize a fork as a fork no matter whether it is lying on a table, standing upright in a dishwasher, or jumbled in with other cutlery in a crowded kitchen drawer. In reading, we know that a *C* is a *C* no matter its size or color, just as we know the configuration of *t-h-e* as the word *the* no matter the style or size of print.

Interpret spatial relationships.   Standing in a room we know which pieces of furniture are closest and can tell where there is space to walk. We understand why a large airplane looks small in the sky. We can read both large and small print, relate uppercase letters to their lowercase counterparts, understand the directional difference between *b* and *d*, and the sequencing difference between *god* and *dog*.

Endow visual images with meaning.   We could probably get around a foreign airport by following the international symbols for baggage, rest rooms, restaurants, or buses. As beginning readers, we endow letters with sounds, see the relationship between a cluster of letters on a page and a word in our oral vocabulary, and gradually learn to absorb information by moving our eyes from left to right along successive lines of print.

VISUAL MEMORY

Having a crisp, reliable visual memory is analogous to having a good mental photocopying machine. The grocery shopper can visualize the misplaced list; the traveler may say, "We're about to come to the intersection where we turn right." In reading, the student with a strong visual memory may need only one or two exposures to lock a word into his sight vocabulary. His visual memory will also help him proofread his spelling. He fixes the word that "doesn't look right."

Paradoxically, reading problems can beset intelligent people whose visual system works well, or superbly, outside school. Their three-dimensional visual skills are as pronounced as their difficulties with two-dimensional printed symbols. If the student's vision is normal, the problem may lie either in visual perception, or in visual memory, or in or both.

Visual perceptual confusion is responsible for *strephosymbolia.* This term was coined by the pioneering neurologist Samuel T. Orton in the 1930s to describe the reversal or transposition of phrases, words, or letters or of any symbols. Afflicted readers may confuse such letter pairs as *b/d, p/q, y/h, m/w.* They may reverse the sequences of letters in a word, reading *was* for *saw,* or, as we shall see later, make as poignant an error as seeing *All Rights Reserved* as *All Rights Reversed.* They may make similar mistakes with numerals, confusing *6* for *9* or saying *17* for *71.* They may interchange words of similar visual configuration, confusing *house* for *horse, could* for *cold* or *cloud, palace* for *place.* One third grader asked, "What's rye beard?"

Some readers with visual perceptual confusion may omit or misread interior syllables in multisyllable words, mistaking *vacation* for *vaccination.* Others may have figure/ground trouble. They may have an easy time with a book made of dark, clear, generously spaced print on opaque paper but be undone by a pocket-size volume of Dickens lightly printed on onionskin paper. Still others with either obvious or residual visual perceptual weakness may be able to read accurately for a short time but then fall apart.

A weak visual memory can produce *wordblindness.* The term was coined by the same Dr. Orton to describe the phenomenon of the intelligent person with good vision who does not remember printed words. Many smart kids with school problems have a weak visual memory for symbols: letters, whole words, numerals, symbols for mathematical processes, or chemistry formulas. De Hirsch says it is as though they are trying to make an imprint in very loose sand. The problem does not vanish with childhood. William James (1842–1910), author, philosopher, psychologist, and brother of the novelist Henry James, was an intellectual giant with perfectly normal eyesight. Yet he said, "I am myself a very poor visualizer and find that I can seldom call to mind even a single letter of the alphabet in purely retinal terms. I must trace the letter by running my mental eye over its contour in order that the image of it shall have any distinctness at all."[1]

VISUAL LEARNING AND READING

Before we can help the student with a reading problem, we need to decide, what is reading? and how do people read?

WHAT IS READING?

Reading is a visual, aural, linguistic process through which the reader takes meaning from print. A reader uses his eyes to recognize in print the same language he has recognized with his ears in speech. To convey meaning, print must represent words the reader understands. It profits little to string the letter sounds *d-a-m-p* together if the word *damp* is meaningless. Although the more sophisticated reader learns some new words from reading, they stick only if they have some element of familiarity: either containing recognizable roots, or representing a concept already understood, or being so vividly descriptive that they convey an instant image.

Reading is a highly integrative process, which draws on all the learning systems, and in which people use varieties and combinations of methods, unconsciously choosing whichever fits the moment. The more methods readers have, the greater their facility. People read by *phonics*: associating letters with sounds, and blending the sounds into words; *look-say*: recognizing whole words; *structural analysis*: combining recognizable chunks of words such as affixes, roots, and syllables; and *inference*: guessing a word from verbal context, from an illustration, or from a linguistic hunch.

HOW DO PEOPLE READ?

To understand smart kids who struggle with reading, those of us who read easily need to recognize the arbitrary nature of the complicated symbol system we take for granted, sometimes explaining points that seem obvious.

Students may need to be shown that just as a spoken word is a unit of combined sounds, a written word is a unit of print, and each cluster of letters on a page represents one word.

Impaired readers often do not realize that there is more than one way to figure out words. When they discover that there are several ways, they still may feel that the method stressed in their classroom is the only proper way and that others are either inferior methods or some form of cheating. Their teachers and parents need to free them from this restrictive approach.

Students who have experienced the instant learning we explored as one of the traits of giftedness in Chapter 1 often feel that being able to read is a lucky accident of fate like having blue eyes, curly hair, or inherited wealth. The instant learner who can't yet read may need to be convinced that reading is a teachable, learnable skill. A former first grade teacher tells the story of the child who said to her, "I can read now. I can read ANYTHING!" She said, "Joey, that's wonderful. How did you learn?" "I didn't learn," he said. "The letters just whisper to me."

All students can be taught to read, at least at a rudimentary level. Although many conundrum kids will never read for pleasure, they can learn to decipher the code.

Caution! There was a time when people hoped that exercises and visual perceptual training would cure or alleviate reading problems. It seemed so logical. However, research shows that this is not so. At this writing, there seems to be a resurgence of quasi-professionals offering a quick fix. Beware of shopping mall charlatans. See the restatement of policy by the Ophthalmologists' Association, developed by the Ad Hoc Working Group of the American Association for Pediatric Ophthalmology and Strabismus, and The American Academy of Ophthalmology, May 7, 1981:

Indeed, children with dyslexia or related learning disability have the same incidence of ocular abnormalities, e.g. refractive errors and muscle imbalance (including near point of convergence and binocular fusion deficiencies) as children without. There is no peripheral eye defect that produces dyslexia and associated learning disabilities. Eye defects do not cause reversal of letters, words or numbers. Indeed recent studies suggest dyslexia and associated learning disabilities may be related to genetic, bio chemical and/or structural brain changes. Further controlled research is warranted.

No known scientific evidence supports claims for improving the academic abilities of dyslexic or learning disabled children, or modification of delinquent or criminal behavior with treatment based on:

Visual training, including muscle exercises, ocular pursuit, opr tracking exercises, or glasses (with or without bifocals or prisms);

Neurologic organization training (laterality training, balance board, perceptual training).

Furthermore, such training frequently yields deleterious results. A false sense of security is created which may delay or prevent proper instruction or remedial therapy. The expense of such procedures is unwarranted, and appropriate remedial educational techniques may be omitted. Improvements claimed for visual training or neurologic organizational training typically result from those remedial education techniques with which they are combined.

VISUAL LEARNING AND WRITING

The visual learning system also includes visual-motor integration. In daily living, visual-motor integration allows us to walk across a room without bumping into the furniture. In schoolwork, many visual-motor tasks involve eyes, hand, pencil, and paper, requiring both analysis and execution.

Copying, a school survival skill, is an example. Young students practice letter formation by copying single letters and then words. Older students copy spelling patterns from the board, they copy early drafts to final drafts on paper, they copy examples of arithmetical processes from textbooks, from blackboards, and from worksheets. They copy geometric shapes in geometry and laboratory experiments in science. They need to copy homework assignments quickly and accurately. The student who writes "read pp. 65–56" will not make forward motion on the assignment.

The first step in copying is analysis. The student either recognizes the object as a whole or analyzes its components. Once he knows what he needs to write, the next step is to carry out the plan: execution. For example, I could copy this page easily because I know each of the words and remember whole sentences. But I couldn't copy a German translation of my page that same way because the language and some of its written characters are unfamiliar. I would have to reproduce each word letter by letter, struggling to put the letters in the correct sequence, learning to put umlauts over vowels but never over consonants, and being careful to leave spaces between words but not inside them.

If I tried to copy a Chinese translation of my page, I might be able to analyze which characters come in which order, but I might not be able to form them correctly. Or I might be able to analyze and execute the character formation adequately as long as the original was there for reference, but not if I had to do it from memory. My errors might be in analysis, in execution, or in both.

Similarly, smart students who have trouble with visual-motor integration may have trouble with either analysis or execution, or in some instances, both. Some students have trouble seeing the small components of a whole design, or word. Others see the bits and pieces perfectly well but cannot make their pencils obey. Some children have trouble with both analysis and execution, whereas others can perform very nicely if the stimulus remains as a reference but be unable to reproduce the configuration from memory. To give appropriate help, we need to know where the problem is.

Students with visual-motor integration problems need to practice their handwriting until the motions are completely automatic. They need short frequent sprints: long sessions for these children means "practice makes worse." They should write on lined, not blank, paper and be taught to use the lines for spatial organization.

PRINCIPLES OF GOOD PRACTICE

Visual learning colors a student's entire academic career. Problems of visual acuity need diagnosis and a corrective prescription followed by regular checkups. Students with problems in visual perception or visual memory need specific training and must be shown how to strengthen their weaknesses with support from their other learning systems. Good training will show the weak visual learner how to manage his problem. It won't go away, but he can survive in school in spite of it.

A teacher or parent can evaluate the student's visual skills in light of the information in this chapter, noting which visual tasks the student does well and which give him trouble. It is important to collect representative samples of work for the master file and to review the student's performance with the overseer, whose role we explored in Chapter 1.

A reminder: fatigue, anxiety, or time pressure will invite the reappearance of past problems. A brilliant professor, who thought she had outgrown troubles similar to the ones in this chapter, was giving a seminar. By the end of the session she was tired and running short of time. Summing up a point she went to the blackboard and, trying to write the word *blackboard,* produced *balckbred.* She was oblivious to her error until everyone had left and she turned around to collect her belongings. Mortified, she erased the evidence and fled.

The student who has been helped to understand and surmount (or circumvent) his difficulty may be able to be as philosophical as William James in the quotation earlier in this chapter. Without such help, the student's self-concept takes a continual battering. A wounded person may direct his inevitable anger inward, deciding he is stupid or generally unworthy, or he may focus his anger on the society that has established requirements he cannot meet. Not surprisingly, there is a strong link between reading failure and juvenile delinquency.

It is never too late to get help. Many people who have hidden their illiteracy well into their adult lives have learned to read through approaches similar to those described in this book. Recent figures show that functional illiteracy (the inability to read beyond a sixth grade level) afflicts some 30 million adults in the United States. Those who do not yet know how to read need reassurance that teaching is available and learning is possible. See the Resources section for materials and programs for older nonreaders (pp. 244, 245).

Folklore says, "There's more than one way to skin a cat." Similarly, there's more than one way to read a word. Smart kids whose school problems are related to disordered visual learning need instruction and practice in each of the following approaches. The smarter the kid the more he needs alternative reading strategies for understanding print, which can nourish his emotions, enhance his aesthetic appreciation, and stimulate his intellect.

We can show students how to read by using a part-to-whole approach: phonics, a whole-to-whole approach: look-say, a whole-to-part approach: structural analysis, and an inferential approach: context clues.

A PART-TO-WHOLE APPROACH: PHONICS

Knowing the sounds of individual letters allows the student to blend them into words. This decoding approach to reading (and its complement, the encoding approach to spelling) works beautifully for many students. According to the 1985 National Institute of Education report, *Making a Nation of Readers*,[2] phonics is the preferred introductory method. Although using it is slower than reading by whole-word recognition, the student who knows phonics always has a reliable strategy to figure out a new word.

A WHOLE-TO-WHOLE APPROACH: LOOK-SAY

Recognizing whole words is the most efficient way to read, and good readers who begin with phonics should learn sight words as soon as possible. However, students with poor visual memory who have tried to learn through look-say have probably felt like unwilling participants in Russian roulette: "Maybe I'll know it or maybe I'll be dead."

In a seeming paradox, students with a weak visual memory who have trouble learning such high-frequency words as *the, one, would, was, of,* or *where* may exemplify what my colleague calls the *Tyrannosaurus rex* phenomenon. Although he misses the common words, he always recognizes *Tyrannosaurus rex.* Its size, shape, and length distinguish it immediately. This seeming contradiction bears on the whole-to-whole approach in two ways. First, it underscores that the little words are frequently the hardest to learn. Second, words that catch the student's interest may be the easiest to learn.

A WHOLE-TO-PART APPROACH: STRUCTURAL ANALYSIS

Figuring out words by going from whole to part is neither more nor less noble than going from part to whole; it is simply a reverse procedure. But students who have trouble with one approach are not always shown its opposite.

The easiest way for some children to learn to read is by finding whole words in recurrent patterns of sentence structure. Such readers may find the "key sentence" technique helpful.

Write out a key sentence such as "Who is here today?" The student parrots the sentence and answers the question. The teacher or parent writes out each answer.

Key sentence: "Who is here today?"

Johnny: "Who is here today? Fred is here today."

As the student reads the key sentence he identifies the words in the recurrent pattern, adds his own contribution, and sees it being written. Then the adult asks the student to find the word *who* or *today* or someone's name. As the reader becomes more proficient, the teacher expands the length and complexity of the key sentence.

Some students learn individual words by looking at the whole and then analyzing its parts. For example, a teacher might show the child his whole name: *Tommy.* "This says *Tommy.* What's the first *sound* you hear in your name? Yes \t\. Where is the letter that makes that sound? What letter makes the \o\ sound you hear in the middle of your name? What letter makes the sound you make when you keep your lips together and hum?" Then the teacher might say, "I am going to make one of the sounds in your name. When I do, I want you to write the letter that makes that sound. I will leave the card with your name on it right here for you to look at if you need to give yourself a hint."

When students master the early levels of phonics and look-say, they are ready to expand their reading powers through *structural analysis*: learning to recognize and isolate such chunks as *ing, ed, re, un*. If they learn to recognize affixes as units of meaning, they can read new unfamiliar words by covering up the familiar chunks, decoding the remainder, and then uncovering the chunks.

Here are some common prefixes: *un, mis, non, re, pre, uni, bi, tri, tele, micro.* Using the "cover up the familiar part" system students could easily read *uncover, misled* (not mistaking it as I did for years as mizled), *nonsense, restore, preview, unicorn, bicycle, tricycle, television,* or *microwave.*

The ability to recognize and isolate affixes both at the beginning and end of a word makes it possible for a young reader to decode such large words as *unforgettable,* making them accessible rather than unmanageable.

AN INFERENTIAL APPROACH: CONTEXT CLUES

Using pictures, inference, linguistic hunch, or a combination of all three, readers establish a context that saves them from having to figure out each word individually. Some students for whom reading is laborious are afraid that this kind of contextual intuition is a form of cheating.

Students should be encouraged to make informed guesses, but as a parallel strategy, they must also be trained to go back at the end of the sentence and check the guess by asking themselves, "Does my word make sense?" and "Are these the letters that spell my word?" A student who guesses the word *election* when the actual word is *electrician* is in for a shock at the end of the paragraph.

It is tricky for parents to try to teach a child to read, and the minute emotional negatives appear, performance will disintegrate. The student, particularly one who is struggling, deserves as much privacy as possible, but still needs to unlock the code of print. The Resources section (pp. 245–46) lists materials that can be used by a teacher, tutor, or parent if necessary.

As we shall see in greater detail in Chapter 6, "Language and

Learning," the richer the student's vocabulary, the more likely he is to anticipate the writer's words, and the less likely he is to be fooled by his eyes. Even habitual adult readers make visual errors. Today the front page of my morning newspaper had two pictures: one of a soldier and one of a ballet dancer. Between the pictures was a headline. At first glance, I didn't know whether it read FATE OF BATTLE UNDECIDED or FATE OF BALLET UNDECIDED. I had two options: I could either read the confusing word by syllables or I could scan the text for a clue. When I saw the words "graceful leaps," I knew the word was *ballet.*

Because I had both the decoding skills and the internal language to correct my error in visual sequencing, I was luckier than my high school sophomore student, alluded to in the beginning of the chapter. Looking at the copyright notice *All Rights Reserved* he asked, "What does it mean . . . All Rights Reversed?" What indeed? Perhaps it means that letters like *b* and *p* that face to the right get reversed to *d* and *q*. Or perhaps it means that his rights, his privileges, such as knowing how to read with all its attendant benefits, are reversed, meaning denied.

A CASE HISTORY: EDNA

Sixth grader Edna wrote: "I wont too du su orsid. I dot kar if I dy. I rid my bik fast so mabe I get hrt, and I klim to the hiist prt of the tre mabe I wil fal an kil misellf. I dont car. i hat been so dum." (I want to do suicide. I don't care if I die. I ride my bike fast so maybe I [will] get hurt, and I climb to the highest part of the tree. Maybe I will fall and kill myself. I don't care. I hate being so dumb.) The paper was returned marked "F. For the last time FIX YOUR SPELLING!"

Her next story said: "I did. I wen up to the ruf an I climd the chimee, an I sed godby an I jumt of. It is betr been ded I dot cy enemor." (I died. I went up to the roof and I climbed the chimney, and I said good-bye and I jumped off. It is better being dead. I don't cry anymore.) This paper was returned marked "F. The dead don't write about it."

Oh yes they do. She just did.

Edna lived in a rural area of Maryland where she entered school as a happy kindergarten child who enjoyed outdoor activities, animals, people of all ages, and numbers.

In first grade left-handed Edna did not learn to read. Each day the teacher would hold up look-say word cards, saying the words for the children to repeat in unison. After going through the new words for the day's lesson, the children would open their books to the assigned page and take turns reading orally, child by child, line by line.

Edna dreaded her turn. She couldn't remember what the words were supposed to be, and she had trouble keeping her place because she couldn't follow what the other children were reading. She would guess words she thought sounded like part of the story and try frantically to remember what words she had heard the teacher read from the cards, but she usually made mistakes. Edna would feel her cheeks get red and hear her own voice tremble.

In second grade, Edna was good in math but her reading difficulties continued. She tried desperately to memorize the words on her spelling list and sometimes could get them right on the test, but when she tried to use them later she forgot what they looked like.

Third grade seemed like paradise; there was no more reading aloud. She would take out her book, run her eyes around the edges of the page, study the picture, see whether she recognized any of the words in the text, and, after what she deemed a suitable time, she would turn to the next page and repeat the process. At discussion time she would listen to the other children's comments and make her own contributions in the form of questions she thought up from the pictures. "Why were Indian canoes always brown?" she would inquire innocently. "What an interesting question; what do you think, boys and girls?" and Edna would be off the hook for another morning.

She slipped through fourth grade, but not fifth. When the math teacher saw that Edna couldn't do the word problems, she uncovered the secret. Edna was a virtual nonreader.

Edna's father was an industrial engineer and her mother was the dietitian at the nearby hospital. Both parents were interested in the scientific aspects of their work, loved the out-of-doors, and loved Edna. They hadn't known about her trouble partly because she disguised it well and partly because they had no warning to be on the lookout. Nonreaders become masters of camouflage.

With the shameful secret disclosed, Edna was scheduled for reading lessons with the second-grade teacher four times a week during recess. The teacher got out the same word cards and basal reader she was using with her own class and tried to teach Edna. But that method had already failed once, and it just made matters worse. Not only was Edna kept in from the playground for lessons, but all the other children knew it, they knew why, and they knew she couldn't read what the second graders were reading. Her classmates were merciless. The second-grade teacher, who had taught many children to read by using these same look-say materials, grew impatient with Edna, and frequently there was a sarcastic undertone to her superficially friendly comments.

By sixth grade Edna's teachers described her as stubborn, uninterested, rebellious, stupid, inattentive, worried, and tearful. Her family didn't understand why she couldn't read and were frightened and ashamed. Edna wrote the two stories about suicide at the beginning of this section. When her mother saw them, she knew she had to act.

She took Edna to the pediatrician, who suggested her eyes be examined. They were perfectly normal. He gave her a comprehensive physical examination. She was perfectly normal. But she didn't feel normal.

Reaching out for comfort, Edna's mother telephoned her sister Martha, a nurse at Johns Hopkins Hospital in Baltimore, Maryland. She wept out the story of Edna's problems, her own anxiety, and the whole family's feeling of being literally and figuratively at a dead end.

Martha had heard about similar situations at the hospital and gave Edna's mother the name of a doctor to call. The rest is history. Edna went to Baltimore for an evaluation. The results are as follows. Her visual acuity is perfectly normal, her visual perception is imprecise and disorderly, and her visual memory is very weak. Her auditory acuity, perception, and memory are strong, as are her general language skills. Her spatial powers are extraordinary, and her scores in reasoning and thinking are in the ninety-ninth percentile.

This is how she was helped. In the seventh and eighth grades, Edna was tutored four times a week in the early morning before leaving for school. Using a multisensory method, her tutor taught her to read, write, and spell, but she was not expected to use these newly developing skills for her schoolwork. Instead, her mother or father read her assignments aloud to her; she listened to stories and books on tape, and she took her tests on the tape recorder.

These modifications of the regular school program were specified by the doctor who had evaluated her, and by the educational consultant who interpreted the test results and, acting as Edna's overseer, drew up the particulars of Edna's educational help. Because they came from a medical doctor's office, the school accepted them just as they would have accepted a plaster cast or a course of penicillin.

By ninth and tenth grade Edna was ready for a new level of tutoring. Although she completed much of her homework on her own, she received help with lengthy reading assignments and was coached in strategies for working with complicated polysyllabic words. She also needed help with her introductory course in Spanish. The doctor had said a foreign language would be hard for her and indeed it was.

In eleventh grade Edna discovered the joy of literature courtesy of the Brontë sisters. She anguished over the thwarted love of Jane Eyre and Mr. Rochester, she imagined Heathcliff on the hills surrounding her town—and she decided to apply to college.

On the advice of the doctor in Baltimore and her educational overseer, Edna requested and received permission to take specially administered SAT and college board exams. (There is considerable information on the hows, whys, wheres, and whats of this in Chapter 9, "Maturation and Higher Education: Getting It All Together"). She was admitted to the state university and plans to become either a psychologist or a medical doctor. When asked why, she said simply, "I know how it feels to hurt."

4

MOTOR FUNCTION AND SCHOOL ACHIEVEMENT

Smart students with mild small-motor weakness can end up with major, school-generated disabilities if their early problems go unnoticed or untreated. Yet the teaching of handwriting, a fundamental small-motor skill, is woefully neglected in many schools. Asking (or requiring) students to use handwriting as a vehicle for expression without giving them sufficient training and practice invites disaster; a student who tries to support strong conceptual work with weak mechanical skills is heading for a full-blown school problem.

"Children who read well but have diminished output or productivity may be misunderstood by parents and teachers, who may not be aware of the possibility that subtle developmental dysfunctions can impair productivity. As a result, a child's chronic failure to complete homework or exhibit enthusiasm in school may be attributed falsely to a poor attitude, a bad home situation or a primary emotional problem."[1]

LARGE- AND SMALL-MOTOR FUNCTIONS

In exploring motor function and school achievement, first we shall consider large- (frequently called gross-) motor function: walking, running, jumping, throwing, bouncing, skipping, batting, tackling, diving, or dancing. Then we will look at small- (frequently called fine-) motor work: cutting, pasting, braiding, knotting, tweezing, whistling, winking, buttoning, coloring or writing.

Both large- and small-motor function depend on muscles, coordination, and memory. These three have direct parallels to the components of visual learning we investigated in the preceding chapter. We might line them up this way:

vision   muscle
perception   coordination
memory   memory

MUSCLE

People need muscles for movement the way they need vision for sight. Just as some people have particularly keen eyesight and enjoy visual activities, some are naturally active and enjoy the feeling of movement. Others, equally intelligent, may be sedentary by choice or because of handicaps. Just as some people need to wear eyeglasses, others may need muscular supports. My aunt was a brilliant psychoanalyst who was crippled by poliomyelitis in her childhood and had to conduct her entire practice from a wheelchair. Muscle power and intellectual power are not synonymous.

COORDINATION

Coordination involves the organization of both large- and small-motor function and thus is parallel to perception in the visual system. Coordination includes spatial awareness, anticipation, and control. A person first learns to control himself or herself in space and then to do the same with materials or objects.

For example, the accomplished tennis player doesn't lunge around the court trying to catch up with the ball. He anticipates where his opponent will aim it and moves there to be ready. He plans where he will hit his return and coordinates his eye, racket, and ball to carry out his plan. Large-motor accomplishments such as these require a high degree of visual-motor organization; the pairing of the two systems is called *visual-motor integration*.

Small-motor organization works the same way: spatial awareness, anticipation, and control. A surgeon uses visual–small-motor coordination to transplant a heart or repair the damage to an injured limb, knowing where to cut, what to watch for, and how to guide his cutting or sewing implements with precision. The same spatial awareness, anticipation, and control are the visual-motor integration skills that produce easy, attractive handwriting.

Poor motor coordination plagues many smart kids and adults. A leader in the field of economics said of herself, "Watching me run is like watching a cow try to fly." Eva, the professor whose success story appears in Chapter 10 (pp. 215–27), still has barely legible handwriting.

MEMORY

Just as a powerful visual memory allows a reader to recognize whole words rapidly and accurately, motor memory permits precision, rhythm, and speed.

Once the motor memory for an action is established, whether it be for serving a tennis ball, for knitting, or for writing, the practitioner can perform the basic operation automatically. Until the motor memory is established, conscious effort must go into learning the necessary motions and arranging them in proper sequence. For example, after my right shoulder was surgically reconstructed several years ago, I had to develop a new large-motor plan for my tennis serve, and I still need to talk myself through the motions: "position, cock, toss, lean, hit." If I don't recite the steps in order, I get partway through my former pattern, realize I can't execute it, try to make an adjustment, forget where I am in the new sequence, and hit my shot out or in the net.

Motor memory opens the way to precision and rhythm, which in turn open the way for speed. Without precision and rhythm, speed is useless; speed built upon them is beautiful. Look at Olympic figure skaters or think of my elderly aunt who knits in the movies. An avid mystery fan, she has knit and purled her way through many a feature film, neither dropping a stitch nor missing a clue. When I told her I thought she was a wonder, she replied, "Nonsense! It saves my money and my waistline . . . you can't eat popcorn when you're knitting."

Many smart kids don't have a strong motor memory for letter formation, yet handwriting that involves no conscious sequence of motions is essential for school success.

MOTOR SKILLS IN SCHOOL

Smart kids with good motor skills bring well-developed large- and small-motor *muscle, coordination,* and *memory* to school, combining them with the visual system. They get on and off the bus without accident, navigate their way through crowded hallways without injury to themselves or others, organize themselves and their possessions, take off and put on their innerwear and outerwear, and claim or challenge the top of the jungle gym. Younger children enjoy cutting, pasting, bead stringing, block building, coloring, and writing.

Older students revel in such visual–gross-motor skills as skating, throwing, catching, running, jumping, or dancing, not to mention the ability of a tardy, well-coordinated adolescent to turn what is normally a three-minute journey into a forty-five-second dash— up the stairs, through the cafeteria, around the corner, into the classroom, and onto the chair before the bell rings. These students play on varsity teams and feel successful.

The fortunate older student will be able to extricate a pencil or pen, open a notebook to the appropriate page, take legible notes, and hand in a paper containing clear thoughts in good penmanship or an exam whose tidy appearance is in harmony with the quality of the content. This lucky soul will use the science lab materials skillfully, function accurately on a computer keyboard, and eat an entire meal without spilling his food or knocking over a glass of milk.

His physical behavior will convey an accurate picture of an intelligent, worthwhile human being.

Smart kids with motor problems are in bad trouble. Because students are called on to use motor skills in their very earliest school experiences, those with either large- or small-motor difficulties suffer blows to their self-concepts at particularly vulnerable moments. The clumsy child meets scorn on the playground as well as in the classroom. As the psychologist Erik Erikson says, school-age children have internalized the judgment "I am what I can make work." The smart kid with a wide discrepancy between his motor competence and his intellectual capacity has nowhere to hide. Curriculum requirements force him to make a public display of his weaknesses, which create an unfair and often inaccurate impression of stupidity.

Fine-motor ease in handling materials has a powerful influence on school success, on the impression a student makes on teachers and other students, on adults outside the classroom, and on a student's opinion of himself. The student who has trouble manipulating materials, be they books or beakers, calculators or keyboards, or, particularly, paper and pencils, has a hard time getting a high grade. Teachers frequently equate tidy-looking papers with accurate content and clear thought; a messy paper may earn a low grade despite good ideas. Orderly written expression predisposes teachers to give higher grades in English, foreign languages, math, science, and history, namely those fields that carry the greatest academic weight.

Many times the student with poor handwriting, who is clumsy with small-motor tasks, is very skillful in combining large-motor function with spatial awareness. The athlete sprints through a chink in his opponent's defense; the actor or dancer uses movement and space to tell a story; and those with social skills use body English clearly and keep appropriate distances between themselves and others. But although these are skills the world admires, and that enhance the overall quality of life, sports, the arts, and social skills are generally thought of as "the extras." They may highlight the Good Joe or earn a student a varsity letter or certificate of commendation, but they seldom influence a grade-point average.

In fact, the student with good large-motor spatial skills and poor small-motor spatial skills is often treated unjustly by teachers or parents who say, "If he can be that precise on the football field (or stage or political rally), he could hand in a presentable paper (write a decent-looking exam) if he only tried."

Meet six smart kids with different types of unusual motor function.

JAKE

Jake is a big boy from a big family. Perpetual motion is the order of the day; Jake and his siblings clamber up and down the stairs of their house, toss balls, sling Frisbees, jump on bikes, pop wheelies, score goals, slide on slides, swing on swings, jump rope—and run!

As an infant, Jake was a rapid creeper and courageous climber. He walked at ten months, and once he got his feet under him, he kept going. His idea of torture is to sit still indoors. Figuratively, his motor is on and running.

Jake enjoyed all the active aspects of his kindergarten year: the playground equipment, the big block corner, the art activities, the singing, and the other children. He was a happy, energetic, popular student.

First grade was a disaster. Jake's handwriting was large and irregular, and he was embarrassed by its appearance. His spelling and reading were very poor. He was often kept in from recess to make corrections or to complete pieces of unfinished work. As the year progressed, his smile faded.

Matters were even worse in second grade, where he lagged far behind his classmates. Jake's letters were poorly formed, his words were illegible, and his numerals drifted out of their columns. He resented sitting at his desk, and his sadness turned to anger.

In preparation for parents' night, Jake's third-grade teacher gave a dictation, planning to hang the children's papers on the wall. The sentences were about a deer. Jake was an animal lover, but he couldn't remember how to spell *deer*, he mixed his *b*s and *d*s, and he left out two key words because he couldn't keep up. He was so discouraged he threw his paper away and was the only student who had no paper on the wall that night. He stopped trying. He began getting into fights on the playground, and the other children became frightened of him. He was big and strong; he became rough and angry. His classmates were wise to be afraid of him.

By fourth grade his work was the poorest in the class, and in November he had to be suspended from school for breaking another child's nose in a playground fight.

In junior high, he became involved in vandalism, and he finally dropped out of high school.

What irony that his motor system, which had brought him such happiness as a young child, was also the system that separated him from his work, from his friends, and ultimately from fulfillment in life.

KEN

Oafish is the only word to describe sixth grader Ken's appearance. He is heavyset and dark-haired, and his corduroy trousers stick in embarrassing places when he gets up from his chair. A boy of very few words, he is sure to bump into at least one desk in any trip down the aisle, his shoes are usually half off, and tatters of paper fall from his pockets like leaves falling off trees in an autumn wind. He wears layers of ill-fitting clothing to protect himself from the cold of the northwestern winters. His eyes are deeply set, giving him the appearance of a perpetual squint, but his visual acuity, perception, and memory are fine.

His teachers complain about his clumsiness and his messy homework papers. He jams them into his desk or book bag without regard. Even though some of his ideas are well thought-out, his handwriting is hard to read and the papers are usually either wrinkled or torn.

Ken needs to be shown how to minimize the effects of his clumsiness. He should keep his papers intact by putting them in notebooks for different subjects, arrange his desk and locker to accommodate them, and have an uncluttered surface to work on. Although his clumsiness makes him look stupid, Ken is actually an extremely intelligent boy who needs help.

Although he cannot move his own body around without collisions, his understanding of spatial concepts is immense and he outstrips many adults in his ability to anticipate and reason: he is chess champion of the entire county. He moves his bishops and knights carefully, he can move his queen with triumph, but he cannot move himself without disaster.

EMILY

Emily was only in the fifth grade when she wrote this beautiful fairy tale.

THE TRAVELER

There was once a traveler on horseback . . . weary, thirsty and with no prospect of shelter. He rode along and along until through the shadows of the early evening he saw the shape of a castle ahead. Comforted, he guided his horse in that direction. When he arrived, he tethered his horse and walked inside. No one was there. It seemed spooky but he was glad to be indoors where he could relax, and so he fell asleep.

When he woke up it was midnight and there was wild revelry. Hags, vultures and creatures were dancing to a wild tune. The traveler looked and was afraid. He looked for the door but for a long time he couldn't find it. Then he found it but it was locked and there was no knob on the inside. He was trapped. Again he was afraid.

Then came the dawn. Through the dusty window came a sunbeam. It looked like a road to the traveler and so he stepped on it, and walked on it out through the window and to his tethered horse which he released, and they rode away together.

This child who could guide her pencil through such intricacies and her characters through such scenery was so poorly coordinated that she did not learn to pump a swing until second grade, and so knock-kneed that getting up and down stairs between classes was a challenge. Gym classes were torture to her, and recess was a nightmare.

Other children isolated her because her motor problems were so obvious. Most of her teachers pitied her but did not think to look beyond her conscientious performance in routine daily schoolwork. When she submitted the fairy tale to the school magazine people were amazed. Emily needed the kind of adult help in finding a showcase for her talent we discussed in Chapter 1. In light of her own motor problems, it is poignant to note the powerful action in her story and the rhythmic quality of the traveler's escape.

MARSHALL AND MICHELLE

Marshall is a tiny first grader with huge ideas. He can read anything and has an immense vocabulary, a wry sense of humor, and original thoughts about the human condition. Although he is highly verbal, he has a noticeable articulation problem that slows his rate of speech, and his large, awkward handwriting makes it hard for his hand to keep pace with his ideas. If he concentrates on his thoughts, he forgets how to form his letters; interchanges *b*/*d*, *m*/*n*, and *i*/*e*; and intermingles upper- and lowercase letters. Letters that should drop below the line (*g, j, y, p, q*) float around as if filled with helium, *i* grows taller than *t*, he forgets to put spaces between words and sometimes puts spaces inside them instead. As a result, his output looks awful and is hard to read.

The parallel between Marshall's speech and handwriting patterns is a common one. Speech is the motor component of spoken expressive language; writing is the motor component of written expressive language. Those with trouble in one kind of motor expression are likely to have equal trouble with the other. This relationship is called a "bocca-lingual-grapho-motor link," from *bocca* meaning mouth, *lingua* meaning tongue, *grapho* meaning write, and *motor* meaning motion. Marshall needs a great deal of extra practice in handwriting until he can form his letters effortlessly. His speech patterns are a symptom of extra vulnerability in his expressive motor system, thus he needs additional reinforcement.

Marshall's classmate Michelle is his opposite. Although it took her a long time to internalize sound/symbol correspondence, she has it now, but resists being rushed. She wants the time to form her letters slowly, deliberately, and exquisitely. When asked to write quickly, she becomes frantic, perfectionist, ritualistic, stubborn, and angry. Rather than hand in a paper she considers substandard, she will throw it away. As a result, she has many pieces of uncompleted work. Although her teacher finds her one of the most interesting thinkers in the class, they are at loggerheads over the pace of her small-motor work.

Like Marshall, Michelle needs a great deal of handwriting practice to get up to an acceptable rate of speed.

ELLEN

Although left-handed Ellen, a first grader, had a difficult time learning to form her letters, she is extremely talented with her paintbrush, her drawing pencil, and her scissors, displaying an uncanny talent for origami. If asked to make an origami Indian tent, or turtle or princess (it didn't matter what), she would tip her head to one side, half-squint, take a piece of paper, fold it in various shapes and layers, make a few cuts with her scissors, and unfold it to reveal whatever had been requested. But when she tried to write letters and words, her hand changed from ally to saboteur. She was fortunate in having a teacher who understood the needs of left-handed students, Ellen in particular, and provided extra instruction, extra practice, and plenty of scope for Ellen's artistic talents. At the end of first grade, with the problem nicely disappearing, Ellen wrote and illustrated this metaphoric autobiography:

"Once there was a terofiing [terrifying] bull. All the men could not kill him, but one girl could fight anything. She bet that she could fight the bull, and she wun the batul. Then she became the queen. The End"

All six of these smart students needed extra attention because of their motor function, and five of the six needed additional training in handwriting. There are many like them in classrooms everywhere, many whose potentially crippling problems are misunderstood or ignored.

The Russian neurologist A. R. Luria coined the expression *kinetic melody* to describe an easy harmony between rate of thought and rate of pencil movement. Having kinetic melody can make the difference between enjoying and dreading written work. Among those who dread it are the avoiders who ask, "How long does it have to be?" Their sparse, sterile product earns a low grade. Others whose labored handwriting gives them good reason to dread writing get caught up in ideas anyway, but their lag-behind hands omit word endings, whole words, phrases, or even sentences.

Let's look at some common patterns of handwriting instruction, noticing why certain approaches aggravate, or even create, school problems.

Kindergarten children learn letter formation, but formation is frequently haphazard. Unchecked, beginners make some letters from the bottom, others from the top, some from the right, some from the left, and intersperse upper- and lowercase letters indiscriminately. In many kindergartens, children write their names and practice their letters on unlined paper and therefore don't learn the relationship of letter to line.

First- and second-grade teachers may emphasize decoding for reading, but often teach spelling separately and give handwriting instruction at still a different time of day. Time is short, there is much to do, and if the general level of handwriting looks fairly respectable, many teachers inadvertently omit formal instruction. This neglects a magnificent opportunity: first, second, and third graders are keenly interested in learning to form their letters well. Whereas fourth graders may think messy is macho, younger students enjoy precision. Consistent instruction during these years, which can easily be integrated with spelling and reading (as we shall see in Principles of Good Practice), trains *muscles,* develops *coordination,* and builds motor *memory.*

In third grade, reading and writing shift from being the goals of the curriculum to being its tools. Students are expected to have an easy familiarity with letters and words, writing them to express thoughts and feelings. This expectation is fine for the child with well-developed expressive language who has a natural ease with a pencil, but there is a sizable group of smart students who aren't yet ready. Many of them are boys: some are left-handed, others are developmentally immature, some were developmentally unready to make good use of the training presented in earlier grades, and others never received any training. These strugglers and stragglers are still trying to remember how to form certain letters, or where letters belong in relation to the lines, and are not ready to think and write simultaneously. When these third graders are also asked to transfer from manuscript to cursive writing, as is standard in many schools, they face an overwhelming combination.

Fourth, fifth, and sixth graders have an increasing flow of abstract ideas and are expected to write with mechanical accuracy and cohesive organization. But at the same time, handwriting instruction is either deemphasized or discontinued. The student whose attentional energy is still drained by the mechanics of handwriting, or whose hand tires quickly because of an awkward pencil grip, is hampered, to say the least. Resource room help, if available, generally centers on reading, and sometimes spelling, but rarely on handwriting, and, anyway, these are the years in which conceptually strong students would rather be dead than suffer the embarrassment of going for extra help. Their after-school hours are consumed by extracurricular interests or just "hanging out." Handwriting, then, is a skill that is required but not reinforced.

From grade seven on, increasing demands for volume and speed are superimposed on expectations of mechanical accuracy and well-expressed content. The student with handwriting problems is in real trouble. In day-to-day work, he is expected to listen, learn, take notes, and copy from the board and simultaneously absorb new ideas. He becomes overloaded. In pop quizzes or exams, his hand lags behind his thoughts, and he doesn't get his ideas across. For all his subjects he has different teachers, most of whom give weight to both content and mechanical accuracy in grading papers, and his marks suffer accordingly. By now the smart kid who started out with a minor problem is in major trouble.

Stephen is an example. He had two undiagnosed problems, each of which was minor in isolation and only mildly troublesome in the elementary grades. But, as he progressed through the educational system and as academic demands grew increasingly complex, his handwriting difficulty, combined with a weakness in auditory memory, caused serious setbacks.

For instance, although he was a conceptually powerful mathematical thinker, Stephen floundered in math class, and he was failing ninth-grade algebra. He said, "The teacher stands up at the board, explains something new, and we're supposed to listen, take notes, and do examples. I get behind in the writing, I have trouble reading what I've written, then while I'm trying to figure out what

I've written on my own paper I realize I've missed some important step in the explanation, I ask him to say it again, he gets mad, and by then I'm so far behind, it's hopeless and I give up. I guess he's right: I'm dumb."

We can often prevent such school problems from developing by including handwriting in the curriculum in the early years of school and being sure to continue the training through the sixth grade, or beyond in special cases. If we don't, difficulty begets avoidance; avoidance destroys the opportunities for practice, which could help correct the situation; poor performance leads to active distaste, to discouragement, poor grades, and a feeling that the whole problem is overwhelming.

Strategies for teaching handwriting are available and inexpensive, as we shall see in Principles of Good Practice. Strategies for large-motor skill development are also available, but it should be emphasized that the research shows no transfer from training in large-motor coordination to academic skills. The student who improves his throwing, catching, or balance-beam walking will enjoy athletics more, and may improve his self-concept as a result, but these exercises will not help him become a better reader or improve his handwriting.

PRINCIPLES OF GOOD PRACTICE

Many students need help with these handwriting skills: forming letters and numerals, developing small-motor muscles, holding the pencil appropriately, placing the letters, gaining accuracy and speed, producing an attractive product, and taking notes.

FORMING LETTERS AND NUMERALS

Because muscle memory for handwriting travels from the large- to the small-motor system, it makes sense for students to begin by using their large muscles in large spaces. In multisensory training the student learns the letter name, sound, and a verbal description of how to form it: "This letter's name is *o*; its sound is usually \o\.

O starts the way *c* starts and then closes the circle. Try it in the air. Hold your writing arm straight out, at right angles to your body, and write the letter in the air while you say its name and sound. Good."

When the student can write his letters in the air, he is ready to use the index finger of his writing hand to form them on the table or desktop, in a box of salt, tray of sand, or on the floor. He should start with large letters, about twelve inches high, and keep reducing the size until the letters he makes spontaneously are the appropriate size to fit comfortably on generously spaced lined paper. No matter the age of the student, the principle is to move from large-motor to small-motor.

DEVELOPING SMALL-MOTOR MUSCLES

When the student can perform the tasks described, he is ready to use his small-motor muscles. He should be given a pencil and lined paper and taught the correct formation of each letter and numeral, always with a verbal accompaniment such as the one cited previously, as well as the letter name, and a sound association to help him attach meaning to the symbol.

HOLDING THE PENCIL APPROPRIATELY

A proper pencil grip is only mildly important for single-letter formation but vitally important for rapid manuscript or cursive writing. An ice-pick grip should be changed to an proper one. We can prevent the development of a hook in left-handed children by angling the paper so the lower right-hand corner of the paper points to the student's belt buckle. (Do the reverse for right-handed students.) If necessary, use masking tape to make a right angle on the desktop as a spatial guide for the paper. This will assure proper paper placement each time, with nothing left to chance.

PLACING THE LETTERS

The student needs to make peace with these four aspects of spatial organization: orientation on and between lines, directionality, letter size, and arrangement of rows and columns. Visual cues help, verbal cues help, but visual-verbal cues really do the trick.

Orientation. Students can learn orientation on and between lines by the Traub designations of attic, house, and basement.[2]

‾‾‾‾‾‾‾‾‾‾‾‾‾‾‾‾‾‾‾‾	attic
‾‾‾‾‾‾‾‾‾‾‾‾‾‾‾‾‾‾‾‾	house
‾‾‾‾‾‾‾‾‾‾‾‾‾‾‾‾‾‾‾‾	basement

Directionality. To teach directionality, have the student put a green dot (for go) in the upper left-hand corner of each paper and a red dot (for stop) in the right-hand corner. This is traffic light language for where to begin and end and gives a point of orientation in describing the directionality of letters: "*b* starts in the attic, comes down through the house space, goes back up through the house space, and swings away from the green dot"; "*q* starts in the house space, swings toward the green dot, goes down through the basement, and makes a little line toward the red dot."

Letter size. To help a student with letter size, the teacher should first ask him to write out the alphabet, then ask him to draw an upright rectangle around all the tall letters, underline all the short letters, and draw an oval around those letters that go below the line. The student should practice each category.

Arrangement of rows and columns. Students need to make accurate use of rows and columns in math. Those who need extra support lining up their numerals will be helped by using graph paper or by turning regular lined paper sideways so the red margin line is at the top and the blue lines become column markers. A simple mnemonic device to remind the student which is a row and which is a column is that the top piece of the letter *r* in *row* is horizontal, as is a row. The *l* in *column* is vertical as is a column.

GAINING ACCURACY AND SPEED

Most students receive handwriting training in letter formation, small-motor practice, pencil grip, and spatial orientation of letters, but instruction frequently stops there. The unhampered student can manage on his own, but the student with handwriting problems is shortchanged without extra training and practice. He needs this maxim: work in short spurts. Three ten-minute periods are far more effective than one of thirty minutes. As the hand tires, practice makes imperfect.

PRODUCING AN ATTRACTIVE PRODUCT

First, second, and third graders care very much about the aesthetic appearance of their written work. As students grow older, particularly girls in fourth and fifth grade, they are likely to want to miniaturize their handwriting. Tiny is cool. The problem is that tiny is hard to read and cramps the hand. We are well advised to reward larger letters.

TAKING NOTES

Those whose handwriting has become effortless can use their hands and eyes to help them remember what they hear. A young friend of mine, an outstanding college student, takes copious notes at all lectures. She says, "I listen carefully, write down key phrases and ideas, look at my notes as I take them, and in between I look up at the professor. At the end of the lecture, I look over the notes for a few minutes, and almost never look at them again, but the act of simultaneously hearing, thinking, writing, and seeing seems to imprint the stuff in my mind. When I'm thinking back trying to remember something, I'll remember where it was on a page of notes and the phrases will pop to my mind's ear. It makes studying for exams a snap. Years later, I'll hear one of those phrases and see where I had written it. I really remember the things I learn that way."

From kindergarten on, schooling places increasing loads on the student's handwriting, and as the levels get harder they require increasing motor proficiency. If the motor system is weak or untrained, it will cave in under increasing demands to combine looking, listening, thinking, and remembering.

In spite of fine training, some smart kids will still struggle with handwriting. It is important to explore manuscript versus cursive writing; mechanical aids: typewriters, word processors, tape recorders; and alternatives to written reports or examinations.

MANUSCRIPT VERSUS CURSIVE WRITING

The battle rages over whether to teach students to print, to write in cursive letters, or to teach first one method and then the other. Some schools teach only cursive, a few teach only manuscript, and most start with manuscript and make the switch to cursive at third grade. Each system has its advocates, its advantages and disadvantages.

Advocates of manuscript say that the letters look more like the letters students see in books; therefore, learning to write manuscript reinforces learning to read print. They say that students find it easier to read their own early attempts at writing in manuscript than in cursive. They say that young students whose hands tire easily can write longer words when forming only one letter at a time. They also point out that printed labeling is a valuable skill for science, for other disciplines that require cataloguing or display, and for everyday life.

Advocates of cursive say that it is easier for a student to learn rhythmic handwriting when letters are connected. They also say that reversals and inversions are much less common in connected letters than they are in manuscript. They claim that students develop a clear sense of the overall shape of a word and an accurate idea of where one word ends and another begins, thus avoiding many spatial errors. Advocates say that students who start out with cursive begin with the system they will always use; therefore, there is nothing to unlearn and relearn.

Advocates of the two-step system claim the advantages of teaching manuscript at the same moment children are learning to read, and making the switch at the same time children need to increase the fluency and volume of their written output. They see the advantages in the students' knowing both systems. The smart kid with handwriting problems should be permitted to choose the style he finds easier, and then receive help to bring it to an effortless level.

MECHANICAL AIDS

Mechanical aids may help the student who has handwriting problems. They include typewriters, word processors, and tape recorders.

Typewriters. They have helped countless numbers of intelligent thinkers with poor handwriting encase their thoughts attractively, but it is important to recognize one truth and explore two concerns.

Smart kids with poor handwriting will certainly benefit from learning to type, but they still need to know how to write legibly with good speed to take telephone messages, write directions for getting to a friend's house, jot a marketing list, or take rudimentary or comprehensive lecture notes.

The two concerns focus on developmental levels. If typing is presented prematurely, the student may find it as laborious as handwriting, developing an aversion to a skill he will really need later. Each child is different, but my experience shows me that the summer between fourth and fifth grade is the earliest it makes sense to begin formal typing instruction, particularly with a student who has small-motor–visual imprecision.

The second concern is that students who develop their own hunt-and-peck systems may have trouble unlearning those motor memories and replacing them with the correct ones, which would be of genuine help. As increasing numbers of young children use typewriter keyboards for computers, we shall discover whether this concern is well founded.

Word processors. In spite of the proliferation of software, a growing body of elementary school teachers are turning away from computerized reading and writing programs for students in kindergarten through the second grade.

Detractors of computer language arts programs for young children say that first and second graders are eager to learn to write with pencil and paper. They feel it is unwise to lure students away from something that interests them, which they will need in later life, just to give them early training on a machine that will be waiting for them when they are older, and for which they may be physiologically, intellectually, and developmentally unready.

Most educators and parents agree that word processing is a technological gift for the middle-school child, the high school and college student, the postgraduate student, as well as authors of any age. A word of caution, here, too, however.

People with good small-motor muscle coordination and memory may pick up keyboard skills quickly. But the conundrum kid who lacks dexterity, and who has had trouble remembering sound/symbol correspondence, may need extra time and overlearning to master the keyboard and the specific commands of his word-processing program. Such students need a block of time to learn to operate the word processor before being asked to use it for writing or editing.

Tape recorders.   An exam taker with labored handwriting receives invaluable assistance from a tape recorder. If a high school or college student with an acknowledged handwriting deficit begins the semester by explaining his problem to his teacher, asking permission to tape-record the answers to exam questions, and offering to answer harder questions than those on the regular test, administrators and faculty members may agree. The willingness of some highly competitive colleges to accept college board scores earned from alternatively administered exams has gone a long way to breaking down the thought that this is a form of mollycoddling. Chapter 9, "Maturation and Higher Education: Getting It All Together," offers examples of alternative ways to take tests, such as extra time allowance, having a reader, or relying on a scribe.

The tape recorder can appear to be a friend to the high school or college student who has trouble taking notes quickly. "I'll just get all those lectures on tape and never have to worry again."

But this ease is an illusion unless the student has enough self-discipline to sit down at the end of each lecture and transcribe the tape into notes. Few students (of any age) anticipate the need for this step; consequently, most find themselves with a handy thirty-six hours of recorded lectures to review for a test or exam—too much for anyone to absorb!

Another illusion is that a smart kid with weak handwriting skills can simply tell his story into the tape recorder and transcribe it afterward. This works only if the student has planned the organization of the story or essay very precisely. If so, the tape recorder will be his friend. But if he has organized it carefully enough to be successful on the tape recorder, he has probably researched and organized it well enough to write it out, so long as he is not under pressure of time. Trying to transcribe loosely organized thoughts is harder, not easier, than writing from scratch.

ALTERNATIVES TO WRITTEN REPORTS

Theodore Sizer advocates "exhibition" in place of written exams or reports. Sometimes teachers behave as if writing is the only way of proving comprehension. Nonsense! The conceptually keen student with poor handwriting deserves to be liberated from this restrictive point of view and helped to find alternatives. Just as some people learn more easily from seeing a demonstration than they do from reading a manual, some people do a better job of sharing their knowledge and concepts through painting, pantomime, cartoons, sculpture, dioramas, models, or oral reports.

A CASE HISTORY: PHILIP

Philip was a normal child born to normal parents in a normal delivery following a normal pregnancy. But he was not an average kid.

From his earliest years he was fascinated by science, math, and history. He would pore over the books in his family's extensive library and, oddly enough for a small child, was particularly interested in their three-inch-thick, eleven-pound book on the works of Leonardo da Vinci. He would spend hours looking at the anatomical and architectural drawings the way other children his age would spend hours with a Richard Scarry book about trucks.

Imagine his and his family's great surprise and frustration, then, when he started school and could not learn to read or write.

Not only could he not distinguish between *b*s and *d*s, *p*s and *q*s, he couldn't even recognize the letters in his name. This boy who could understand Leonardo's design for an airplane, which he called Birdman, couldn't tell the difference between the words *Philip* and *Edward*, his brother's name. He spent first grade as a reasonably content nonreader, in a relatively undemanding school with an unsophisticated teacher who didn't understand the significance of what he could and could not do.

In second grade he was as perplexed by his classmates' facility with schoolwork as he was annoyed by his own difficulties. His parents were concerned, but because his teacher wasn't alarmed and they knew Philip was bright, they didn't panic.

It was not until they moved and he changed schools in third grade that they discovered the severity of the problem. The head of his new school required that he be given a thorough, individual psychoeducational evaluation, part of which was the Wechsler Intelligence Scale for Children, Revised (the WISC-R). We shall explore such tests in Chapter 8, but for now we shall simply note that Philip's demonstrated ability in verbal reasoning was at the top of the scale but his ability to manipulate unfamiliar symbols quickly, with pencil and paper, was well below the national average. Clearly, here was a conceptually brilliant child with a severe mechanical deficit.

He was assigned to the resource room for reading, writing, and spelling help five mornings a week for thirty minutes a morning with a teacher who was both understanding and demanding. She said, "Yes, you have a difficulty, but it is in mechanics, not thinking. I'll help you overcome your weakness, but because you are so intelligent, I'm going to make you work even harder than other kids." Using a multisensory approach, she taught him the interrelated skills of reading, writing, and spelling. As is customary, reading fell into place first. His teacher gave Philip a phonics workbook, which he found both difficult and boring, but she also went to the library and got a copy of a book of Leonardo's drawings to keep at school. The agreement was "Phonics, handwriting, spelling, dictation, then Leonardo. No skills, no Birdman."

By the end of sixth grade Philip was reading at grade level. His teachers (and by now he had a different one for each subject) didn't know about his earlier problems, so they took his reading for granted. They were keenly appreciative of the conceptual levels so evident from his participation in class discussion, and they were equally appalled at the unacceptable quality of his handwriting and spelling. These, as is customary, lagged far behind his reading despite good, consistent help. His difficulties were aggravated by any kind of pressure, particularly timed tests or exams. The severity increased as academic demands expanded and as his rate of ideas accelerated.

In seventh grade he got caught in a perfect example of academic irony. For his science project he chose to investigate and illustrate hibernation, incubation, and migration. He used his own fund of general information and located new information in the library. The way he wove the old and new facts together into these three categorical headings was extraordinarily sophisticated. For each category he made a series of meticulously drawn illustrations and fastidiously correct labels. It was a stunning work of art as well as a thorough piece of investigative science. He handed it in in December and received an A.

In late January, he failed his science exam. Across the top of the blue book the teacher wrote "F: I cannot read one word of this exam."

In an exam, under combined pressures to remember, to reason, to explain, and to hurry, his handwriting reverted to its most primitive levels. He interchanged lowercase and capital letters, his letters floated high up and crashed down, he wrote with no regard to lines on the paper and left no spaces between his words but lots inside them. For example, in spite of his interest in the concept of hibernating and his familiarity with writing the word, when he tried to use it in the exam, he wrote "h nti ng." Spatial confusion resurfaced to obliterate his recently acquired but not wholly internalized manual skills.

When Philip had the time to work slowly at home, he could write legibly. He enjoyed putting his brilliant thoughts together in novel combinations. In a classroom, he contributed his ideas to group discussions, he was faithful about handing in his homework assignments, and he didn't complain about the amount of time they required.

In tenth grade, Philip took a remedial-level typing course and mastered the skill. When it was time for college boards, Philip was given permission to take untimed tests and to give his answers to an amanuensis, a scribe who wrote down what he said.

Philip was admitted to a highly prestigious northeastern university, where he was permitted to use either an amanuensis, a tape recorder, or a portable word processor to take his undergraduate exams. He graduated with high honors in biology and is now in graduate school training for a career in genetic engineering. The weakness in his mechanical muscle and memory is insignificant compared to the contribution he will make through his conceptual muscle and memory. Both will be with him always, but effective compensations or substitutions break the power of the weakness.

5

AUDITORY
LEARNING

LEARNING TO LISTEN,
LISTENING TO LEARN

"Listening—even smart kids don't know how!" is what I hear from elementary and high school teachers when I ask them where their students have trouble.

Many school problems in intelligent older students are extensions of minor or unrecognized auditory distress from earlier years. A look at auditory learning in infants and young children will help us understand how the system works.

The young child with an intact auditory system absorbs the sounds of his environment, gradually connecting them to what he sees, identifying the source, meaning, and implications of each. An infant learns to recognize the voices of the people in his family and responds by looking in the direction of the speaker. He distinguishes his mother's voice from his brother's. He learns that the sound of the door opening at the end of the day followed by approaching footsteps heralds Daddy's return.

The word is the infant's introduction to verbal abstraction. This miracle occurs the first time he isolates a cluster of sounds from the running stream of speech, recognizing it as a unit with consistent meaning. Although the word may arise in different contexts or be spoken by different voices, the child learns to recognize the cluster of sounds as a consistently reliable representation of a person, thing, or action. Using hearing, auditory perception, and auditory memory, the child learns to listen and then listens to learn.

Last summer I watched and listened as eighteen-month-old Luke, a city child, discovered the beach. I did a double take when I realized he was doing exactly what I was writing about: he was identifying the sources and implications of unfamiliar environmental sounds, gradually relating them to new words that he learned to understand and then tried to imitate. By attaching the new sounds and words to what he was seeing and doing, he developed a whole new set of concepts.

He looked up from his digging at the sound of the engine of the approaching lobster boat, pointed, and responded with his own engine noise. I said, "lobster boat," and when I repeated it later, he looked out across the water to where the boat had been. He listened and watched as the water lapped against the rocks and the little waves rolled up on the shore. He looked up at the sound of splashing. I pointed to where some boys were jumping off a raft, told him what they were doing, and he moved his hands up and down the way he does when he splashes in the tub, saying his own approximation of the word *splash*.

He was absorbing the vocabulary for new objects and activities and responding with his own umbrella term, "sand-a-wadda" (sand and water), which he used in various inflections depending on intent. Declarative sentence: Sand-a-wadda. Question: Sand-a-wadda? Victory: Sand-a-wadda! He issued an imperative from the breakfast table, sand-a-wadda, and crooned a memory from his crib, sand-a-wadda.

It seemed so simple until I realized how many new words he was learning from listening, and how accurately he was absorbing them despite their similar sounds: *sand, sand and water, shovel, shell, seashore, sea gull, surf* (with its synonym *waves*), *seaweed, sailboat, lobsterboat, pail* (with its synonym *bucket*). Luke, the baby beachcomber, like other children with good auditory systems, was learning a whole new vocabulary. He was discriminating similar-sounding words (*big/dig, shovel/shell*) without confusion; he was hearing and combining what he heard with previous and present associations; developing concepts about water, sand, and holes; and storing his experiences and words away for subsequent reflection and use.

He was doing just what older learners do: using his hearing, auditory perception, and auditory memory to label, catalogue, and interpret his environment. A smart child with any malfunction in auditory processing is at risk not only for comprehending schoolwork but for understanding life as a whole.

AUDITORY LEARNING

Normal auditory learning incorporates *hearing* for the reception of sounds, *perception* for organizing and understanding them, and *memory* for storing their messages. These are analogous to the components we investigated in the visual and motor systems:

VISUAL	MOTOR	AUDITORY
vision	muscle	hearing
perception	coordination	perception
memory	memory	memory

It is important to stress, again, that although learning systems are interdependent and mutually reinforcing, we need to explore them separately.

HEARING

Just as visual acuity ranges from blindness to excellent eyesight, auditory acuity goes from deafness to excellent hearing. Normal acuity allows the listener to hear sounds of different volume, in different pitch, at different distances, and from different directions.

The smart kid with depressed hearing acuity may seem stupid, stubborn, or unfriendly, and, frequently, hearing-impaired children develop unpleasantly loud voices themselves. In cases of suspected hearing problems, the child should have a complete audiological examination.

Later in the chapter, we shall explore some reasons for the increasing incidence of hearing loss in young children, and its impact on learning.

AUDITORY PERCEPTION

Through normal auditory perception the listener learns to recognize words and extract meaning from speech. The poet W. H. Auden said, "I like hanging around words listening to what they say."

Inaccurate auditory perception undermines every kind of learning, including reading. A smart kid's school problem may originate with poor auditory perception of single sounds, words, syllables, phrases, or concepts.

Single sounds. When sounds are indistinct, words lose their meaning. Jim had trouble discriminating between the sounds \th\ and \f\. In the early days of reduced airline fares there was an economy ticket called No Frills. Returning from a weekend trip to Florida, Jim reassured me, "Don't worry, it wasn't too expensive; our family flies 'no thrills.' " To him, the sounds were the same, and since he didn't care much about either word, he was unaware of the substitution. Pity anyone who doesn't know the difference between a frill and a thrill.

Words. Word substitutions are cute in little children; in older students they are gateways to ridicule. Annette told me she was going to take her sick dog to the vegetarian.

Friendly listeners intuitively understand the speaker's intention and eventually don't even notice the errors. Annette is safe with her family—and with me—but not always with her peers. Trying to impress a group of other fifteen-year-olds at a restaurant, she put on her most sophisticated air and, meaning gazpacho, ordered a bowl of gazebo. She was mortified when everyone laughed. Gazpacho and gazebo were all the same to her. Ridicule hurts.

Syllables. Students prone to misperception of syllable sequence may say they eat "bizgetti," look at "mazagines," or admire the "ephelant" at the circus. Such errors aren't limited to little children.

Jane Holmes, a neuropsychologist from Children's Hospital in Boston and Harvard Medical School, was giving a lecture in which she made frequent reference to graphomotor skills. Fatigued toward the end of her talk, she delivered her punch line on "the vital role of grotomapher skills."

Dr. Holmes's slip revealed an underlying proclivity for which she usually compensates very well. Fatigue or anxiety, however, frequently revives old patterns.

Students who persistently tangle syllables in speech are showing unsteady perception of sound sequence that will probably hamper their ability to read polysyllabic words and to sequence their sounds in spelling.

Phrases. Auditory perceptual confusion can distort whole phrases. In administering a phrase repetition test I asked a nine-year-old boy to repeat "sheets and pillowcases" three times. He obliged: "sleeps and pillowcateses." When questioned, he said, "Yes. Sleeps. You put them on the bed where you sleep. In our house the sleeps and pillowcateses are different colors for different rooms. My Mom says it makes it easier to sort the laundry."

Concepts. Inaccurate auditory perception can skew whole concepts. A listener with imprecise intake stores sounds, syllables, words, or phrases in incorrect mental categories and therefore retrieves inappropriate pieces when trying to build concepts. Smart kids with imprecise auditory perception, who do not read enough to have their eyes teach them the concepts their ears have misinterpreted, may make ludicrous spoken or written errors, particularly when they use figures of speech or when they try to show off. Tenth grade Martha said, "I don't like big parties. . . . I get lost in the shovel." A high school senior trying to sound impressive in a college application essay wrote, "The character suffered from an edible complex."

These errors differ from ordinary slips of the tongue because they reflect the student's thinking. For people with poor auditory perception it as if a prankish homunculus is running between their ears and their minds, making confusion of what should be clarity.

AUDITORY MEMORY

The smart student who has trouble remembering verbal explanations or following directions deserves our sympathetic understanding for a legitimate difficulty that can cause horrendous and heartbreaking school problems. Reading and writing are language laid out in space, always available for another look. Listening and speaking are language laid out in time, there for an instant, but then gone for good.

Anyone who has ever stopped to ask directions and after following the first two (turn left at the corner of Maple Avenue; go three blocks to a blinker and . . . and . . .) forgets what comes next knows what it feels like to have an auditory memory lapse. An adult can simply hail the next pedestrian and ask again, but smart school kids are stuck. They are often scolded, ridiculed, or punished for "not listening," "not trying," or "acting spacey."

Often an annoyed adult makes the kid feel ashamed. Here's a classic scenario. The teacher says, "Today we will continue our study of the Middle Ages. Please collect your textbook, three pieces of lined paper, a pencil, and two colored markers." When the student with a weak auditory memory misinterprets the instructions or says "What?" the adult glares, and says, slowly, "Listen. Get your textbook (pausing to hold up a copy), three pieces of lined paper (holding up three fingers and a piece of lined paper), a pencil (waving one at the student), and two colored markers" (gathering two in her hand). Unwittingly, but often with sarcasm, she has provided ideal memory support; she has broken the task into small steps and provided visual accompaniment. When the student finally follows the directions correctly, she may say with exasperation, "If you'd only listen, you'd get it right the first time."

SIX FACTORS THAT INFLUENCE AUDITORY LEARNING

To understand the general level of auditory skills in today's classrooms (from nursery school through college) we need to investigate the implications of six seemingly unrelated factors prevalent in our current culture. Smart kids, those whose auditory skills are perfect, and those with problems ranging from minor to severe, are, directly or indirectly, influenced by these factors, which singly or in combination may create or aggravate auditory problems. They are ear infections, allergies, day care, non-English-speaking care givers, weary parents, and multimedia stimulation and instant gratification.

EAR INFECTIONS

A series of ear infections in infancy and early childhood may be the unrecognized cause of learning and behavior problems that wreak havoc in later life. Because middle-ear infections (otitis media with effusion, or OME) can cause intermittent, fluctuating, or permanent hearing loss, they may lower the child's acuity or disrupt his perception, causing him to miss or misinterpret individual words, verbal explanations, or general conversation. Diminished auditory function can have a devastating effect on the child's vocabulary development and the acquisition of general information and concepts that are the foundations of his developing intelligence. However, the hearing losses or fluctuations that frequently follow middle-ear infections often go unnoticed by the child's parents or pediatrician at the time, and their deadly effect is only understood in retrospect.

The parent and pediatrician of a child with an earache are concentrating on the acute pain and fever phase of the illness and not looking ahead to school and behavioral or learning problems. If the child is comfortable and seems to be functioning normally after the acute phase has subsided, no one may notice temporary or fluctuating hearing disruption for months, often years. Hearing disruption has no visible symptoms: no rash, no limp, no scar to act as a danger flag. It is a silent crippler.

Ear infections, one of the most common childhood ailments, need to be seen as acute-phase illnesses whose secondary consequences may have serious long-term implications for later learning and school. Research studies such as those reported over the past few years in *The Journal of Learning Disabilities* show increasing incidence of the causal link between middle-ear infections and problems with behavior as well as learning.[1]

> children with otitis media exhibited more maladaptive behaviors such as high dependency, short attention span and weak goal-orientation (observed by psychometrists). Significantly more mothers of the otitis media subjects described their children as restless, fidgety, destructive, not liked by other children and often disobedient.[2]

Understanding the impact of recurrent ear infections is important for two reasons. First, students with resultant learning and behavioral patterns will be a negative influence in their classrooms. Their distractions and short attention spans often disrupt other students with minor problems who find it hard to focus and learn in the presence of distraction.

Second, children who are (or were) susceptible to ear infections, whose Achilles' heels are their ears, need a thorough audiological examination to determine whether their hearing is normal in each ear individually and when both ears are used together. It is important to decide whether treatment is indicated or special accommodations are needed in school. For example, if a student has normal hearing in his right ear but depressed acuity in his left ear, he should not sit on the right-hand side of the room beside the window; he should sit so the teacher can speak to his right side.

In cases of significant hearing loss the student may require medical treatment or a hearing aid. But help must not stop there. He should have a language evaluation to discover the specifics of any resultant language impairment or gaps. These should receive remedial attention as soon as possible so that missed patches can be caught up.

ALLERGIES

Allergies, along with colds or flu, can disrupt learning and school behavior in similar ways. Allergic reactions are commonly respiratory, affecting ears (and therefore hearing) as well as throats, noses, and eyes. In addition to hearing poorly, the allergic student may be distracted from intellectual work by his overall physical discomfort. Furthermore, the medicines given for allergies have systemic as well as specific effects that often impede learning. For example, many antihistamines given to relieve sneezing and itching make the student drowsy, and cortisone and cortisone derivatives frequently affect energy levels, emotions, and appetite.

Teachers and parents understand how colds or flu inhibit learning but often underestimate the effect of allergies. Let us see how allergy seasons intersect with the rhythm of the school year.

September is time to establish the rules of the classroom, lay out the plans for the coming year, and review skills and concepts in reading, writing, spelling, and math. Much review is presented orally. What happens to the student whose hearing is fluctuating, depressed, or missing in whole or part, on one or both sides? What happens to the child who is restless and has a hard time concentrating either because of allergies themselves or the medicine given to relieve them?

From mid-October through March or April, the prime season for presenting and developing new concepts, the windows in the school building are generally closed, dust balls grow in the corners of classrooms and halls, blackboard erasers send off clouds of chalk dust, hamsters multiply among the cedar shavings in elementary school classrooms, and woolly sweaters with hairy souvenirs from Spot and Puff spill out of cubbies and lockers. What happens to the student who is allergic to dust or animal dander?

The spring term brings review, exams, and pollen.

Allergies have a direct and an indirect effect on all the students in a classroom through the distractions they inflict on the victim and the onlookers (onlisteners). Students with minor difficulties in hearing, attention, or concentration may work much less efficiently and require extra support and structure during allergy season. It is as if they are allergic to allergies.

As mentioned in Chapter 1, neurologists are noticing the frequent coexistence of allergies and learning differences or disorders. In trying to understand the paradox of smart kids with school problems, we must recognize that some students have an allergy that causes school problems, a single set of cause and effect. Others are doubly vulnerable. They have both allergies *and* learning problems; double cause and double effect.

DAY CARE

Any thorough discussion of auditory learning should explore the effects of day care on the listening skills of small children. We know that auditory learning develops through sustained, individual conversation. Listeners learn labels, nuances, and cadence of language; they expand their vocabularies and absorb models of correct usage of increasingly complicated language. As Luke did at the beach, they learn to listen and listen to learn.

The primary obligation of day care is to provide the greatest possible amount of physical safety and emotional security in a tolerable noise level. In spite of the best of intentions, the average adult/child ratio prevents sustained individual attention; opportunities for one-to-one conversation are limited. Day-care center directors wrestle with frequent staff turnover, and it is very difficult for them to train (and then retain) a staff to give a high priority to such an invisible skill as listening. Day-care wages are low, and workers, although dedicated and kind, are seldom highly trained.

Because of constraints imposed by space, time, and adult/child ratio many of the labels, phrases, and sentences children hear in day care are those that simply govern routine: "Time to go outside," "No-no," "Let's all have crackers and juice," or "Here's our story."

In addition, a group setting exposes its members to colds, flu, or viruses, which frequently turn into ear infections in small children.

Parents who use day care are well advised to pay particular attention to earaches. At the same time, they should take every opportunity to expand their children's listening experiences and conversational opportunities. Parents have a big role to play in early learning. Preschool, kindergarten, and first-grade teachers whose students have been in day care may need to leave extra time in their lesson planning for the development of accurate auditory skills.

NON-ENGLISH-SPEAKING CARE GIVERS

A child who is just learning to associate single words with the objects in his environment, and learning to understand connected speech, needs consistency in order to avoid confusion. Each lan-

guage has particular sounds and rhythms as well as its own syntax
and vocabulary. If the smart child who is just learning to understand
speech hears one set of words, rhythm, fluency, and level of so-
phistication from a parent and then a different set from a non-
English-speaking care giver, his language acquisition may be
delayed, disorganized, or disrupted. The results may be devastating.

Although some young children manage two or more languages
skillfully, a significant number cannot. The difficulty lies in predicting which children fit which category. Hindsight tells the tale
fully, but after the damage has been done. Boys, who are generally
later than girls in developing language, are particularly vulnerable
to double-language distress, and instead of becoming bilingual, they
may be semilingual.

To use Luke as an example again, suppose he had heard *sand,
shovel, lobsterboat,* and *pail* from me on his introductory trip and
then had returned to the beach with someone who had named those
things for him in Spanish, German, or any other language. The
labels would have been different, and in addition he would have
heard the lilt and mechanically different speech sounds and constructions of a foreign tongue, one that perhaps puts verbs in different places and that attaches gender pronouns to objects as English
does not.

Until the child's primary language has jelled, it is frequently
overwhelming and destructive for him to hear conflicting linguistic
messages. They are "double-talk."

There are three main groups of children whose early auditory
learning is in more than one language: those whose families spend
some time out of this country, those whose families have come to
the United States from other countries, and those whose families
employ non-English-speaking domestic help.

In the first category are children of military personnel, children
of civilians in the foreign service of the government, children of
those who work for organizations with plants or offices in foreign
countries, and children of parents who want to live abroad and
choose their jobs accordingly. In the second category are children
whose families have come to this country for temporary or permanent relocation. In fortunate circumstances, these children become
truly bilingual, but a significant minority are separated from their

native language before they consolidate it. Even in seemingly trouble-free situations, highly intelligent bilingual students frequently need extra work in reading comprehension.

In the third category are children whose working parents use domestic help instead of day care. In many cities, the pool of domestic help is non-English-speaking, or uses English as a marginally developed second language, or speaks an English dialect. There is usually a big wage difference between those who speak English well and those who do not. Even though young working parents who use domestic help rate child care as one of their highest expense items, as well as highest priority, many, even those with two incomes, may feel able to afford only the lower wages of a non-English-speaking care giver.

A preponderance of children whose auditory learning has been in two languages tips the balance of a class, necessitating extra and different help from a teacher. In considering auditory learning in students of all ages we need to understand the direct and indirect effects of language confusion on all the teachers and learners in our schools.

WEARY PARENTS

In more and more two-parent families both parents work (the current figure is close to 60 percent), and almost all single parents work. A working parent is tired at the end of the day, and it takes enormous energy, self-discipline, and understanding of child development for a weary adult to converse with a preverbal or newly verbal child. It's much easier to give a kiss and a hug, to give something to eat, to be physically demonstrative and physically nurturing than to be verbally engaged. The temptation is to let them watch more television. This is particularly true of parents who are not overly verbal themselves.

Margaret said this: "I leave Mark at day care at seven-thirty and get the train to work. I have to be ready for action as I cross the threshhold; that's the way my job goes. I either have lunch with a colleague, or I eat a yogurt, and exercise at the health club. On the way home I read the paper and try to sort out the day's experiences. Then I pick up Mark, and usually have to stop and do some sort of errand, even though I try to do all the grocery shopping on Saturdays. By the time we pull in, I'm shot and we're both hungry. I talk to him as much as I can, but sometimes when I think I'm listening, I know I've been daydreaming and just saying 'Mmm.' I cook something for both of us, feed him, and have my own bites in between. Then I give him a bath. That's one of the best times. He loves the water, I love to watch him play, I love toweling him and putting him in his pajamas. He looks so cute. I sing him a song or sometimes we look at a book, and then he's down for the night."

Mark has been a cooperative, healthy, well-adjusted little boy, and Margaret is clearly a conscientious, loving mother, but there's not much opportunity for verbal exchange, for learning to listen and listening to learn. And now there is a new problem.

As all children do when first exposed to groups of other children, Mark is picking up the current bug of the week. In his case it often starts in his nose and throat and works its way around into his ear. He has had four ear infections in the last five months. The head of the day-care center says that ear infections are the most common cause of illness among her charges; that would not surprise any experienced nursery school teacher or parent of young children.

Mark's auditory learning is in triple jeopardy: he has recurrent ear infections, goes to day care, and has a weary parent. He is a deeply loved, intelligent child who may be accumulating the invisible seeds of school problems. In Utopia, his financially secure, professionally fulfilled, energetic, verbal parents would play and converse with him, guarding his health and monitoring his hearing. But Mark doesn't live in Utopia; he lives in Rhode Island, where his divorced mother is doing her enlightened best.

She has scheduled an audiological examination. She has bought some story and song records for him and is going to make a special effort to talk with him about the things they do together, attaching words to what they see and do on their weekend outings. She has talked with Mark's father about the importance of conversation, reading aloud, and verbal interaction. He has promised to reinforce her efforts when Mark is with him.

The young child's auditory nourishment has a profound effect on his vocabulary growth, concept development, and academic achievement. The smart school-age kid with insufficient auditory skills is hampered himself and indirectly affects the others in his class.

MULTIMEDIA STIMULATION AND INSTANT GRATIFICATION

Ours is a heavily visual, increasingly alingual culture of instant gratification. From the home computer to the videocassette recorder to the television, visual messages appear rapidly in response to the touch of a button. We want, we press, we receive. Young children, and students of all ages, are now accustomed to having visual imagery provided for them through television or films and are soon crippled in generating their own imagery. They have trouble digesting oral presentations in the classroom partly because they are used to motion pictures (instead of words) for imagery, musical accompaniment for mood, and canned laughter for setting a frantic pace. Although they respond to the cues that govern the watching-and-listening routine, they are seldom learning to listen or listening to learn. The effects of this dependency reach into every classroom in the country.

When they do listen, what do they hear? Contractions and fast-food lingo: "uh-huh," "waddyawant?" "wudja-gunna-get?" or "'s up?" Students whose intake consists predominantly of such verbal shortcuts have trouble understanding sentences containing negatives, passive constructions, or dependent clauses.

A recent research study charted the average sentence length in television scripts as being between four and six words. If this is the bulk of what our students are accustomed to hearing, it is no surprise that they have trouble when trying to comprehend whole paragraphs of information.

In other times and cultures, musical lyrics were interesting, intricate, or poetic. W. S. Gilbert, Cole Porter, Oscar Hammerstein, and Stephen Sondheim, more recently, put fresh vocabulary and imagery in the ears of their listeners. But most of today's popular music lyrics either are repetitions of single words or phrases or are submerged by rhythm.

Our culture reinforces dependency on pictures and music as accompaniments to words while also promoting the habit of nonlistening. The high level of environmental noise (jackhammers and horns in cities, or other students' stereos in college dorms) means that survival lies in tuning out or at least tuning down. So students learn to watch-listen to television and films, thump-listen to music, or tune out completely. <u>Because school learning requires real listening, the student is caught in a push me–pull you of cultural habit and academic requirement.</u>

All students can be affected by any one or any combination of these factors. <u>The more the child has to bear, the greater the chance of his being impeded in learning through his ears.</u> If this is true of children who have no inherent trouble with auditory acuity, perception, or memory, what happens to the student with genuine auditory processing difficulty? He lives in a culture that requires auditory skills but doesn't teach or reinforce them, and he receives diminished help in his area of greatest need. If, in addition, he has the bad luck to have a teacher whose preferred method of instruction is verbal explanation, he is in real trouble. How can he learn to listen and listen to learn?

PRINCIPLES OF GOOD PRACTICE

First of all, adults need to be on the lookout, or on the "listen out," for auditory problems. It is all too easy to assume that a smart, healthy-looking kid is totally intact.

Second, in any case of suspected auditory problems, teachers, parents, and the educational overseer should consult (or establish) the child's master file, looking for recurrent patterns of distress in hearing, perception, or memory. Has the student been adversely affected by any of the six factors that impede auditory learning? It is important to do the following.

REVIEW THE CHILD'S EARLY HEALTH HISTORY

<u>Look for patterns of respiratory difficulty or ear infections. When indicated, the student should have an audiological examination. This</u>

should be more than a small part of a general pediatric checkup. If there is, or has been, a hearing loss, the school should be notified and the student should also have a language evaluation.

CHECK FOR ALLERGIES

Try to eliminate sources of allergic reaction or request appropriate medication, noting any side effects.

EXPLORE THE CHILD'S EARLY LANGUAGE DEVELOPMENT

The language of his caretakers, his interest in hearing stories, and his ability to understand and remember them are indicative. Was it easy for him to develop imagery to accompany what he heard? Was he dependent on illustrations or film; could he listen to learn?

Here are some suggestions for helping students with weak hearing, perception, or memory.

SUGGESTIONS FOR PROBLEMS WITH HEARING

Smart kids with hearing problems need both medical and management help. First they need a medical diagnosis and prescription, which may range from surgery to a hearing aid. In severe cases, special schooling may be necessary. Mainstreamed students, or those with manageable or mild impairment, still need careful management in school: appropriate seat location, visual accompaniments to verbal explanations, and opportunities to learn through their eyes and their hands. Other students need to be told the reasons for what their intelligent hearing-impaired classmate can and cannot do.

SUGGESTIONS FOR PROBLEMS WITH PERCEPTION

Listening skills are demolished by perceptual problems that distort individual sounds, single words, syllables, and phrases. In order, here are some ways to help.

Individual sounds. To teach auditory perception of sounds

within spoken words, use Jerome Rosner's Test of Auditory Analysis Skills in Helping Children Overcome Learning Difficulties. The student is asked to hear and repeat a word, then to say it again, omitting one piece. Here are two examples, one from the earliest and one from the hardest levels.

"Say *cowboy* . . . say it again but don't say cow."

"Say *stale* . . . say it again but leave out the \ t \ sound." Once the student's accuracy and level are determined, the teacher or parent can move to the appropriate group of Rosner's clearly explained, sequentially arranged exercises designed to develop this fundamental skill. Students enjoy them, and furthermore they work. (See Annotated Bibliography for Chapter 5, p. 240.)

Single words. A smart kid can use his eyes and his language system to compensate for auditory-perceptual confusion of single words.

Not only is seeing believing: seeing can mean understanding. Many of the words these students hear are slippery and elusive; the words they see can become reliable. Think of the confusion implicit in Annette's conversational gaffes: taking her dog to the vegetarian and ordering a bowl of gazebo. Visual analysis (vegetable, *-ian*: "one who") might have saved her from humiliation.

For example, for three years I taught a talented young scientist and mathematician whose severe spelling and reading problem was tied to a fluctuating hearing loss caused by recurrent colds, ear infections, and an allergy to dust. He wrote *I sall* for *I saw*, *chrane* for *train*, *buckees* for *monkeys*, *I em* for *I am*, *rēn* for *reading*, and *lant* for *landed*.

We would often begin our lessons with my exhortation: "Blow your nose for better spelling." When his head was clear he could begin to connect letters with sounds and then arrange them in correct order. He could also clarify the reverberating words in his head by literally *seeing* their *sounds*.

Misperception of word endings, such little items as plural *s*, *ing*, *ed*, or *er*, distorts the meaning of an individual word, undercutting true comprehension of language. We shall discover more about this in the next chapter, "Language and Learning."

Because accurate anticipation, "word-hunch," helps the listener clarify incoming words, a well-developed language system is a boon to the student with auditory perceptual problems. But language development and auditory learning are partners. Trouble in one system affects the other. We shall learn more about this in the next chapter.

Teachers and parents of students with auditory-perceptual confusion are well advised to anticipate the content of each particular course and make a glossary for the student to preview.

Syllables. Smart students with imprecise auditory perception frequently omit, substitute, or transpose syllables in what they hear or say. To overcome this problem, the teacher or parent should say a word, then ask the student to listen, repeat, count the number of syllables, and hold up a matching number of fingers. When he can do this accurately, the adult should give him a word, ask him to repeat it, and then to pronounce only the first, second, or third syllable. When he can isolate and pronounce individual syllables, he can be asked to spell a designated one. For example, "Say *magnification*. Pronounce each syllable in succession (*mag-nif-i-ca-tion*). Isolate and spell the fifth syllable." If necessary, let the student see the word as he is segmenting it. He should learn to use his eyes to help his ears.

Phrases. Smart kids with imprecise auditory perception should be taught figures of speech through their eyes, not their ears. This can spare them the ordeal of trying to "take the ball by the horns" "in the store that brought the camels back."

SUGGESTIONS FOR PROBLEMS WITH MEMORY

Help the student with a weak auditory memory bring his handwriting to the level of a reflex. As they grow older, students with auditory memory problems rely on note taking, but they need to save all their attentional energy for listening. None of it must be drained away in remembering how to form letters. Although it may sound strange to stress handwriting in a chapter on auditory learning, it is vital.

To help people remember what they hear, teach them to make a mental movie; repeat; use pantomime, draw a rebus, or write words; and request a graphic accompaniment.

Make a mental movie. Students in today's world have little practice generating their own imagery because television routinely provides standardized pictures for them. As is true with narrative, they need to practice getting a picture in the mind's eye to accompany directions like "Go to the next traffic light: turn left" or instructions like "In the blue math book, do the first three problems at the top of page 54." The mental image may be easier to recall than the vanished spoken words.

Repeat.   Repeat the directions aloud: "Left at light, go three blocks."

Use pantomime, draw a rebus, or write words.   When I am given traffic directions, I gesture with my hand (out of sight to save my pride) pointing left, holding up three fingers for three blocks, and so on. It works. Other people jot a personal pictographic shorthand of arrows, dots, or whatever is quick and easy. Others list key words. Any of these memory aids is a fine preliminary to full-fledged note taking.

The student who uses these strategies is already harnessing his other senses to assist his auditory memory. He develops a multisensory habit: hear it, see it (mental movie), say it (repeat), write it.

Request a graphic accompaniment.   Many teachers use visual aids in their teaching. Charts, graphs, maps, and examples help the student with a weak auditory memory. Teachers who don't use such aids routinely are often glad to incorporate them if asked. A very verbal teacher often forgets. Most teachers are willing to write assignments on the board instead of simply dictating them. Many teachers, particularly in high school and college, give their presentations from an outline and are willing to share the outline with their students. Listening to a presentation while looking at an outline is an invaluable aid to a student with a weak auditory memory.

An older student should explain his difficulty to his teachers at the beginning of the semester *before* any problems arise: "Sometimes I have trouble remembering things if I only hear them. Will you give a graphic accompaniment as frequently as possible? Also if I need to have a comment or assignment repeated, please understand that I am not trying to be annoying."

Many students with auditory memory troubles do better with whole ideas that they can then break down into components than they do with little increments that they must assemble. But from phonics to history, much schoolwork is presented in parts for the student to build into a whole. When teaching and learning styles collide, educators are wise to scrutinize the method rather than calling the student "at risk," "at fault," or "disabled."

We can help smart kids by remembering and reinforcing the link between listening and language. Listening nourishes language; language facilitates listening.

A CASE HISTORY: STUART

Stuart, an eighth grader, has always been an agile runner and strategic soccer player, and on family camping and boating trips he has been outstandingly good with maps, charts, and compass.

Because Stuart seemed comfortable and ready, he started school early. He was a tall, competent child who loved the playground, the gym, art, music, the block corner, and the cooking projects but had trouble following directions. If the teacher said, "Please get a blue crayon, a red crayon, and a piece of paper and line up at the door," he would hotfoot it to the door, smile engagingly, and wonder why she was cross. When reminded, he'd say "Oh, okay," as if hearing the instructions for the first time.

He was a gregarious, verbal boy with a mild articulation problem, pronouncing \r\ and \l\ like \w\. One of his favorite songs was "Wed Wivoo Vawee."

In first grade he had a rigid teacher who used only one textbook series and one approach to teaching reading. Stuart couldn't string sounds together into words; by the time he finished saying *b-a-t* he forgot where he started. Trying to blend *m-u-s-t* he said, "stamp?" He spelled *dup* for *dump*, *hepl* for *help*, and *fst* for *fist*. He was in the lowest reading group and he did poorly on pencil-and-paper math, although he was good with money and counting at home. His teacher said that he was inattentive and that his handwriting was clumsy. By his sixth birthday Stuart considered himself a failure.

When he entered second grade, approaching seven, his fame had preceded him: his teacher assumed he would become a disciplinary problem, and he obliged, frequently disrupting the class with silliness and mimicry. He was a playground leader and his teacher's bane.

When he was in third grade his parents gave Stuart permission to walk to and from school alone. He was proud of his independence and navigated his way through pedestrian and motor traffic as skillfully as he wove through the opposition on the soccer field. At home and on the street he was wiry and winsome, but in school he continued to be restless. His grades were low and dropping. His only moment of glory came in the class play, where he played his minor role superbly. His report card read, "If only Stuart would give the attention to his academic subjects that he gave to the play, we would have a star student."

That summer Stuart took diving lessons, and after a hiatus in the fall to continue in his soccer league, he enrolled in an after-school diving program at the neighborhood Boys' Club for the winter term. He was an excellent diver, once again demonstrating his extraordinary ability to position his body in space.

In school he was excited about science and problem solving. In art class he learned to do macramé (the sailor's embroidery) and made a beautiful wall hanging. In reading and language arts, however, he was in the lowest group.

In fifth grade his classmates elected him captain of the soccer team, but the position was taken away from him because of his poor grades in reading and spelling. He was required to take extra work in those subjects in place of sports. Needless to say, he was angry, rebellious, and in no mood to learn, particularly because there was no attempt to vary the approach; it was just more of the same.

To save his sanity, his parents allowed him to continue the diving. By January everyone was concerned over his unhappiness and worried about his lack of academic progress.

His parents took him to the pediatrician, who found him normal. The reading specialist who evaluated him reported that his work was below grade level and suggested he should read for pleasure . . . an unlikely possibility! The psychologist who tested him found him an intelligent boy with low self-concept, at high risk for school failure. He also remarked on Stuart's minor articulatory difficulty and suggested a speech checkup.

Thus it was that Stuart arrived at a speech, hearing, and language clinic, where the evaluation showed significant auditory problems: his acuity was low, he had some perceptual confusions, his auditory memory was very weak, and in addition, he suffered from a chronic infection known informally as "swimmer's ear." With this discovery, the pattern became clear. He was a smart boy with superior visual-spatial skills and a serious auditory deficit.

Realizing that he had some catching up and patching up to do, Stuart and his family agreed that he should repeat the sixth grade and receive tutoring for four forty-five-minute sessions per week after school. The learning specialist assigned by the school to oversee Stuart's program said that the boy's retraining and remedial work would be very different from what he had received previously.

Stuart was eager to improve, eager for success, and afraid to try wholeheartedly in case the plan didn't work. It wasn't until January of the new year before he really began to trust himself and to see the strength he was gaining. Once he sensed that, the last ice of his resistance melted away and he made giant strides. That spring Stuart exhibited a piece of his work in the school science fair and was elected a team member for the group who entered Olympics of the Mind. He has continued his soccer and given up diving. His extracurricular hunch about his own intelligence has been confirmed in school. He knows he is smart, and so does the rest of the world.

6

LANGUAGE
AND LEARNING

INTELLECT, LANGUAGE,
EMOTION

Language disorders can paralyze smart kids in school, causing reading problems in word recognition, rate, fluency, or comprehension; blocked or scattered spoken or written expression; disorganized ideas, possessions, or work habits; trouble with word problems in math; unsatisfactory relationships with other people; psychological distress and poor self-image; impoverished concept development.

Yet because everyone uses language, and because it is invisible, many people take its sources, structure, and power for granted.

Leon Eisenberg, professor of child psychiatry at the Harvard Medical School, says, "Linguistic competence stands at the very center of what is crucially human in each of us. We are as we think, we think as we read, we become human as we understand each other through language."[1]

A look at the functions of language, and the normal progression of receptive and expressive language development, will help us understand what happens to learning when language goes awry.

LANGUAGE FUNCTIONS

The developing child joins the rest of us in using language for expression, for organizing, for mediation, and for reasoning.

FOR EXPRESSION

Through language people can express their ideas and feelings, share their insights, transmit and receive knowledge, and formulate questions, abilities unique to humans.

FOR ORGANIZING

Language is the great organizer, allowing us to sort our ideas, emotions, and experiences first for storage, then for retrieval, and finally for making useful or imaginative combinations. If we think back to the intellectual traits of gifted thinkers, we can understand why divergent thinkers who are alert to pattern, who have heightened perceptions, who delight in originality need to develop effective linguistic filing systems.

FOR MEDIATION

Language is the mediator between fantasy and reality. In early childhood, fantasy is a force that controls the child. At around the age of five, the child establishes the boundary line between fantasy and reality and gains dominion over fantasy by separating the two. He needs language to accomplish this vital task. As we saw in Chapter 2 the fantasy/reality border influences formal academic work, but more important it helps the child stabilize his universe, allowing him to distinguish between the probable and improbable, the likely and the ludicrous.

All of us use language to distinguish between the wishes and the oughts of life. Resisting a piece of chocolate cake, I said, "I talked myself out of it." Giving in, I said, "They talked me into it." When a small child is first learning to use language to control his own behavior, his actions and words may be contradictory. When our son, Angus, was at this stage I heard him in another part of the house emphatically saying, "No! No! No!" Following his voice, I found him shouting "No" while using a fat red crayon on a freshly painted white wall.

FOR REASONING

Language is a tool for reasoning, for the embellishment and extension of original thought, for disagreement with others, and for defense of opposing positions. Growing children who are trying to make sense of what they see around them need language to keep their assumptions on target.

When Angus the crayon criminal was three-and-a-half, I had an important appointment for him with a doctor in New York. The drive from our house to the medical center generally takes about an hour, but, as the day came nearer, my chronophobia made me fret about being late, missing the appointment, and having to wait another two months for the next one.

We left home at 8:00 A.M. and walked in the door of the medical center at 9:00, two full hours early. I had brought a big tote bag stuffed with animal crackers, toy cars, Richard Scarry books, and other paraphernalia and said to the innocent child, "Oh good, we can sit right here on this nice wide bench and play with the stuff in the bag." And we did.

People went in and out of the elevators across from the bench, and there was the general scurry and bustle of a big organization starting up a new day. Finally, with a bare forty-five minutes to go, I gathered up our things and said, "Okay, time to get in the elevator." He looked first at the elevator and then back at me and said, "No." Surprised, I said, "Yes," and the more I said "yes" the more he said "no." Finally, I asked why. "Don't you see?" he said, pointing to the elevator, "Everybody going in there comes out different!"

In our vigil he had watched people go in and seen the elevator doors close. When the doors opened again, Presto! there were different people . . . some of them in wheelchairs.

I had been too caught up in my own concerns to recognize that this country child didn't know that inside the elevator door was a moving box that would save us from climbing up thirty-three flights of stairs. Without the language of verbal explanations to lead him beyond his visual threshold, his observations told him it was a change-box.

LANGUAGE DEVELOPMENT

Language is both receptive and expressive, the relationship between the two being like that between seed and crop. Skimpy planting brings skimpy growth. Just as flowers and vegetables grow best with generous amounts of light and water in tilled, fertilized ground, the child's language crop grows best when it is cultivated and supported. Just as extremes of weather can damage plants, a harsh or cold emotional climate can wither language.

The lifelong process of language development begins as the developing child absorbs the rhythm and melody of the rushing stream of sound surrounding him, trying to imitate what he hears.

Gradually the child recognizes recurrent clusters of sound, identifying them as words. Adults consciously and unconsciously encourage the process. A mother talking to her baby spontaneously speaks in short sentences, repeating key words slowly and frequently. "Hi, Jesse. Hi, big boy. Jesse is a big boy! Let's play 'How big is Jesse?' 'Soooooo big!' Wow, Jesse, what a big smile!"

Sometime during the second year of life, the child learns to speak the single words he has absorbed. The baby who says "Dada" or "Mama" discovers he can stop the world!

The child first understands words and then uses them to communicate with himself as well as with others. In her book *The Magic Years*, child psychologist Selma H. Fraiberg talks about the child who has been put to bed and is heard chanting "Mama," "Mama," "Mama" in his crib. There is neither urgency nor petulance in his voice. He has discovered that by using the word *Mama*, the label for that all-important figure, he can summon her presence without her having to be there physically. This discovery, seemingly minor, gives the child instant access to every person, event, emotion in his experience for which he has a label. He accumulates vocabulary through his receptive language capacity, and through the abstraction of words he becomes the organizer of his own experience.

In every child, the growth of expressive language follows this progression: gesture; labels; two words; articles, pronouns, and affixes; word order; and semantics.

As the language learner progresses from one stage of expressive language to the next, he builds on the earlier, more primitive levels, incorporating them into his speech. Let us take them one by one.

GESTURE

The baby's first intentional smile starts him off on the road to communication. He smiles, and the world smiles back. The infant learns to hold up his arms to be picked up, to point or reach for what he wants, to purse his lips against unwelcome foods, and to flirt in peekaboo. Adults as well as children communicate through body English. From the stamping of a two-year-old foot, to the message of a wink or the comfort of an arm around a shoulder, expressive opportunities abound without reliance on a single word.

LABELS

Labels allow the language learner to catalogue his world. Once a child discovers single words or phrases within streams of sound, he begins to use them: *Dada, Mama, car, cookie.* He wants to find out what everything is called; the process becomes a passion.

The growing child learns actual labels and invents others to describe things he can't yet name. Three-year-old Amy showed her father a nearly invisible cut on the fat pad of her thumb, saying, "It's on my thumb-stomach." Sometimes the child's original labels are difficult for adults to understand. This same Amy would say, "Amy do the 'gwinner' " every time she approached the entrance to her house and would cry when her mother opened the door. It took several tearful episodes before her mother understood that Amy wanted to turn the knob and push open the door herself: "Amy *do* the go-in-er."

A single label, *gwinner,* can convey an entire concept, and, as is true with gesture, people of all ages use labels for verbal short-hand. Depending on inflection, the student may use the label *home-work* to express gloom (weary voice, "homework"), inquire about plans ("homework?"), vent outrage ("homework?!"), or accept the inevitable ("homework"). Labels used as epithets can extend the meaning of a word well beyond its dictionary definition, as in "Chicken!"

Later on we shall see what devastation comes of not being able to label.

TWO WORDS

The child's language capacity explodes when he discovers how to pair words with one another. The single word *ball* can become *red ball, my ball, Mommy ball, big ball, little ball, new ball, ball go, ball now,* or *ball bye-bye*. Nouns can pair with adjectives, other nouns, or verbs, and markers of such properties as size, color, and location, sparing us the impossible job of using a separate word for each possession, experience, or emotion.

ARTICLES, PRONOUNS, AND AFFIXES

So far so good. Most of us from the age of two to ninety-two can express ourselves through gesture, labels, and two-word com-binations. The next stage is the ability to use articles, pronouns, and such affixes as *s, er, er/est, s, ing,* and *ed*. This level, *mor-phology,* has a profound effect on the child's ability to understand what he hears and what he reads, the seeds of what he will say and write. Because many smart kids have unrecognized weaknesses in this language level we will give it extra scrutiny.

These little words and word endings are small and may look simple at first, and yet they build the base for comparison, cate-gorization, and analogy, the foundation of advanced intellectual ex-ercise. They help the learning child understand and express the language of space and of time, two vital concepts.

Comparing and categorizing. Articles and pronouns such as *a, the, this, these, that,* and *those* distinguish between singular and plural and indicate location in space: *a cat, the dresses, this apple* (here) and *these apples* (plural, or over there), *that box* (over there), or *those boxes* (plural, or in another place). Simple as they seem, these are tools for comparison, categorization, and spatial placement.

Personal pronouns mark the difference between self and others, distinguish among genders (masculine, feminine, and neuter), as well as indicate singular and plural: *I hope, you deserve, he went, she won, it was red, he fasted, they ate.* Like articles, they allow comparison and categorization.

The ending *s* changes a singular object to a plural: *cat, cats.*

The ending *er* can change an object into an agent: *paint, painter, farm, farmer* (but not *moth, mother!*), another tool of comparison and categorization.

The endings *er* and *est* establish degree: *fat, fatter, fattest; near, nearer, nearest.* When they are used to describe size and location they function as the language of spatial organization, another way of saying the language of mathematics: relative position, size, shape, interval, and ratio. These, too, are tools for comparing and categorizing.

Analogy. Articles, pronouns, and affixes, the language tools that allow comparison, categorization, and spatial and temporal organization, open the door to analogy, the foundation and the tool of higher-level abstract thinking.

Young children practice with such simple analogies as

$$paint : painter :: farm : \underline{\hspace{2cm}} \text{ (farmer)}$$
$$prune : prunes :: elephant : \underline{\hspace{2cm}} \text{ (elephants)}$$
$$I : we :: you : \underline{\hspace{2cm}} \text{ (us)}$$
$$taller : tallest :: more : \underline{\hspace{2cm}} \text{ (most)}$$
$$jumping : jumped :: going : \underline{\hspace{2cm}} \text{ (went)}$$

The words in parentheses must be supplied by the student.

Higher-level students use more complicated analogy to explore history, literature, philosophy, religion, mathematics, science, music, art, political science, and economics.

Verb tenses and time. The endings *s, ing,* and *ed* are the language of present and past: verb tenses. They mark temporal organization: she jump*s*, the computer is run*ning*, the plane land*ed*. Time, being invisible, is difficult to grasp. The child who understands the separation between the present and the past can store his experiences away for later reflection and sort them chronologically, giving himself a window on cause and effect.

The child who understands the difference between the present and the past can develop realistic anticipation of the future. The language learner who hasn't grasped the implications of verb tenses lacks the tools to organize the past, the present, and the future. He remains a prisoner of the present, and probably behaves accordingly, taking what he wants and filling the needs of the moment as they arise.

The ability to postpone gratification, a prerequisite to success in school as we saw in Chapter 2, depends on the child's ability to anticipate realistically. The child who understands the *will* and *next* in "You will get the next turn" can tolerate watching another child playing on or with something he wants.

Time is the language of sequence; sequence is the language of both memory and planning. College sophomore Eleanor laid out her study program for her political science course this way: "First I will read *The Federalist Papers*; then I will choose either Madison, Hamilton, or Jay as the subject of my term paper. Meanwhile, I will keep watching the evening news and see whether federalism is evident today."

Second grader Pete had a different agenda. "First I'll take out the trash and pick up my room. After I do that Mom will let me go over to Sammy's. We're going to put Lego motors on our space machines."

The language of time and sequence allows us to understand cause and effect. "If . . . then" depends on understanding a sequence. For this the student needs verb tenses.

Verb tenses and temporal markers put time into words. Without time and words students cannot explore the higher-level concepts that beckon smart kids.

Why do so many young people have trouble at this language level? Think back to the six factors disruptive to auditory learning that we explored in Chapter 5: weary parents, day care, non-English-speaking care givers, allergies, ear infections, and a culture of multimedia stimulation and instant gratification. Consider their potential impact on this level of language acquisition.

Weary parents keep their conversation simple and unembellished.

Day-care personnel have to limit their language to what most young children will understand quickly.

People who are just learning English, or who speak it poorly, may use verb tenses, pronouns, articles, and affixes incorrectly or omit them entirely.

The child whose hearing acuity is impaired, temporarily or permanently, from ear infections, allergies, or respiratory ailments may be unaware of word endings. If he doesn't absorb them in speech he will overlook them in reading and omit them in speaking and writing. If his perception is imprecise he may misinterpret them.

In our visually oriented, verbal-fast-food culture the linguistic niceties of this language level are often omitted or misused.

Although surrounded by noise, even by words, children who do not consolidate this level of language are cut off from important concepts. The smarter the kid, the greater the loss. If these influences affect the linguistically sturdy, think of their impact on a linguistically vulnerable student.

WORD ORDER

Word order, or *syntax*, refers to the rules that govern the order of words in sentences. Syntax changes a declarative sentence into a question: "The dinner is scorched again" "Is the dinner scorched again?" This syntax is uncomplicated and obvious. With complicated constructions it is not. The child who has absorbed rich syntax will be able to express complicated thoughts in appropriate constructions, but many children have not had this linguistic exposure. Think back to the six factors that inhibit auditory learning and consider their effect on this language level.

SEMANTICS

Semantics involves the way words hang together to make sense. A comedian talking double-talk uses real words in familiar inflections and cadence. The double-talker creates the illusion of intelligibility, but what he says doesn't make sense. Language without meaning is useless.

Not everyone reaches the highest semantic levels. Some smart kids whose gifts lie in working with their hands are comfortable with concrete language but stumble over metaphor and figures of speech. They may understand each individual word in "A rolling stone gathers no moss," but they don't understand what the phrase means.

LANGUAGE PROBLEMS

Difficulties in learning language, or in using language as a learning tool, can properly be called "the dyslexias." The singular form, *dyslexia,* has previously been used to describe one particular type of reading problem; however, language-based difficulties have more than one manifestation. Increasingly, neurologists, pediatricians, researchers, and clinicians use the plural *dyslexias.* As we saw in Chapter 1, the brain organization thought to underlie the dyslexias often also underlies great talent in such fields as science, the arts, and mathematics.

In his monograph *The Advantages of Being Dyslexic,* Richard H. Masland, the Columbia University neurologist, quotes Albert Einstein, who is commonly regarded as having been dyslexic: "The words of the language, as they are written or spoken, do not seem to play any role in my mechanism of thought. The psychical entities which seem to serve as elements in thought are certain signs and more or less clear images which can be voluntarily reproduced and combined. . . . Conventional words or other signs have to be sought for laboriously only in a secondary stage, when the mentioned associative play is sufficiently established and can be reproduced at will."[2]

We shall explore five types of language disability: receptive disability, coding difficulty, expressive disability, emotional interruption, and difficulty with abstraction or organization.

RECEPTIVE DISABILITY

Receptive language is intertwined with auditory and visual learning. It is nurtured by listening and reading, and what the reader has absorbed through receptive language determines the level at which he will read with ease and comprehension.

Young children normally absorb words from their surroundings, but the child with a receptive language disability (whose hearing is normal) does not understand the full meaning of language and learns to ignore it or tune it out. This child may have a hard time establishing rapport with other people.

People are not attracted to a child who seems uninterested in what they have to offer. Apparent coolness on the child's side makes others less inclined to seek him out. The child misses the feeling of being attached to the world through comprehension and conversation: explanations, admonitions, stories, jokes, the gift of big new words to keep and use. A sad picture emerges of a lonely child connected to the world around him by a thin string instead of a stout intertwined line.

Departures from the following general guidelines for normal receptive language development are warning signals.

By one year, most children understand gesture and such simple labels as *Mommy, Daddy, cookie, doggie, peekaboo.*

By two years most children understand and use two-word combinations. They enjoy being shown picture books and may "read" them independently.

By three years most children enjoy hearing a story and sit still to listen.

By the age of five, most children can understand articles, pronouns, prepositions, and verb tenses as well as passive and negative constructions. They can carry out a three-part command, "Please hand me a pencil, put the rubber toy on a chair, and go touch the window." Much of elementary schoolwork depends on listening to and following directions. The child who understands single words or very short constructions but cannot process larger chunks of language has trouble in every area of school life. He may appear to be listening, but when the words are finished and it's time for action, he may have to copy his neighbors.

By first and second grades most students learn to take meaning from print just as they previously learned to take meaning from speech. Receptive language is visual as well as auditory: reading is listening through the eyes. Through decoding words and short sentences ("The cat is black"), they learn to take meaning from printed symbols.

From third grade on, reading shifts. No longer primarily a conscious process of visual pattern decoding and recognition, it evolves into one of automatic linguistic recognition. Good readers take in whole phrases at once. People used to think that language growth was a product of reading, but current research tells us the opposite. Language must exist inside the child to give incoming information something to stick to. With language inside, the child connects the new information to his existing supply, and the two join together like two sides of a closing zipper.

Third graders use language as a social as well as an intellectual tool. They are more likely to argue than hit; they instigate and resolve their disputes verbally; they play with homonyms and tell riddles.

Fourth graders join language with numbers to solve word problems. Exercising and relying on the seemingly simple skills discussed in the section on articles, pronouns, and affixes, they experiment with the structure of language. From fourth grade through adulthood, readers (and listeners) are expected to remember facts, arrange events in sequence, absorb new vocabulary, identify main ideas, anticipate outcome, and understand inference as well as fact.

Because accurate, fluent reading is a result of anticipating what is to come, and then letting the eye match the probability, marginally developed syntax prevents a child from reading with rhythm and fluency and impairs his comprehension. Familiarity smooths the way, allowing the reader to "cast a linguistic shadow." Nancy has a receptive language difficulty and, consequently, poor linguistic hunches. Haltingly, she reads out, "Be quite, there's a hung elephant, wait for my single." Abigail, whose decoding is shaky but who has grown up drenched in stories, reads it correctly, "Be quiet! There's a HUGE elephant. Wait for my signal."

Here are comments from actual reports on students with receptive language disability.

Kindergarten: "Tim's a doer not a talker. He prefers blocks to stories."

First grade: "George has trouble following directions."

Second grade: "Ellen is a gentle, quiet child who lets others go first, watches what they do, and then tries her own hand."

Third grade: "Billie gets in fights on the playground and disrupts classroom discussions."

Fourth grade: "Barbara is so interested in everything that she just plunges in without waiting for instructions. A little more restraint would be helpful."

Fifth grade: "Mary does well in social studies projects but seems lost in discussions and explanations."

Sixth grade: "Allen uses the present tense in telling about his experiences. His vocabulary is small and he is a weak reader."

Seventh grade: "Jack could do good work if only he'd try harder. He is good with numbers but doesn't apply his knowledge to word problems."

Eighth grade: "Mark is failing French this term."

Ninth grade: "Francie has one of the lowest grades in this history class. She seems to have no sense of cause and effect and can't keep events in their proper order."

Tenth grade: "Unless there is major improvement, Terry should be seen by a psychiatrist."

Eleventh grade: "Charles is too old for this restless behavior."

Twelfth grade: "Tom's spelling is still dreadful." Comments such as these deserve red-flag attention.

CODING DIFFICULTY

Coding difficulty can make trouble in either decoding (reading) or encoding (spelling) or both. Few difficulties frighten parents more than a reading problem. Often they panic, wondering whether they themselves are to blame, whether the child is stupid, and whether there is any hope.

As we know from the preceding chapters, there are several ways to try to crack the code that connects written and spoken words.

The dyslexic who has trouble with decoding may reverse or invert letters (*b/d, p/q, h/y, n/u*) or words (*on/no, was/saw, dog/god*) and may confuse words of similar configuration (*cold/could, house/ horse*). Obviously such confusions distort meaning. It is important to distinguish between "he was a god" and "he saw a dog." Similarly, "a cold house" and "a cold horse" require different remedies.

The student with encoding difficulties may forget which letters represent which sounds, and, once having remembered, may still be uncertain how to form them correctly. His handwriting may range from the unattractive to the illegible. His spelling may show incorrect sequence of sound order, missing letters, or omitted syllables.

It is important to separate the student's intellectual challenge from his training in coding. He needs both, but they can seldom come in the same lesson. Teachers need not pretend that phonics is intellectual enrichment, nor should they frustrate the student by offering tantalizing concepts in words he cannot decode.

EXPRESSIVE DISABILITY

We should consider the following expressive language difficulties: sparse output, incorrect pronunciation and spelling, conversational shyness and fear of writing, atypical rhythms in speaking or writing, and word-finding difficulty.

Sparse output. If sparse output results from a small vocabulary or unfamiliarity with complex linguistic constructions, the student needs opportunities and exercises in language development. He needs to hear well-developed language in conversation and in the classroom. Ideally someone will read aloud to him, individually or in a group. If this is not feasible his parents should be encouraged to involve him in story programs at the local library. Stories on records and cassettes are often available at libraries, and Books on Tape has many selections available for rental or purchase (see p. 245).

Inaccurate pronunciation and spelling. Many young children may lisp or have other forms of imprecise articulation until their second teeth are in place. The sounds for \th\, \l\, \r\ frequently present difficulty. For instance, many children as old as six say \y\ or \w\ for \l\: *yittu* for *little*. They may say *w* for *r*, *wuv* for *love*, *wed* for *red*, *vewy* for *very*. They may use \v\, \f\, or \d\ for \th\; *wiv* or *wif* for *with*, *du* or *vu* for *the*, *dis* or *dat* for *this* or *that*. These errors are within normal limits until age seven, and many children outgrow minor articulation problems. However, if the child has trouble making himself understood, he should receive language therapy as soon as possible. A smart child whose communication is blocked suffers profound frustration.

Spelling difficulties harm written expression, making the writer appear stupid. The student who relies on a weak visual memory may write *nieghber* or *niehgbor* for *neighbor*. The student with auditory confusion who tries to spell phonetically may write *dup* for *dump*, *kafyujan* for *confusion*, or *azgeti* for *spaghetti*. The pattern of spelling errors will dictate what kind of help is needed.

Conversational shyness and fear of writing. Some students are reluctant to contribute their ideas to classroom discussions; other original thinkers who are just plain shy in verbal situations may do very well on paper. Conversely, many students who enjoy talking are intimidated by writing. They might be called "paper-phobes": the sight of a blank piece of paper waiting to be filled paralyzes their ideas. These may be students who spell poorly, who have poor handwriting, or who are simply untaught, unpracticed writers.

Atypical rhythms in speech and writing. Slow speech may be a symptom of word-retrieval difficulty or it may be the hallmark of a speaker with a large vocabulary who selects his words carefully. In either case the speaker is likely to use fillers (and um, the um, you know) that make it hard for the listener to stay tuned in. Other speakers talk very quickly, their thoughts seeming to come in rushes that they spit out in rapid-fire clusters. Their speed sometimes makes them hard to understand. Fatigue or pressure will accentuate atypical rhythms.

Rhythms in speech are likely to be mirrored in written work. The careful speaker can often write a letter or paper on the first try. The rapid speaker often blurts his thoughts out on the paper and has to eliminate, reorganize, and rewrite.

Word-finding difficulty. A subtle, common cause of expressive disability is frequently overlooked or misunderstood. It is word-retrieval difficulty, sometimes called *dysnomia* (from *dys* meaning poor or having trouble with, and *nomen*, to name) or *aphasia* (from *a*, meaning not, and *phatos* to speak). It disrupts all communication: speaking, writing, listening, and reading.

Anyone who has momentarily forgotten someone's name knows what dysnomia feels like. The dysnomic may have trouble retrieving the name of a person, the location of a battle, the title of a treaty, a date in history, or the label for a common object. The reader who has ever said "Hand me that thing" or "Look! There's a whatcha-callit" has used some classic dysnomia-dodgers. All of us have experienced this at one time or another. We are perfectly familiar with the object or person, but the label won't come out. "It's right on the tip of my tongue," we say. "I can't remember it right now, but I'll know it at three in the morning" or "When I tried to introduce him, I drew a complete blank!"

While the speaker (or writer) is still searching for the elusive word, its absence creates what William James called "an intensely active gap." No other word will quite fit in its space, and when it finally floats into grasp, it fits in the gap as snugly as a piece in a jigsaw puzzle. So far, it sounds like a mild social inconvenience, and for most of us it stays that way. But the afflicted student suffers in school, where many teachers do not understand the disability and its manifestations.

Monica studied hard in her eighth-grade history course. She understood the concepts and enjoyed her homework readings, but she had some trouble in classroom discussion, did very poorly on pop quizzes, and failed three important tests.

Recently I visited her class. Monica, conscientiously prepared as usual, took her seat. The teacher began, "I want to review some of the events in last night's homework that preceded the declaration of war. We know that the people on both sides were going hungry, we know that there was a boundary dispute and that there was a violation of a treaty. What was the name of that treaty . . . Monica?"

Monica froze. She had studied it the night before. In her mind's eye she could see the name in italics halfway down the left-hand page of her book, but she couldn't remember it. "Wait, wait, oh I know it," she said. "I knew it last night." The teacher interrupted, "Monica, if you knew it last night, you'd know it today." Penciling a mark in her record book, she turned to another student, saying, "Mark, how about you? Can you remem . . ." "Oh I've got it now," Monica blurted. "It's the Treaty of. . . ." The teacher cut her off. "Monica, how many times do I have to ask you not to interrupt? You had your turn. If you would study more carefully, you'd pass this course, you know."

The tears welled up in Monica's eyes. She *had* studied carefully; she just forgot when she was called on to answer quickly. When she got scared she forgot, and when the pressure was taken away, the answer came bubbling up.

Monica was struggling with dysnomia, a specific disability. It didn't trip her up when she was able to choose her own topics. Using familiar vocabulary she could express herself adequately. When she wandered further afield, she relied on time buyers and fillers, description, and function: "the—um—you know——the thing over the door" (she meant transom); and "the, the um, the . . . razor blade," "hand me that blue doohickey over there" (the blue photograph album on the chair); and "Let's get 'em with the water-shooter" (the hose).

Single-word answers are hard for the dysnomic to deliver, but they are simplicity itself compared with trying to summarize or trying to write a test answer. For example, in recapping a short story, Monica's classmate said, "Maude, who was the main character, realized that unless she delivered her brother's parka to the hockey rink, he wouldn't have it for the trip. The team was due to leave directly from the rink without stopping back at school." In trying to sum up the same story, Monica said, "She tried to figure it out and stuff, but she didn't think she could get it over there, and if she didn't and he left, well, like, it would be really bad."

The problems created by dysnomia multiply when the student is required to write, particularly under time pressure, as in a test or an exam. Tension and anxiety are normal parts of test taking, but anxiety is the enemy of memory.

Students working in workbooks may do nicely when filling in

the blanks or when answering questions from multiple-choice answers. When they are asked to write extemporaneously, however, their work is either brief or disconnected or their papers are swiss-cheesed with erasures. When the workbook provides the word, there is no problem. But when the student has to retrieve, think, and write simultaneously he becomes overloaded.

Dysnomics are likely to be either poetic or rambling. For example, Harvard linguist Anthony Bashir uses the example of the high school student who, in writing an exam, was trying to refer to a migrating flock. Lost for the words, he wrote "a flying wedge." Metaphor is beautiful, but it may not earn a high grade on a science exam.

Dysnomia creates trouble in both listening and reading. The dysnomic listener forgets the words he has heard and often has trouble remembering oral directions accurately.

Dysnomia takes its toll in both early and more sophisticated reading. Reading means taking meaning from printed symbols. The reader who has trouble with word retrieval may look at a word, recognize its configuration, know that it represents a hairy four-legged creature who whinnies and jumps over fences, but have trouble retrieving the label *horse*. Whereas the reader with problems in visual learning may make a *horse/house* error, this reader may make a *horse/pony* error. His errors will be within categories instead of outside them. This is the reader who would read *salt* as *pepper*, in contrast to the reader with visual confusion, who would see *salt* and say "slat."

The competent reader actively generates language in anticipation of what's coming next. The reader who has trouble retrieving a target word is on the spot and may tire easily. Research by Denckla and Rudel has shown that such a student may retrieve the needed word the first or second time he meets it, the third try will be slower, and the fourth and fifth slower still and less accurate. This reader's retrieval ability is rapidly exhausted. It has no relation to visual perception, physical energy, native intelligence, or good attitude. It's as if he is driving a large car with a very small gas tank.

Of course not all people who forget names, speak slowly, or say "and um" or "like" are dysnomics prone to *horse/pony* errors.

All of us use time buyers and fillers, and we read inaccurately on occasion. The tip-off is frequency. If we know someone, particularly a child, who depends on gesture, inflection, a smile, time buyers, and descriptive terms instead of labels, we owe it to that child to probe for dysnomia. Once we understand, we can help. Until we do, we will continue to offer inappropriate remedies or fruitless threats and exhortations to "do better."

EMOTIONAL INTERRUPTION

Emotional difficulty can interrupt or block language development. In the metaphor of a staircase, the young language learner starts out with two feet firmly planted on the floor. As he begins his ascent from one language level to the next, it is as if he climbs a staircase. With both feet on one tread his linguistic balance is pretty secure. But, as he reaches for the next level, one foot stays on the familiar tread and the other is traveling the riser to the next level. One foot gives half the balance of two. If an emotional upset or interruption coincides with a transition from one language level to the next, the child's language may regress or not reach the next level as quickly as expected. What could cause this?

The child who starts school too soon may revert to earlier language levels as a signal that he is in over his head. Recurrent illness can encourage helplessness, which shows in baby talk. An older child who loses his place in the family hierarchy with the arrival of a baby or a set of step-siblings may regress to an earlier language level. The pain of parental separation, divorce, or remarriage frequently affects the developing child's or adolescent's language level. The budding orator may drop back to "factory outlet" expression.

A change in a child's language level is a warning signal. Regression needs to be met with patience and understanding. In cases of serious or prolonged difficulty a language clinician should be consulted.

Because we shall explore the effects of emotional difficulty on schoolwork in detail in the next chapter, "Psychological Availability for Schoolwork," here we only mention the way it interweaves with language development.

DIFFICULTY WITH ABSTRACTION OR ORGANIZATION

Many smart kids who are reaching out to learn new things don't take the time to distinguish main ideas from irrelevant ones in what they hear or read and may have trouble arranging their spoken and written thoughts. They need to allow the linguistic filing system to make its contribution. Orderly storage makes retrieval easier, thus helping the student organize his spoken or written output.

Students with trouble in abstraction and organization are often those who did not consolidate the preanalogy skills of comparison and categorization (see the section on articles, pronouns, and affixes, pp. 113–16) and don't really understand the concept of time.

Unfortunately, specific language disabilities aren't limited to one to a customer. An artistically gifted student may struggle with coding and also have word-finding problems. A young scientist with expressive problems may also face an emotional interruption. The more the conundrum kid has to contend with, the harder the task, and the greater the need for specific, on-target help.

PRINCIPLES OF GOOD PRACTICE

Many reading problems spring from a disorder in the language system and can afflict highly intelligent students.

When a parent or teacher suspects the existence of a language problem, the student should have a thorough language evaluation. Although learning specialists and psychologists are trained as testers, many have not been trained to evaluate the specifics of language development and are not tuned in to the academic implications of subtle language disorders. Therefore, this kind of evaluation should be made by someone trained in speech, hearing, and language. An evaluator can be found through the school system or the medical profession.

The child's pediatrician may make a referral, or help may be found by inquiring at the nearest large hospital. Many hospitals have a department of speech, hearing, and language staffed by people qualified to diagnose and prescribe. Failing these sources, The American Speech, Language and Hearing Association, 10801 Rockville Pike, Rockville, Maryland 20852, has regional listings of certified practitioners.

In preparation for the evaluation, parents should consult (or start) the master file described in Chapter 1 (pp. 18–19). It is important to reconstruct the child's history, noting the age at which he reached developmental milestones, particularly the onset of speech. It is also vital to note family history. If Great Uncle Ernie had a hard time learning to read and write, he may be casting a generational shadow. The teacher should contribute samples of current work and descriptions of classroom behavior, mentioning specific instances of success and failure. Cooperation among the student's parents, teachers, and the overseer whose role we probed in Chapter 1 (pp. 16–18) is essential.

The student needs to learn the reason for the evaluation in an age-appropriate way. It may or may not be helpful to refer to "the dyslexias." Some students are more comfortable having a name for their problem; others feel that the label is a confirmation of disease. An honest and positive approach goes a long way to banishing the student's spoken or unspoken fear that he is stupid. The gifted thinker who sets high standards for himself and struggles with learning problems may have difficulty understanding or using the words to deal with such fears.

If professional language therapy is indicated the clinician prescribes the particulars, but parents and teachers can make immense contributions too. Following the order in which we explored the language difficulties, here are suggestions for help.

RECEPTIVE LANGUAGE DISABILITY

To help a student with receptive language problems we may need to lighten the language load. Giving him more words, more quickly, or more loudly (the way some people shout at foreigners) only aggravates the problem.

Starting with gesture and labels, and moving through the other levels of language growth, we can determine which words have meaning for the child, how many he can handle, how long he can remember them, and whether he can transfer them from one context to another.

We can connect interesting vocabulary with his actual activities. Memorized vocabulary lists don't stick.

We need to use active and passive constructions and dependent clauses as he is able to understand them.

We should be sure he understands those little words that shift meaning: *if, unless, whenever, nevertheless,* and so on.

Always we can encourage him to generate visual imagery to accompany what he hears.

It helps if we use the terminology of time precisely: we shall be leaving *in half an hour,* or *right after lunch,* or *at 12:30.*

Of course we want to read aloud and get books on tape.

Probably we need to help him sort his vocabulary. He needs to hear and categorize words. He needs to be taught the meanings of figures of speech, idioms, and proverbs. He needs training in listening. The specific strategies in Chapter 5 on auditory learning will help. He needs short, frequent language stimulation, with change of pace. He needs specific training in reading comprehension. He needs to reinforce the link between language and mathematics.

Many outstanding mathematicians are weak in certain kinds of verbal work. Many highly verbal people are more skillful with words than with numbers. But students, and thinkers of all ages, need both words and numbers to use math for asking questions and solving problems. We need to be sure he understands such words as *each, diameter, circumference, area, volume, ratio,* and *every other.*

We should investigate his understanding of time, not just noticing whether he can read the face of a digital watch. We need to find out whether he knows the meaning of the terms *morning, noon,* and *evening* and why *afternoon* is called *afternoon;* the feeling of elapsed time: how long ago does your birthday seem, the worst day of your life, the first time you saw your baby brother, and so forth; the anticipation of elapsing time: whether he knows he is going somewhere in twenty-five minutes, whether he can be ready in time without looking at his watch; that human beings use the language of time to organize thoughts and experiences into present, past, and future.

Above all the student needs sympathetic acknowledgment that his difficulty is a legitimate one that others have had and overcome.

CODING DIFFICULTY

An intelligent child who has not learned to read or write in spite of exposure to traditional teaching methods needs something different. More of the same will continue to produce disappointing results: frustration or failure.

To help a student who has coding problems, teachers or parents should arrange for him to receive multisensory training. If this training is available in school, the student is fortunate. For the parent who is not sure how to ask, it may be described as Slingerland; Orton-Gillingham; Traub, *Recipe for Reading*; or Alphabet Phonics. If it is not provided in school, the teachers need to recommend outside help, and parents need to provide it much as they would eyeglasses, a hearing aid, or physiotherapy.

A smart kid struggling with coding difficulties is like a singer in a soundproof room or an athlete in shackles.

EXPRESSIVE DISABILITY

Here are some ways to help the student with word-retrieval difficulties.

Help the child use words with as many associations as possible: opposites, synonyms, categories, and so forth. A word stored alone has only one handle by which to grab it. A word stored in a pair has two. Storing in pairs, then, doubles the shot at retrieval.

Provide verbal accompaniment to label the items and experiences in the child's life: "Here, hold your mittens while I zip the zipper and tie the drawstring. I'll button my sweater, and put on my down vest. Then we can go on the sled" instead of "Okay, hang on, we'll get set, here, see? Okay, let's go."

Expose the child to different kinds of experiences, using the vocabulary for each. Language uses different sets of words for different purposes. Even young children can tell the difference between the language of a television commercial, the language of a bedtime story, the language of a scolding, or the language of a secret. Each one has its own words. By helping the child (or student of any age) to pay conscious attention to differences he understands subliminally, we expand the number of lexicons to which he has access.

Invite eye contact that makes a bond between the speaker and the listener. It will buy time (and patience) from the listener.

Make special preparations for taking a test or writing a paper. The dysnomic student preparing to write a paper, or take a test, should sit down with his books beforehand to list the labels and terms he thinks he's going to need. Generating the list is one more way of underscoring and overlearning the words. Then he can leave the list out on his desktop while he's writing the paper so the words are all neatly captured.

He should prepare for a test in the same way. In the process of compiling the list, he's actually sorting important from unimportant, a valuable comprehension and study exercise. With explanation of his difficulty and a sympathetic teacher, he may obtain permission to take the list with him to the test or exam. Just knowing that *primogeniture, photosynthesis,* or *Phoenician* is right on his card will allay his anxiety about retrieving the term. He will be able to spend his time thinking, instead of chasing through his own mind with some verbal net trying to catch elusive words.

Open-book exams are a release for these students and are more and more often used in high school history and English courses.

Foreign languages are particularly difficult for these students, and high school or college students may need to try to have that requirement waived or simplified. As we saw in the case of the college student in Chapter 1 (p. 23) whose dean suggested she be tested to effect such a release, understanding of the problem is increasing.

EMOTIONAL INTERRUPTION

Although teachers and parents can help, the student whose work and language are disturbed by emotional interruption needs a checkup from someone trained in mental health. This is no place for the well-meaning amateur.

The distinctions between the roles of educational and psychological therapist mentioned in Chapter 1 are important to bear in mind. As Katrina de Hirsch points out in her monograph "Interactions Between Educational Therapist and Child," the educational therapist allies herself with the student's intactness and reality, the psychotherapist with the student's pathology and fantasy. We shall explore this further in Chapter 7, "Psychological Availability for Schoolwork." Meanwhile parents need to be aware of this distinction, understanding which kind of help is needed and what it is intended to accomplish.

We shall explore how to help the student with emotional interruption more fully in Chapter 7.

DIFFICULTY WITH ABSTRACTION OR ORGANIZATION

The student needs to learn how to outline, using major headings, subheadings for successive topics, and subheadings to the subheadings: Roman numeral I, subheading A, subheading i, subheading a, and so forth.

Conceptually strong students with poor organization or verbal abstract thinking profit from "Supermarket School." There are boundless opportunities for cataloguing, remembering, choosing, comparing, selecting, and describing: in other words, putting language to practical use. Students who have trouble with the school language they consider esoteric can often be lured, and then helped, by practical language exercises connected with everyday experience.

Supermarkets provide endless opportunities for exercising receptive or expressive language:

Labels: oil, vinegar, dishwasher detergent, cantaloupe
Two words: baby carrots, fresh peas, french bread
Categories: starches, preserves, canned goods, fresh produce
Comparison: new potatoes, Idaho potatoes, frozen french fries
Analogy: plum : prune :: grape : raisin

Parents can help their children hone their organizational skills in the supermarket:

We are doing our grocery shopping for the whole week. You

are the dessert king. Please pick out enough to last us until we return.

We are taking a picnic to the beach tomorrow. Please pick out enough rolls, hot dogs, relish, napkins, fruit, soda, plastic forks, napkins, paper cups, and plates for six people.

We shall have three age groups tonight: Grandpa, Aunt Edith, and second grader Sammy. Please find a snack for each of them.

All students, and particularly those who struggle with language problems, grow through being read to. In addition to enhancing language, reading aloud has other benefits that, although important to all students, are vital for intelligent students who struggle with the dyslexias. Reading aloud:

soaks the listener in complex language. Language is more caught than taught.

enhances concept development, delivers new information, and promotes opportunities for philosophical reflection. Through literature the dyslexic can meet the questions that have puzzled and delighted juvenile and adult thinkers throughout history.

helps the listener recognize the existence of, and differences among, such genres as biography, poetry, adventure, romance, and satire, to name but a few, and provides the comfort of bibliotherapy when needed.

gives the listener the feeling of belonging we explored in Chapter 1. In hearing a story, the young listener (or the adult playgoer) can identify with characters and share responses with others in the group, be it his family or a class in school.

A CASE HISTORY: LAVINIA

Lavinia, the youngest of three girls, admired her three male cousins. When she was three, one of them gave her an outgrown baseball cap, which became her trademark. She wore it whenever she could, or carried it around the way another child might tote a security blanket. She was a beautifully coordinated blue-jeaned tag-along who loved physical adventure.

Other people would catch their breath at some of her stunts, but her parents learned not to worry. Oddly, for all her physical daring, she had very few bruises, never broke a bone, and probably wore fewer Band-Aids than any other child her age.

In contrast to her talkative sisters, Lavinia was a quiet child who could entertain herself for hours playing with the blocks at her cousins', making things with clay, drawing, painting, creating collages, or making adventures for her stuffed animals.

Her passion for the jungle gym, the tricycles, the blocks, and the art corner flowered in nursery school. She was an active, hands-on doer. Her beloved baseball cap was with her always, pressing down on her curls but not concealing them.

Toward the middle of the year, however, her sparkle dimmed. She pulled her baseball cap down over her ears and became an unhappy, aggressive group member who hit and pushed whenever she didn't get her way. The other children began to pull away from her. They were afraid.

Late in the spring her class did a project with shadows, which culminated in the teacher's making life-size silhouette portraits of each child. Lavinia slashed hers with scissors. When reprimanded, she cried but wouldn't explain why she had done it.

In kindergarten she contributed little if anything to group discussions and pinched or found some other way to disrupt when the talking went on too long. Her classmates isolated her, and the lonelier she was, the more demanding and physically abusive she became. Her artwork lost its joyful quality. She pulled down the brim of the cap that had become her emotional barometer. The only time she was happy was when she was in gym. Academically, she had a difficult time trying to learn her letters, and, even though she was a whiz with money, she had had trouble with paper-and-pencil math.

The kindergarten teacher requested testing, and the first results were alarming. Lavinia's receptive language was above average, but her expressive language was far below the national norm, near the level of many retarded children. The second round of testing revealed another side of Lavinia. In all measures of nonverbal reasoning she scored in the highest possible range. Here was a child of immense nonverbal intelligence.

Her parents agreed to a language evaluation, and the results bore out the school's hypothesis that Lavinia was an extremely intelligent child with a genuine expressive language difficulty. Her natural inclinations had led her to block building, sports, arts and crafts, and away from words and abstraction. This had been fine during the early years of preschool, when the emphasis was on action, but when words became the medium of exchange, she was isolated. Competitive but unable to get to the top, she resented those who usurped what she considered her rightful place, and her anger took physical form. She had trouble using letters and numerals because they were abstract verbal symbols.

The discrepancy between her nonverbal and verbal reasoning was creating anger and pain. The gap between her comprehension and her output was forcing her into more and more antisocial behavior. The angrier she grew the more she needed a way to express herself, but her only way was through physical aggression. The greater the anger, the greater her need, and the greater her need the greater the anger at not being able to do anything about it.

Her parents agreed to take her three times a week for language therapy, and the miracle began. As her words came, her smile crept back. She pushed her cap back on her head so her face could be seen. As she found ways to explain her ideas, her feelings, and her plans, she began to take joy in her artwork again. Although she was hesitant about trying to make friends with her classmates, she made such good progress in her individual language therapy sessions that she was soon able to join a therapy group, in which she socialized with increasing ease.

Returning to Leon Eisenberg's phrase "we become human as we understand each other through language," Lavinia became human, and she became human through language. She learned how to ask for a turn, she learned how to invite another child to play, she learned to use *if*, that tiny powerful barter word: "If I give you this block, will you let me have the green clay?" She learned to use "Trade ya" as an offer instead of as a claim. Last week she said, "If you'll be my friend, I'll invite you to my birthday at my house and let you use my best bike."

PSYCHOLOGICAL AVAILABILITY FOR SCHOOLWORK

AROUSAL, ATTENTION, ACTION

Arousal, attention, and action are the Get Ready! Get Set! Go! of psychological availability for schoolwork. Just as the athlete gets ready by warming up, the student prepares by arousing himself physically and intellectually. The athlete tenses his muscles, poises his body, and gathers his energies to get set; the student gets set by focusing his attention. The athlete gets ready, gets set, and then goes into motion; the student converts his combined arousal and attention into the action of active learning.

Those of us who know how to Get Ready! Get Set! and Go! may be puzzled by others' difficulty, yet many smart kids with school problems cannot accomplish this seemingly simple sequence and are not psychologically available for schoolwork. In exploring why, we should bear in mind the intellectual traits of gifted thinkers and also the social-emotional needs we explored in Chapter 1.

In addition, we should be on the lookout for the impact of the factors disruptive to auditory learning discussed in Chapter 5 (pp. 91–100). We should recognize their power to prevent arousal, divert attention, or block action.

AROUSAL

Arousal is the first phase of attention. "I could teach him if I could only get him *with* me." The student who has trouble arousing himself is literally unavailable. His parents, teachers, or educational overseer should talk together about sleep, food, allergy and hearing, boredom, and emotional resilience.

SLEEP

Luther was an outstanding student until November of sixth grade, when his midterm grades dropped dramatically. His math teacher recommended tutoring, his English teacher threatened academic probation, and his guidance counselor suggested a comprehensive psychoeducational evaluation. Common sense and a conference found the cause and the cure.

It turned out that Luther's father had started a new job, which required frequent travel; his mother was taking evening graduate school courses; and the sitter-housekeeper was lax about discipline. Luther was watching TV until 10:30 or 11:00 P.M., and trying to do his homework on the bus on the way to school. Arriving tired out, and sitting in an overheated classroom, Luther found it hard to stay awake. When the facts emerged, TV was banned on weeknights, Luther's bedtime was reestablished, he was ready to learn again, and the problem melted away.

FOOD

It is virtually impossible for a hungry child to rouse himself to a symbolic task. This has always been true, but the number of children who come to school without breakfast is increasing to include many from affluent and middle-class families.

As the number of women in the work force increases, the number of traditional breakfast makers decreases. Independence is the mealtime theme, particularly in the morning, when family members rush to keep to their various timetables. The child is often expected to prepare his own dish of cereal, muffin, or whatever. If there are several children and both parents, or the single parent, are trying to get to work on time (sometimes with the added scheduling problem of dropping a younger child at day care), the schoolchild's breakfast habits may be overlooked. In many households that rely on domestic help, the housekeeper who comes in for the day arrives after the children's departure for school.

A child who goes to school hungry may be all right for the first period or even the first hour and a half, but the two periods before lunch are worthless. When physical energy wanes, psychological availability wilts.

ALLERGIES AND HEARING

Allergies are the enemy of arousal for two reasons. First, the allergy itself causes physical distress: stomachaches or upper respiratory ailments. A child whose physical well-being is disturbed rarely has the energy left over to "get ready" to learn. Second, many allergy medications cause drowsiness or lassitude. Allergic reactions may also affect hearing acuity or perception, interfering with responsiveness.

BOREDOM

Sometimes, sad to say, lessons are just plain boring. Smart kids are sedated by boredom, which may spring from genuinely uninteresting material or presentation, or from a mismatch between the type of presentation and the learning style of the listener. It is hard for the visual learner to stick with a primarily verbal lesson.

EMOTIONAL RESILIENCE

Although only a trained psychologist or psychiatrist can diagnose and treat an emotional problem, a parent, teacher, or concerned adult can often make useful guesses. Parallel to the questions raised about his physical condition, we can ask, Does the student seem psychologically refreshed or weary, nourished or hungry, irritated or at peace? In the section on Action we shall explore some emotional factors that drain the student's psychological energy and block his availability for schoolwork.

Without arousal the would-be learner is merely a passive observer. The unroused child may be extremely intelligent, active in other types of situations or at other times of day, but he will continue to have school problems until he can "Get Ready" to "Get Set" to "Go." Educators and parents can plan appropriately if any of these conditions seems to be the cause of the problem. Often, as in Luther's case, the remedy is simple. If the cause is difficult to pinpoint, the student should start with a medical checkup.

ATTENTION

Adults are so aware of the student's need to *focus* his attention that they frequently minimize the importance of the flip side: the ability to *shift*. Unhampered students do both, but some smart kids can't.

In medically diagnosed cases of attentional deficit, medication can have a dramatic, positive effect on the student's concentration, but not all students need it. Some developmentally young children are interested in so many things that it's hard for them to settle on one. If these children are young for their grade level, smart but unready, they may be misdiagnosed by impatient adults. These children don't need medicine; time and training are the appropriate remedies.

Sometimes a smart kid can focus his attention but has trouble shifting it. If he is exploring a concept or project, he likes to pursue it to its outermost limits and resents interruption. As we know from the traits discussed in Chapter 1, sustained concentration can be a hallmark of gifted thinking. A student with this capacity needs free time for projects at home, he probably needs to strengthen his concept of time, and he needs to be teased into flexible thinking. Let's look first at *focus* of attention, and then at *shift*.

To focus his attention the student needs arousal, a filter, language, and appropriate work.

AROUSAL

Arousal awakens the attention, which then needs to be focused.

A FILTER

A filter keeps out external or internal distractions. External ones may be sounds, sights, uncomfortable temperatures, hard chairs, or poor lighting.

Some students have a hard time filtering out sounds that others don't even notice. For four years I worked with Eugene. A brilliant thinker, he used his native intelligence and high motivation in trying to overcome his reading problem. Everything would be fine until a telephone would ring, the furnace would go on, or the maintenance crew would turn on the snow blower. Eugene would give a start, shake his head, and try to discern the source and meaning of the sound, and he would need to remark on it before he could settle back to work. His alertness to environmental sounds was paradoxical, considering his difficulty with phonics and blending sounds together to make words. He would say "s\t\a\n\d . . . stand? . . . Yes. Stand" and, in the same breath, "That's the third ambulance that's gone by this week."

Other smart students may have trouble filtering out visual distractions: someone walking along the side of the room, a piece of paper fluttering, or a simple environmental change.

Hughie is an accomplished fourth-grade mathematician who has trouble with reading comprehension. Last week his teacher gave him a sheet and said, "Hughie, here are the questions that go with today's reading. Read the questions first, think about them, then read the passage, and we'll work on the questions together when you're through." Halfway through the short passage Hughie looked up, saying, "Why did you move the red books to the other shelf?" Glancing up in the middle of his reading, he had noticed the change and needed to be told the reason for it before he could continue reading.

Eugene and Hughie are keenly alert to environmental detail, and would be great exploring a desert island or solving a crime, but in school they get in trouble because their filters aren't strong enough to screen out environmental distractions.

An effective filter also blocks out internal distractions: fatigue, hunger, the kinds of irritable sensation that accompany allergies, or that insidious thief of concentration, daydreaming.

Daydreaming is a silent, seductive interruption. In severe cases, the student should have a checkup by a psychologist or psychiatrist. But here's something to try first, which I learned from Katrina de Hirsch. Often the person isn't aware of the onset of daydreaming but, instead, comes to with a jolt, realizing, "Oops, I don't know what's been going on." When you work with a daydreamer, sit beside him. When you feel him slipping away, touch him and ask, "Are you daydreaming now?" If the answer is yes, ask whether he can remember what it felt like just *before* his attention slipped away. The first time or two, he probably won't be able to answer, but, simply through having had the question raised in a friendly, non-threatening way, he will begin to recognize the premonitory sensation. The student who understands his own warning signals can be on guard against daydreaming, the internal intruder.

LANGUAGE

Language organizes thought; organization allows the student to focus his attention. As we saw in Chapter 6, the language of time is a framework for planning: first, next, finally. The student uses language to break down a large task into manageable pieces, to anticipate cause and effect, to categorize and to sort ideas according to their relative importance. Some students who appear to have trouble paying attention actually lack the language to structure their work. They don't need pills or extra workbooks; they need language help.

APPROPRIATE WORK

Sometimes the label *attentional deficit* is applied to a student who is merely in over his head.

Sandy's second-grade teacher called his parents for a midyear conference and suggested he be taken to the pediatrician with a request for medication for attentional deficit. She said, "He's out of his chair, swinging around on the rows of desks, talking to his neighbor; he doesn't pay attention, and he disrupts the other children with his comments, jokes, and general restlessness."

In looking over his work folder, Sandy's mother found fourteen sheets of seat work (five pages of arithmetic word problems and nine of reading), all of which she knew were too hard for him to read. Sandy was chronologically young for his grade, had had chicken pox and two episodes of severe bronchitis in first grade, and consequently had missed a lot of instruction. Not surprisingly, his reading was quite far below grade level, and yet his work folder contained standard fare for second grade. Here was a young, insufficiently prepared child being chastised for being unable to solve problems he couldn't read and being a candidate for drug therapy to reduce hyperactivity when the root problem was a mismatch between skills and tasks.

SHIFTING ATTENTION

Language prods and helps verbal shifts. Students need to learn to use one word in two ways, either in homophones (*steel/steal*) or homographs (*present/present*).

Parents and teachers can encourage children by playing with riddles and puns. The student also needs to interpret figures of speech and metaphor, understanding both the individual words and overall meaning of "two heads are better than one."

Language prods and helps the student to shift attention as he increases his accuracy and speed in sorting, filing, and retrieving ideas. Awareness of different styles and rhythms of language helps him shift among categories of spoken or written messages, differentiating among television commercials, fiction, business letters, and journalism. Each has its own vocabulary. Parents and teachers can point out these differences, helping students become consciously aware of categories they recognize subliminally.

Here is yet another instance of how understanding the language of time influences behavior. To be willing to shift attention, students need to grasp the meaning of such words as *now, later, tomorrow, before, after, until.* People with a hazy grasp of time are understandably reluctant to leave something interesting; they are not sure when they can return to it. "Later" and "after math and science" may have no more real meaning for them than "in an hour." As we saw in Chapter 6, many smart kids are in this category.

ACTION

The student who can channel his arousal and attention shows psychological availability for schoolwork. Action, active learning, depends on willingness to take risks, acceptance of the error half of trial and error, and openness to ideas.

Action can be slowed or halted by fear, disorganization, depletion, helplessness, guilt, or depression. These operate like a sea anchor, as a brake below the surface.

It is important to remember that when one family member has a psychological problem, fallout spreads to the others. One family member's problem can flush up guilt, resentment, anguish, jealousy, despair, or bitter warfare among the others. As we consider psychological distress we need to think, then, of secondary as well as primary victims.

The Center for Preventive Psychiatry, White Plains, New York, offers the following Table of Trauma, listed in order from most to least devastating: (1) death of parent, (2) divorce, (3) separation, (4) visible deformity, (5) death of brother or sister, (6) jail sentence of parent, (7) remarriage of parent, (8) hospitalization of child, (9) involvement with drugs/alcohol.

Here are some blocks to active learning I have seen over years of teaching smart kids with school problems: fear of failure, disorganization, fear of depletion, learned helplessness, guilt, and depression.

FEAR OF FAILURE

Smart kids from high-achieving families sometimes become prisoners of perfection. When such a child enters school, the unspoken expectation might as well be chiseled over the front door: GO TO THE HEAD OF THE CLASS. A little child pleases his parents by smiling, walking, talking, and doing other expected things. Schoolchildren know that academic success pleases their parents and think that scholastic failure may cause withdrawal of parental love, a child's deepest fear.

As we know, smart kids have very high expectations for them- selves, can anticipate the complicated nature of unfamiliar tasks, and hate to do poorly. When the stakes are academic success and parental approval, it is tempting to abandon a novel idea in favor of a sure shot.

Fear of failure can prompt either "If I don't try I can't fail" or "I'll only do it if I'm sure I'll get it right."

DISORGANIZATION

Clear organization is conceptual cartography. It requires being able to pick a starting point, aim for a midpoint, anticipate a con- clusion, and create a mental map to get from one to the other. Whether the cartographer starts with lots of details and builds them into a whole or starts from the whole and assembles the parts, the goal is the same: organizing material to fit inside the contours of the idea or the project. In the absence of a mental map the reader, listener, watcher, interpreter—whoever—doesn't know which way to go.

It is hard for some students to think in an orderly way if their personal possessions are disorganized. A colleague in California said it this way: "So many of my students are from split-custody families. They're with their mothers on Mondays, Wednesdays, and Fridays, and their fathers the other days. They alternate weekends. These kids don't know where their sweaters and tennis rackets are, but worse than that, they sometimes can't seem to find their thoughts. It's as if their touchstones are in misplaced backpacks: not lost, not stolen, just not handy."

FEAR OF DEPLETION

I learned about fear of depletion at a medical lecture and felt as if each word were a brush stroke in a perfect portrait of a student I had never really reached. This is what I learned.

Some children who have suffered painful loss set up psychological safeguards against having to reexperience the feeling. They remember how they felt before "it" (whatever it is) happened. Now the loss has taken away a part of them, leaving a hole. Unconsciously they think, "Something valuable is gone. I don't want that hole to get any bigger, so I'm going to hang on to whatever I have left, including my ideas. If I share them, I might use up my whole supply and hollow myself out even more."

Children who have lost a parent through separation, divorce, or death are particularly vulnerable to fear of depletion, and as the divorce and separation statistics mount, so do the incidences of this fear and its effects on schoolwork.

These students are reluctant to share original thoughts in class discussion, to generate new ideas for written work, or take intellectual risks. A smart kid, adept at spotting patterns, a divergent thinker, one with heightened perceptions, has natural impulses to be inventive. When fear of depletion cripples his imagination, a paralysis that works against the child's nature and delays the healing of the original pain results.

Loss through death, though terrible, has a finality. Margo was a second grader when the car in which she and her father were riding was struck broadside at an intersection by a drunk driver. Her father was killed instantly. As the family tried to accept the shock, everyone remarked on Margo's ability to cope. She kept to her previous schedule, took care of her little sister, and was "a perfect little grown-up."

In a handwriting project she copied four poems out of a book and traced their illustrations. This, in spite of the fact that she had previously been an accomplished artist and creative writer. Her deportment was so considerate and tidy, and she seemed to have accepted the death so well, that it was a long time before her mother saw Margo's manners and coping skills for what they were: a deadening of emotion, a denial of grief over something she couldn't bear to accept, and a hoarding of ideas. She was happy to copy and recite but afraid to release original thought.

With the encouragement of a perceptive teacher, Margo's mother enrolled her in an after-school drama and arts program. She learned her lines quickly and well and began investing them with emotion and powerful body English. Margo discovered that the more she gave out, the more her power increased. She made the same discovery in her painting and drawing and finally began to contribute her ideas to classroom discussions. She found that replenishment came steadily, and she is now a vigorous contributor.

Loss through divorce may, paradoxically, be harder for the child to accept than sudden death because the coming and going of the absent person keep alive the hope of permanent reunion. Children of any age have trouble with "here today and gone tomorrow," and they may lay a burden of perfection on themselves, attempting to bring back the absent parent. "If I am better, Mommy will come home for good." "If I get all As, Daddy will be so proud he won't be able to stay away." This can add fear of failure to fear of depletion, doubling the problem.

LEARNED HELPLESSNESS

Martin E. P. Seligman, M.D., coined the term *learned helplessness* in his research as a clinical and experimental psychologist at the University of Pennsylvania. According to Seligman, learned helplessness develops in animals and people whose efforts have no impact on their circumstances.

For instance, if animal number one, placed in a water tank in danger of drowning, thrashes around and then is plucked from the water, he associates his own efforts with the rescue and will struggle again the next time he is in danger. Animal number two, also about to drown, thrashes around and is only rescued later, after he has stopped thrashing. He does not connect his rescue with his efforts.

The first animal learns that what Seligman calls the *locus of control* is inside him: effort brings rescue. The second animal learns that quixotic fate may be cruel (jeopardizing him to begin with) or benevolent (arranging the rescue), but that the locus of control is outside, beyond his reach. Animals who learn helplessness give up when danger comes; they drown quickly.

As Seligman illustrates, learned helplessness, unchecked, leads to passivity, depression, and, in extreme instances, death.

For some of our students it's not such a long step from the experimental drowning tank to the mainstream classroom. The student who has difficulty doing what others around him do easily can either thrash around or give up. When a child in difficulty thrashes around trying to save himself, but nothing changes, he "learns" that the locus of control is outside him.

Where is the locus of control in most school settings? The teacher plans the lessons; the student does them. The teacher sets the standards; the student must meet them. The teacher gives the assignments; the student completes them. The teacher grades the product and the effort; the student is measured. When the match is right, each success fuels the next endeavor. In a mismatch, who feels the pain? The student. Who struggles? The student. Who has the power to change the circumstances? Seldom the student.

Which children are particularly vulnerable to learned helplessness?

The child whose early health history contains major illness, hospitalization, or chronic poor health may develop a fundamentally passive approach to life. During the years he should be exploring and gaining dominion over his world, the ill child who survives by taking medicine, breathing oxygen from a machine, having transfusions, having things put into or cut out of his body learns that strength is external rather than something that can grow from within. The unhealthy young child survives and recuperates through obedience, rest, and restraint. These early experiences of helplessness can deplete psychological availability for schoolwork.

Once in school, the athletic child with a weak visual memory sinks in look-say reading instruction. The mathematically powerful student with slow visual-motor integration gasps for air trying to take dictation. The verbal reasoner with a weak auditory system drowns in words in classrooms that emphasize listening. The intelligent child with receptive language disability grasps at straws, trying to learn through reading. The poetic child with visual-spatial confusion loses ground trying to solve math problems by using manipulative materials. These are a few examples of students at risk for learned helplessness.

Smart kids with school problems who are powerful in areas that are not acknowledged in school live at two simultaneous psychological extremes: power and helplessness. Swings between such distant poles are confusing and debilitating.

What diminishes the risk of learned helplessness? Giving students a sense of control over their own learning. Students need to learn strategies more than they need to learn facts. If a struggling student is given tutoring in the facts that everyone else around him already knows, is given the "whats," he is receiving information that he feels he ought to learn independently. He sees his success as coming from the benevolence of his tutor; the locus of control remains outside. If, on the other hand, the student is taught strategies, the "hows," he can begin to take charge of his own learning. The locus of control moves inside.

With the locus of control outside, life teaches the lesson of learned helplessness. With the locus of control inside, life reinforces the lesson of learned competence.

GUILT

The preschool child sees the world as an extension of himself, believing that external events occur because of his internal wishes and emotions. As he grows older, the machinery of cause and effect becomes more apparent, and he trades omnipotence for common sense. While it is painful to relinquish total power, it is also a relief to shed its responsibilities. In normal development, the child makes the trade at around age five and goes on about his business, constantly learning "If I do this, such and such will happen" and "If I do not do this, such and such will or will not happen."

If a child suffers a traumatic loss through death, divorce, or separation when he is still an omnipotent thinker, he feels responsible for the event. If the little child says "I hate you" to a parent (as perfectly normal children do from time to time) and the parent subsequently packs up and leaves because of a marital problem, the child nevertheless feels responsible and therefore guilty.

If a father dies or leaves home at the height of a little boy's struggle to resolve an Oedipal complex, the child unconsciously feels guilty that what he wanted has come to pass.

The statistics show an increasing number of divorces and separations among the parents of preschool children. Unconscious and inappropriate assumption of guilt can make the child afraid to explore questions of cause and effect. Who needs public confirmation of secret shame? Because active learning involves cause and effect, this fear can set up new learning problems or aggravate existing ones.

Erik H. Erikson says the child's psychological growth follows a preordained sequence of internal crises, using the word *crisis* to describe the tension between negative and positive forces. The resolution of the crisis, negatively or positively, determines how the child will react to the next stage of his life and tips the balance for the outcome of the next "crisis." The infant's crisis is basic trust versus mistrust. The preschool child's tug-of-war is autonomy versus shame and doubt. The mounting statistics on parental departure during these years when the child considers himself omnipotent tip the balance in favor of shame and doubt, which has a powerful influence on the resolution of the schoolchild's crisis: industry versus inferiority.

DEPRESSION

Educators and parents need to acknowledge the phenomenon of childhood depression, recognizing it as a serious problem requiring professional care. Although a concerned adult can sense sadness or inturned anger, only the professional is qualified to confirm the existence of clinical depression, only the professional should try to assess the depth and scope of the illness, and only the professional should apply the treatment. Kind people with common sense are allies who must recognize their limits. Sigmund Fraud is a dangerous imposter.

The teacher and psychotherapist play separate and distinct roles. The teacher is the student's ally in the realm of reality and keeps him in touch with his own intactness by conveying "This is what you *can* do," "These are things you *have* learned," "Here are ways for you to help yourself." The student needs acknowledgment of his competent side in order to keep faith in himself. The psychotherapist meets the student in the realm of fantasy and pathology. Without pathology there would be no need of treatment. The child needs to know there is someone who will help, respect, and accept him in spite of his confusion. If the teacher, who is meant to hold the child in the realm of reality and intactness, glides over into the realm of fantasy and pathology, the child loses his guide. This is a profound betrayal.

Depression deserves volumes to itself, and any attempt to cover it in a chapter, or part of a chapter, would be both presumptuous and unprofessional. There are, however, two ways in which depression and school overlap that are particular perils to smart kids with school problems. One is mourning and schoolwork; the other is the chicken/egg question of school problems and depression.

A school-age child may mourn the death of a person or pet or the departure of a parent through separation or divorce. As mentioned, the reappearance of the separated parent may prolong the grief. Reappearance denies finality, yet the acceptance of finality is a prerequisite of true healing.

Children mourn, too, for less obvious losses. The child, particularly one with the intellectual traits of a gifted thinker, may mourn his own infancy and childhood when things seemed easier. He may also mourn his departing sense of competence or his access to those activities and areas in which he finds joy and success.

During a time of mourning, the student's schoolwork may suffer because of these symptoms: diminished powers of concentration, trouble with short-term memory, shortened attention span, and distractibility, not to mention sadness. Mourning children need reassurance that these symptoms are both normal and temporary. According to Louise Conley, Ph.D., a guidance counselor whose specialty is mourning through death, separation, and divorce, a healthy period of mourning takes roughly one year. Educators and parents need to understand the length, depth, and full effects of this healing process.

Depression can be either the result or the cause of school problems. Clearly, the smart kid whose heightened perceptions cast a terribly bright light on his own shortcomings, whose big dreams seem blocked by his own incompetence, and whose divergent thinking is being confined and forced down through the narrow end of a funnel is vulnerable to the feelings of anger turned inward and helplessness that fuel genuine depression. The anger at not being able to accomplish what others accomplish effortlessly, the anger at being asked to do what cannot be done must go someplace. It may go into depression.

As noted earlier, the smart kid with school problems may be angry with himself or at the society that imposes requirements he cannot satisfy. The depressed student's anger turns inward, putting him at risk for harm, ranging from deliberate troublemaking, to substance abuse, to suicide.

It is also true that depression can be the cause of school problems, affecting all three levels of psychological availability: *arousal, attention,* and *action*. As depression drains psychological energy it inhibits arousal. As depression prompts introspection it steals attention. As depression is the companion of passivity and pessimism it blocks action. The depressed student is not free to mine his own assets.

Recently I heard a guidance counselor from a competitive university lecture on the high incidence of depression among intelligent, attractive, affluent adolescents. He emphasized that "having everything" confers no immunity. In fact, material comfort may be a contributing factor to depression in a child who feels helpless, discouraged, or inadequate. Being showered with the benefits of someone else's competence can reinforce the passivity and learned helplessness from which certain depressions arise.

He explained further that many students with indulgent parents seldom face the consequences of their own actions: the boy who turns off the alarm clock and goes back to sleep is driven to school by a parent who doesn't want him to miss breakfast or be late. This kind of parent may write a health excuse note to explain away incomplete homework. The list goes on. The guidance counselor showed how some depressions have their roots in this pattern.

When the catered-to adolescent tries to rebel, his parents excuse, overlook, or cover up his attempts to strike out: "My Sammy was with a bad crowd that day," "Beer missing? No I didn't notice," or "Julia, we'll say you were with us if you'll promise never to do such a thing again." These responses to rebellion steal the adolescent's power, saying, in effect, "Your actions aren't worth my strong response," the extension of which is "I really don't care about you."

Depression and powerlessness go hand in hand. When indulgent parents try to spare a child the consequences of his own actions, they deny him the power to provoke, then reciprocally, the power to please. They reduce his assaults to flying marshmallows.

This counselor urged his listeners to expand their awareness of adolescent depression and self-destruction beyond suicide to include drug (including alcohol) abuse, withdrawal into solitude, and non-completion of work.

If the smart kid without school problems is vulnerable to depression and its serious fallout, his hampered counterpart is in double jeopardy.

PRINCIPLES OF GOOD PRACTICE

When a student is psychologicallly unavailable for schoolwork, the school and family should join forces to investigate possible physiological causes and should share anecdotal information with one another as well as with the child's doctor. Such symptoms as circles under the eyes, persistent congestion, bad breath, constant yawning, or restlessness need to be pinpointed and investigated. The school and family can help by offering specific examples: "After lunch, it is hard to get his attention," "Noises in the hall disrupt him easily," "He does better when he sits near the person who is speaking," and "Making eye contact helps him focus" are much more helpful than a generalized "He doesn't seem to stay with the group," "He never finishes anything." Be specific as to when and where the child has a particular type of difficulty.

In preparing for a joint conference, the parents, teachers, and educational overseer will want to review the master file, noting his strengths and weaknesses in the learning systems explored so far. A student with seeming arousal problems may not hear well, one whose attention wanders may have trouble filtering out visual distractions, another who doesn't hand in his assignments may have trouble with handwriting or organization. Appropriate notations should be added to the master file.

Much can be learned from a classroom observation. A teacher, the learning specialist, the school psychologist, or, if none of these is available, an adult who knows the student should sit in the classroom and observe him for a half an hour three times during a day, with no other obligations during this time. It is surprising how much information can be gathered by an observer who is free to focus on one person, who has the time to notice the student's concentration span, and the types of situations in which he is psychologically available or unavailable. What is the thread? Where is the pattern?

If a student has difficulty with arousal, the alert adult will notice when he laughs and when he relaxes. Knowing what he cares about helps parents and teachers incorporate these interests into the activities in which he is lethargic, building a bridge from one to the other. If he is interested in rock music, he can be asked to make up a math word problem for each morning's math class about bands, groups, hits, instruments, or whatever. If the student laughs over riddles, he can be the master of ceremonies of the Riddle of the Day. Real learning is active and energetic.

The student who has trouble focusing attention needs to learn the strategies for listening outlined in Chapter 5 (pp. 101–105). During explanations he should sit near the front and maintain eye contact. When he is expected to work independently, he may need a desk away from the window and door, perhaps even a carrel.

The student who has trouble shifting his attention needs variations of activities. Mind benders, word problems, and logic exercises tempt smart kids. "What if" questions require flexible thinking. Word play promotes it. Asking students to invent math word problems stimulates it, as does telling three-fourths of a story and asking the child to invent an ending.

The old-fashioned parlor games I Spy and Twenty Questions, which can be adapted to family or classroom use, are a quick way to stimulate flexible thinking with a group. In I Spy, "It" selects something in everyone's full view and gives one description: "I spy something yellow." The guessers then try to identify the object by asking questions with yes or no answers: "Is it in the left half of the room?" "Is it bigger than a breadbox?" In Twenty Questions, "It" thinks of a person, place, or thing that the guessers must identify by asking no more than twenty yes or no questions.

If a student has trouble with action, here are some suggestions to release the brakes.

To reduce fear of failure, parents and teachers can honor originality over conformity by offering open-ended questions, giving assignments that have no correct or incorrect answers, such as writing a poem, inventing a conclusion to a story, or building a diorama to illustrate a concept. Adults can try new things themselves with the students, teaching willingness to take risks through personal example.

To help overcome disorganization, teachers and parents should be certain the student really understands the language of comparison, categories, space, and time.

Adults can diminish a student's fear of depletion by engaging him in brainstorming exercises in which everyone thinks and shares: How many things can we name that are found in most kitchens? Let's get as many adjectives as we can to describe a fish. Discovering the feeling of replenishment, particularly if it is connected with laughter, will encourage the fearful student to let go.

Adults can help the student replace learned helplessness with learned competence by putting the locus of control within his reach. Teaching him strategies as opposed to giving him correct answers gives him a chance to direct his own attempts and makes a link between effort and success.

We can help students avoid some unnecessary guilt by verbalizing the causes and effects of events in daily living:

"I dropped the glass of milk because my hand was slippery from the soap."

"You hurt your toe because you were so busy trying to carry the box that you forgot to look."

"Your daddy is in the hospital because he hurt his shoulder on the camping trip, and the doctor needs to fix it there."

Educators and parents should be aware of the possibility of childhood or adolescent depression and seek professional diagnosis and treatment as quickly as possible. This is no place for amateurs.

Literature can lead people of all ages to psychological availability for learning. Rich stories allow us to play with elemental themes and questions with no verifiable answers. To find that other cultures and other peoples have wrestled with the ambiguities of the human condition is a reassuring discovery to everyone, and particularly to students in psychological distress.

Creative writing, at home or in school, can tweak arousal, capture attention, and channel action. Recently, during a three-day workshop for parents, administrators, and teachers of gifted children, I invited a large group of local students to participate in an exercise I had used in our school. We started with a brainstorming session on stars: where do we hear about stars in nursery rhymes, popular music, fairy tales, religion? What do they symbolize? Are they near, far, hospitable, dangerous, inhabited? Are they like one another?

Moving from Twinkle, Twinkle Little Star to pondering e. e. cummings's "I would rather learn from one bird how to sing than teach ten thousand stars how not to dance," to reading selections from Antoine de St. Exupéry's *The Little Prince*, we explored the students' memories and associations, comparing them to other authors' ideas. Then it was time for them to invent their own stars. One brilliantly original sixth-grade thinker, who had been hiding and hurting in formal academic settings, wrote:

"My star can be as cold as a stare, hot as hatred. It is located in the back of my mind, far as infinite but as close as a wink. You visit only when you fall asleep, leave when you awake. All speak strange, yet you understand them. You may find friends but may not. Anything can happen, limited only by your imagination. You never eat, drink, get hurt, or die. Those distant stars are my dreams. I hope they never burn out."

A CASE HISTORY: LARRY

Larry is the youngest of four children whose parents are frequently busy in the evenings, leaving him in the care of his older brothers and sister. If they have plans of their own, Larry is left alone. He is never quite sure who will be where, when. His brothers are strong and enjoy contact sports. Larry does not and reports being "scared of Eddie . . . he knocks me around." His sister considers herself "above" the male horseplay and doesn't intervene unless there is a bad fight.

Larry's nursery school teacher reported that he had trouble paying attention and following directions. "He's in outer space," she said, coupling his distractedness to his fascination with astronauts and space shuttles. He needed constant reminders about the simplest routines, and she would often have to call "Earth to Larry."

His spaciness continued in kindergarten, and in spite of his obvious intelligence, he seemed at risk for failure in first grade. Although he could build anything with his hands and had gathered extensive knowledge about the space shuttle from studying pictures and diagrams, he couldn't stay in his seat for more than a few minutes at a time.

In second grade, Larry had trouble with spelling, doing pencil-and-paper arithmetic, and following directions. His teacher said, "Larry is frequently silly, disrupting other children and distracting himself from his own work. His time-on-task record is very poor." His erratic work habits annoyed her and, truth to tell, she didn't like him very much. She tried to be more sympathetic in February, however, when he lost the index finger of his left hand in an accident.

He and a friend had been playing in Larry's yard on an old toy with spinning seats anchored to a center post. When it wouldn't spin, Larry put his finger down the center of the post to see whether anything was stuck. At the same moment, his friend started pushing the seat around by hand. Larry's finger was caught; the friend pushed again, hoping to free his finger but cut it off instead. No adults were home, and although the boys finally got help it was too late to restore the finger. Larry was terrified by the accident and ashamed of his hand.

He was in considerable physical pain for at least six weeks, and, to no one's surprise, showed little interest in his schoolwork for the rest of second grade.

In third grade Larry had serious problems with reading comprehension, his handwriting was sloppy, and although his understanding of math concepts was good, his columns drifted and he added the wrong numbers together.

His parents were impatient: "He's perfectly bright; he just isn't trying. . . ." His teachers were irritated: "If that kid would pay attention he'd be a top student." The school learning specialist said that he was disorganized, did not know how to tell time, misunderstood such spatial markers as *every other*, and showed spatial confusion in letter formation and placement. Her report read, "This seems to be an intelligent child who is not performing well in school. He should have a comprehensive psychoeducational evaluation."

Larry's scores on the testing showed very high abstract reasoning, barely average visual-motor skills, and sequential skills well below the national norm.

The evaluating psychologist wrote that Larry had a poor self-concept and his sense of physical intactness had been badly shaken by the accident. He was embarrassed by the appearance of his hand, felt abandoned by his parents, and was afraid of his siblings. He felt overwhelmed by the requirements of his schoolwork and didn't know how to ask for extra help because he couldn't tell what it was he didn't know. He had no idea how to organize either the problem or the solution. He said, "It doesn't matter what I do. I just can't do any of it."

With this information in hand, the psychologist and the educational team arranged a conference with Larry's parents. They also shared some of the results of the testing with Larry, who was surprised and proud to hear about his high reasoning ability. The educators and parents discussed the implications of the testing with the psychologist and planned appropriate instructional measures.

A private tutor, provided by the parents, met with Larry in school three times a week to work on his handwriting and review concepts of time and space. She gave him strategies to organize his materials, ideas, and homework. They practiced techniques for strengthening his reading comprehension, and gradually Larry's day-to-day work improved. He agreed to take a six-week summer academic skill-building program as long as he could be allowed to continue playing in the soccer league. Everyone knew that his athletic successes were important in helping him overcome the trauma of losing his finger.

His parents made some family rules: an older sibling was to be at home with Larry any time his parents were out. Bullying was prohibited. They also instituted a Saturday morning family marketing trip. Each week, each person was charged with collecting the necessary ingredients for one night's dinner and then responsible for preparing it. The one who cooked didn't have to wash the dishes.

Larry loved to fix pizza and salad, which turned out to be Eddie's weekly favorite, and the others enjoyed it nearly as much. Providing a way for Larry to make a contribution to family living was an example of confirming a child's worth not by praising him, but by depending on him.

Larry received a supportive combination of academic help, emotional support, security in his daily living, and appropriate opportunities for responsibility. It took a while for the benefits to show, but he bloomed.

8

TESTING DEMYSTIFIED

SCORES, INTERPRETATION, PLANNING

This chapter is designed to demystify testing and to show how test scores can work *for* a conundrum kid. Many teachers' experience with testing is limited to the classroom. Some administrators are accustomed to looking at whole-class or whole-school test results and have less experience with assessing individual profiles. Most parents are bewildered by a collection of test scores and unfamiliar terminology.

Because we learn more from patterns than we do from any single score, the emphasis is on identifying *clusters* of strength, *types* of behavior, *kinds* of weakness, and *areas* of difficulty. Recurrent themes emerge when we join anecdotal material, school records, and the results of an individual evaluation.

But expecting the uninitiated to collect these different materials is as unfair as asking a hungry noncook to shop for the ingredients of a satisfying dinner. He may know he needs to eat; he wants a nourishing, tasty meal; but he doesn't know how to check the cupboard for what's already there, where to go to get what is lacking, how much of what to buy, which things are fine ready-made and which need to be made from scratch, how to combine the ingredients, when he can manage on his own, or when he needs to hire a cook.

THE TESTING PROCESS

We shall explore a glossary of testing terms, types of tests, reasons to test, hazards of testing, benefits of testing, and variables in testing.

A GLOSSARY OF TESTING TERMS

The terms are listed in the order most general to most specific.

Norms.   Norms are the results of the typical performance of the group of individuals to whom a test is administered when it is being standardized. National norms are derived from a nationally based population sample. Independent school norms represent scores attained by applicants to, or students in, independent schools. Local norms are developed from the testing results within a given school. Norms indicate average performance as well as degrees of deviation above and below the average.[1]

Percentile.   The term *percentile* comes from *percent*, meaning per hundred. A percentile shows where one student scores in relation to ninety-nine other students. The ninety-ninth percentile is the highest. Because this score shows relative performance, it is not to be confused with getting a score of 99, 69, or 31 on an exam.

Stanine.   Stanines are standardized scores that go from 1 to 9 in the sets of 10 between 1 and 100. The ninth stanine is the highest. A score of 7 would be in the first stanine, 14 in the second, 28 in the third, and so forth.

Mean.   Mean is an average. The mean score of 65, 76, and 84 is 75, derived from adding the scores together and dividing by 3.

Median.   Median is that which is midway between the highest and the lowest.

Standard deviation.   Standard deviation is the amount by which scores can be above or below the mean without major statistical significance. If the standard deviation is 10 on a test whose mean is 100, scores from 90 to 110 do not mark as major a difference as scores from 80 to 100 or 100 to 120.

Numerical score. The numerical score tells how many answers a student had right. If he had 73 correct on a test with 85 items his score would be 73, or 73/85.

Raw score. The raw score is the test taker's numerical total. Alone, it has no significance on instruments that have converted scores.

Converted scores. Converted scores are derived by putting raw scores into a conversion table to compare a student's performance with that of others of his age, sex, or grade level.

Grade equivalent. Some test results give a grade equivalent (GE). If a fourth-grade student has a GE math score of 8.5, it means he has performed on that test as well as a student in the fifth month of eighth grade. It does not mean that he is proficient in eighth-grade math.

Mental age equivalent. Some test results deliver a mental age equivalent (MAE). If the same fourth-grade student has an MAE of 17 on a particular test, it means that his performance matches that of seventeen-year-old students. It does not mean that he is ready to go to college.

IQ. These letters stand for intelligence quotient, a number derived from the student's scaled scores on a standardized test (defined in the next section). It is intended to measure how smart someone is.

TYPES OF TESTS

Standardized tests. A standardized test is one whose results are tabulated from criteria to compare students' performances. Scores are reported in norms, percentiles, stanines, and the other ways listed previously. They differ from teacher-made tests because they compare students from large groups.

Achievement tests. Achievement tests are standardized instruments that measure what the student has learned.

Aptitude tests.   Aptitude tests are standardized instruments that purport to measure the student's aptitude for learning. Theoretically, acquired knowledge doesn't enter in. Some disagree.

Intelligence tests.   Intelligence tests try to tell how smart someone is.

Diagnostic tests.   Diagnostic tests try to tell something about the student's learning style. Their titles are usually self-explanatory: Slingerland Pre-Reading Screening to Detect First Grade Academic Needs, Wepman Test of Auditory Discrimination, Beery-Buktenica Test of Visual-Motor Integration. Projective tests are psychological diagnostic tests.

Group tests.   Group tests are given to whole groups at once.

Individual tests.   Individual tests are administered to each student individually.

Timed tests.   Timed tests must be completed within a time established by the test maker, time being a factor in the test's standardization.

Pencil-paper tests.   Standardized pencil-and-paper tests require the student to mark his answers, usually multiple choice, in a test booklet or to mark an accompanying answer sheet.

Verbal tests.   Verbal tests measure verbal skills.

Performance tests.   Performance tests require a student to manipulate materials.

Quantitative tests.   Quantitative tests measure mathematical skills.

Multiple-choice tests.   Multiple-choice tests have questions that the student must answer by choosing one of the (usually four) answers provided. The student cannot offer his own answer.

Essay question tests.   The student provides his answer in his own words in essay form.

In most schools, students take a set of standardized achievement tests in reading and math once during each year. Some achievement tests include aptitude sections; others do not. The results report individual students' scores and the scores for each class as a group. They are recorded in norms, percentiles, stanines, and the other ways described previously.

REASONS TO TEST

Three good reasons to test are to find out something not already known, to confirm a hunch, and to support recommendations.

When a kid is struggling in school, the first suggestion often is "Let's get him tested." That may or may not be necessary. Look first in the file to see what's already there. This is analogous to checking the kitchen shelves before going out to shop for dinner. School files are filled with test results gathering dust.

When unknowns remain after checking the records, or when it seems time for an update, appropriate testing should be arranged. We shall explore the specifics shortly.

Sometimes a parent or a teacher has a hunch about a kid but would not feel responsible in making a diagnosis without objective or professional information. The teacher who is concerned about a student's hearing wants the verification of an audiological examination. The parent who is worried about developmental readiness wants clinical evidence to help with a school placement decision.

Sometimes numerical test results are needed to support a recommendation. Numbers talk.

"Mr. Smith, Johnny's teachers don't feel he's solid enough to go into first grade" is less effective in buying Johnny the extra year he needs than "Mr. Smith, although we all know Johnny is bright, he scored below the fiftieth percentile in all subtests of the standardized testing. With another year under his belt he could be at the top of the class."

HAZARDS OF TESTING

Dr. Seuss, the philosopher who writes books for children, wrote a poem for a class of college seniors: "The Art of Eating Popovers." It might as easily have been written for people who interpret standardized test results: "Do a lot of spitting out the hot air and be careful what you swallow."

For reasons explored throughout this book, many smart kids score poorly on standardized tests, creating an incorrect impression of low overall ability.

In today's cultural climate, test scores are taken seriously, but the tests themselves are often insufficiently analyzed. For example, one section of a well-known test is called Spelling, but the student is not asked to spell. He is asked to find the correct spelling from among four alternatives; this is proofreading. Some clumsily designed test items test two, or even three, separate skills within one question. Well-designed test items probe discrete areas separately.

Group-administered or "quick-to-give, easy-to-score" IQ tests are dangerous as well as inaccurate: the picture they give is shallow, and the result is usually a numerical score, which gives no indication of patterns. Many such tests require the student to read the questions. One of my students, an intelligent poor reader, received an IQ score of 74 (national norm 100). In this era of data banks, numbers that do not represent what they purport to represent are dangerous. Once a number is on a transcript there is no control over who sees it, what interpretation is given, and what use is made of the interpretation. Intelligence tests and diagnostic tests should be administered individually.

BENEFITS OF TESTING

Well-planned, well-used testing has many benefits. First, today's kids need to be familiar with the process. The sooner they start and the pleasanter the initial experiences, the more they will take testing in stride.

Standardized testing can protect creativity in the classroom. Being able to say "The students in Mrs. Smith's room, who do such magnificent projects, also score well above the national norms and even above the local community norms on their standardized tests" enlists support for the projects from even the most conservative onlookers.

A cumulative record of test scores is an invaluable addition to the student's master file. Historical perspective highlights patterns.

VARIABLES

Three variables deserve close attention. Changes in the child's external environment may influence his daily performance or his performance on a test. Changes within the child (as he moves from one linguistic, developmental, or psychosocial level to another) may influence his performance. Changes in the focus of the curriculum may influence the quality of his performance, as we have seen throughout the book.

A test measures a student's performance on one particular instrument on one particular day in one particular situation. If the results don't ring true, educators and parents should probe further and should not let test results own the student. He should own them.

INDIVIDUALIZED TESTING

If you, the adult reader, think the student should have individual testing, what do you ask for, where do you get it, when should you have it, what does it look like, how long does it take, what are the results, and how do you use them?

WHAT DO YOU ASK FOR?

You ask for a comprehensive psychoeducational evaluation, which should include the child's developmental history, current achievement levels, an IQ test, screening for learning disabilities, and psychological or neurological testing if deemed necessary by the examiner or examiners.

WHERE DO YOU GET IT?

You can arrange for testing through the school system or have it done by a private organization. There are advantages and disadvantages to each. If the student is in the public school system, the testing will be done by an evaluating team, which usually includes a school psychologist and/or a learning specialist. Testing will take place in school without extra charge. If you have faith in the school personnel, this is fine. If you, as a parent or teacher, feel that the student is not well understood, you may prefer an outside opinion.

If the student is not in the public school, but you are a taxpayer in the district, you are entitled to an evaluation, by the school team, without charge. However, you have no choice as to who will administer the tests. This is either risky or safe, depending on the district. Check. Because the evaluation will be the foundation of a great deal of subsequent planning, quality is vital.

If you choose to have this done outside the school, there are several ways of finding people to do it. Ask the guidance department in the school, check the pediatric or neurological departments of a nearby hospital (a teaching hospital if possible), or ask the student's own doctor. Failing these, you could contact the regional representative of The Orton Dyslexia Society, 724 York Road, Baltimore, Maryland 21204, to ask for the name of a doctor or psychologist near you. Remember the caveat: if the results don't ring true, probe further. The test results should mirror the child's performance. Because costs vary widely, it is impractical to address that question here.

WHEN SHOULD YOU HAVE IT?

Although some excellent diagnostic tests are available for use with preschool children, IQ tests are of dubious merit before the age of six. A smart child with school problems should have an individual diagnostic screening for learning disabilities at the first hint of trouble. A smart, healthy child, working under a good teacher in appropriate grade placement, who has trouble mastering what others are learning easily should have an individual evaluation, ideally before entering second grade.

An evaluation should be given as soon as the family, the student, or the school becomes concerned. If one was given when the student was in first grade, it is appropriate to have another around fourth or fifth grade, and perhaps again at around tenth. These suggested intervals are suitable but not mandatory. Although individual subtest scores may vary, the pattern of learning style within the test results usually remains consistent: fingerprints don't change.

WHAT DOES IT LOOK LIKE?

For older students as well as younger ones, it will seem like conversation, games, and puzzles with a friendly person.

HOW LONG DOES IT TAKE?

The examiner will probably schedule one intake session with the parents; two or three testing sessions with the student, lasting roughly one hour apiece; and then a final interpretative session. If not all three testing sessions are necessary, it is easy to cancel one.

WHAT ARE THE RESULTS?

Skillfully interpreted, they highlight not so much *what* the student has learned, but *how* he acquires information, and whether he can manipulate as well as acquire it. The scores will be reported in percentiles, stanines, norms, or in the other testing terms listed in the glossary.

The parents and school should request a written report to accompany or follow the oral, interpretative session. They should inquire ahead of time whether the examiner is willing to put the findings and interpretation in writing; if not, they should obtain permission to tape-record the session and write down any and all numerical scores. It is important to have the subtest numbers. Later in the chapter, we shall look at ways of using these numbers to understand the student's learning style and make some educational decisions. The interior, subtest scores are much more helpful than the numerical total.

HOW DO YOU USE THEM?

The results can form the platform for short- and long-term educational planning: choosing the best type of academic setting from the available choices, tailoring the combination of courses best suited to the student's learning patterns; and selecting areas of study which will exercise talents, shore up weaknesses, minimize frustration and failure while encouraging interest and success.

Let's look at one test battery, and one recently published book, which suggests an entirely different look at intelligence and measurement. They are the Wechsler Intelligence Test for Children, Revised (commonly called the WISC-R) and *Frames of Mind: The Theory of Multiple Intelligences*, by Howard Gardner (New York: Basic Books, 1983).

Why these? The WISC-R has stood the test of time, there is a great deal of interpretative data on each subtest, and interesting research shows new and additional ways of interpreting the scores. Because it is familiar to educational, psychological, and neurological evaluators everywhere, the results are transferable among disciplines.

In *Frames of Mind: The Theory of Multiple Intelligences*, Howard Gardner bases his hypotheses on work done in three areas. He works with victims of brain disease and injury at the Boston Veterans Administration Medical Center, he is an associate professor at the Boston University School of Medicine, and he is a codirector of Harvard Project Zero, in which he studies the artistic and intellectual development of normal and gifted children. He feels that restricting intelligence measurement to verbal and performance categories, or linguistic and logical/mathematical categories, results in rapid, prejudicial labeling of smart and dumb and gives an unfairly negative appraisal of many who, under different, expanded standards would be superior. A review of his book said:

> There is an increasing tendency to restrict the measure of students' intelligence to the numerical scores they can earn on standardized tests. The simplistic illogic that a high score equals an intelligent, worthy human being carries with it the fallacy that a low score equals an unintelligent, unworthy human being. When these ideas take hold, social critics, educators, and parents cry out for higher scores and the activities of young minds are restricted in response. In effect, students are pushed down through the narrow end of a funnel. Now, in contrast, Howard Gardner inverts the funnel, inviting an expanded and

benevolent yet scholarly and explicit model of human intelligence.[2]

Let's take a deeper look at each of these.

THE WISC-R

Although the WISC-R is an intelligence test that can be administered only by a licensed psychologist or tester, the scores may be interpreted in several different ways by specialists and nonspecialists alike who understand the significance of the numbers.

A WISC-R delivers a *full-scale number* representing the student's overall IQ. This number is derived from the scaled combination of two sets of subtests, Verbal and Performance. Each of these two categories has its own total, which is derived from the scaled combination of six subtest scores:

VERBAL	PERFORMANCE
Information	Picture completion
Similarities	Picture arrangement
Arithmetic	Block design
Vocabulary	Object assembly
Comprehension	Coding
(Digit span)	(Mazes)

VERBAL SUBTESTS

All verbal subtests are presented orally and are intended to be given in this order:

Information. This is a test of general information. Good readers and students with rich cultural background usually do well here.

Similarities. This subtest is often considered the most valid predictor of academic success. As the name implies, it requires comparison and contrast on an abstract level. Good performance here can indicate facility with abstraction and manipulation of concepts, poor performance the opposite.

Arithmetic.   This subtest is an oral presentation of counting and word problems. Students with weak auditory memory have a hard time, and anxiety works against good performance.

Vocabulary.   This subtest requires word knowledge and the ability to give definitions. Critics complain that it is culturally biased; also, auditory-processing problems may lower vocabulary levels.

Comprehension.   This subtest probes the student's knowledge of social conventions and the way the world works.

Digit span.   This exercise in auditory memory and concentration tests the student's ability to hear and repeat (forward and backward) a meaningless string of numbers. It is sometimes omitted and sometimes not factored into the verbal subtotal.

PERFORMANCE SUBTESTS

No performance subtest requires the test taker to read, and only Coding requires writing.

Picture completion.   The student must discover what is missing. A good score indicates sharp eyes, alertness to detail, and common sense.

Picture arrangement.   The student arranges a group of pictures to tell a story in correct sequence. Poor performance in this subtest indicates susceptibility to certain types of language and reading problems.

Block design.   This subtest is considered to be a highly accurate indicator of spatial intelligence. Students who do well here grasp spatial relationships and abstractions quickly, exercise good small-motor coordination, and often become talented engineers, scientists, and mathematicians.

Object assembly.   To score well, the student must put puzzle pieces together quickly and adroitly to form a picture.

Coding.   This subtest requires deft visual-motor integration. Students with strong visual memory have an advantage. Concomitantly, students with weak visual memory, anxiety, and difficulty with concentration or pencil manipulation are penalized.

Mazes.   This subtest requires the student to use a pencil to find his way out of a maze. This subtest may be omitted and is not required for a performance score.

Each subtest delivers a scaled score, which may range from 1 to 19, 19 being the highest and 10 being the national norm. In addition, each numerical score falls into both a descriptive category (dull-normal, superior, and so on) and a percentile. A perfectly normal profile (that is, the norm) would be 10 on each subtest, a verbal IQ of 100, a performance IQ of 100, and a full-scale score of 100, intelligence falling in the fiftieth percentile. But people are seldom so consistent. *Discrepancy* is the key word for conundrum kids. Witness Miranda.

The opening paragraph of her individual evaluation reads, "Miranda was referred for testing because of her uneven school performance. While she sometimes contributes sophisticated comments to classroom discussion, her written work is poor. Her teachers and parents question her overall endowment and wonder why her performance is so erratic."

WISC-R
Miranda X
Full-Scale: 122

VERBAL: *128*	PERFORMANCE: *109*
Information: 14	Picture completion: 13
Similarities: 18	Picture arrangement: 12
Arithmetic: 11	Block design: 15
Vocabulary: 15	Objection assembly: 12
Comprehension: 15	Coding: 5
Digit span: 12	Mazes: no score

Miranda received a verbal IQ of 128, placing her in the Superior range; a performance IQ of 109, or Average; and a full-scale IQ of 122, also in the Superior range. Of note is the 19-point discrepancy between the two categories. Of even greater note is the internal scatter, or discrepancy, among her performance subtests, which range from 5 to 15. And we see a span of 18 to 5 from her highest to her lowest subtest scores across the categories: 18 on the verbal Similarities and 5 on the performance Coding. Because a discrepancy of 3 points from the student's own mean (Miranda's would be 12.5+) is considered significant, Miranda's scores are very revealing.

What do the totals tell us? Miranda's verbal house is in good order, and she is less adroit with performance tasks. Does the number 122 tell us very much? No. It is a much lower number than she would have had without the Coding score, but there is no little warning flag saying, "Watch out; this is not the whole story."

We can see a great deal by looking inside the totals. Miranda is a good thinker whose mechanics are weak. She is comfortable with abstraction (see Similarities and Block design), has a good understanding of the world around her (see Information, Vocabulary, Comprehension, Picture completion), and relative "freedom from distractibility" (see Arithmetic and Object assembly), but she has miserable visual-motor integration (see Coding). Her verbal strengths are easy to spot, but her spatial conceptual ability does not show in the Performance score, which was lowered by her poor coding.

It is informative to rearrange WISC-R scores according to the student's own mean score, figuring any deviation of plus or minus three (± 3) as significant. Making the individual's own set of clusters highlights strengths and weaknesses. Miranda's show the following patterns:

MARKEDLY LOW	IN THE MIDDLE	MARKEDLY HIGH
Coding 5	Arithmetic: 11	Information: 14
	Picture arrangement: 12	Vocabulary: 15
	Digit span: 12	Comprehension: 15
	Object assembly: 12	Block design: 15
	Picture completion: 13	Similarities: 18

What do we learn? There are many more significant strengths than weaknesses, and the strengths are all in conceptual and acquired knowledge tasks, auguring well for learning new information and enjoying intellectual work.

Much early schoolwork requires memory and speed, and Miranda's rote memory work is only slightly above the national norm (see Arithmetic and Digit span). Her high conceptual levels, however, will help her develop her own compensatory strategies. The analysis of clusters points an imperative finger at the need to shore up the weakness in Coding, a debilitating problem, dangerous to both self-concept and output if neglected. A numerical grouping such as the one here paints a clear picture. Thank you, Miranda.

"Memory-Myra," whose full-scale score puts her in the Superior category, scores high in the mechanical and memory subtests of Coding, Digit span, and Arithmetic. Her middle scores are in acquired information subtests, and her low scores are in conceptual areas. She was a strong student in the early years of school: she learned sight words, memorized number facts, and recited the capitals of all the states. But when the curriculum shifted to abstract thinking, she began to sink through no fault of her own. Her parents, and some teachers, assumed her full-scale IQ certified giftedness and needed to be let down gently.

Edward's conceptual scores are high, but his scores for acquired information are low. This was the tip-off to an auditory processing problem and hitherto undetected hearing loss.

Full-scale, verbal, and performance are the traditional ways to categorize WISC-R scores. Bannatyne[3] suggests an additional way to interpret them by allocating subtests to the following three categories:

SPATIAL	SEQUENTIAL	CONCEPTUAL
Object assembly	Digit span	Comprehension
Block design	Coding	Similarities
Picture completion	Picture arrangement	Vocabulary

Bannatyne shows that the subtest scores of many smart kids with school problems cluster together within these categories. Here are some examples.

Mickey does well in math and science and is a good athlete, but his language weakness shows in reading comprehension and trouble with figures of speech. He scores high on spatial tasks, and low on sequential ones.

Conversely, Adam, the potential English major who does poorly in math, scores high in sequential/conceptual work and low in spatial tasks.

By adding two more categories, Acquired information and

Memory, to Bannatyne's trio we could contrast acquired information with conceptual manipulation, and conceptual manipulation with rote memory.

Dr. Jane Holmes, a neuropsychologist at Children's Hospital in Boston and adjunct faculty member at the Harvard Medical School, points out another cluster. She calls it the "green beans phenomenon."

Numerous children with difficulty in concentration, selective attention, and rote memory show clustering scores in Arithmetic, Coding, and Digit span. She and her colleagues became tired of saying the whole phrase "low in Arithmetic, Coding, and Digit span"; abbreviated it to Ari., Co., D.S.; and then realized that the French word for green beans is *haricots* (pronounced "arico"). Because children with this pattern jump around a lot, she connected green and jumping beans and nicknamed them "Green Beans." Thank you, Dr. Holmes, for one more pattern. Meet Big Boy Smith.

VERBAL	PERFORMANCE
Information: 16	Picture completion: 15
Similarities: 19	Picture arrangement: 13
Arithmetic: 10	Block design: 13
Vocabulary: 19	Objection assembly: 13
Comprehension: 19	Coding: 7
Digit span: 4	

Here are two conundrum kids' WISC-R scores for the reader to interpret and recategorize.

ICHABOD Q. STUDENT
Full-Scale: 139

VERBAL: *135*	PERFORMANCE: *135*
Information: 15	Picture completion: 19
Similarities: 18	Picture arrangement: 16
Arithmetic: 17	Block design: 19
Vocabulary: 13	Objection assembly: 16
Comprehension: 14	Coding: 5
Digit span: 13	

Where is Ichabod strong, where is he weak, what does he need, what academic situations will present problems, and where will he shine?

JOE X

Full-Scale: 113

VERBAL: *125*	PERFORMANCE: *96*
Information: 13	Picture completion: 10
Similarities: 15	Picture arrangement: 8
Arithmetic: 12	Block design: 10
Vocabulary: 12	Objection assembly: 12
Comprehension: 19	Coding: 8
Digit span: 8	Mazes: 15

See what happens when we recategorize Joe's scores as Bannatyne suggests:

SPATIAL	CONCEPTUAL
Object assembly: 12	Comprehension: 19
Block design: 10	Similarities: 15
Picture completion: 10	Mazes: 15
	Vocabulary: 12

SEQUENTIAL
Digit span: 8
Picture arrangement: 8
Coding: 8

It is easy to see where Joe X is strong, where he is weak, and why he thought he was stupid in the early years of school.

Familiarity with these patterns is useful for educational planning as well as understanding of current function. We might flip the coin, using the scores and categories prescriptively as well as descriptively to hypothesize that a student whose scores are high in one area will be good at particular types of studies.

For example, if a class is going to be studying the exploration of the American West, a student with a high score in Block design and a low score in Vocabulary might make a significant contribution by creating and interpreting relief maps, increasing his vocabulary along the way as he uses words to describe what he is trying to depict. He can use his spatial conceptual strength to shore up his linguistic weakness.

A well-administered WISC-R, interpreted in several different ways, is a solid foundation first for understanding and then for helping a smart kid with school problems. As this student moves through school, it is wise to get another. The first one sets the stage; subsequent ones show consistency in pattern and evidence of growth. An eleventh grader with two or three in his file has solid ground on which to base curriculum choices and college decisions.

FRAMES OF MIND: THE THEORY OF MULTIPLE INTELLIGENCES

If no standardized test accompanies Gardner's book and there is no curriculum syllabus, why does it deserve our space and time?

First, the interested reader deserves access to the neuroanatomical reasons for learning styles. These patterns, and the intelligences Gardner describes, are precisely those that we have explored in the students whose stories are in this book.

Second, he explains from a medical and scientific standpoint that unusual talents can be hidden and damaged by single-dimensional educational values.

Third, this is one of those rare works that draws together literature, high-level scientific research, and human understanding.

Fourth, the parent or educator who develops the student's master file, plans his curriculum, and attends to both talents and weaknesses needs to describe the student in light of Gardner's intelligences. This view adds an important dimension.

Throughout *Frames of Mind*, the author's language is so precise that I have frequently quoted it, because it is hard to paraphrase without blunting his points.

Impatient with the limiting quality of existing methods of measuring intelligence, and moving well beyond current Western ideas of what intelligence is, Gardner expands to seven the number of separate "intelligences" that should be explored in evaluating individual potential and achievement.

> I argue that there is persuasive evidence for the existence of several relatively autonomous human intellectual competences, abbreviated hereafter as "human intelligences.". . . In ordinary life these intelligences typically work in harmony, and so their autonomy may be invisible. But when the appropriate observational lenses are donned, the peculiar nature of each intelligence emerges with sufficient (and often surprising) clarity. . . . I have reviewed evidence from a large and hitherto unrelated group of sources: studies of prodigies, gifted individuals, brain-damaged patients, idiots savants, normal children, normal adults, experts in different kinds of work, and individuals from diverse cultures.[4]

Gardner describes each of the seven intelligences scientifically, historically, and anecdotally. They are linguistic intelligence, musical intelligence, logical-mathematical intelligence, spatial intelligence, bodily-kinesthetic intelligence, and interpersonal and intrapersonal intelligences.

LINGUISTIC INTELLIGENCE

Readers of Chapter 6 will feel at home in this section. A Gilbert Islander, Lillian Hellman, T. S. Eliot, Robert Graves, and Stephen Spender are the voices that summon us into this chapter. Through them we are privy to the arduous process of searching and sorting that results in the perfect metaphor or the pleasing phrase.

Gardner explores four major uses of language: the rhetorical aspect whose purpose is persuasion, the mnemonic potential whose purpose is memory for items and methods, the role of language in explaining ideas and phenomena, and the uniquely human ability to use language to explain and reflect on its own activities.

These four functions of language depend on the linguistic foundations we explored in Chapter 6: gesture, labels, two words, articles and affixes, word order, and semantics. Gardner adds *pragmatics*, the uses to which language may be put.

He gives examples of high linguistic intelligence through the words and experiences of both budding and mature authors and demonstrates the influence of neurology on language through descriptions of the linguistic consequences of disturbance in various parts of the brain.

The relationship between human language and the auditory-oral tract receives considerable attention, both for itself alone and for its role in separating language from spatial forms of intelligence.

My belief in the centrality of the auditory and oral elements in language has motivated my focus upon the poet as the user of language par excellence and my citation of the evidence from aphasia as a strong argument in favor of the autonomy of language. . . . Reading is invariably disturbed by injury to the language system, while, amazingly, this linguistic decoding capacity proves robust despite massive injury to the visual-spatial centers of the brain (p. 98).

MUSICAL INTELLIGENCE

Throughout this book, we have met many smart kids who have both school problems and musical talent. Gardner believes that musical intelligence, in a performer, a composer, or an active listener, is a separate entity, neither part of language nor part of mathematics.

The core components of music, as Gardner explains them, are pitch, rhythm, and timbre. He points out that rhythm can exist independently of auditory competence. For example, deaf people can begin to comprehend music through feeling or watching rhythm. (As an aside, anyone interested in "visual music" should read Douglas Hofstadter's article in the July 1983 issue of *Scientific American*.) Through these, together and separately, music holds powerful sway over affect. Music can serve as a way of capturing feelings: "Of all the gifts with which individuals may be endowed, none emerges earlier than musical talent." "Except among children with unusual musical talent or exceptional opportunities, there is little further musical development after the school years begin." Although these observations have been made before, people concerned with co-nundrum kids cannot read them too frequently.

Gardner says,

> Investigators working with both normal and brain-damaged humans have demonstrated beyond a reasonable doubt that the processes and mechanisms subserving human music and language are distinctive from one another. . . . Whereas linguistic abilities are lateralized almost exclusively to the left hemisphere in normal right-handed individuals, the majority of musical capacities, including the central capacity of sensitivity to pitch, are localized in most normal individuals in the right hemisphere. . . . As the names promise *amusia* is a disorder distinct from *aphasia*. . . . What is really crucial is whether other abilities predictably occur together with music such that when musical ability is destroyed, so are the others. So far as I am aware, none of the claims with respect to musical breakdown suggest any systematic connection with other faculties such as linguistic, numerical or spatial processing: music seems, in this regard, *sui generis* (p. 118).

LOGICAL-MATHEMATICAL INTELLIGENCE

As is the case with musical intelligence, logical-mathematical intelligence appears early, and "the major work of most mathematicians is over by the age of twenty-five or thirty." The hallmark of this intelligence is a love of dealing with abstraction, asking questions, identifying problems, and finding ways of solving them. Throughout this book we have seen instance after instance of gifted mathematicians who were struggling in school. To jeopardize their gifts is criminal.

SPATIAL INTELLIGENCE

Many smart kids with school problems have unusual spatial function, either in talent or in difficulty.

Spatial intelligence, unlike language, music, and the abstractions of mathematics, is tied to the objects in the real world. People use spatial intelligence to identify objects whose positions have been changed or rotated, to orient themselves, and to navigate their way. Spatial intelligence is fundamental to sculpture, architecture, painting, navigation, and some kinds of scientific thinking. Reflecting Gardner's interest in abnormal functioning is his documentation of what happens when parts of the brain controlling spatial intelligence are damaged. Here as in other instances he makes his case for the existence of a discrete intelligence by describing its absence as well as its presence.

Then Gardner takes us on one of his philosophical vaults. "In my view the metaphoric ability to discern similarities across diverse domains derives in many instances from a manifestation of spatial intelligence. For example, when gifted essayist Lewis Thomas draws analogies between micro-organisms and an organized society, depicts the sky as a membrane, or describes mankind as a heap of earth, he is capturing in words a kind of resemblance that may have occurred to him initially in spatial form." This reminds me of the irony of the physically clumsy fairy-tale writer in Chapter 4.

Gardner concludes this section with cheerful news indeed:

> My own view is that each form of intelligence has a natural life course: while logical-mathematical thought proves fragile later in life and bodily-kinesthetic intelligence is also at risk, at least certain aspects of visual and spatial knowledge prove robust, especially in individuals who have practiced them regularly throughout their lives. There is a sense of the whole, a gestalt sensitivity, which is central in spatial intelligence and which seems to be a reward for aging. . . . Perhaps wisdom draws on this sensitivity to patterns, forms and whole (p. 204).

BODILY-KINESTHETIC INTELLIGENCE

Marcel Marceau, the noted mime, is the guide Gardner selects to usher us into an exploration of bodily-kinesthetic intelligence. "I treat these two capacities—control of one's bodily motions and the capacity to handle objects skillfully—as the cores of bodily intelligence." His exemplars, then, go beyond the predictable athletes, dancers, and hunters to include artisans, instrumentalists, inventors, and actors. Fine-motor skills rank alongside gross-motor in this discussion. Readers of Chapters 3 and 4 in particular will resonate to Gardner's words.

And just as the reader feels a subversive inclination to say, "Wait a minute, maybe this isn't a separate intelligence at all," Gardner says,

> Buttressing my claim for a separate bodily intelligence, it turns out that injuries to those zones of the left hemisphere that are dominant for motor activity can produce selective impairment. Neurologists speak of the *apraxias*, a set of related disorders, in which an individual physically capable of carrying out a set of motor sequences, and cognitively capable of understanding a request to do so, is nonetheless unable to carry them out . . . limb-kinetic *apraxia*, ideamotor *apraxia* or ideational *apraxia* (p. 212).

Tucked in the middle of the text is this simple statement with profound implications for educators: "The fact that some individuals prove skilled at this kind of learning, but that it is accorded a low priority, may help explain why many promising young performers and dancers in our culture become alienated from school at an early age." This is a group the educational system can ill afford to lose. The reader may remember this when meeting Peter Boal, the dancer whose story appears in Chapter 10.

INTERPERSONAL AND INTRAPERSONAL INTELLIGENCES

Gardner explores personal intelligences from the points of view of both interpersonal and intrapersonal life, saying, "The core capacity here is access to one's feeling life."

"I feel that these forms of knowledge are of tremendous importance in many, if not all societies in the world—forms that have, however, tended to be ignored or minimized by nearly all students of cognition." (He footnotes a bouquet to Wechsler.)

He describes the development of the personal intelligences in the infant, the child aged two to five, the school-age child, and the periods of middle childhood, adolescence, and maturity. The section on the school-age child is particularly clear and poignant as he describes the growing sense of self that is rooted in "I am what I can do." His points here are in close agreement with Erikson's and tie in closely with many of the case histories at the conclusion of each of the chapters in this book.

Gardner is the originator of a term that should be used in education and in the study of intelligence. He talks of people as being "at promise" for certain kinds of tasks.

> What recent research has shown, virtually incontrovertibly, is that whatever differences may initially appear, early intervention and consistent training can play a decisive role in determining the individual's ultimate level of performance. Conversely, and perhaps more obviously, even the most innately talented individual will founder without some positive supporting environment. Discovery of an individual's inherent intellectual profile, which I believe may be possible, need not serve, then, as a means of pigeonholing the individual or of consigning him to an intellectual junk-heap; rather, such discovery should provide a means for assuring that every individual has available to him as many options as possible as well as the potential to achieve competence in whatever fields he and his society deem important (p. 116).

> Although Gardner's view of intelligences has not yet become a part of formal evaluation procedures, it adds a critically important way of understanding human beings. Intuitively, clinically, and intellectually Gardner's assessment rings true. To the mind's ear, it is like the sound of a ting on fine crystal.

PRINCIPLES OF GOOD PRACTICE

When a smart kid has school problems, educators and parents should review the master file, bearing in mind the intelligences Gardner cites and making additions to the file accordingly. They should review test scores, arrange for an individual evaluation, and study the results carefully, using some of the methods suggested in this chapter. If the test results do not ring true, it is important to probe further. A tester sees the student a few times; educators and parents see the student over a long period.

Familiarity with testing terminology, types of testing, and test interpretation frees educators and parents to ask better questions, understand the answers, and be full partners in planning what comes next.

Test numbers should work *for* the educators and parents. After all, considerable time, effort, and money (even if it's the taxpayer's) has gone into accumulating them. They should do more than sit on a piece of paper or rest in a file drawer.

Insofar as possible, concerned adults, with the help of the educational overseer, should try to arrange for instruction that harmonizes with the student's preferred method of learning.

The student deserves to know his own patterns of strengths and weaknesses and benefits from learning test results in an age-appropriate way. Starting with strengths and their implications, the adult can move to weaknesses, always mentioning the available strategies for overcoming them. Self-knowledge and self-acceptance lead to healthy self-concept.

A CASE HISTORY: JODY

Jody is a bright eighth grader with a poor academic record. From early childhood he has been physically agile and daring, impatient with "scaredy-cats," eager to learn, and reluctant to be put on the spot. His strongly developed social sense (*personal intelligence* in Gardner's words) and knack for telling jokes have kept Jody in the "in-group" all along despite academic failure.

In kindergarten, Jody missed many school days because of recurrent ear infections, flu, and his grandparents' offer to take the whole family on a three-week trip to Spain in April. "After all, it's only kindergarten," his parents said, so off they went.

Jody finally learned individual letter sounds in first grade, but he had trouble trying to blend them into words; by the time he got to the end he had forgotten the beginning, would try to start over, and became badly discouraged. One day he threw his book on the floor, saying, "This dumb book doesn't work." Sometimes he would try to make the other children laugh to distract attention from his own failures.

Although he had a fine innate sense of numbers and was accurate with money in his extracurricular life, numerals were almost as hard for him to manage as letters. He wrote them backward or out of sequence, writing *96* for *69* as often as he wrote *was* for *saw.* His teacher believed in compartmentalized language-arts instruction, teaching reading during one period, spelling in another, math in another, and handwriting twice a week. Once a week the children were asked to copy a poem from the board and illustrate it. Jody responded enthusiastically to hearing the poem, as well as to memorizing and reciting it, but, although his illustrations were lovely, his copying was awkward and inaccurate.

In second grade his seeming improvement in reading proved to be an illusion; Jody was memorizing the morning's selections by having another child read them to him on the bus ride to school. His behavior grew increasingly disruptive, and although the other children laughed at his jokes, his teacher was not amused. Jody began to apply his powerful social skills to intellectual tight spots.

In the middle of the year an assistant teacher arrived, a young woman finishing her graduate degree in learning disabilities who needed one more semester of student teaching to complete her requirements. She chose Jody for her case study. She reviewed his records, screened him for learning disabilities, and identified some specific weaknesses. From watching him in class she knew he was smart and decided he would profit from multisensory training. She began working with him individually, in the classroom, during the time the other children were doing their seat work. She arranged with the head teacher to excuse Jody from some of his regular seat-work requirements, because, of course, it would be ridiculous to penalize him for being given extra help. He bloomed.

Everything improved. Jody was a highly intelligent little boy whose brightness helped him learn the strategies she taught him, and, because they made sense and he could apply them right away, he absorbed them all and reached for more. By the end of the school year, he was reading on grade level, his numbers were well formed, he had memorized all his math facts, and he was considered "cured."

When he started third grade, everyone assumed that "the trouble" was like chicken pox: having had it once, he would be immune for life.

Jody's native intelligence, social skills, naturally competitive streak, and new but unsolidified academic skills supported him through the first part of third grade, but as January closed in, the curriculum shifted, and life did too. Jody tried to make his pen keep pace with his ideas, and his jokes. It wouldn't. He began to flounder. Because he had a new friend, one his teachers and parents disapproved of, his slide was attributed to the "evil companion" and his parents tried to break off the friendship.

By the middle of fourth grade Jody's family was told that he was sinking to the bottom of the class. They were worried, he was frightened (though he tried to conceal it), and his teacher thought he wasn't trying. They dropped him down to the lowest reading group and put him into a remedial spelling class twice a week during the time the others went to art.

His standardized testing showed a wide discrepancy: verbal aptitude in the ninety-fifth percentile, verbal achievement in the fifty-sixth; quantitative aptitude in the ninety-eighth percentile, achievement in the sixtieth.

Well-meaning people tried persuasion, threats, bribery, and withdrawal of privileges without success. In retrospect, his best time had been his half year with the graduate student, but real life isn't a one-on-one teaching/learning setup.

His parents agreed with the school's suggestion to get an individual evaluation. In addition to some psychological testing that showed a wobbly self-concept, he was given a WISC-R. The results of the WISC-R were remarkably similar to Miranda's. In other words, he was very high conceptually (a cluster of 19s) and very low mechanically (a 5, 6, 7, and 8). His rote memory was weak, and his visual-motor integration both slow and imprecise. He impressed the examiner as being humorous and self-protective: "He will do beautifully in life but suffer through school."

The educational overseer, in this instance the learning specialist, scheduled two meetings: one with Jody and his parents, one with his current teacher, his next year's teachers, and his academic adviser. Together they discussed which subjects were likely to be difficult and laid out their teaching plans, incorporating many of the ideas that have appeared throughout this book.

Jody has access to a word processor for his written work, he uses manipulatives as well as paper and pencil for math, he is getting spelling help from a tutor twice a week at home in the afternoons, and he is working alongside his classmates.

Although the meetings took some time, they required a lot less than would otherwise have been spent discussing the whys and whats of a failure. By involving Jody himself in the program planning, they ensured his cooperation and gave him a feeling of being an agent of his own destiny rather than an object of fate.

Jody feels smart. He will never outgrow his learning style, but he has made friends with it.

9

MATURATION AND HIGHER EDUCATION

GETTING IT ALL TOGETHER

Last week a friend invited me into her darkroom to watch her develop a roll of film. I had been with her when she took the pictures, but because I hadn't been looking through the camera, I didn't know what shots she had or what angles she had used. We had been at a beach picnic, so I assumed we would see sand, water, blankets, and people. I could anticipate the general ideas but not the specifics. The outside of the roll of film certainly gave no clue.

As she did her alchemy with solutions and pans, images began to appear, general patterns of light and dark first, then human shapes, then human features. The negative, showing black where there would be white and space where there would be shape, was ready to print. Looking at the positive print, I could identify the same face under a hat, in the sun, in the shade, scowling, smiling, close-up or farther away. Yet, even though those images had been on the film the whole time, I couldn't tell what they were until the developing process was complete. The same is often true of the student between sixteen and twenty-one.

Intellectually and emotionally these are years of maturation and negative or positive consolidation. Erik Erikson calls the internal struggle of this age "identity versus role confusion." In the adolescent, the outcome of the "crisis" of identity versus role confusion is weighted by the outcomes of the previous crises. The child with a positive resolution of basic trust versus mistrust is well positioned for the pull between autonomy versus shame and doubt. A positive ratio for autonomy predisposes a healthy outcome in the push me– pull you of initiative versus guilt and industry versus inferiority. The influence of these cumulative ratios touches the entire course of the individual's adult life, sometimes treacherously. In the smart kid's journey through school, he may have accumulated shame and doubt, inferiority, guilt, and role confusion. In the most solemn sense of the phrase, this is a matter of life and death.

Adolescent suicide is increasing at an alarming rate. Reports submitted to the Senate Judiciary Juvenile Justice Subcommittee in October 1984 say that "suicide is the third-leading cause of death among 15–24 year olds, whose suicide rate rose dramatically from 1960 to 1980. In 1980 one of five suicides was a 15–24 year old male. . . . The experts said teen-agers with family troubles, low grades and overly high expectations were more prone to suicide, as are drug and alcohol abusers, those who lost a friend, and those trying to adjust to a new town or country."[1]

We know from the traits explored in Chapter 1 that smart kids set extremely high standards for themselves, have heightened perceptions, and are keenly aware of patterns. Smart kids with school problems feel tremendous pain from the gap between their expectations, their own ideals, and the work they actually produce or the grades they receive. The pressure from this pain is sometimes unbearable.

Although the pressure sometimes comes from adults, often it is self-generated. The pressures vary: to be accepted by the group, to do well enough to avoid being noticed, to give birth to an artistic or intellectual dream, to escape the ridicule of an unsympathetic teacher, to please a beloved teacher. Whatever the reason, self-generated pressure to close the gap between external demands and internal capacities is a force powerful enough to kill.

When the combination of high intelligence and school problems brings despair, we see throwaway kids who shrivel. When it generates violence we see throwaway kids who boomerang.

Studies such as those by Hogenson, and Hernnstein and Wilson, show the correlation between learning disabilities and delinquency, both urban and rural. It makes sense that the smart kid who cannot get what others are getting from society (and a student's society is his school) will either be angry at himself or at the successful others and the institutions that confer that success. Studies of inmates in penal institutions point over and over again to the high rate of illiteracy and the correlation between illiteracy and crime, also pointing to the high level of abstract intelligence in master criminals. In adolescents the combination of high intelligence with school failure is a loaded gun.

In less dramatic situations that bring neither physical death nor incarceration, other kinds of death occur: the death of concentration and the death of hope.

What kills concentration in the adolescent? The same processes we explored at length in Chapter 7. Hope? The future can seem bleak to the smart adolescent with school problems he doesn't understand. He needs explanations of why schoolwork is hard, reassurances of help, an internalized locus of control, and some power of choice. But there are happy fulfilled adults who used to be smart kids with school problems.

A marketing manager in New York has risen quickly to very responsible positions because in her boss's words, "She'll sell the world to the world." She says of her school career, "I hated doing all that bookwork. I was a slow reader and I wanted to get on with things, not sit inside chained to a desk reading about them. I loved athletics (figuring out strategies as well as physical movement), being out-of-doors, and being with people." Asked how she survived as well as she did, she said,

> My family never bugged me about grades. I had lots of opportunity to do the things I liked after school, and the summers were wonderful.
>
> When I was sixteen I went on a five-week National Outdoor

Leadership School trip in Montana. I learned I was a good decision maker. I also knew I enjoyed being with people and discovered I could get along with many different kinds. On a trip like that you learn to trust yourself as well as others. I even went on to college, although I had sworn I'd never crack a book after I graduated from high school. I loved college. It was for ideas instead of for memorizing. People I respected thought my ideas were good. When I got my first real job, I started to believe what my parents had said all along: "You're one smart kid!"

Higher education can open new worlds or be a tunnel. College-bound students, even those with impeccable academic credentials, face bewildering decisions. They must ask themselves

What courses should I select to get or maintain a good grade-point average?

Should I risk lowering my GPA by taking a course I may not be good at?

How many times should I take the SAT?

If I take it several times will my scores go up or down?

Should I take an SAT coaching course?

If I do, will it really raise my score?

If I take one, should I admit it to my school and prospective colleges?

How do I know whether I'm college material?

How many colleges should I apply to?

How do I select a long shot, a likely shot, and a sure shot?

How should I present myself?

Should I choose extracurricular activities with an eye to what looks good on an application?

Supposing I get into college, will I survive academically, emotionally, socially?

If these issues are perplexing to students with strong academic records, how doubly perplexing they are for smart kids with school problems. To help them make good decisions about higher education, we need to explore issues and plans.

ISSUES

As we did with testing, let's begin by clarifying some terms.

Grade-point average. A grade-point average (GPA) is just what it says, an average. It may raise up low scores and flatten high ones. Conundrum kids have profiles more like a cross section of the Alps than a side view of gentle hills. A poor or failing grade in one subject pulls down the grade-point average, leaving no place to show an outstandingly high grade. Our students frequently do poorly on tests and exams while doing beautifully in three-dimensional, hands-on work. But as noted throughout the book, art, music, sports, leadership, photography, school club activities, these "extras," are seldom factored into the GPA. Because of this, it is virtually impossible for a smart kid with school problems to have a high GPA, a score that is included on a college application and is supposed to be evidence of a student's ability to handle academic work.

SAT and achievement tests. The Scholastic Aptitude Test (SAT) is a multiple-choice, group-administered, timed, pencil-and-paper test that purports to measure scholastic aptitude. Critics, whose numbers are increasing to include college admissions officers, see it as one indicator of a student's ability to manage course work in the first year or two of college but not as an accurate measure of aptitude. The difference between GPA and SAT is the difference between evidence and prediction.

Students with many of the intelligences Gardner cites may do poorly on the SAT. The student who reads slowly may not finish; one who reads inaccurately may misperceive key words. The ruminative student may think about individual questions and forget to race through. A brilliant student may think beyond the test designers and be unable to find a palatable answer in the proffered multiple choices. In addition, the setting and the format of the SAT are anxiety-provoking to many students. Throughout this book we have seen those who think clearly in class, contribute to class discussions, and enjoy learning who score poorly on timed, standardized pencil-and-paper tasks. Although, as we will see in a later section of this chapter, the SAT hammerlock is gradually being broken, for now, many college applicants feel they must submit this test score. We shall explore SAT coaching courses shortly.

Achievement tests, although presenting some of the same problems as the SAT, are fairer. They do not pretend to measure aptitude; they give a student a chance to show what he has learned in the courses he has taken. The residual dyslexic, the slow or inaccurate reader may still have trouble managing a large amount of material in a small amount of time, but the smart kid with school problems generally finds it easier to do well here than on the SAT.

If SAT scores don't do the job, what are more reliable predictors of success in higher education and beyond?

Douglas Heath, sociologist, psychologist, and professor at Haverford College in Pennsylvania, has studied this question extensively. His findings, garnered from teaching his own students, from wide reading and research, and from a longitudinal study in which he interviewed his subjects at three different times, are particularly encouraging for smart kids with school problems.

Heath's longitudinal studies show little correlation between high scores on standardized tests early in life and feelings of fulfillment and success in later life. He finds that high scorers on timed, pencil-paper tests are more likely to experience dissatisfaction, frustration, intellectual atrophy, and a high instance of mental health problems. This is no wish list from a flower child: these are the research findings of one who revels in intellect.

Using his longitudinal study as a backdrop, Heath goes on to project which qualities will bring satisfaction to adult lives in the year 2000 and beyond. He says that as the nature of work changes, and as traditional sex roles lose the rigidity of their former boundaries, interpersonal skills, managerial skills, and skills in juggling and sorting information will assume increasing importance, as will the ability to be a self-educating person and to sustain intellectual curiosity.

According to Heath, the qualities found in, and valued by, people who were functioning at a high level of success, who felt fulfilled, and whose emotional health was very sound were sense of humor, self-confidence, enthusiasm and energy, honesty, self-dis-

cipline, intuition, empathy, ability to be a good listener, self-awareness, persistence, and willingness to take risks.

What about conundrum kids? We know from our own experience and from the preceding chapters in this book that, in addition
to areas of vulnerability, our students frequently have extraordinary
interpersonal sensitivity, open-mindedness, persistence, and ability
to get an idea across and are divergent thinkers who welcome questions as well as answers. They are alert to patterns and take delight
in testing out new ones. Having been bruised themselves, they are
often tolerant. Having had to struggle, they have self-awareness.
Having survived, they probably have humor. In short, if not discouraged by failure, they have in abundance the qualities Douglas
Heath's studies show to be the ones that really count in college and
later in life.

Other voices join with Heath's. Former Yale president A. B.
Giamatti wrote a letter to the incoming freshman class in 1981. He
said,

> I believe a liberal education is an education in the root meaning
> of "liberal"—"liber"—"free"—the liberty of the mind free to
> explore itself, to draw itself out, to connect with other minds
> and spirits in the quest for truth. Its goal is to train the whole
> person to be at once intellectually discerning and humanly
> flexible, tough-minded and openhearted; to be responsive to
> the new and responsible for the values that make us civilized.
> It is to teach us to meet what is new and different with reasoned
> judgment and humanity. A liberal education is an education
> for freedom, the freedom to assert the liberty of the mind to
> make itself new for the others it cherishes.[2]

Theodore Sizer, former dean of the Harvard School of Education and author of *Horace's Compromise: The Dilemma of the
American High School*, regrets what he considers the national "collection of schools in pastel colors" and decries their vernacular of
donation: "we give courses," "we deliver services," "we offer." "High
schools must respect adolescents more and patronize them less. The
best respect is high expectations for them, and a level of account-
ability more adult in its demand than childlike. We should expect
them to learn more while being taught less. Their personal en-

gagement with their own learning is crucial; adults cannot 'give' them an education."

The common threads linking Heath, Giamatti, and Sizer with Gardner, Erikson, Seligman, and many other voices in this book are the importance of active involvement, willingness to take risks, self-knowledge, and self-respect.

Three particular personal qualities in some high-scoring students augur poorly for success in higher education and fulfillment in life thereafter: passivity, dependence on high scores for self-esteem, and premature or pseudo-sophistication.

Real learning is aggressive exploration. Passive absorption of predigested ideas may permit tidy performance on a test or term paper, but it will generate few original discoveries.

In exploring dependence on high scores, Heath discusses the student accustomed to As and high scores on standardized tests. Often these students, according to Heath, enter college with their goals established. They have already determined what they will study, their class rank, where they will go to graduate school, what salary will buy them the life-style they have selected, how to go about earning that sum of money, and how to stay on the top of the pile.

At each step up, success is harder to capture because the pyramid narrows. But the student whose identity is bound up in grade-point average can't abandon the chase for high grades without risking annihilation. The pressure intensifies, placing iron bands around the student's intellect at just the time it should be expanding.

Premature or pseudo-sophistication is as restrictive as dependence on high scores. It is a mask that controls the wearer.

Between the ages of sixteen and twenty, a blessed phenomenon may occur. Some troublesome aspects of the student's learning style may simply dissolve through maturation. The young child's developmental readiness for school is well charted: metaphorically and actually he loses his baby teeth and steps up to a new level. A less-documented developmental shift often occurs in late adolescence. Educators, parents, and students who are aware of this possibility can avoid premature rejection of higher education.

Betsy had been plagued by poor spelling throughout her early years of school. She never checked her words against a dictionary because, she said, "How do I know which ones to check? They all look right to me, and if I think about it too long, none of them look right." During her sophomore year of college, she suddenly knew which words to check, and many of her habitual errors fell away. Never again did she write that she was "re-nude." She was renewed!

Andrew who had avoided reading anything but assignments and the sports page discovered spy stories and tales of horror. When his mother took his jacket to the cleaner recently, she was amazed to find a John Le Carré paperback in one pocket and a volume of Edgar Allan Poe in the other. When she returned them to him, he said, "Thanks. I've been looking all over for those books. I've got to find out what happens next."

All of a sudden, Sam could identify a main idea in a story and do word problems in math. Terms such as *area, ratio, volume,* and *mass* became friendly words in addition to being concepts he had understood intuitively since his childhood block-building days.

Amelia, a college freshman, has discovered child psychology. Finally free of the foreign language and algebra courses that had been torture to her, she carries her textbooks as badges of honor and reads them eagerly. Her smiles are ready and her contribution to the professional field may very well be outstanding.

Jackson can concentrate. That simple three-word sentence is a miracle. He thumped, zapped, rocked, wiggled, bumped, and irritated his way through grades one through ten and gradually calmed down in the middle of eleventh grade. In the days when many young men, particularly boys with school problems, served a post–high school stint in the military, people would notice their new maturity, saying, "Soldiering brought that boy around." And although uniforms, structure, and responsibility undoubtedly played a part in the maturational process, there were other internal battles being fought and victories being won.

Even though the issues are complicated, the conundrum kid may do as well as or better than problem-free students if he has acquired self-knowledge, reinforced self-respect, received good compensatory training, and nourished his gifts and talents.

What an irony it is that the person who ultimately stands to make great good use of higher-level education may be the one who initially has great trouble gaining access to it.

PLANS

Getting from here to there requires good use of test scores, maturity in three areas, and appropriate choices.

TEST SCORES

How much weight do standardized test scores actually carry, what factors outweigh or counteract them, what about coaching courses, and are there some shifting patterns?

How much weight does an SAT score carry? In October 1984 William C. Hiss, dean of admissions at Bates College, wrote,

> Three recent efforts can help us address these questions. First, our staff has just completed a three year study of the relation between statistical predictors and personal qualities under a grant from The National Association of College Admissions Counselors. . . . Second we sent a questionnaire on SAT coaching to 100 colleges . . . 74 were returned: 41 private colleges, 21 private universities, 6 state universities and the rest anonymous or unsure what to call themselves. . . . Finally we can draw upon our own discussions and talk with guidance counselors.

The findings point to a diminished reliance on SAT scores and an increased reliance on the combined achievement test scores, written work, and a transcript reflecting a demanding course load. "Many deans sensed some swingback in high school transcripts toward tougher courses. I recall seeing three courses on one transcript with the bewildering titles 'Rocks and Ropes,' 'Things Russian,' and 'Things British.' This, all agreed, is often the kiss of death in the admissions office."

Personal qualities matter very much.

We found that a number of self-rated personal qualities added significantly to our formula for prediction of grade-point average. "Energy and initiative," for example, is often as strong as any single statistical measure in predicting variation in grade point average. Many other personal evaluations . . . creativity, independence, widening of perspectives, insight and humor . . . added to the prediction formula. . . . To allow anxiety over SATs, and sustained, intense coaching to set the tone of the junior and senior years is to misdirect seriously one's energies. These personal qualities, and not simply the standardized testing, are an integral part of being a good student and therefore a good candidate for top colleges. . . . Many felt that the SATs, if they do not control school curricula, very often distract a student's attention . . . and thus real growth as a student . . . from those factors that do control admission decisions: tough courses, good grades, hard thinking, good writing and significant other achievements.[3]

Where does this leave a conundrum kid? It diminishes the influence of the SAT, on which many of our students do poorly for the reasons cited earlier. It gives more power to the achievement tests on which our students may do well, particularly if they take advantage, where necessary, of the options for nonroutine administration of those tests. It gives our student a chance to demonstrate his intellectual power through written work and verbal expression, at which he may excel if he has received the kind of training and help suggested in this book. It puts the question of GPA in good perspective; a transcript that shows high performance in physics, algebra, and precalculus with lower performance in language is an accurate picture of a learning profile, showing areas of a student's interest and willingness to tackle tough subject matter. It indicates active involvement in learning.

Someone may argue, that's all very well to say, but does it really happen that way, and if an SAT score is going to be part of the record, why not take a coaching course? If they seem to work, why not get the benefit of the doubt? If they don't help, what harm has been done? If the school doesn't recommend it, why not just do it on the side without telling anyone?

Dorothy Dillon, assistant head of Kent Place School, Summit, New Jersey, wrote an article citing the research on actual gains from coaching courses and the time/numerical gain ratio involved.

> For example, eight hours of mathematics coaching is needed for a 10 point gain, nineteen hours for 20 points, the equivalent of two additional problems on the SAT. In the verbal area, twelve hours of coaching will yield a 10 point gain, 57 hours a 20 point gain or the difference of three correct answers. . . . Carrying these figures farther, we find that 300 hours would be necessary for a 31 point verbal gain and another 300 hours for a 53 point gain on the mathematics section.[4]

If the ability to use time well is one important predictor of success and fulfillment, what does this use of time suggest?

Is it a worthwhile trade-off to take this much time for possible numerical gain on one single instrument? What gets pinched or cancelled in such a regimen? Very often it is the music, the art, the photography, the athletics—in short, the talent—that must be sacrificed. Ridiculous! In later life, once college admissions decisions are history, no one will know, much less care, what an individual got on the SAT. Dillon continues, "As far as college admissions officers are concerned, the solid commitment in time to a hobby or job or homework has far more influence than any small gain in SAT points obtained by hours away from constructive pursuits."

There are some practical guidelines to giving a student the best possible shot at his best potential score. Dillon lays them out clearly:

> We need to let our students know what the SAT is all about, give them sample tests, let them practice analogies and antonyms, go over their PSAT [Preliminary Scholastic Aptitude Test] performance, and share with them the College Board booklet "Taking the SAT." . . . We must take the initiative in informing our parents and students about the results of research on the impact of coaching for the SAT, as follows.
>
> They can expect without any review an average SAT score gain of about 18 points on the verbal and 15–20 points on the mathematics section between junior and senior year.
>
> The expected gain varies with the initial score. For a

score of 700, a decrease of 7 points is expected; for an initial score of 500, an increase of 7 points; for a 400 score, plus 18 points; and for an initial score of 300 an increase of about 36 points.

In schools where students take advanced mathematics courses, the effect of coaching is negligible, even though the mathematics section of the SAT has been shown to be more responsive to coaching than the verbal.

The analogies portion of the SAT is the most responsive to short-term instruction. Even brief practice and instruction in this area can help "highly able students."

"Familiarity with the test . . . should assist them in attaining scores better representative of their abilities."

Although the mathematics required to answer SAT-M items is intentionally limited to ninth and tenth grade content, mathematics beyond that level serves not only as review but also to facilitate answering SAT-M items.

The general level of developed ability largely determines a student's SAT mathematics or verbal score.

What does all this have to do with conundrum kids? We can consider what Dillon says about analogies and antonyms in the light of Chapter 6. We can listen to what she and Hiss, as well as other college admissions officers, say about the use of time and reflect on the gifted thinker's need to keep his talent alive. We can interpret Dillon's comments about natural gain in the light of what we know about spontaneous growth. We can consider the frequent discrepancy between doing well on standardized tests and possessing one or many of Gardner's intelligences. We can remember Heath's fulfilled and unfulfilled adults.

Words from these experienced professionals can free our students from hours of needless, pointless drudgery. The following shifting patterns will benefit our students, particularly as these procedures become standard practice.

At a growing number of competitive colleges a student may submit an extra achievement score in place of the SAT. Almost all colleges will accept the results of specially administered achievement tests. It may be untimed, a reader may read the questions aloud to the student, an amanuensis may write out the student's answers for him. College admissions officers say that the need for a special administration does not jeopardize the chance for acceptance. However, some college advisers suggest that the student take a regular form of the test the first time and request an untimed or special administration a second time. This demonstrates the student's willingness to tackle regular work and also allows for a comparison of the two scores.

In August 1984 the Harvard Business School announced that applicants would be asked to submit essays in place of standardized multiple-choice test answers. This is one more example of growing disaffection with standardized tests as predictors of ability and increasing reliance on *how* the student thinks, his ability to put his thoughts into words and organize words into clear exposition.

MATURITY IN THREE AREAS

How can we help smart kids with school problems develop social/emotional maturity, intellectual maturity, and linguistic maturity?

Social/emotional maturity. In reaching for social/emotional maturity, young people between the ages of sixteen and twenty struggle with internal and external ambiguities. They want desperately to conform; at the same time they long to glory in their own individuality. They must try to develop self-control at the same time they have no control over the ways their bodies change daily. Developing aesthetic and athletic tastes whet lifelong appetites, yet scholastic requirements may absorb most of the available time and energy. Students this age are subject to the societal pressures of drugs, alcohol, and sexual experimentation. Their decisions may have irreversible consequences, yet they receive conflicting advice from all sides: "Stick with your friends, be loyal, don't tattle." "Be responsible for the well-being of other people; caring for your friends means helping them stay out of trouble." "Real learning depends on the willingness to take risks." "Don't take chances." "Listen to the voice of experience." "Be your own person."

External forces set requirements: courses a student must take, hours of driver education to be completed, minimum balances for a checking account. These externals are superimposed at the same time the young adult needs the locus of control.

If these forces pull the trouble-free student in opposite directions, how do they affect a smart kid with school problems? He may be ahead of the game. If he has been raised with understanding and has received appropriate training, he may have already accepted himself as different and feel free to join others without disguise.

Social/emotional maturity comes from self-respect, self-knowledge, and an attribute that can be described in a four-letter word.

Self-respect grows from competence. A student who is competent in a particular field, academic or nonacademic, has something to dream about and hang on to. We need to remember Gardner's intelligences here. The very existence of an area of competence contributes stability to the adolescent's internal gyroscope.

Self-knowledge is what this book is all about. The student whose parents and teachers revere his strengths and understand his weaknesses experiences the acceptance that allows him to know himself without fear.

The four-letter word comes from the British neurologist Macdonald Critchley, who writes, "Lastly, and perhaps most important of all, a personality trait on the part of the patient: sheer dogged determination to succeed. . . . This is what American psychiatrists call ego-strength; in Great Britain we prefer the simpler term 'guts.' "[5]

Intellectual maturity. Intellectual maturity comes from exposure to ideas and from practice with comparison, abstraction, and patterns. These are magnets to original thinkers. Yet frequently the kids who are the subject of this book are pulled in the opposite direction by educational requirements for factual recitation and rote memory.

Conundrum kids need remedial training, but not at the expense of intellectual stimulation. As we have seen, they need opportunities to join music with words, words with art, art with music, art and music with dance, or dance with language, using their strengths to support weaknesses.

Linguistic maturity. Linguistic maturity grows with social/emotional and intellectual maturity as we saw in Chapter 6. The absorption and exercise of all the levels of language development foster linguistic maturity. Language is the verbal medium for explanation, request, permission, compromise, planning, anticipation, mediation, and congratulation. Our kid may need to dicker, tinker, barter, and tailor. He needs to be able to express his self-awareness and determination through language.

APPROPRIATE CHOICES

This section is written as a checklist for the student. Those who don't want to read it probably don't think they want to go to college. That's one choice. But it is unwise to rule out higher education because of fear of rejection. Choosing a college and being chosen are more than a petal-plucking game of "loves me, loves me not." Here are some steps to take to reduce the complications and increase your chances of being admitted and succeeding once you begin your college career.

Know your own interests and strengths. Pick a school that emphasizes those areas and disciplines. Don't pick a place for its prestigious name or because someone you know went there. This choice is for you.

Know your area of difficulty and what courses and requirements you will need to meet in order to graduate. Don't pick a college with a four-year language requirement if you can't do Latin.

Find out as much specific information about the college as possible. Learn its size, faculty/student ratio, and whether freshman and sophomore courses are taught by full-time professors, part-time visiting firemen, or graduate students. Although this is a generalization, smaller institutions are likely to be more responsive to individual needs. Graduate students are likely to be the most inflexible grade givers, and full-time professors have a deeper investment in the institution than visitors or graduate students. In addition to reading the catalogue, talk to students who have been there. If at all possible have a personal interview.

Lay your cards on the table. Be forthright about your strengths and open about your weaknesses. Don't try to slide in and patch things up afterward. You are shopping for an education just as much as colleges are increasingly shopping for students. The only way to expect a good fit is to be honest with one another from the very beginning. Show that you have self-knowledge and strength and that you have done your research thoroughly. This will mean much more to an admissions officer than a 10- or 20-point difference on an SAT.

Find out what extra help the college offers or would be willing to offer. Susan Vogel, Ph.D., writes in her article "On Developing LD College Programs," "Depending on the stringency of the admissions requirements of the institution, there are some gifted LD students who are presently enrolled or who have completed degree programs in undergraduate, graduate and professional schools. There are far more however who are average or above in ability, and who, after a year in college, are in serious academic difficulty, have dropped out, or who have been asked to leave."[6] Ask whether the college offers study skills classes, tutors (and at what price), flexibility in core requirements, the possibility of waiving or trading a requirement, computers or word processors and training in how to use them, alternative formats for taking exams, curriculum specifically designed for dyslexics or different learners. There are some colleges designed specifically for the learning disabled; Curry College in Milton, Massachusetts, and Landmark College in Putney, Vermont, are two of many. (The Bibliography for Chapter 9 and the Resources list offers sources for finding others.) In addition, many art and engineering schools are now adding remedial and developmental reading and writing programs to their offerings because many of their most spatially gifted students are deficient in this area. Don't be embarrassed to inquire.

Get your study habits well organized ahead of time. They won't develop spontaneously. It's hard to catch up once you get behind. The principles will stand you in good stead all your life. See the section on Principles of Good Practice for specifics, and the Resources list for references.

Choose with an eye to recreation time too. Don't put yourself into a situation in which bare survival will consume all your time and in which success is a question mark even when you are working your hardest. Save time for nurturing your strengths, for friends, for fun, and even for a little frivolity.

Although this type of educational planning is complicated, it represents the ability to identify and work out an intricate pattern. In and of itself, this is an extremely valuable life skill and one at which conundrum kids, with their alertness to pattern, may excel.

PRINCIPLES OF GOOD PRACTICE

Consult the master file and add to it. Consult with your overseer. Keep the file up to date with evidence of talent as well as admissions of weakness. If it is an accumulation of many years it will be a real help to you. If you have a summer job or an after-school job or have done some volunteer work, be sure to get a letter from your boss or supervisor when the job ends. Put it in your record.

Plan your courses with an eye to balancing your strong and weak areas. If you are a slow reader or a residual dyslexic, do not take a reading course in Tolstoy and Dostoevsky in the same semester as philosophy and world history. Spread them out.

Be flexible in your planning and be willing to bargain. Take tough courses one at a time in a January term or over the summer.

Follow the study skills suggestions outlined by Milton Academy in conjunction with Harvard University, those outlined by the Forman School, those in the paperback book *Study Smarts,* and those outlined in the articles in *The Journal of Learning Disabilities.* Although the sources are as different as can be, the principles remain constant. (See Resources list). Some specifics follow.

Organize your belongings, your materials, your time, and your obligations. Keep a calendar with dates assignments are due. Hang it above your desk.

Transcribe your lecture notes daily. This will help you keep a tidy notebook and will also serve as a double review.

Develop a note-taking shorthand for high-frequency phrases.

Have a separate notebook for each course. Keep all notebooks in one backpack or briefcase.

Discuss your needs with your professors the first day of the semester. Do not wait until you are floundering.

Sit in the front row away from your friends. Keep eye contact; write notes as accurately as you can. Raise your hand if things go too fast.

Make a course outline. This will serve as the organizational grid on which to slot incoming information.

Learn the vocabulary for each subject. Don't skip new words even when you are tempted to do so.

Arrive before class starts, get your materials organized, and preview the topic. Do not leave class if there is anything you have not understood.

Line up your support systems before the semester starts. It's always easy to discard them, but don't put yourself in the position of having to scramble around trying to find a tutor after you're already in trouble.

Get to know the librarian. She could be your best friend.

Set up outlines, grids, previews in as many ways as you can, for the reasons we have discussed throughout this book.

Get enough sleep.

Keep your gifts alive and well. Exercise them and enjoy them.

Trust in yourself.

Returning to the metaphor of the photographer's darkroom, how clouded the images are of those in transition between childhood and adulthood. And how obvious the patterns seem once the salient features emerge. The next chapter offers three such portraits.

THREE
SUCCESS STORIES

In spite of obstacles, in spite of the lifelong nature of learning styles, success is possible, even inevitable, if greater emphasis is placed on children's strengths than on their weaknesses. Let these three stories speak for themselves.

PETER

Peter's story is one of a brilliant student whose high school transcript would appear to be work of a mediocre (at best) student, one who would in no way meet federal or local numerical criteria for inclusion in programs for the gifted. Yet Peter Boal (his real name) is a member of the New York City Ballet, founded by George Balanchine and now under the direction of Peter Martins and Jerome Robbins. At nineteen he is the youngest male ever to have been given many of the roles he has danced. In the fiercely competitive world of the ballet, Peter's rise to the top has the same certainty and precision as his physical leaps and jumps.

As a young child, Peter was a sensitive, highly intelligent child, skillful with words; a rapid, precise learner; a lithe athlete; and a young boy with an extraordinary sense of justice. Others' suffering gave him pain in a way far beyond his years.

All schoolwork came readily: reading, writing, spelling, math, science, art, social studies, and athletics. He was popular albeit reserved. He listened generously to others but kept his own counsel.

In third grade he enrolled as a student in the School of American Ballet, commuting daily for dance classes from his home in the country, an hour outside New York City. Because he was a boy in a predominantly jock community, he concealed this activity, saying he "took gymnastics."

His cover was blown when, in sixth grade, he starred as the prince in the well-known annual production of *The Nutcracker*. He danced the Prince for three years, all the while managing to stay afloat academically. His innate sense of order kept him on the track for his homework assignments, which he completed on the train, and his contributions to classroom discussions added depth to any and all topics.

But as his interest in ballet grew, and as his emotional attention was drawn more and more in that direction, the world of words lost its previous fascination for him. Already at eleven and twelve he was trying to live two lives, each demanding. His high personal standards would not let him be comfortable with slipshod performance in anything he undertook, yet satisfying the demands of both an academically demanding school and an art form such as ballet seemed nearly impossible to the adults in Peter's life.

At thirteen he had to make a choice. He could turn away from dance, relegating it to "something he did in his childhood" and something he would always enjoy watching. That would free him to pursue his studies in the best of schools and universities. He had the intellectual muscle to move in any abstract direction he chose.

Or he could turn to ballet as a serious pursuit, recognizing that it would be all-encompassing. He was told that his was the kind of talent that comes perhaps once in a century, but that, no matter how great his dedication, adolescence was going to change his body, perhaps allowing him to grow into an even finer dancer, but perhaps turning his talent to mediocrity. There was no way to predict, no exercises to do, no guarantees that single-minded study would finish his preparations and allow him to continue his high performance level.

His parents left the decision to Peter. As he climbed into the sleigh for his last performance as the Prince no one knew whether his journey was away from dance, to what some would call "the real world," or into dance for the realization of a dream.

Peter chose dance, knowing that it would be extraordinarily difficult to keep on with academic study at any kind of acceptable level, yet realizing that his mind as well as his body needed continuing training.

It is interesting to note his standardized test scores at the end of seventh and eighth grades, the years just preceding his decision. On the Secondary School Aptitude Test (SSAT) his quantitative scores were medium to high, reflecting his mathematical ability and, doubtless, his spatial awareness. But his verbal score was much lower than one would have anticipated from his early schoolwork and his capacity to think. Peter likes to work slowly when precision is important, and all his standardized test scores were lowered by his reluctance to rush.

His scores on standardized achievement tests were respectable, but not remarkable, reflecting the same patterns as his standardized aptitude tests. Nowhere in these numbers was there any indication of his extraordinary talent and reasoning ability and high personal dedication and standards. Anyone looking solely at his numerical transcript would have had no hint of the person behind the scores.

Peter moved into an apartment in New York, managed his own marketing and daily living (he had just turned fifteen), and enrolled in a school that strove to meet the needs of students who were also performing artists. But while "ought" was attached to academics, his heart was in his dancing. He found little time to study, and when he did crack the schoolbooks, either fatigue or his love of dance pulled his attention away.

His mother was insistent that Peter at least pass a high school equivalency test. Not having a high school diploma is reckless in today's world.

As Peter struggled to complete the requirements he was not interested in, he also struggled to discipline his growing artistic competence and to resist temptation to capitalize on it prematurely. He was offered a contract for a piece of work that would have brought him a large amount of money and public exposure. It was the kind of offer many performing artists dream about, and yet Peter turned it down. He made the decision himself, telling his family after the event. He knew, somewhere in his artistic soul, that he needed more training, that using his talent before solidifying it would jeopardize the long run for short-term glory.

As the competition grew more intense, and others were eliminated or moved sideways, Peter kept moving up. His body was powerful now as well as graceful, sinewy as well as slender, his artistry was maturing with depth and breadth. But the studies, the hateful requirements wouldn't go away. For all his ability to land precisely at the end of a predetermined arc, he didn't have the book learning to do formal geometry. For all his ability to see and move himself in relation to others, ratio and area were obstacles on paper. In spite of his capacity to communicate in English words and the additional language of space and movement, he couldn't pass French. For all his ability to be friends with many different types of people in the ballet world, he had no grade in civics or deportment to codify his leadership and personal integrity. There is no space in the professional dance world for the adolescent rebellion to which others his age feel entitled. Perhaps in academics he snitched a bit of the teenage irresponsibility denied him elsewhere.

At this same time that he was wrestling with the high school equivalency requirements, he voluntarily signed up for a college level literature course. A paper he wrote discussing a point in *Six Characters in Search of an Author* was praised by his professor as one of the most insightful pieces of criticism he had ever read. But how to pass social studies?

Peter's story has no tidy ending, thank goodness. He has finally passed his high school equivalency and is free to think, to learn, and to dance. Unshackled from academic requirements, he can soar in intellectual leaps, delighting his watchers and satisfying his soul.

In the summer of 1985 he performed in the amphitheater in Taormina, Italy. He described the moon rising behind the dancers, the powerful presence of Mount Etna, the look and feel of the stones, the sense of history of those who had seen and given performances here, century after century. He was not just one dancer in one time, but part of the magic alchemy between audience and artist, part of a tradition of movement and expression, part of a whole and greater power—from the past and of the future.

RICHARD

Richard Strauss told his story at the Twenty-eighth Annual Confer-ence of The Orton Dyslexia Society in 1977 in Dallas, Texas. The son of a locally and nationally prominent family, Rick is now a husband and father himself, as well as being president of the Realty Development Corporation in Dallas. His story comes from a time when understanding of learning styles was limited and help un-available.

When I was asked to give a speech at the annual conference of the Orton Society, I said that if I had to prepare one to read, it would take me an hour and a half to get through what would take a normal person only ten minutes. Rather than do that, I decided to tell a little bit about my life, about some of my educational experiences, and about some of the good and bad in it.

I started in public school in the first grade like most people. But by the fourth grade, my teachers called in my parents to inform them that I was totally unable to read or write and for that reason, they suggested, I should not progress into the fifth grade. At that time, my parents enrolled me at St. Mark's, a very fine private school with small classes. I was still unable to compete with the other students. I can remember that in the fourth grade there, the teacher had to write my last name on the bulletin board for me because I could not spell it.

I went to St. Mark's from the fourth grade through the eighth grade and continued to have great difficulty in competing with the rest of the students. In fact, the more difficulty I had, the more I cut up in class. I was probably the leading juvenile delinquent in St. Mark's history, and I was asked not to return for ninth grade for disciplinary reasons. I had spent more time skipping classes than in attending classes. I would have gotten away with that except when I skipped classes, I would go into the different classrooms and steal pens and pencils out of the desks and sell them to other kids on the campus to make a few dollars. One day on the way home on the bus, I sold back to a guy his own pen that I had stolen that day. That was the end!

In the ninth grade, then, I went back to public school for another try. At the same time, I was being tutored just about every afternoon. Off and on, I was taking speed reading courses, and I was spending most of my life in summer school. Finally we found a doctor who "realized" what my problem was. He suggested that I buy bifocal glasses and that would cure it all.

So, wearing my bifocals, being tutored, and taking my speed reading course, I was making great progress! In fact my parents thought that I was making exceptional progress until one day my Latin teacher (I had started Latin in the ninth grade) called them about midway through the semester and said, "Mr. and Mrs. Strauss, I'll make a deal with you. I'll pass Rick in this semester if you will promise—in writing—that he will never take another foreign language until he gets out of high school. This is the dumbest kid I've ever seen in my life." He said, "I've had him for nine weeks and he doesn't know one word of Latin and I'm not sure that he knows many more in English." This sounded pretty good to me at the time because it looked as though it might be the only course I was going to pass that year.

As time went on there were still problems with my conduct, or at least my parents seemed to think so. I seemed to think I was having a lot of fun. I was out of school more than I was in. I was caught riding go-carts through the halls of the school. I did all the usual things!

Every morning, announcements would come over the loudspeaker mounted high on the wall of the classroom. In my classroom there was a bolt missing from the bottom of the mounting which would always shake a little. One day when it snowed in Dallas, I put a snowball on top of the speaker. The teacher sat down beneath it, and as soon as the morning announcements began, down came the snowball . . . and out went Rick!

I finally wrapped up my high school career with my second attempt at my senior year when I took woodshop, speech, and— for the third time—freshman English. I took those three courses and finally got out.

It was early during that senior year that my father contacted a person in New York who was supposed to be one of the leading people on learning problems in children. He suggested that I go to the Scottish Rite Hospital in Dallas to be tested for dyslexia. I did get tested and for the first time was made aware of exactly what my problems were. I was then tutored by Mrs. Bywaters in the Orton-Gillingham method all through my last year in high school.

Then it was time for me to try college, so I sent my applications off to ten schools thinking that I would get four or five acceptances and then pick the one I wanted to go to. When all ten rejected me we found an organization that, for $250, would enroll a student in any [sic] college or university in the United States. We paid the $250 and I received three acceptances, one of them from a college that received a lot of publicity about 12 years ago. It was Parsons College but when *Life* magazine did a cover story on it, *Life* called it "Flunkout USA." As long as your father was willing to pay the high tuition, you could go there no matter what your grades were . . . and nobody had ever failed out. Well, I proved them wrong in twelve easy months!

From Parsons I went to another school, Henderson County Junior College in Texas. There I managed to do in six months what had taken me a whole year at Parsons. After about six months there my father took me into the sunroom one day and said, "Son, you know some kids are born students and some aren't, and you definitely fall in with the latter. Maybe we ought to try something else." So I got into the Air Force Reserves and, after a short time of active duty, was stationed near Dallas. I went back to Mrs. Bywaters and was tutored some more.

After my period of service, I went to work for a real estate brokerage firm in Dallas. At the age of 22, I opened my own real estate firm. That was ten years ago. Since that time I have built over 5000 apartment units in four states and have managed over 10,000 units. We have done the corporate restructuring for a major American Stock [Exchange] company after it went through bankruptcy. The company had 900 stores and 250 million dollars in assets and liabilities. We represented another American Stock Exchange company in the acquisition of a third American Stock Exchange company which was doing 80 million dollars a year in business and making a little over $8 million a year in profits. I am Chairman of the Board of a bank in Dallas and also chairman of the loan committee.

All of the successes I've had were possible to me for a few simple reasons. I learned that every person has strengths. For some it is in finance, being able to study financial information; for others it is being able to read well; for others it is writing well; and for others it is common sense. Every person has certain strengths. What is most important for students with dyslexia—or adults with dyslexia—is to locate those strengths and learn how to capitalize on them, and learn how to do the things that come naturally to them, and not to spend their whole lives concerned about the things that are the most difficult.

Another important reason for my successes is that I was very fortunate in having understanding parents. They understood that I was trying. They understood that I could spend two hours studying for a test on which others would need to spend only fifteen minutes. The others would get an A on the test and I would get an F. My parents did not concern themselves as long as I was applying myself and trying. The more trouble I got into, the more understanding they were. The worse I did in school the more understanding they were. They understand that some people are born to be students and others are not born to be students. When I was having my most difficult time in high school, when I was on my third round with freshman English, and when I couldn't pass any of the courses, I would go home at night and sit down with my father and compute the depreciation schedules on his radio station with him and do the budget for the next month. Yet, at the same time, I could not compete in my class with kids who were fifteen and sixteen years old.

Another thing is important for people with dyslexia. At an early age they must have explained to them what their problem is and that they are not mentally retarded, and that there isn't anything that makes them much different from other kids. They have got to know what their problem is, and it's got to be explained to them in a way that they can understand. There is nothing worse than not understanding—and I know because I went through it.

In my opinion the disciplinary problems come from not being able to compete in class with others or to get the attention of other students or feel equal to them. You've got to do something else whether it is cutting up in class or becoming the fastest runner on the track team or the best passer on the football team. If you are five feet seven and a half, as I am, with short legs, you aren't going to be a great football player or track star, so I thought cutting up was best. Had I known myself, had I not had the problem of wondering why I couldn't compete with the kids next to me, why I couldn't answer the questions they could answer, couldn't make the grades they could make, and couldn't achieve scholastically like them—had I understood all this, then I believe I would not have had so many disciplinary problems. The problem must be recognized and must be explained to children.

There is something else I think we need and that is important. I came from a very fortunate situation in that my parents did not believe there was something mentally wrong with me. They could afford to spend the time and the money and the effort—a lot of years and a lot of work—trying to find out what my problem was and why I could not read or write. Not many children in our school systems today have that opportunity. Therefore we must give that opportunity to them. We must teach teachers in the public schools to be able, first, to recognize children with dyslexia while they are in class and second, to teach them to read and write in that class along with the other students. If you do that in the schools where the children are—the children who do not have the opportunities I had or the parents who understand the problem and can afford the special help—then, in my opinion, this will help the children with dyslexia more than anything else I that know of. Dyslexia is real, and it can be dealt with, and the most important thing a person with dyslexia can have is the understanding of the people around him.[1]

EVA

Eva's story is also in her own words, a forty-five-page manuscript. For this book, with Eva's permission, I have included only those parts that bear on school problems. One day, when she reveals her identity, perhaps her whole story will be published. For now, Eva (a pseudonym) is a nationally respected authority on child development. She titles her story

MEMORIES OF A BRIGHT CHILD WHO COULD NOT—
WOULD NOT—LEARN: THE DOUBLE MASK

This is the story of a double mask.

The disabilities, at first particularly the speech defect, served to hide from other people my ability to think so well. At times it even made ME doubt that I was so bright, although at other times, the enforced unintelligibility increased my sense of arrogance. Later on, the wretched handwriting and spelling and other difficulties with the mechanical part of learning masked my ability to think and acquire material. That was the first mask.

The other mask was one I could don. Increasingly, after I learned to speak clearly, I would use my fine intelligence and wide range of knowledge to bemuse people to camouflage my various disabilities. With these two masks coming on and off I often felt like a sham and would speculate who the Real Me was.

The double mask bewilders the child herself and is also hard on adults. As a child I had no margin of sympathy for grown-ups: my own woes were too big. In retrospect, I sympathize with my parents and even my nefarious teachers Ms. Clyde and Ms. Shaw.

This is not a full autobiography, but the focused story of a selective portion of my life, dealing with academic and physical skills. My early learning was a complex interaction between a mind, a family, and a cultural background that were operating on one level and a neurophysiological structure with lags and deficits.

Everybody talked in my family, and talked very well. My father was a minister and my mother a professional lecturer and writer. The sound of their voices was beautiful even when they were saying very ordinary things. And they both used words that had all kinds of colors and tones about them that I enjoyed hearing even when I didn't know what the words meant. My parents talked to me and my brothers (one older, one younger) the way they talked to other grown-ups, which made it even better to listen.

It was different talking to other children, or other grown-ups, than it was at home. Father and Mother tried never to be angry or to make me hurry when they couldn't understand me, but would wait patiently and ask me to try the word again or say it with other words. When I finally got the word out correctly, if I could, they would suggest I practice it so next time it would come out better. But the next time I might be so excited about what I wanted to say that I would stumble again.

I was in a hurry when grown-ups talked in an exasperatingly overdetailed manner; long before they had finished a sentence I would anticipate the ending and, in my arrogant way, try to finish the sentence for them. When my words came out jumbled I would be accused of interrupting with silly sounds. I learned to finish the sentences inside my head, simultaneously exulting in being so much smarter than they were, and fuming at not being able to talk right.

In the early 1920s, the time of which I am writing, schools did not expect children to read before first grade and most parents thought that children should wait until school to be taught. My parents, intellectual, constant readers, gave us beautiful picture books and read aloud to us, but did not expect us to master our letters until "the time was right."

I had trouble with coordination as well as speech, but since my parents were not athletic they did not notice my difficulty learning to ride a tricycle, jump rope, or play jackstraws. Jump rope started around the first grade, and paralleled the exclusion my garbled speech produced in kindergarten. It seemed so easy when I watched the others, but when I tried to jump over the rope, I would trip and fall. Instead of knowing how to arouse compassion in my peers, I would go into a rage, denouncing them for turning the rope the wrong way, and become excluded again. Even when I took a turn at rope turning, I could not synchronize with the other rope turner, the jumper would get mad, and there would be another fight.

Playing jacks, or jackstraws, overlapped with jumping rope, but lasted well into third grade. I alternated between making a fool of myself trying to learn from other girls in a group and trying to practice alone. My cat was fascinated by the little rolling ball and the tiny jacks he could field and hide so that at least was a little fun. But jackstraws never worked for me. The girls I tried to play with were as impatient as the jump ropers. Once a kid screamed at me, "What's the matter! Are you a cripple or something?" As usual, when I was upset or lost my temper, my retort came in garbled speech. So they added jeers that I couldn't even talk right. Unfortunately, I had to face these same girls in class every day. I always thought of them as "The Other Children."

When I was around five, an optometrist who had come to our house as a visitor watched me trying to pass a plate of cookies to our guests. When he saw how often I bumped into the furniture, he said to my parents, "Bring that child to my office in the morning."

The glasses he prescribed meant a whole new view of life. I had heard people talking about the way leaves looked, but up to then they had been a mass of green. Now, suddenly, leaves took on different shapes as if they were flowers. I could even see the way they were attached by twigs to branches. The American flag, which we had to salute in school daily, was now a clear set of red and white stripes and definite five-pointed stars on a blue background. The 1920s was a period of unabashed patriotism and I had heard the song "The Stars and Stripes Forever" many times, but for the first time I saw what they were.

The acquisition of glasses also led to some of my first metaphysical speculations. I would look at something with my glasses on, seeing a clear and sharp image, and then take my glasses off, seeing a vague and fuzzy image but sometimes one whose colors seemed more vivid in the absence of contour. I would wonder which image was real and what other people saw.

It would be good to report that the improvement with vision solved everything. It helped me avoid some accidents and embarrassment at breaking things, but I remained awkwardly unable to do, even with GREAT effort, what other children could do easily. Late in second grade, I still couldn't tie my shoes, a disgrace in class when everyone else got up from "rest," put on and tied his own shoes. I had to ask the teacher to do mine, and she would invariably respond that someone as smart as I could do it if I tried.

First grade taught me that there was no place for a left-handed child. Until then I had not been bothered by my handedness or even paid it much attention. The very first day of first grade, the teacher whose name I still remember as one of the ugliest words in the language, Miss Clyde, leaned over me when I was trying to copy a letter from the board, yanked the pencil from my left hand, and thrust it into my right hand, making a little speech about why I should always use the right.

We had wide-lined paper for practicing our letters. Mine went off the line and were too high or too low, too big or too small. I soon learned that certain letters and numerals were as troublesome as certain sounds, b, d, p, q, and s, and my 3 always went in the wrong direction. Fortunately there were 40 or 45 "Other Children" in the classroom, so Miss Clyde was too busy to pay much attention to me, but suddenly she would descend to insist that I change back to my right hand if I was sneaking in a little left-handed work or criticize what I was doggedly accomplishing with my right hand.

In hindsight, I wonder why I never told my parents about this, but it never occurred to me that what went on at school and at home had anything to do with each other.

Then came the reading. Or, rather, it did not come. In this particular school in the 1920s each child was furnished with a box of letters printed on small cardboard forms, much like Anagrams or Scrabble, except that they were cardboard. Miss Clyde would write a word, or a "family" of words, on the blackboard (*at, cat, bat, sat,* etc.) and we were to copy them on paper or make them with our cardboard letters. Miss Clyde would say the word "B-at" and the class would chant back "B-at." The whole morning seemed to go by while we were doing one "family."

Often, even with my glasses, I couldn't see her words on the blackboard. My mind would wander, and since I had always liked to nibble on things, I might chew on one of the letters. Without realizing it, I might chew up a dozen or more during one interminable recitation. Then, when I looked for a particular letter, I would realize it had gone down my gullet.

School got worse and worse that whole first grade. Besides prowling around to change my pencil from my left to right hand, Miss Clyde caught on to my habit of "Eating School Property" and chastised me publicly. She wrote to my family and they had to pay for a new box of letters. I was so ashamed that they knew, but I still went on eating letters because that was all I could do with the terrible boredom and not knowing what was going on with the reading.

Although I was not reading yet in school, at home I was learning poetry at a great rate simply by listening to my parents recite it. My mother could not carry a tune well, and so, when she sat by our beds at night, she would put us to sleep by reciting poems. Many we would request again and again, and before long I found that I really had them for my own. I still loved to hear her say them because of the sound of her voice, but I could say them with her under my breath.

In school, the children were now called on to "recite." Miss Clyde would fire a question at me in a way that made it impossible for me to answer coherently. While The Other Children were answering I knew in advance what they ought to say and corrected them in my own mind if they made mistakes, but when I was called on, garbled speech was all that came out.

One very cold morning I refused to eat my oatmeal and went out fortified only with milk, juice, and a piece of toast. I remember with complete vividness that my habitual path through the empty lot was bumpy and the white frost was over all of the weeds and the frozen earth. My knees burned with the cold, I had lost my mittens so my hands hurt too, but most of all I remember the pain of my face. My metal-rimmed glasses cut like fire into my cheeks. Tears kept coming. I could envision being in the classroom with Miss Clyde scolding me for saying things wrong or eating some of my letters. Suddenly I knew I could NOT make it to school. I turned and stumbled home.

My father grasped that the problem was more than physical cold, but he did not let on. He rewarmed the oatmeal, and I ate it slowly. Probably he added an extra portion of brown sugar and raisins. By then it was obvious that I was terrified of going back to school. Father carried me on his shoulder, took me up to the classroom, and explained my lateness to Miss Clyde in a way that kept her from scolding me more than usual that day.

But this one moment of rebellion and flight did not dispel the anguish of first grade. I vented my frustration by going into tantrums at home. My parents had been quite lenient when we had cried or screamed as little children, isolating us in our rooms until we had cooled off. But six was too old for tantrums, particularly when the triggering events were so trivial. I would flail around on the floor, "kicking and screaming like a four-year-old" as one adult put it. Another would say, "Calm down and tell us what's wrong; don't howl like an animal." But I went on howling and flailing.

Even in those far-off days of the 1920s there were some psychologists in this country. My parents did not have much money but felt a consultation would be a wise investment. They took me to Dr. Jessie Taft, one of the first practitioners of child psychology in this country. I remember meeting a very kind, white-haired lady who knew how to listen to children. The way she listened helped me talk clearly enough for her to understand.

Dr. Taft saw that the current school situation was getting cumulatively worse. Since one could not alter a school, she said the best thing would be to take me out for "medical reasons" until the end of the term and give me a new start in the fall.

She not only suggested I leave school, but that there be some time with me and mother alone. Mother started the rental on our summer beach cottage in early April and took me there alone, except of course for my cat. Father came down midweeks to see us, but otherwise I did not see other members of my family until after the Fourth of July. By then, in those three months, much of the cure had been accomplished.

For my mother, as a working writer, this time in the cottage with only one small child was a godsend. She wrote, and wrote, and wrote; the sound of the typewriter was as constant in my ears as the sound of the waves on the beach. We both loved the ocean, the beach, and the dunes and explored them freely. Mother had time for me when I needed it.

Since there were only the two of us, we took turns cooking and I learned on a kerosene stove, and a pump instead of running water, to do practical cooking effectively. I was responsible for many of the supplies by picking blackberries and walking the half mile to the nearest farm to bring back fresh milk and fresh-churned butter. Visiting the farm people an hour or two each day was a joy. I saw how much wonderful work got done with so little talk. I learned the songs of the butter churn as the old woman sang them. Here, too, I talked much more clearly.

An awareness began to dawn. During those long, miserable days in school, with the dreary repetition of letters on the board and the cardboard messes, in spite of myself I had learned to associate sound and shape of letters, and even ideas of sound blends, word families, and patterns. But I had kept this skill in the back of my mind because I was so scared and furious. Also, with a number of beautiful fairy tale books at home, I had often sat looking at the books, the pictures and the words together, and may have learned to recognize many words by sight without realizing it. So I had all of these sound and sight recognition techniques buried somewhere within me, if only they had a chance to come out right. And in one afternoon they did.

The previous week my mother had read "The Ancient Mariner" aloud to me, all the way through. Some educators would have questioned the suitability of this for a six-year-old, even a bright one, but that didn't bother my mother. She loved the poem for the rich imagery, the moral, and she also felt that living within sight of the ocean was good reason to read things connected with the sea. I was enthralled and wanted to go over it again and again, hoping I could memorize it and make it all mine. The sheer length seemed no obstacle because it was all so wonderful.

When I decided I needed another exposure, Mother was typing, and I knew she was only to be interrupted for a severe emergency. So I found the book myself and started looking at it. It happened not to be an illustrated edition but a very small little paperback copy. With this little book, I began reading, filling in from my memory, deciphering, decoding, and probably using what we would now call context clues. I was keenly attuned to the rhymes, and if a final word needed one, I could supply it. I have seldom in my entire life had the same heady, exhilarating experience, and it mounted and mounted as the poem went on. When the sound of the typewriter stopped and Mother came in to see what I was doing, I had completed the poem all by myself.

I exultantly told her and asked if I could read it to her. She was as happy as I and listened all the way through, and only on the rarest occasion did she tactfully interject a correction when I had grossly altered or mispronounced a word. I compare this moment of having finished "The Ancient Mariner" with the same kind of incredulous excitement I had two years earlier, discovering a whole new world by wearing glasses. But now it was my own mind that had the sharp vision. There was nothing artificial I had to put on.

The rest of the summer I read and read. Most of the books were for children, of them we had a great store, but I was allowed to read anything I saw, and there was no end to things.

All of this made me happy, but the greatest happiness was in the written page itself and where it would take me. I would often stop in the middle of reading and "see" what I was reading ("and it grew wondrous cold, and ice, mast-high, came floating by as green as emerald"). And I would look out at the ocean, now so bright blue in the June sunlight and see those mast-high deep green icebergs. I never stopped reading "The Ancient Mariner" the rest of the summer, but each day added one or two other things. Before tackling a new poem, I would often reread one or two from the previous days so each day I built up the number with which I was thoroughly comfortable.

At the same time I was reading poetry, I started writing. I started by writing postcards or letters to Father or my brothers. Mother was endlessly patient about spelling the words for me. She offered to have me dictate letters to her on the typewriter, but somehow, once I could read I felt ready to write also. My letters must have been a terrific job of deciphering for my father. With my poor coordination and using my right hand, bad as it felt to use it, the letters were enormous and scrawly, and when I made a mistake, I tried to mark over it, not erase. Miss Clyde had not approved of erasing. Still, it felt wonderful to see a letter being folded up in an envelope, knowing it would take my words to Father before I saw him again.

It would be nice to end here and say that when I entered second grade I had my tools well enough in hand and that whatever early difficulties I had been suffering were all over, but it wasn't so. Elementary school and all the rest of the way was a hard pull.

In second and third grades, when we studied reading, each child would get up in turn and read one paragraph with the teacher correcting any errors. This took a great deal of time, so I would go ahead on my own and read the rest of the book. When I was called on, I might be on page 18 while the paragraph I was meant to read was on page 3. I tried to use a finger to mark the paragraph I had figured out would be mine, but that method never seemed to work. If the story was really good, I would be so involved with how to get the hero out of danger on page 19 that I would stumble in my reading aloud, exposing my speech difficulty to the whole class.

Writing and spelling have continued to be painful problems into adulthood. My spelling is a joke among my colleagues; I do as much as I can of dictating rather than writing. Many things contributed to my difficulty learning to spell. They were all there together making each other worse. One was my terrible handwriting. I really didn't know what a word looked like after I put it down. Like many bright children who are poor spellers, I would foul up my handwriting deliberately so people might give me the benefit of the doubt in judging the correctness of a word.

Spelling and handwriting became a power struggle between me and whatever teacher I had. I would be furious because I knew that my poems, stories, or compositions were the best in the class, yet the teacher would return them with comments such as "Disgraceful handwriting for a fourth grader" or "Copy this over with NO spelling mistakes." I was seldom given credit for fine content or rich ideas because teachers harped on technical trivia. Growing up in a family of writers, I knew that content and style are what matter.

I decided to teach myself to type. We had a little portable my father had used in World War I which we children were allowed to use. I was thrilled with my first half-page double-spaced composition and confident the teacher would eat her previous cruel words, finally praising me for my true worth. My parents suggested I "proofread" my page. I used a pen to correct what errors I thought I saw but must have chosen one with a bad nib and managed to make great blots. When I handed the paper to Miss Shaw (not quite as ugly a name as Clyde, but it comes close), she held it up to the whole class as an example of unacceptable work.

Although I used the typewriter at home for my personal writing, it wasn't until high school, when I had a very different relationship with the faculty, that I dared hand in another typed paper.

As a result of several years of speech therapy and spontaneous growth, my speech improved so much that by sixth grade few people were even aware of the problem, but in adulthood I still must be careful, especially when tired or upset. At certain points of fatigue, I am vulnerable to malapropisms, spoonerisms, and other mistakes. But because I am adult I can pass them off as intentional jokes.

Around sixth grade I got involved with children's theater, and found to my delight that when I was acting a character, reciting memorized lines, my speech would be flawless. This is a common phenomenon among people with speech defects, and I put it to use when I had to meet new people socially or speak out in a difficult class situation. I would cue myself by pretending to be someone else and the speech would come out clearly.

The physical awkwardness was a much harder and longer thing. While other kids learned to whistle, I could never make more than a tiny gasp. My brothers and I climbed trees, went on long hikes searching for fossils, bird's nests, or arrowheads. We were active but not in the way of other kids our age.

When, at my request, I received a bicycle for my fifteenth birthday, I was too proud to ask to be taught how to ride it and did not know about the coaster brake. I managed by some kind of image of having seen other people ride to get going, riding straight along until I came to a hill. Going down, I didn't know how to avoid an approaching vehicle, rode myself into a parked car, and broke my leg. So it went, one accident after another, but I didn't give up.

The after story is predictable. I seemed doomed by family background and my own values to enter some field of intellectual endeavor. I have loved it, done well, and, in the words of educators, "adequately compensated" for many of these early disabilities. But the adequate compensations are sometimes only partially successful.

In the pursuit of my Ph.D., I was required to take a French exam and reverted to the agonies of first grade. I was enraged that the university required me to pass a French exam that had nothing to do with successfully completing the doctoral program and writing a first-rate thesis. I failed the French qualifying exam three times and finally passed it with an average mark, one of the few "averages" I have received in my entire academic career. On the matriculation examinations for my doctoral program, I failed the multiple-choice questions more miserably, I was told later, than had any graduate student in the history of the program. I had trouble keeping my place on the separate answer sheet and felt insulted by the stupidity of the questions. At the same time, I made one of the very top ratings on the essay questions.

Part of my success on the essays was knowing the extent of my own disabilities. I knew that if I had to write for four hours with a pen, the sheer fatigue and preoccupation with ideas would make my handwriting increasingly illegible and invite all kinds of misspellings, omissions, or even reversals. Therefore I petitioned the department to let me write my essays on a portable typewriter. If I had had to write all that material in one stretch by hand, I might have scored as low on my essay questions as I did on multiple choice, although for different reasons.

My current professional life requires a considerable amount of telephoning, which I try to do in the morning when I am refreshed. If I must do it later in the day, I hold the number right in front of me and dial slowly. Otherwise, out of seven digits, I am likely to get at least five of them scrambled.

Somewhere in adolescence, I tried to settle on a few aids to orientation so I would not be caught going the wrong way. I wear my wristwatch on my right arm and a bracelet on my left. When I remember to look at either one before saying anything or turning one direction, I am usually all right. I say "usually" because there still seems to be some sort of gap between the word and the actual physical direction. I can be driving home in a taxi in the neighborhood where I have lived for twenty-five years and tell the cab driver, "Turn right at the next block" when I mean he should turn left.

Along with this I have better than average orientation in the physical world. Having once been to a place, I can revisualize it and have a good mental map. If I must drive a car in unfamiliar territory, I memorize the map ahead of time.

I do not want to conclude this narrative on a note of bewilderment about right-left orientation; it is such a small portion of the life that intellectually, professionally, and personally has become increasingly productive and joyful.

I began with the image of the double mask. The masks remain. It is no accident that even now I do not wish to use my name for this account. However, along with the concealment that has become such a way of living, when I look back over my sixty-seven years I see continuity and conviction. My early love of language, and the images language can create, has persisted. I have never lost the ultravivid eidetic imagery of childhood. A single phrase, in the words of John Donne, "Makes a little room an everywhere."

The experience of living with a double mask extends the boundaries of empathy. Feeling cut off from human communication, such a frequent part of my early childhood, has helped me communicate with the learning disabled, the intellectually limited, and the psychotic. Even the agony of having such teachers as Miss Clyde has helped me learn what teaching should not be and to recognize that whenever a student fails I must look beyond her errors to her intentions.

Whichever mask is on, the other one is still available. Yet I am slowly growing to where I can have an open face.

Peter, Richard, and Eva are child, man, and woman, representing the configuration of the human family. They are from the worlds of commerce, academia, and the arts and cut across many socioeconomic layers. Together their triumphs and their tribulations represent the universality of conundrum kids.

As their personal stories speak more powerfully than any description from a distance could, so the voices of two young poets tell what education can be to an atypical learner.

This first poem was written by a high school senior in Alton, Illinois, two weeks before he took his own life.

ON EDUCATION

He always wanted to explain things
But no one cared

So he drew.
Sometimes he would draw,
And it wasn't anything.
He wanted to carve it in stone
Or write it in the sky,
And it would be only him and the sky and
The things inside him that needed saying.
It was after that he drew the picture.
It was a beautiful picture.
He kept it under his pillow
And would let no one see it.
He would look at it every night
And think about it.
When it was dark and his eyes were closed,
He could still see it.
When he started school,
He brought it with him,
Not to show to anyone,
Just to have along like a friend.
It was funny about school.
He sat at a square brown desk,
Like all the other square brown desks.
He thought it should be red.
And his room was a square, brown room,
Like all the other rooms.
It was tight and close and stiff.
He hated to hold the pencil and the chalk,
His arms stiff, his feet flat on the floor,
Stiff,
The teacher watching and watching.
The teacher came and spoke to him.
She told him to wear a tie like all the other boys.
He said he didn't like them.
She said it didn't matter!
After that, they drew.
He drew all yellow.
It was the way he felt about morning,
And it was beautiful.

The teacher came and smiled at him.
"What's this?" she said, "Why don't you
Draw something like Ken's drawing?
Isn't that beautiful?"
After that, his mother bought him a tie,
And he always drew airplanes and rocketships
Like everyone else.
And he threw the old picture away.
And when he lay alone looking at the sky,
It was big and blue and all of everything,
But he wasn't any more.
He was square inside and brown,
And his hands were stiff.

He was like everyone else.
The things inside that needed saying
Didn't need it any more.
It had stopped pushing.
It was crushed.
Stiff.
Like everything else.[2]

The second poem, "The Wall," was written as a tribute to Henry Collis, for many years Director of The Association For Gifted Children in London. The author was an eleven-year-old boy who prefers to remain anonymous.

THE WALL

They laughed at me.
They laughed at me and called me names,
They wouldn't let me join their games.
I couldn't understand.
I spent most playtimes on my own,
Everywhere I was alone,
I couldn't understand.

Teachers told me I was rude,
Bumptious, overbearing, shrewd,

Some of the things they said were crude.
I couldn't understand.
And so I built myself a wall.
Strong and solid, ten foot tall,
With bricks you couldn't see at all,
So I could understand.

And then came Sir,
A jovial, beaming, kindly man,
Saw through my wall and took my hand,
And the wall came tumbling down,
For he could understand.

And now I laugh with them,
Not in any unkind way,
For they have yet to face their day
And the lessons I have learned.
For eagles soar above all birds,
And scavengers need to hunt in herds,
But the lion walks alone,
And now I understand.

Concerned adults, working together, have the power to choose what
education will be for
Smart Kids with School Problems.

NOTES

1. RECOGNIZING, UNDERSTANDING,
AND HELPING CONUNDRUM KIDS

1. Norman Geschwind, "The Brain of a Learning Disabled Individual," *Annals of Dyslexia* 34 (1984).
2. G. H. Parkyn, Remarks presented at the World Conference on Gifted Children, London, England, 1975.
3. Shel Silverstein, *Where the Sidewalk Ends* (New York: Harper & Row, 1974).

2. THE YOUNG CHILD:
DEVELOPMENTAL LEVELS AND ACADEMIC REQUIREMENTS

1. Jerome Rosner, Test of Auditory Analysis Skills, taken from *Helping Children Overcome Learning Difficulties*, rev. ed. (New York: Walker, 1979).

3. VISUAL LEARNING

1. LLoyd J. Thompson, M.D., *Language Disability in Men of Eminence.* Orton Monograph 27 (1969).
2. The Report of the Commission on Reading, *Becoming a Nation of Readers,* prepared by R. C. Anderson, E. H. Heibert, J. A. Scott, I. A. G. Wilkinson for The National Academy of Education, The National Institute of Education, The Center for the Study of Reading, 1985.

4. MOTOR FUNCTION AND SCHOOL ACHIEVEMENT

1. Melvin D. Levine, F. Oberklaid, and L. Meltzer, "Developmental Output Failure: A Study of Low Productivity in School-Age Children," *Pediatrics* 67, no. 18 (1981).
2. Nina Traub, Francis Bloom, et al., *Recipe for Reading,* rev. ed. (Cambridge, Mass.: Educator's Publishing Service, 1975).

5. AUDITORY LEARNING:
LEARNING TO LISTEN, LISTENING TO LEARN

1. Julie Reichman, M.S., and William C. Healey, Ph.D., "Conductive Hearing Loss Involving Otitis Media," *The Journal of Learning Disabilities* 16, no. 5 (May 1983): 272–78. "The most common cause of hearing loss in children in developed countries is Otitis Media with Effusion, OME, an unresolved middle ear inflammation . . . [which] may arise insidiously and painlessly, may produce only low-grade discomfort . . . a number of studies have been reported that show relationships between OME and impairment in intelligence, reading, speech and language; additionally increased behavior problems have been found in children with OME. It was concluded that the relationship between middle ear pathology and learning disabilities deserves intense and critical study because of a possible causal link."
2. P. A. Silva, C. Kirkland, A. Simpson, I. A. Stewart, and S. M. Williams, "Some Developmental and Behavioral Problems Associated with Bilateral Otitis Media with Effusion," *The Journal of Learning Disabilities* 15, no. 7 (August/September 1982): 417–21.

6. LANGUAGE AND LEARNING:
INTELLECT, LANGUAGE, EMOTION

1. Leon Eisenberg, M.D., "Psychiatric Aspects of Language Disability," *Reading, Perception and Language, Papers from the World Congress on Dyslexia* (Baltimore: The Orton Dyslexia Society, 1975).

2. Richard H. Masland, M.D., *The Advantages of Being Dyslexic*, Orton Monograph 72 (1976).

8. TESTING DEMYSTIFIED:
SCORES, INTERPRETATION, PLANNING

1. National Association of Independent Schools, *Glossary of Selected Terms for Testing*, compiled by Alice Jackson (Boston, 1982).

2. Priscilla L. Vail, Book review, *Independent School* (February 1984): 46–51. Many of my remarks on Gardner's work are taken from my review of his book, which appeared in *Independent School*, and are reprinted here with their kind permission.

3. A. Bannatyne, H. B. Vance, and M. G. Singer, "Recategorization of WISC-R Scaled Subtest Scores for Learning Disabled Children," *The Journal of Learning Disabilities* 12, no. 8 (August 1979): 63–66.

4. Howard Gardner, *Frames of Mind: The Theory of Multiple Intelligences* (New York: Basic Books, 1983).

9. MATURATION AND HIGHER EDUCATION:
GETTING IT ALL TOGETHER

1. *The New York Times*, October 9, 1984, sec. C, p. 11.

2. *The New York Times*, September 6, 1981, sec. C, p. 25.

3. William C. Hiss, "Coaching for the SATs: What the Colleges Think," *Independent School* (October 1984): 51–53. (Boston: National Association of Independent Schools)

4. Dorothy H. Dillon, "SAT Preparation and Independent Schools," *Independent School* (October 1984): 45–49. (Boston: National Association of Independent Schools)

5. Macdonald Critchley, M.D., *Dyslexia Research and Its Application to Education* (London: Wiley & Sons, 1981).

6. Susan A. Vogel, Ph.D., "On Developing LD College Programs," *The Journal of Learning Disabilities* 15, no. 9 (November 1982): 518–28.

10. THREE SUCCESS STORIES

1. Richard Strauss, "Richard's Story," *Bulletin of The Orton Dyslexia Society* 28 (1978): 181–85. (Baltimore: The Orton Dyslexia Society). "Richard's Story," in its entirety, is reprinted here with his kind permission.

2. *Scholastic Magazine* (October 10, 1970).

ANNOTATED
BIBLIOGRAPHY
AND RESOURCES

ANNOTATED BIBLIOGRAPHY

The following books and articles are pertinent to the contents of the entire book as well as to the specifics of Chapter 1, "Recognizing, Understanding, and Helping Conundrum Kids." Orton monographs are available by mail from The Orton Dyslexia Society, 724 York Road, Baltimore, Maryland, 21204.

Clarke, Louise. *Can't Read, Can't Write, Can't Talk Too Good Either*. New York: Penguin Books, 1973. This is the clearly written personal story of a parent who kept faith in her son, who struggled with severe school problems and who has gone on to have a rich professional career.

Erikson, Erik H. *Childhood and Society*. New York: W.W. Norton, 1950. Particularly Chapter 7, "The Eight Ages of Man," which describes the psychosocial stages of human growth, showing the influence of the child's experiences on his developing self-concept and view of the world.

Featherstone, Helen. *A Difference in the Family*. New York: Basic

Books, 1980. This book describes the ways in which one child's disability affects the rest of the family. It is simultaneously a personal and universal story.

Galaburda, Albert M., M.D. "Developmental Dyslexia: A Review of Biological Interactions." *Annals of Dyslexia* 35 (1985): 21–33.

Gardner, Howard. *Frames of Mind: The Theory of Multiple Intelligences.* New York: Basic Books, 1983. This scientific work is difficult reading for those unaccustomed to scientific terminology. But Gardner weaves in literature, anthropology, human understanding, and humor with his neurological research and offers tactful shortcuts to keep the lay reader from getting too bogged down. It offers an exciting and optimistic view of human intelligence.

Hampshire, Susan. *Susan's Story.* New York: St. Martin's Press, 1982. This gifted actress tells the story of her early attempts at learning to read; how her mother kept her artistic talents blooming; and how, in spite of poor reading, she learned to survive tryouts and new scripts and has enjoyed a career as an internationally known actress at peace with herself and at home in the world.

Healy, Jane M. *Your Child's Growing Mind: A Parent's Guide to Learning.* New York: Doubleday, 1987. This commonsense book by a neuropsychologist, who is also a teacher, learning specialist, and parent, is a gold mine of good advice and child-centered suggestions.

de Hirsch, Katrina. *Interactions Between Educational Therapist and Child.* Orton Monograph 53 (1977). (Baltimore: The Orton Dyslexia Society).

Masland, Richard L., M.D. *The Advantages of Being Dyslexic.* Orton Monograph 72 (1976).

Sapir, Selma G., and Wilson, Bernice. "The Selection of Special Educators and Learning Disability Specialists." *The Journal of Learning Disabilities* 15, no. 3 (March 1982).

Simpson, Eileen. *Reversals: A Personal Account of Victory over Dyslexia.* Boston: Houghton Mifflin, 1979. This is the first-person account of the author's disastrous, misunderstood school problems; her marriage to the poet John Berryman, who first diagnosed her difficulty; her triumph in earning a graduate degree in psychology, and her becoming a therapist.

Sizer, Theodore R. *Horace's Compromise: The Dilemma of the American High School.* Boston: Houghton Mifflin, 1984. This study of high schools, written by the man who was dean of the Graduate School of Education at Harvard University and headmaster of Phillips Academy, Andover, Massachusetts, is a call for reform in which practical suggestions interweave with educational philosophy, human understanding, and clear writing.

Smith, Sally L. *No Easy Answers: The Learning Disabled Child at Home and at School.* New York: Bantam Books, 1979. This readable, clear introduction to learning disabilities is a reliable handbook for parents or professionals working in the field.

Vail, Priscilla L. "Pardon Parents and Pardon, Parents." *The Orton Dyslexia Society Newsletter* (February 1983).

————. *The World of the Gifted Child.* New York: Walker, 1979. This book was written for professionals and parents. A combination of theory, practical suggestions, and case studies, it explores Who They Are, How They Live, What Else They Need, and What They Say.

2. THE YOUNG CHILD: DEVELOPMENTAL LEVELS AND ACADEMIC REQUIREMENTS

Ames, Louise B. *Is Your Child in the Wrong Grade?* Available from Gesell Institute of Human Development, 310 Prospect Street, New Haven, Connecticut 06511. The title of this book is self-explanatory. They also publish *A Gift of Time,* a brief, jargon-free pamphlet summarizing the reasons for basing school-entry decisions on developmental criteria, which is very helpful in reassuring perplexed parents and educators.

Elkind, David. *The Hurried Child.* Reading, Mass.: Addison-Wesley, 1981. This important book has clear messages for both parents and educators.

Jansky, Jeannette J. *The Marginally Ready Child.* Orton monograph 68 (1975). The title is self-explanatory. Jansky is a careful researcher and experienced, intuitive clinician. This is for all audiences.

Rosner, Jerome. *Helping Children Overcome Learning Difficulties*. rev. ed. New York: Walker, 1979. This practical guide to identifying specific levels of difficulty in visual and auditory analysis is written for parents as well as educators and contains carefully sequenced exercises to help children overcome problems in these two areas.

Vail, Priscilla L. *Gifted, Precocious or Just Plain Smart?* New York: Programs for Education, 1987. (1200 Broadway, New York, N.Y. 10001.)

———. *The World of the Gifted Child*. New York: Walker, 1979. Chapter 1 describes the perils of acceleration (overplacement) through a case history.

3. VISUAL LEARNING

Cox, Aylett R. *Structures and Techniques: Remedial Language Training; Multi-Sensory Teaching for Alphabetic Phonics*. Cambridge, Mass.: Educator's Publishing Service, 1967, 1969, 1974. This highly detailed, technical manual of the structure of our language is an invaluable help to the teacher who wants to learn more about the rules that govern the decoding and encoding of English and wants to learn multisensory techniques.

Hogenson, Dennis. *Reading Failure and Juvenile Delinquency*, Orton monograph 63 (1974).

Keogh, Barbara K., and Pelland, Michele. "Vision Training Revisited." *The Journal of Learning Disabilities* 18, no. 4 (April 1985): 228–36.

Lieberman, S. "Visual Perception vs. Visual Function." *The Journal of Learning Disabilities* 17, no. 3 (March 1984): 180–81.

Orton, Samuel T., M.D. *Reading, Writing and Speech Problems in Children*. New York: W.W. Norton, 1937. Available from the Orton Dyslexia Society. 724 York Road, Baltimore, Maryland 21204. Dr. Orton's book is technical, but the general reader can also enjoy and learn from it.

The Report of the Commission on Reading. *Becoming a Nation of Readers*. Prepared by R. C. Anderson, E. H. Heibert, J. A.

Scott, I. A. G. Wilkinson for The National Academy of Education, The National Institute of Education, The Center for the Study of Reading. 1985.

Rosner, Jerome. *Helping Children Overcome Learning Difficulties.* rev. ed. New York: Walker, 1979. This clearly written, practical book is for parents and educators. Rosner's exercises work and students enjoy them.

Traub, Nina, and Bloom, Frances, et al. *Recipe For Reading.* rev. ed. Cambridge, Mass.: Educator's Publishing Service. 1975. This practical manual offers step-by-step lessons combining decoding, encoding, and handwriting. It is less complicated than Cox's *Structures and Techniques* (cited previously) and dwells more on practical exercises than on the research.

Welty, Eudora. *One Writer's Beginnings.* Cambridge, Mass.: Harvard University Press, 1983. This is the beautifully and simply told story of a romance with reading, writing, and language.

4. MOTOR FUNCTION AND SCHOOL ACHIEVEMENT

Duffy, Joan. *Type It.* Cambridge, Mass.: Educator's Publishing Service, 1974. This is a manual for teaching typing to students in grades one through twelve.

Levine, Melvin D., Oberklaid, F., and Meltzer, L. "Developmental Output Failure—A Study of Low Productivity in School-Age Children." *Pediatrics* 67, no. 18 (1981).

Plunkett, Mildred. *A Writing Manual for Teaching the Left-Handed.* rev. ed. Cambridge, Mass.: Educator's Publishing Service, 1967.

5. AUDITORY LEARNING:
LEARNING TO LISTEN, LISTENING TO LEARN

Lash, Joseph P. *Master and Teacher, the Biography of Helen Keller.* New York: Delacorte Press, 1980. Helen Keller's story belongs in any discussion of listening, learning, and alternative routes to language.

Oliphant, Genevieve. "The Lens of Language." *Bulletin of The Orton Dyslexia Society* 26 (1976): 49–62.

Rosner, Jerome. *Helping Children Overcome Learning Difficulties.* rev. ed. New York: Walker, 1979. This book for teachers and parents contains the test and exercises referred to in this chapter.

Vail, Priscilla L. *Clear and Lively Writing: Language Games and Activities for Everyone.* New York: Walker, 1981. Particularly the section on listening. This book for teachers and parents offers games and activities for developing listening, speaking, reading, and writing skills in students from kindergarten through twelfth grade.

Welty, Eudora. *One Writer's Beginnings.* Cambridge, Mass.: Harvard University Press, 1984. Particularly the section on listening. This 104-page volume is Harvard's first best-seller. It is a must for anyone who cares about words, children, learning, language, and listening.

6. LANGUAGE AND LEARNING: INTELLECT, LANGUAGE, EMOTION

Blachman, Benita A. "Are We Assessing the Linguistic Factors Critical in Early Reading?" *Annals of Dyslexia* 33 (1983).

Denckla, M. B., and Rudel, R. G. "Rapid 'Automatized' Naming (R.A.N.): Dyslexia Differentiated from Other Learning Disabilities." *Neuropsychologia* 14 (1976): 471–79.

———. "Rapid 'Automatized' Naming of Pictured Objects, Colors, Letters and Numbers by Normal Children." *Cortex* 10 (1974): 186–202.

Eisenberg, Leon, M.D. "Psychiatric Aspects of Language Disability." *Reading, Perception and Language.* Baltimore: York Press, 1975, 215–29.

Fraiberg, Selma H. *The Magic Years.* New York: Charles Scribner's Sons, 1959. This book, written for parents, is filled with warmth, wisdom, humor, and insight into the nature of the young child.

Geschwind, Norman, M.D. "Why Orton Was Right." *Annals of Dyslexia* 32 (1982): 13–30.

de Hirsch, Katrina. *Language and the Developing Child.* Baltimore, Md.: The Orton Dyslexia Society, 1984. This collection of de Hirsch's articles and papers is written for professionals, but anyone interested in the topic will find it readable in spite of its technical language, and helpful because of its profound understanding of language and the child.

Kastein, S., and Trace, B. *The Birth of Language.* Springfield, Ill.: Charles C. Thomas Publishers, 1966. This is the true story of an anguished mother who, guided by the renowned, warm language therapist Dr. Shulamith Kastein, helped her child, originally diagnosed as retarded, to acquire language. In addition to being a moving story, it is a step-by-step model of how to teach language to a language-disordered child.

Rawson, Margaret B. *Adult Accomplishments of Dyslexic Boys.* Cambridge, Mass.: Educator's Publishing Service, 1968, 1978. This is the true story of Rawson's dyslexic students at the heterogeneously grouped school in Rose Valley, Pennsylvania, and what they have done with their lives.

———. *Self Concept and the Cycle of Growth.* Orton Monograph 62 (1974).

The Report of the Commission on Reading. *Becoming a Nation of Readers.* Prepared by R. C. Anderson, E. H. Heibert, J. A. Scott, I. A. G. Wilkinson for The National Academy of Education, The National Institute of Education, The Center for the Study of Reading. 1985.

Selfe, Lorna. *Nadia.* New York: Harcourt Brace Jovanovich (by arrangement with Academic Press, Inc., London), 1979. This is the story of a nonverbal child with extraordinary ability to draw, particularly horses. This shows examples of her work and tells what happened to her art when she developed language.

Vail, Priscilla L. *Clear and Lively Writing; Language Games and Activities for Everyone.* New York: Walker, 1981. The title explains the contents, which are specific, detailed, and classroom- and family dinner table–tested.

———. *Limerence, Learning, Language and Literature: an Essay.* Orton Monograph 77 (1978).

Vygotsky, Lev. *Thought and Language.* Cambridge, Mass.: The MIT Press, 1962. This is the brief but powerful work of the Russian learning theorist and linguist. It is dense reading but important.

7. PSYCHOLOGICAL AVAILABILITY FOR SCHOOLWORK:
AROUSAL, ATTENTION, ACTION

Bowlby, John. *Loss, Sadness, and Depression.* New York: Basic Books, 1980. This excellent resource gives professionals and concerned adults a solid foundation of information and research.

Erikson, Erik H. *Identity: Youth and Crisis.* New York: W.W. Norton, 1968. Although this is not light fare, the interested reader will find wisdom and illustrative cases.

Francke, Linda Bird. *Growing Up Divorced.* New York: Simon & Schuster, 1983. This well-researched book is written primarily for the popular market.

LeShan, Eda. *Learning to Say Good-bye: When a Parent Dies.* New York: The Macmillan Company, 1976. This short, highly readable book written for the popular market is a wise, warm, practical exploration of a painful subject.

St. Exupéry, Antoine. *The Little Prince.* New York: Reynal & Hitchcock, 1943. Because this beautiful story can be read or heard on many levels, it is appropriate for students roughly from second grade on through old age. It should be read aloud *to* most children below fifth or sixth grade, giving them the chance to soak up the language and imagery.

Seligman, Martin E. P. *Helplessness: On Depression, Development and Death.* San Francisco: W.H. Freeman, 1975. This book is written for both the professional and popular markets, and although the subject matter is gloomy, the presentation is concise and interesting.

8. TESTING DEMYSTIFIED:
SCORES, INTERPRETATION, PLANNING

Bannatyne, A., Vance, H. B., and Singer, M. G. "Recategorization of WISC-R Subtest Scaled Scores for Learning Disabled Children." *The Journal of Learning Disabilities* 12, no. 8 (August 1979).

Gardner, Howard. *Frames of Mind: The Theory of Multiple Intelligences.* New York: Basic Books, 1983.

International Reading Association. *How to Use WISC-R Scores in Reading Diagnosis.* Newark, Del., 1986.

National Association of Independent Schools. *Glossary of Selected Terms for Testing, Commonly Seen Tests. Appendix: Test Publishers.* Prepared for NAIS by Alice Jackson. Boston, 1982.

Wechsler Intelligence Scale for Children, Revised, and its companions the *Wechsler Preschool and Primary Scale of Intelligence,* normed for children age three years, ten months, fifteen days, and the *Wechsler Adult Intelligence Scale,* normed for persons aged sixteen and above, are published by The Psychological Corporation.

9. MATURATION AND HIGHER EDUCATION:
GETTING IT ALL TOGETHER

Ansara, Alice. *Language Therapy to Salvage the College Potential of Dyslexic Adolescents.* Orton Monograph 78 (1972).

Bright, George. *The Adolescent with Scholastic Failure.* Orton Monograph 33 (1970).

Brown University. *Dyslexics at Brown: A Student Perspective.* One of a Series of Occasional Publications of the Office of the Dean of the College, Providence, June 1985.

Cordoni, Barbara. "A Directory of College LD Services." *The Journal of Learning Disabilities* 15, no. 9 (November 1982): 529–34.

Cowin, Pauline, and Graff, Virginia. *Comprehensive Treatment of the Older Disabled Reader.* Orton Monograph 28 (1977).

Dillon, Dorothy. "SAT Preparation and Independent Schools." *Independent School* (October 1984). (Boston: National Association of Independent Schools)

Gillespie, Jacquelyn. "The Pushouts: Academic Skills and Learning Disabilities in Continuation High School Students." *The Journal of Learning Disabilities* 15, no. 9 (November 1982): 539–40.

Heath, Douglas. "Academic Predictors of Adult Maturity and Competence." *Journal of Higher Education* 48 (1977): 613–32.

————. "Adolescent and Adult Predictors of Vocational Adaptation." *Journal of Vocational Behavior* 9 (1976): 1–19.

————. "Some Possible Effects of Occupation on the Maturing of

Professional Men." *Journal of Vocational Behavior* 11 (1977): 263–81.

————. "Teaching for Adult Effectiveness." *Journal of Experiential Education* 1 (1978): 6–11.

Hernnstein, Richard J., and Wilson, James Q. *Crime and Human Nature.* New York: Simon & Schuster, 1985. This complicated, somewhat controversial book is intended for the professional.

Hinds, Katherine. "Dyslexia." *Brown Alumni Monthly.* Providence: Brown University, December 1984/January 1985.

Hiss, William. "Coaching for the SATs: What the Colleges Think." *Independent School* (October 1984).

Howe, Bill. "A Language Skills Program for Secondary LD Students." *The Journal of Learning Disabilities* 15, no. 9 (November 1982): 541–44.

Kesselman-Turkel, J., and Peterson, F. *Study Smarts.* Chicago: Contemporary Books, 1981. This eighty-five-page paperback is a concise and funny gold mine guide to study skills. The kids who need it will read it.

Liscio, Mary Ann, ed. *A Guide to Colleges for Learning Disabled Students.* Orlando, Fla.: Academic Press, with Grune & Stratton, 1985. The title is self-explanatory.

National Association of Secondary School Principals. *College Study Skills Program.* Reston, Va. Developed by Milton Academy and Harvard University, this is available in student texts and instructor's guides, and offers high-class practical advice from top-quality schools. It says in more solemn and thorough terms what *Study Smarts* says briefly and humorously.

Ostertag, B., Baker, R. E., Howard, R. F., and Best, L. "Learning Disabled Programs in California Community Colleges." *The Journal of Learning Disabilities* 15, no. 9 (November 1982).

Rawson, Margaret. *Dyslexics as Adults: The Possibilities and the Challenge.* Orton Monograph 22 (1977).

Vogel, Susan A. "On Developing College LD Programs." *The Journal of Learning Disabilities* 15, no. 9 (November 1982).

RESOURCES

ORGANIZATIONS

The following organizations, through their publications, conferences, and research, are valuable resources for the concerned educator or parent.

The Alexander Graham Bell Association for the Deaf, 3417 Volta Place N.W., Washington, D.C. 20013, offers many materials that are suitable for students with marginal to moderately severe problems with auditory learning, as well as those whose hearing is severely impaired. Their catalogue is available free of charge.

The American Association for Gifted Children, 140 East Monument Avenue, Dayton, Ohio 45401.

Association for Children with Learning Disabilities, 155 Washington Avenue, Albany, New York 12210.

The Association for the Gifted (TAG), c/o Council for Exceptional Children, 1920 Association Drive, Reston, Virginia 22091.

Books on Tape (catalogue), P.O. Box 7090, Newport Beach, California 92660. Through Books on Tape, weak readers can hear books they can understand and enjoy but cannot yet read.

Educator's Publishing Service, 75 Moulton Street, Cambridge, Massachusetts 02238.

The Foundation for Children with Learning Disabilities, 99 Park Avenue, New York, New York 10016.

Literacy Volunteers of America, whose tutors are trained to work with adults, has branches all over the country. For information, contact their main headquarters: 404 Oak Street, Syracuse, New York 13203.

The National Association of Independent Schools, 18 Tremont Street, Boston, Massachusetts 02108.

The Orton Dyslexia Society, 724 York Road, Baltimore, Maryland 21204.

World Council for Gifted and Talented Children. Papers from their annual conference are published yearly by The Trillium Press, Box 921, New York, New York 10159.

PERIODICALS

Gifted Children Monthly. 213 Hollydell Drive, Sewell, New Jersey 08080. Articles and activities for roughly preschool through fifth or sixth grades.

The Gifted Child Today (formerly *G/C/T*), A Magazine for Parents and Teachers of Gifted, Creative and Talented Children. P.O. Box 6448, Mobile, Alabama 36660-0448.

School Success Network. Rosemont, New Jersey 08556. This newsletter, published three times a year, is written for parents and teachers of young children. Its title explains its emphasis.

INDEX

Index

THE GOOD BODY

THE GOOD BODY

A Novel

Bill Gaston

A Cormorant/Stoddart Book

The publishers gratefully acknowledge the support of their publishing programs by the Canada Council for the Arts and the Ontario Arts Council. The publishers also acknowledge the financial support of the Government of Canada through the Book Publishing Industry Development Program.

Published in 2000 by
Cormorant Books Inc.
RR 1, Dunvegan, Ontario, Canada K0C 1J0
&
Stoddart Publishing Co. Limited
34 Lesmill Road, Toronto, Ontario, Canada M3B 2T6

Cover design by Angel Guerra.
Printed and bound in Canada.

Distributed in Canada by:
General Distribution Services Ltd.
325 Humber College Blvd., Toronto, Canada M9W 7C3
tel (416) 213-1919   fax (416) 213-1917
E-mail customer.service@ccmailgw.genpub.com

04 03 02 01 00   1 2 3 4 5

Canadian Cataloguing in Publication Data
Gaston, Bill, 1953-
The good body : a novel
ISBN 1-896951-21-X
I. Title.
PS8563.A76G66 2000   C813'.54   C99-901528-1
PR9199.3.G38G66 2000

For R. A. Gaston
"Gaspipe"
1924-1999
Basketball Player

I

... on a sheet of clear ice, each man
can skate his name, cleanly as by hand
—Milton Acorn

... it is this delight, not yet known,
that takes you through the seasons.
—Rita Donovan, *Daisy Circus*

"I'm not the type of person who likes
to have a lot of operations."
—David Adams Richards, *Road to the Stilt House*

Doing seventy, pointing north, window wide open and elbow on the edge. The falling night rushed and pounded the left ear like loud flux, like chaos itself. Here we go, what's next.

Good to blow out the cloying perfume reek — yesterday he'd hung a second pine freshener from the rearview, and this morning in the car's enclosed heat he'd snapped its string and tossed it, wincing in the smell. It was like someone had spilled Mr. Clean in the seats. He'd left the old one up and dangling. Drained of scent and almost grey, a cardboard antique, it was a talisman that had come with the car, with him a decade now. Longer than any one person.

The old tree cut-out twirled in the car's night wind. Bonaduce looked higher into the rearview itself, the dark Maine interstate rushing away in the wrong direction, back to his old life. His gut flipped at the notion of steering with this sight alone.

North out of Bangor, five hours to go, there began a whacking on his roof so he pulled over to check things. The autumn cool felt okay on his neck. Stars were out and glaring in this clean air but he had no time for them. Funny how on trips you relax less the closer you get. He stuffed the flapping tarp under a suitcase corner and tightened the bungee cord, thinking he probably should have crammed more of this stuff in the back seat. But he loved using this roof rack, the gypsy load up there straining full, giving him a feeling in his body he could not name. Something like, home was where the car was. Something like, he was free and life was lucky. Loose Bonaduce.

When next he floored it to pass a car, the tightened cord howled in the wind. He passed another car and there it was, a shrieking steadiness, loud right over his head. The next time he passed he opened the window, reached up and grabbed the cord, but his grab only changed the tone, upping it an octave. He decided then to hear it not as noise but as a note, and smiled at the possibilities of this, the kind of smile rare to him since he'd heard his news and made his decision.

Playing the bungee cord meant he had to stay at speed, at least eighty for a clean tone. The road slicing the middle of Maine was fine and straight, but when he found himself falling into a downhill curve it took some teeth-clenched cool to keep the speed and the music going. It also cost him two tickets. These he tossed the second the cop was out of sight, for they were American tickets, and he was leaving for good. Between tickets he learned, by pinch, the cord's nearly three octaves. Its lowest notes were lost in the engine's drone, while its highest shriekers buzzed and thrilled his fingers in a way almost ticklingly sexual. By the time he crossed the border, and got his first Canadian ticket, which he kept, he'd roughed out "American Woman" and "Blue Christmas." He wondered if Jason would like, or even know, either song. He was well into the stupid arena-pleaser, "La Macarena" (he hoped Jason didn't like this one), when up came the lights of the small city he had decided would be home again.

Fredericton, there it was. He could admit he was nervous. The good butterflies. Only amateurs aren't nervous.

When to call Jason, when to announce himself? And would he call Leah at all?

In any case, here he was, Bonaduce back in town. After twenty years. Middle of the night, guitar on the roof, skates in the back, maybe two months' grace in the wallet. In the head, a doctor's news jockeyed for space with his plan.

At passing speed, squinting into the next few months, he hit the city limits, playing on his howling bungee an improvised, humble, speculative tune.

He woke. It was a Monday morning. He knew where he was, even the motel's name.

He did his stretches in front of the window, hanging on to the air conditioner. Okay. So what was all this worry about school? He'd done it before and always got himself over the hump. Ten, fifteen years had passed, so what. He had the way with words. Half Irish, half Italian — if that didn't make a poet, what did? If it took a while to get the pen looping and the tongue flapping, he could fall back on profs' mercy. Sir, I haven't thought seriously about literature or any of this in, let's see. Haven't really read a serious book in, let me think now.

Sir, it'll take a while to get the brain in game shape.

Start on push-ups today. He dropped to the brown shag, deciding to begin with two reps of thirty, add five more each day. Good it was a Monday. Monday was when you began something. And fall. A fall Monday was when you started school, or training camp, where — one of his favourite things — you put on the new uniform and looked down your chest at the unfamiliar colours of your new second skin. You read the upside-down emblem, which in the old days was embossed with heavy luminous thread: Express, Americans, Indians.

The secretary looked decent. Thirty, lanky, henna in the hair, baggy sweater, string of clunky wooden beads. She threw him a little smile while she dealt with two younger types ahead of him. He smiled back, meeting her eye over these kids keeping two adults from doing business. If he was a "mature" student, then by extension these two in front would be immature. Maybe she'd laugh at that.

Profs buzzed through, heads down in sheets of fresh xerox, rolling their eyes at some nuisance or other. It was going to be strange here, no question. A few looked younger than him. He hoped he wouldn't have to call them "sir." Jesus, could he physically, actually do that? "Doctor" would be even worse. Doctor Paragraph, heal me. There goes Doctor Comma, off to lunch with Doctor Diphthong.

Better if he got women. For some reason the power struggle had different rules with women. Too often during his part-time undergrad stints the manprofs had seemed less than comfortable with the basic look of him, the scarface and Bonaduce bulk, maybe the perceived readiness of his muscles, who knows. In any case, they had been driven by some urge to give him grades lower than deserved, to meet him not in the alley but with a chickenshit mark in the mail. His essays were decent enough. That one course, the Modern British, a seminar affair with about ten of them around a table — he'd been at the weights all summer and wore a T-shirt the first day and the reedy prof had had furtive eyes for his chest and whatnots and at the end of it all he'd received the shittiest mark of his life.

"Bobby Bonaduce?" The secretary looked up from the file folder that no doubt held record of that very mark.

"Robert."

He had decided to be "Robert" here. He must have signed his forms out of autograph habit. In grad-school world the "Bobby" would not help his already shaky credibility. He wasn't exactly a goon at a tea party, but he wasn't not that either. Forty-year-old named "Bobby." Neck thicker than any other two around here.

"I'm definitely 'Robert.'"

"Well" — she handed him a course list — "I'm definitely 'Lorna.' Since you're so late — we're a week and a half into classes—"

"Guess I'll have to buy a couple essays off somebody." He

gave her a deadpan she didn't see.

"—since you're so late you have to get the professors' permission, so you'd better choose fast and go and—"

"Can you tell me which of these are women?"

"Sorry?"

"There's just initials here." He rattled the course list at her. Only when he saw the look on her face did he realize how the question must have sounded. Maybe she thought that he thought he was sexy or something and wanted women profs for that reason. Or that she had in front of her some stiff old throwback who wouldn't be taught by a woman. Jesus, Lorna was looking at him hard. Maybe it was only that his morning five o'clock shadow was upon them both, and the scars were coming out bright white, and she had no clue about him, whatsoever.

He woke up surprised at any number of things.

At the window's view he did his stretches, which sometimes did and sometimes didn't affect the stupidity in his right foot, and considered the town below. The cathedral had recently gotten a new copper roof. The newest part was still shiny, while the older part was already turning black, on its weird way to that green.

Yesterday's drive through town had sparked so much memory, things he hadn't thought about for years. The butcher shop where Leah had insisted they buy their meat. The church where the wedding was, all those quiet Moncton relatives of hers he didn't know and met only the once. That tavern, now a pizza chain, where the owner had set up a used electroshock machine on the bar, some customers laughing, others wary of it.

Up the hill, a glimpse of the hospital where Jason was born had put Bonaduce right back in that yellow room. Light from that window falling on that tiny squinty face. *My god it's a little old wrinkleman.* He'd watched it all, a fairly daring thing for the dad to do in those days, though apparently it was strange not to do it now. Impromptu, the doctor asked if he wanted to cut the cord. Scissors were handed over and he'd stood hesitating long enough for the doctor to ask if he was shy of blood. He shook his head, unable to voice questions to do with the cord there, its pulsing, its unearthly colour — because, because whose was it? Leah's or Jason's? Who would it hurt, the cutting? When the doctor reached for the scissors Bonaduce went ahead and did it, it was tough like steak sinew. The blood came rich and thick, and neither mother nor son seemed bothered.

Down the hill from the hospital was the corner gas station where on Christmas Eve they'd bought a tree, Bonaduce home from a road trip for the only Christmas the three of them would spend together. Gripping the crook of the lowest branch, he'd dragged it home over the sidewalk snow, a perfect winter night, the heavy quiet. Leah carried Jason, who peered out from his ball of soft blankets, wide awake, watching it all. Two new parents agreeing that from the staring look in his eyes you could tell he was listening even harder, he was hearing more than seeing.

Twenty years later, driving in traffic, Bonaduce could see that look of his baby boy listening.

He hadn't meant to drive by her old place, but there it was, the tiny upstairs apartment, her window you could see from the street. All those early times there, her awful little bed, not much sleeping to do anyway, they couldn't get enough of each other. And that time — Bonaduce smiled, speeding up — her apartment door was unlocked and he'd walked in and surprised her at the kitchen table eating that unbelievable stuff right out of the can. Which had explained the mints she sometimes munched at the start of a date. A few months later that sober evening at the same table, her pregnancy news, his monotone proposal. Hustling out then after hugs and laughter and her tears, late for the team bus, shaking his head at life and breathing hard, fleeing this building, now painted a flaccid green, used to be white.

The station wagon was chugging a little, ominous. It missed the highway, it didn't like this city stop-and-start. For a last taste of nostalgia he kept going, up to the arena, and the boxy old thing made him feel his first job again. He'd been twenty, Jason's age.

The pride. Paid to play. Paid to *play*. People buying tickets to watch. He'd gone straight out and bought the Datsun 240Z, grinning into debt. He was making a living that would only get better, the NHL only a year away, for sure. For now, the Fredericton Express. He'd had trouble keeping down the grin as he checked out the dressing room, shook hands with the guys, found his stall with his jersey hanging in it. For days he sang about it in his head, singing his jersey number to the tune of the Bee Gees' "Stayin' Alive." *Ha. Ha. Ha. Ha.* Number *five*, number *five*.

Stretching at the window, he scanned Fredericton's rooftops. She lived on Grey Street now. Where was Grey Street? Jason's addresses had been different from hers the last couple of years, good; he'd left the nest, no mamma's boy. Did he live in a party house, wading through pizza boxes, cracking rude jokes with the boys, or did he have solo, studious digs? There was so much to find out about Jason, so much of it so basic. The ever-kindling guilt of the wayward Bonaduce.

He packed the car, checked out, found a cheaper hotel, unpacked again. Cheaper was better so long as the bed was hard. After a lunch of cheese, crackers and two apples, he drove down Waterloo Row to park by the river. Nice fall day. He recalled fall here to be a good one, breezy clear blue days, just the kind that helped the fresh start.

He got out of the car, looked at the river, took a breath. He'd done it. Fredericton. Here he was.

He had his jogging stuff on; he dipped down into groin and ham stretches before the run. It was stupid to be afraid of bumping into either of them, it wasn't that small a town. Though it hadn't grown much. A few more red-brick buildings downtown, a few fewer elms. Of course the river hadn't changed at all. Twenty years ago he'd parked here in the same spot, doing what he was doing now — getting ready to jog but also watching, smelling, this moving mass. Feeling the weight of it, the dark authority of a big river, the hugeness of its intrusion and, as it swept by, the impersonal departure. No hello or goodbye. Rivers were essentially foreign. Almost eerie. Bonaduce had always thought of rivers as the place people drowned.

Watching the water leaving town, he found the names coming unbidden: Rochester, Kalamazoo, Tulsa, Las Vegas, Utica. Fredericton again. Some by trade, some by choice, in two decades the places he had called home.

Staying down in a toe-touch, he tightened his shoes. Blood filled his head, he wasn't in shape. But some months ago in Utica his right hand had bungled this job of tying a shoe. Today the hand was a magician again, fingers so fast you could hardly follow them.

He erased the phony poetry thought about a river once taking him away and now bringing him back.

Jog. *Jog.* Onomatopoeia, a litword he remembered. Buzz, whack, yodel, they sound how they mean. *Jog.* Jog the legs, the spine, the body into a pleasant stupor, hardbreathing. Jog the brain into a memory he should have had but didn't, Jason with him here, jogging this forest path, puffing along behind, unbearable sound of your child's pleading breath. *Hey, Jase, you, lookin', forward, to, puttin' on, the skates?* No answer but the boy's noncommittal grunt, the boy in pain, hung over from a night out with his buddies, and a non-jogger to boot, in youth scornful of these maintenance measures. But jogging anyway, knowing the truth of the father's example. *Son the, mortal coil needs care, the bone-rig needs, tending for the, long haul.* Parking lot in sight, the dad does the corny thing, letting his puffing boy catch up and pass him at the finish.

. . .

Pen and blank sheet of paper on the tiny formica table. Large McDonald's coffee. Printed at the top of the sheet:

TO DO:

He felt cold and crusty under his clothes from the run. And ridiculously winded — two days of solid driving, the body falls way out of tune. But full feeling in the feet. Running, he'd felt almost bloody graceful. Doctors are best at arrogance.

Sad to end up in a food court. He'd cruised the town hungry, passing little pasta parlours and coffee bars, for some reason not stopping. Why not just accept it as a comfort that you feel at home in a food court? In this mall, with this coffee, you were anywhere on the continent. To get a bit cosmic with it — or "postmodern"? He had to get to the bottom of "postmodern" — he was everywhere on the continent at once. McDonald's had done this, and Ted Turner had done this too, hiring his unidentifiably clean Yankee voices. These Fredericton mall kids wearing Nike hats — shoe company conquers the planet's feet and now does the head. It was like something out of *Batman* — Sameness Drops diabolically added to the water supply.

1. skates sharpened

Aside from these Freddie kids looking less dangerous than American kids, scowls a little less earned maybe, and almost no kids of colour, the people of Fredericton looked just as stunned as they did in Springfield or Kalamazoo.

Impossible not to look stunned in a mall. Automatically tired, skin pale under fluorescent sky. Suggestion of mouth agape. A dumb hunt. You could imagine a scene a million years ago wherein some Cro-Magnon entrepreneur stocked a forest clearing with tethered hare, mudpools of carp, mounds of fruit, a few big-ticket U-Kill antelope, and let the Neanderthals in to "hunt," provided they had the shiny rocks to exchange. This the birth of the Mall Age. Of the Vicarious Era, marked by rapidly devolving human muscle. Which led to sports fans, to people paying others to play their hard-body games for them, thus giving Bonaduce a job, and so what was he complaining about.

2. place to live

A question of balance here. If he went for the one-bedroom over the bachelor, he'd need a part-time job. If he got the meanest shared flop he could find, he could maybe make it on the assistantship they'd promised him today. He could get a thousand for the car if anyone believed him that it came from south of the Rust Belt. But carless he'd have to rent closer to campus, higher rent, vicious cycle. And how could you go carless? How, when midnight came and your foot started tapping, could you not have your car out there waiting with its roof rack and headlights and map of the big picture ...

Maybe he should sell the car as a gesture to roots here.

There was still the chance, a small chance, of the cheque. The Utica courts might come through. How could Wharton get away with it? How could a guy declare bankruptcy, fold a team and renege on the payroll, even as his car dealership stayed open and looked healthy as hell, rows of shiny Japanese cars and dayglo pennants flapping in the breeze? So what if during the period in question Bonaduce hadn't been quite up to playing. A contract was a contract. Eight thousand dollars — almost twelve Canadian — would be just fine. Fournier was still with his girl-friend in Utica and he'd promised to keep Bonaduce posted.

Rent, books, food, money money money. He'd never had a secure thing but here he was at forty thinking week-to-week. Hand-to-mouth Bonaduce. But a thought: while Canadian schools couldn't give athletic scholarships, there were rumoured "subsidies" for the best players. So maybe he'd get some under-the-table. He'd go see the coach, stick out his hand and announce his intentions. Bob Bonaduce, I'm back in school, I'm thinking of playing for you. Or, "trying out." Best be humble, polite. There was no question of not making it. The floppiness had almost left, the motor was fine thank you. At his age he had a good year or two left at this level, no sweat.

3. Get coach's name, call coach

Though once he announced himself to the coach, the cat was out of the bag. A less-than-cool way for Jason to find out about any of this.

4. Call Jason

Writing this, he caught himself feeling almost comically nervous. Jesus. So what else?

5. Buy books

He'd scanned the reading lists. Regardless of what courses he took, the number of books he was to have read over the summer was enormous in itself, and the number he was to read between now and Christmas was similarly impossible.

He studied number 5. What about not buying any books at all, see how that went. He crossed out number 5.

Jason's letter had done it. The letter had come during one of those days, the kind which tell you from the start you're having a turn under luck's big magnifying glass: traffic lights would either all turn green for you, or all turn red; you could win the lottery, walk on water, or be singled out in a mall and executed by a maniac. Anything *would* happen today.

First — he was just going out the door, to the doctor for test results — a call came from Fournier about Wharton folding the team and skipping out. Season over, no pay, no job. Then — he was back from the doctor, just in the door, feeling hollow and cold and shaking his head in recognition of what a lifespan is — Jason's letter clattered through the mail slot, hitting his knee, making him jump. Jason, whose letters came maybe every two years, one letter for every three of his. Bonaduce would've written more but hadn't wanted to force the relationship more than his unanswered letters did already.

He picked up Jason's letter, looked at it, waggled it for weight, announced to its return address, "Hey, Jason. Dad's got multiple sclerosis."

He was being dramatic of course, in the throes of fresh news, not belief. He read his son's letter, barely skimming the surface of its content, seeing more the texture of his boy's typing, feeling its effort and intent, amazed that his boy could think, decide, punctuate. A recent big decision, said the letter, was to quit his last year of junior in favour of university, playing there. More and more guys, Jason explained, had been jumping into pro from college.

And Bonaduce, seconds later, phoning the University of New Brunswick for registration forms. It was one of those things you couldn't put much thought to. He knew it was utterly corny every whichway. Tiny Tim territory. In no direction could you escape the corn of it. While Bobby Bonaduce could still skate, he was going north to enrol in school and play on the same team as his long-abandoned son.

God bless him, every one.

He unhooked the roof-rack bungees and lugged his stuff inside. The guy named Rod had disappeared upstairs but the big girl, Margaret, helped. Things were finally taking a good turn — after six ugly days he'd found himself a place. Town full of students, what did he expect. But here he was, and you couldn't argue a hundred-forty a month. Over on the north side, or wrong side, of the river, and a few miles out of town, the old house was paint-thirsty and gap-shingled, and right on the highway. He'd be sharing its one bathroom with three girls and two guys. His room was so small that, in his head, he was thinking quotation marks around "room." He suspected his housemates were making a secret buck off the landlord by renting out what was perhaps an old sewing room — but you couldn't argue one-forty a month. Heat included. No closet, but furnished. Or, "furnished." He could find a board to put under the mattress. You could *panhandle* one-forty a month.

"We each keep our own food like, separate," Margaret was saying as he slid a suitcase under his bed. "But I mean, sometimes we make meals together. Not that much. Weekends. You could keep your food, I don't know, in like, a box or something."

Margaret probably thought a bit about food. She was fairly tall but up around the one-seventy, one-eighty mark it looked like. But nice, smirking and gum-chewing like a guy. She was leaning on his door frame and he could smell her minty breath. When certain people are nice you feel bad noticing their body.

"Marg? I like your earrings." She had what must be ten of them, mostly small hoops, in her right ear.

"Of course you do." Smiling, chewing her gum, her sarcasm including her as much as him, and nothing but pleasant.

"Whatcha got, about ten in there?"

"About. I could make us some tea?"

"Great. GREAT." A roaring *whoosh* from the highway made him repeat himself. It wasn't rush hour yet.

"Herbal? Black? Gunpowder?"

"Herbal, great." He was tempted to go Gunpowder to see what he got, maybe some in-crowd concoction. Booze or drugs even, you never knew. Not hard to tell from Margaret or the decor what sorts his roomies were. Probably casual smokers. A little tokahontas never hurt anyone, he might even join them. Each room had a couple of arty candles. The rooms themselves were painted in the clash-colours of past tenants. Not overly clean. Without looking for them you could see cobwebs in ceiling corners, and the smell of incense armwrestling mildew. Rod and Margaret had been asking one-fifty but dropped it ten when they saw his car and he said sure to her question, "Some of us are like, students too, and could we maybe get a ride in when you go?"

Margaret shouted from the living room that the tea was ready. Absurdly, first he checked his hirsute self in the mirror strung up on a hook on his wall. It would be too utterly bizarre to dig out his razor and shave. But he patted his hair down.

They sat blowing politely into their teacups. Margaret had closed a window, but they still needed to talk loud to overcrow the *whooshing*s, especially the semis, whose shadows also pounded into the room, preceding the *whoosh* by a split second. In the silences Margaret seemed a little nervous, and Bonaduce's stomach hollowed as he recalled the formula: three girls, two guys ... Now three guys, even-steven. Newly alert, he looked up at Margaret just as she looked up at him too. He looked blinking back into his tea. Well, Jesus, don't be an asshole. Forty, broke, roughish face. No catch himself. Anyone studenting at his age had obviously foundered on one of life's more basic reefs.

"Actually at night I love it. My room's like, right above yours. Puts me to sleep."

"Sorry? It?"

She jerked her head toward the window. "Truck-noise."

"Ah." Bonaduce exhaled. "Well I keep a little fish bonker beside my bed for the same purpose." Bonaduce made as if to whack himself two hard ones on the bean and Margaret laughed.

"No, they're spaced apart at night. You can hear one coming, a low like, sort of something way in the distance. I pretend I'm sleeping on the beach in Maui and it's like, this wave coming, and it comes roaring in just like a breaker, *whoooOOOSSSSHHhhhh* ... So where'd you like get the scars? Rod said you were either an axe murderer or a hockey player."

The room had a pastel, thickened feel from the layers and layers of paint, the latest one pale lemon. Floating dust added a dreaminess. Margaret chewed her gum with confidence, eyeing him with an off-kilter but intelligent glint.

He rasped like Brando, "Rod was right. See, I never did get the hang of skating." He waggled demonic brows at her. She smiled, no more afraid of any of this than he was. She'd be fun, she'd be okay. He could play guitar and sing in front of her, no problem.

"So Marg. What sort of student are you?"

"Not good, if that's what you mean."

"What are you taking?"

"Archaeology, only they don't really have a program here."

"Ah."

"I'm thinking of packing it in."

"No way."

"Well, yes."

"Marg? There's this saying. And as your elder, you have to listen and obey."

"I have always obeyed you."

"Marg? 'You sign your name, you play the game.'"

"Okay, sure," she said, not considering the Bonaduce maxim for more than a second. "And so like, what if the game's the shits?"

"Doesn't matter. Quitting feels shittier. It's true."

Unconvinced, or maybe she'd stopped listening, she pointed out the window to the stand of trees across the highway, near the river.

"Look. A pileated woodpecker. *Wow* they're big. I think it is one."

He tried to picture Marg in the academic world and couldn't quite. It wasn't just the way she talked. It was her humanness. He imagined her walking the halls head down, ashamed, insulted. Perhaps there were some human profs there too, but this morning he hadn't met them.

. . .

He'd sought out his preferred profs and got in to see two. First, Doctor Gail Smith and her "Canadian Writers of the British Diaspora." He liked CanLit.

Bonaduce had long ago become wary of that brand of person who strategically doesn't say much, leaving you to stammer in the articulate pressure of their gaze. Some reporters tried that. But reporters you just played dumb with.

Her door was wide open. He knocked anyway and she watched him do this. She was maybe five years his junior. He stated his business. After a silent stare of ten seconds or so, sizing him up, she turned to her computer screen to ask, "Why do you want to take my seminar?" She hadn't exactly emphasized the "you" in her question, nor was its tone quite "What is two plus two?" but nonetheless it threw Bonaduce for a loop. First he answered her silence with some of his own. No way a joke or knowing smile (she still wasn't looking at him) or chummy reference to their shared age would deflect the question. There were correct answers, and there were honest answers, and as usual the honest ones were ridiculous: Because I need to take something. Because you're a woman. Because, though the doctors are wrong, I might not have much ice-time left and I want to play hockey with my son.

"Because I wanted to find out, you know, more about it."

"It ...?" Staring harder into her computer and starting to type.

"Canadian writing. And—"

The typing stopped. The room froze with intelligence.

"—and, you know, the, the British diaspora."

"*Dee*aspora?"

"Well, tom*ay*to, tom*ah*to. But, sure, *die*aspora." He knew that she knew that asking him the word's meaning would be cruel, and of course fruitless.

Typing and reading her screen, speaking in a monotone that suggested jowls-to-come, Professor Smith used whatever portion of her brain it took to say, "Lowry this week. *Volcano*. Brian Moore next." She pronounced Brian *Bree*an. "Lorna has the reading list."

He held up his xerox sheet and smiled. "I already have ..."
She was so busy not noticing him now that he didn't finish.

Maybe if he had shaved.

Professor Daniel Kirk, his course called "New Traditions in the Carnivalesque," was perhaps fifty. He leapt to his feet, he stuck out his hand, he was all bootlick and smile, saying, "Dan Kirk! Read your application! Used to go to the Express games!" but Bonaduce knew he'd be calling him "Professor." He was the kind of eager, buttclenched male animal who would smile and meet your eye while checking out everything about you, alert to danger. His office felt like a lair of radical pettiness.

Bonaduce felt himself mirror Kirk's beaming smile. Shaking the man's hand, he knew a shitty mark when he saw one.

A Coke in his fist, cubes rattling, he went table to table in the Student Union Building cafeteria asking questions. The team name had just been changed from the "Red Devils" to the "Varsity Reds," this reportedly having something to do with Fredericton being a fundamental notch in the Bible Belt. The season started in two weeks, a road trip to Nova Scotia against Dalhousie, then Acadia. The coach was Michael Whetter, and he could probably be reached through the Athletics Department. He was believed to be quite young, maybe even late twenties. No one knew if he had played any pro.

Bonaduce had hoped to find at the helm an old crony, or at least someone who'd heard of Bobby Bonaduce. At worst, and this might be the case here, it was some youngster who'd kept all his teeth, played college and then gone to coaching school to learn the European stuff: the jogging with medicine balls, the five-man rotating unit, the playing flimsy and falling down howling if somebody nudged you.

It's not like you wanted to be handed a spot on the team. It's just that when you're not in the greatest shape it would be easier for all concerned if you were dealing with someone who knew what you could do. Because in training camp you don't go out and bash. These guys were going to be your buddies; you had their knees, shoulders to worry about; you saved the bashing for the enemy. This was a concern because, from the look of things, he might be forced to go out and impress someone, show what he could do. And what he could do was bash.

The meal had an edgy, formal quality to it, and Margaret seemed almost nervous. Nervousness didn't suit someone like her. Bonaduce suspected she'd gone backstage and campaigned to have everyone eat together tonight and welcome the new guy. Not present was the other woman, Joyce, who apparently almost never left her boyfriend's. So much for Bonaduce's mating-math.

It was him, Marg, Rod, and he was introduced to the two others. One was a poor guy named Toby who had a withered arm held like a fleshy hook against his chest. Toby was a smiler, but behind the smile was that brand of whatever hell it was to grow up with an arm like that. The other person, Beth, turned out to be Marg's sister, and Beth was even bigger, and six feet at least.

Margaret brought their plates out two at a time. Unlike the others, Bonaduce waited for her to sit before he began, though he didn't think she noticed.

Marg looked beautiful next to her sister, Beth. Beth wasn't quite walleyed, wasn't exactly hulking, but those were words you'd use. She hunched over her plate, protective of her food. Her thin, tightly curled hair made Bonaduce imagine her bald when old. He looked at Marg and saw her being bald too.

"So where's 'Ralph'?" Toby asked Beth, taking some bored pleasure in overpronouncing this name. Bonaduce had heard Toby refer to the boyfriend as "Ralph the Forestry Ape." He'd surmised too that Beth doted on him, and that Marg was a bit worried that her sister's love seemed desperate.

"At a funeral," Beth answered, shovelling a forkload. "One of his profs." She spoke with her mouth full, and Bonaduce had to look away.

They were eating something Marg had cooked and called "student gourmet" — mac and cheese with extras thrown in. Bonaduce embarrassed himself commenting on what tough but tasty tomatoes they had here in New Brunswick, meaning this as a sort of compliment, and Marg having to explain about sun-dried.

"So. Robert." Marg cleared her throat for the rehearsed question. "So like, what brought you up here? To do English lit."

"Well, that's" — he chuckled for her, shaking his head — "that's a complicated one."

"Oh, the chain," Toby said slowly, mocking no one in particular, "of pain."

"Well, yeah, it's always complicated," Bonaduce offered. "But I guess here I could say it was either push rust in Utica, or English lit here."

"'Push rust' ...?"

"Sell cars."

"Sounds like a bad name for a band," said Toby, making a show of buttering with his good hand while holding the bread to the table with his bad elbow. "'Push Rust.'"

"No," continued Marg, "but like, why here? You've been all over. And apparently unencumbered. I mean, *New Brunswick*?"

"What you do is this." He smiled to tell them he was both joking and not. "You turn forty. You find an atlas, have a few beers, close your eyes and go" — he closed his eyes, twirled his finger, then stabbed — "Hey, New Brunswick!"

He dipped his head and ate. Dinner would soon be over. Things would settle in a week and be just normally friendly. He had no doubt now that this was Marg's work. She had asked Rod, who'd been reading a book in his lap, to put on one of his classical discs. It played quietly now in the background, making you want to sit up straight. Toby, proud to know, announced Vivaldi. Bonaduce had heard it before, it was a common one, almost elevator. Toby announced further that they were listening to "Spring." When Rod told him it was "Winter," Toby said it should be "Spring," because those plipping sounds were so totally like icicles melting.

This guy Toby, amazing. Suggesting Vivaldi had gotten his seasons wrong.

It was Krieger who changed Bonaduce's outlook on hockey as a job.

Krieger was finishing his career in Kalamazoo just as Bonaduce got there. A basher and a crasher and the team captain, he was one of the characters you meet. He'd had his nose broken a bunch of times and was fond of saying that on windy days he didn't know what side of his face his nose would end up on. If asked about his scars, Krieger might say someone had put out his face fire with a shovel. If you sat next to him at the restaurant and displayed an appetite, you might hear your dining style likened to a starving man sucking a dog through a keyhole. Krieger's hyperbole.

Bonaduce's second year there, Krieger retired but stayed in town as a car salesman, which is what lots of guys did, cashing in on what local popularity might have accrued. Also they were essentially homeless otherwise. Certainly jobless. Bonaduce easily pictured Krieger selling cars, leading a customer around, nodding at the car's back seat and making some outlandish sex joke, and the customer feeling included in the panache of professional sports.

The team missed the bruising Krieger. Certain tough guys come to be mother hens more than anything else. When play stops they check for scuffles, concern on their faces, protective. They are respected and don't have to fight much any more. In any case, with Krieger freshly gone, Bonaduce said what the hell and stepped up his grit to fill the void. He had to try something. He hadn't climbed leagues and he was twenty-five.

Slash, spear, elbows always up. I'm meaner than you. Drop the gloves first, get in the first punch. In front of the net be a constant menace, a fucking monster. Your goalie's your helpless naked mother and nobody gets near. It wasn't so hard: you'd been living on the edge of malice to begin with.

Though the face got messier, the style paid dividends. That first year he came close to the IHL penalty record, he got the loudest cheers at home and the loudest boos away, the local paper said it was like he'd miraculously come out of nowhere, and once suggested that if Bobby Bonaduce ran for mayor, well, hey. Until he was traded again two years later, a few of the guys called him "Mayor," or even "Your Worship," which is what the mayor of Kalamazoo was referred to, politics being as full of hyperbole as Krieger. But even though violence didn't get Bonaduce the phone call from above, he was now a known commodity, a leader, a mature influence some team would need. He'd been made captain.

Though what had really fuelled his new violence, if the truth were told, was the sight of Krieger selling cars. Bonaduce drove past on his way to the rink and he'd see Krieger in the floor-to-ceiling window, sitting there at a communal desk, waiting for customers, Krieger's boredom clear even at this speed and from this distance. It was the "Used" lot — they generally stuck the ex-players there, the idea being that hockey fans were more the Used than the New market. Krieger would probably sell a few cars, but still.

What Bonaduce had seen through the window was that, when

you quit the minors, selling cars was about as good as it got. He'd seen a few retirees jump into assistant coaching, but they were the keeners, the hockey-Eddies. He'd seen others go into what turned out to be shady business deals. Some went into security, donning fake cop gear to walk empty malls at night. And he'd seen guys keep at the beer like they'd always done while playing, only now they ballooned, adding forty, fifty pounds in a few years. Some drank more than ever, more than beer, and some — you heard stories — got into dealing dope. Rumours of downtown violence, detox, bad guys from Colombia. Some of the names you heard had faces. You could remember crashing corners with some of them. You could remember the grace of so-and-so's stride, and you could understand the bitterness that maybe helped take him down, because he and everyone else knew he should have been in the NHL from the start but management was too stupid to see it.

You'd heard of other teams offering career counselling for older players. While it may have been coincidence, two weeks after an old 'Mazoo alumnus, a guy named Al White, was found dead in a Boston alley, such counselling was offered to a few of them, including Bob Bonaduce, who was now twenty-six, an *older player*. This was about as mood-enhancing as writing your law-school finals and on your way out being handed an application for employment at McDonald's. To attend a session was to finally admit you were not going to the bigs. No one signed up.

What Bonaduce did do by way of career enhancement was enrol in an English course.

His third prof he met the next morning in class. He stumbled in late and she rose from her chair in greeting.

"Jan Dionne" was all she said, giving him her hand in a clumsy, human way. Finally, a professor who didn't have to act like one.

"Jan? Bob Bonaduce."

This was "Creative Writing: Longer Narrative Forms." Bonaduce was registered in the creative-writing option, meaning this was his speciality, this was what he would do next year's thesis in. He had already decided to write a novel. According to her thumbnail bio, Jan Dionne was primarily a poet. This fact made Bonaduce sweat a bit, thinking of his application. But what were the chances?

He sat and took stock. A seminar, there were only three other students, and Jan Dionne, around a table. Hard to hide in this one.

The other male in the room looked maybe Jason's age, and he wore traditional artist's gear — tight black refuse and a glower. Name of Philip. Serious business, this guy. One young woman was uncomfortably pretty, blonde, with unforthcoming but potentially wild eyes, hard to read. Her name also happened to be Jan. (Bonaduce dubbed them "Big Jan" and "Little Jan," an age thing, because they were the same size.) And there was Kirsten. Glasses and, though she may yet turn out to be nice, she cast upon the room a constant lip-length sneer, one that wrinkled her nose and bared her upper teeth. They were never not bared. It was like she'd once been struck snarky by one of youth's big sticks and her face had set this way. Kirsten didn't look at him long enough for him to nod to.

"You look lost." Big Jan was smiling at him.

"Well, you know. I'll catch up."

"We can get a coffee after this and I'll fill you in?"

"Great."

Big Jan explained that they were doing "plot-building exercises" begun last week. She invited him to jump in if he cared to. She had given them a scenario whereby a person turns a corner and hears a scream. The idea was to come up with what happens next, the goal being something called "artful incongruity" — which Little Jan, perhaps seeing in Bonaduce's face something other than comprehension, explained was "some plot device that's unexpected but not so out there that it's just bizarre."

They went round the table with their incongruous plots and

Bonaduce heard nothing too good in any of it. Kirsten's was actually sort of stupid, in that a woman screamed because the guy was naked, which was fine, but then she had the guy wake up, it was all a dream. Big Jan pointed out that using a dream to end a plot was clichéd and a cop-out, to which Kirsten, lip lifting and nose wrinkling, asked whether fiction wasn't a cop-out by definition. To which Big Jan said, while that may be true, such discussion lay in literary theory, whereas this course was about craft, about what worked dramatically. When Kirsten fell into an unconvinced, talentless stare, Bonaduce found relief in the knowledge that her presence in the class would take some of the pressure off him.

This relaxed him enough to contribute when his turn came. They were about to move to the next exercise when he half-raised his hand.

"Bob?"

"This is off the cuff."

"That's fine. So: fellow comes around the corner, there's a scream and— First, your character's name? And occupation?"

"He's, you know, unemployed. Newly unemployed. Name of — Robert."

"What happens next?"

"Okay. First, it's his own scream. It's him screaming."

"Okay. Good. So what's he screaming at?"

"Well, everything. The details."

"What sort of details?"

"Well, it's sort of random. Just all the shitty stuff. All the details that sort of work at you—"

He put his hands up and worked his fingers like chaotic worms, half-noticing that those on the right hand weren't going as fast as those on the left ... *and depending on the pattern of plaque it'll be one hand or the other, one foot or the other, thankfully not both ...*

"—the details that suddenly get you. Make you scream."

"Okay, so what happens next?"

"He dies. Boom. Totally unexpected."

Jan's eagerness fell. "Well, cop-out. It's like Kirsten's dream, a convenient—"

"It's not the end. It's the beginning of a story about his after-life."

Big Jan looked willing to be eager again.

"It's been done in movies and stuff, I know," Bonaduce continued modestly, "but if you write it really straight, the reader won't expect it, won't even know he's there, because there's no trumpets and stuff. That's your incongruity. That it's just ordinary."

"An afterlife ..." Jan Dionne shrugged at the size of this.

"Another incongruity is that the same shitty details are there, but now he knows what they mean. He feels foolish for blowing it all his life. His main feeling in the afterlife is embarrassment, and" — what was that word — "atonement."

Bonaduce took in the details of Philip shutting down, Little Jan's ass shifting, Kirsten's teeth watching him.

Jan laughed again. "You've done some thinking about this."

"Jan? You hit a certain age."

Jan Dionne would be workable. She was an eye-to-eye prof, one who began by respecting you and then you could blow it or not. Over a coffee in the English Department lounge, surrounded by some definitely non-human types, she filled him in. The course was a workshop. You brought in your stuff, everyone discussed it, you took it home and fixed it. At year's end she had to — Jan whispered this bit — assign your stuff a grade, but only because academe — she shot the others in the lounge a dismissive look — demanded it. It's a struggle for us here, she added, meeting his eye, the "us" including him, and meant "writers." Her gaze lingered into uncomfortable silence, and it was in this moment that Bonaduce became aware of her hairless chin, her facebones, her breasts, and the rest of her difference and unknowability — her as a woman. He felt this as both a bridge and a distance.

"I forgot to mention that I enjoyed your poetry," Jan said as they stood. So sincere she wasn't smiling. "Very much. I didn't read the whole portfolio, but enough to know it was extremely good. 'Eclectic' is right."

"Hey." A slight shrug. What were the chances. Don't meet her eye. Let her misread fear as humility.

"'Till Death Do Us.' The sex/cannibalism ironies were so layered. 'My flesh, the salt of your kiss, the teeth of time...'"

"Hey." Jesus, quoting the stuff. He hardly remembered typing that one. "Do you remember one called 'Blades'?"

"No. Sorry." She paused apologetically. "But I remember lots. Have you thought about a collection? What I saw was certainly publishable. Here and there I was intimidated, to tell you the truth. That one, 'Aeolia,' my goodness, and so different from—"

"Stuff I worked at over the years. Long bus trips, not much else to—"

"That's right! I know! You're a hockey player! People are talking about that."

A shrug, a dull look away to deflect this direction. Afraid as he was, it was disappointing watching her turn into a hockey fan.

"Any newer work you'd like me to see? Poetry is my area."

"Actually I think I've packed it in. Fiction is all I do now. My new area. Writing a novel for my thesis."

"You've started it?"

"Thought I'd get the jump on it."

"You going to bring it to the workshop?"

"Why not."

To get into the creative-writing option, which let you do two fewer academic courses, he'd had to submit "a portfolio of recent creative work." He had no such work, recent or otherwise, save for two old poems, and no time to write more. He could write, he knew he could write. In the meantime, there in the college library in Utica were all these literary journals — *Mississippi Review*, *Ploughshares*, *Alchemy* — a slew of unread anthologies of unknown poets' unknown poems.

It took him an afternoon and evening to select and type twenty-eight pages of poetry. And his own two, "Blades" and "Black Hogs." Describing his work in the cover letter, he used the words "eclectic range," and "postmodern."

As arranged, he met Marg outside the library, where she'd been studying, and they walked out to the student parking lot together. An almost balmy night. He remembered that Maritime weather was nothing but change, consistent change. Also that the extremes could be entertaining but you got sick a lot.

He took off his sweater and carried it in his hand. His other hand squeezed two books. He had to get a briefcase. Time to hit the yard sales. Marg was bookless, her long arms dangling not quite in rhythm to her pace.

"Haven't quit school yet, eh?" he asked as she waited at the locked passenger door. He searched for the key.

"Not yet." She smiled as he opened her door for her. "You know, like, not a lot of people lock their cars here?"

"I've been in the States for twenty years."

"Especially, I mean," she continued, and he was already wincing with the punch line, "cars like this."

It was warm enough to ride with the windows down. Marg marvelled at the eight track, and played with the old air freshener. She brought her nose to it.

"I think this has lost its power."

"Well, it's acquired new ones."

"Oh — this is your rabbit's foot." She nodded and seemed happy, like this was her territory.

"That's it." He paused. "Keeps me a lucky mess."

She looked genuinely interested in the grey cut-out now, fingering it with respect.

Lucky mess. It was Fournier who had called him this. That accidental way non-native speakers make poetry. Fournier, his best friend ever? Who knows. And why decide such a thing. But Fournier, Fournier and his watch exactly three hours late. Ask the time and it took him that little calculation. It was one of those many-buttoned watches with beepers and such, and Fournier would go into pidgin English to explain how he didn't know how to set it. But it had been perfectly three hours late for years. Out of the blue, in a rare insecure moment, Fournier had confessed to him that he'd set it this way when he was still Vancouver property, playing for their farm club, Hamilton, three time zones away. He'd bought this watch and set it and kept it at Vancouver time. The silly hopeful bastard, it had probably cursed him.

It was eleven when they pulled off the highway into their gravel drive. A motion-sensing light over the kitchen door shone in their faces. Bonaduce envisioned a year of this: arriving home, this light, Marg beside him, the old-oil smell of the gravel. Arriving "home."

"You're limping."

"Stiff." He hadn't realized he'd been helping himself along, one hand on the car.

Inside she asked if he wanted tea and he said okay and took a seat on the couch. Rod nodded to him and went back to his reading. Rod was always reading. You could hear someone in the shower and, mixing with the musk of an old house, smell the distant steam and soapiness.

He may have nodded off. Marg delivered his tea. She put a disc on, some soft Celtic instrumental. He picked up the case, The Irish Descendants. Not your most imaginative name. What he felt like, he didn't know why, was some Shirelles. Even some Supremes.

"Do you play Yahtzee?" Marg asked.

"Well, I don't know."

"It's dice, but sort of like poker."

"I know poker."

Marg located score sheets and two pencils, and what looked like a handful of dice. This was okay, this student life. Late night, tea, music, good company, no real worries. Yahtzee. He'd missed all this.

Bonaduce asked Rod if he wanted to play Yahtzee. Rod declined, smiling. Rod said almost nothing but you could tell he was a good guy.

"Do we bet?" he asked Marg, who was rattling the bones, warming them up.

"We could bet."

The taskmaster morning sunlight of fall. It didn't sound like any of his housemates were up and there was no evidence of them yet in the kitchen. Moving quietly, still a stranger here, he plugged in the kettle. Or tried to, missing the socket, his eyes still fastened more to dream details than to those of the waking world.

It was the kind of dream that shapes your morning and fills it with feeling long after it's forgotten. Jason was a Jason the father hadn't known, a boy of a prime sixteen, and they were all in bed together: Bonaduce, Jason, Leah. Dad in the middle. He could feel their heat. They'd all been jogging, in bright white track suits, though his own was muddy-dirty. In bed they still had these track suits on, and they were covered with a heavy comforter. It was hot but Bonaduce kept the comforter gripped to his neck in case anyone wanted to throw it off. No one said anything. Jason seemed concerned with food, and Bonaduce and Leah shared a proud knowing look at their son's appetite.

Three adults lying in bed together. Bonaduce shook his head, smiling gently, blowing into his coffee cup. He took the coffee to his room and sat on the unmade bed. He put a hand down, the bed still warm from the heat of him sleeping, the heat of his dream. Out the window, the maples were hinting at red, the poplars at yellow. The start of their pretty death.

He had the name and number scrawled on a napkin scrap. This piece of paper felt so electric in his pocket after two days, he had to smile at himself, how nervous he felt, how like a teenager afraid to call the special someone.

He decided that when he did call he would leave a message, and not have to talk. Ashamed of this cowardice, he plotted nonetheless to call on a Saturday night, a time any healthy young guy would be out-and-about. Hey — the message would say, and its tone would be neither pathetic nor too clever — Hey, guess who? Well, you sitting down? I'm in town. And I think maybe here for a while. Anyway, got some weird and wacky news. Gimme a call. Let's have a coffee or whatever. Be great to see you! Hope things are good and all that. It's been a while, eh?

Something along those lines. There was no telling how he'd be, how they'd be, if the call happened live. Even worse, way worse, if it happened in the flesh, face-to-face. That could be a stammering, awkward disaster. Better get the boy on the phone, leave a message, let him prepare.

Noon public-skate. The Lady Beaverbrook Arena. He'd practised here with the Express a few times. Outside it reminded him of a swimming pool because of its low contours and walls of blue tile.

He hadn't public-skated since he was a child. Outdoors in Winnipeg, at night. Lights strung up, music piped through bad speakers — Juliette, Rosemary Clooney — and couples skating hand in hand. Once in a while the Beatles as a treat for the kids, and a sudden licence to go wild. The young Bonaduce flying around, near misses, showing off. He remembered being grabbed mid-wildness by the coat scruff, yelled at by some old hero whose wife had her hands hidden in a white fur muff, like in a Hollywood movie.

He laced his skates. The smells always got to him. The water-melt on wood or rubber, the Zamboni fumes, sometimes ammonia, the old socks or wet cigars, or just the after-stink of your buddies. You always knew you were in an arena. How long had it been, six months? This would hurt.

The wall sign said noon was an adult-skate, no kids. Through the glass doors he could hear piped music, "Maggie Mae." And it *was* late September and, hey, he was back in school. The nice coincidence, the teenage astrology, of music. A whiff of a song like that from the window of a passing car could make you feel her skin, smell her shampoo, see the bark of the tree she braced against.

You can smell ice. The broad white sheet in front of you. He stepped on, the tiny vertigo of first-time-in-a-while. Mostly middle-aged and old men, here for exercise, skating a slow circle. Two couples. No muffs, but both were doing the fancy hand-hold. Born of Holland. Maybe Hollywood.

It was cowardly coming here, public-skating before reporting to the Varsity Reds. But he had to get the worst kinks out. He'd never not been in shape but he had to admit he was forty. And doctors were sometimes right, whatever; something grim had indeed attacked him, who knows what. But the legs felt decent. Right calf wasn't all there but it seemed to be suffering no loss of thrust. Better slow it down in fact, some people were watching. Public-skate protocol. Awful that they might think he was showing off, like there was a need to. He pictured himself losing his mind, doing some bashing here at the geriatric noon skate, something out of Monty Python. "Berserk Skater Maims Twenty Before Turning Blades On Self." Did they still have the *Daily Gleaner* here?

Actually it was a challenge to skate this slow.

Nor was there any doubt now. She was fighting not to look at him. Marilyn Bauer. Had to be. The veiled way she was eyeing back. They'd partied together two decades ago. Leah's friend Marilyn Bauer. Husband Dale? Dave? Marilyn and Dave. Dave had been with Leah before Bonaduce arrived on the scene, then they'd continued as friends. This now-platonic connection had nonetheless given Marilyn coy reciprocal claims on Bonaduce and, that's right, they'd had that flirt once under the table with their feet.

Marilyn Bauer looked ready to break into a smile the next time he chugged near. Fredericton had suddenly shrunk. Bonaduce left the ice, an early exit he would not read about in the Sports pages.

Time to suck it up and make some phone calls. What could either of them say? He was respectable. He was a grad student. He was a published poet.

He'd actually often thought of writing. Writing something. And not just when bored — the road trips, the bus, Jesus, the endless bad TV in the what-town-we-in hotel. Sometimes he was simply inspired. He'd write a bus-poem, usually a funny rhymer, and maybe set it to guitar for later, or maybe he'd show it to the guy beside him, depending who the guy was. He wasn't hiding anything, it wasn't that, they already all saw him as a freak, it's just that only certain guys would appreciate the clever lines.

How many times had some guy, knowing he'd taken another English course over the summer, yelled at him across the dressing room: So when you gonna write a book about us? They'd laugh and mock him for the booky weirdo that he was, but in their eyes you saw that they did feel their lives were worth writing about, and that they hoped maybe he would.

Maybe he would.

Getting "home" that evening he saw tacked to his door frame, hanging from a leather thong, a many-coloured spiderweb thing in a metal hoop. A few feathers dangled from it. It looked Indian, and it was apparently a gift. A taped note said: For your window, Margaret.

He took it down and rehung it in his window. And in doing so realized that he'd be seeing sunsets from this room, here was an orange one now. It wasn't a bad view altogether, he hadn't noticed this. Early peerings out had depressed him a little because it had looked so barren — unkempt fields and stunted trees fronted by a neighbour's heavy-equipment trailer permanently parked there, the trailer barren too. Greys and browns and the dying greens of fall. The scene had made him think of Jan Dionne's term "emotional landscape," which was where the main character found himself, and into which the clever author would plant traps and rewards. Well, if this scene was his emotional landscape, there were no rewards in sight, and probably no traps either, and it looked like it'd been decades since any author had come scheming by.

He scraped a crusty smidgen off the glass with a fingernail. If you wanted to, you could see this lack of drama out there as simplicity. This lack of colour as subtlety. More fuzzy than stark, like a watercolour. You could see it as an empty stage waiting for something to happen. Birds. Deer. They had to come. In two months, snow. There were worse things to watch than an empty stage. For now, this decent orange sunset. This Indian thing from Marg.

In the SUB cafeteria he thumbed through the *Daily Gleaner*, Fredericton's rag, searching for Sports, wanting to check up on the stats and lives of a few buddies. He couldn't help but notice the spelling mistakes, and the wildly bad headlines — "Seniors Pursue Recreational Pursuits" — and letters to the editor, half of which quoted the Bible while railing against a gay group's attempt to hold a Pride parade. Where was he, Montana?

Today's paper had a Health section, which he scanned, trying not to read "Kidney Symptoms and—" "Bowel Disease the Scourge of—" You get into reading this stuff and you turn hypochondriac, fearful every time you pee and things feel a little off. "Pancreatic Cancer Rare But—"

That's what Coach Murphy had had. Pancreatic. A fast one. The Tulsa players had taken turns in groups, it was easier that way, Murphy being a coach no one liked. Half-dozen guys shuffling around, trying to hide behind each other, no clue what to say. How ya doin' Coach. Can we get you anything Coach? We lost to Phoenix again last night, blew it in the third. Lame jokes about who blew it, shoulders punched, Coach Murphy manages a smile. In it you can see his corny gratitude and terror both. He cries, or maybe it was just pain, his face squeezing up like a baby's. He looked so weak, completely used up, no say about whether he cried or not, a leaf in some fatal wind. It didn't exactly cancel out their former sense of him, all that macho dressing-room bluster — it just made it seem pointless. The last time Bonaduce saw Coach Murphy, his head was turned to the window and he was unresponsive to them. He'd fallen to an even more basic state. Though *fallen* wasn't the word. His intelligence as such appeared gone, but you could see that his feeling for what he looked at — the light in the window — was deep. A yearning, but not even that complicated. A plant's basic connection to the sun.

One *Gleaner* article that caught Bonaduce's eye had him actually laughing out loud as he chewed his last french fry, kept him smiling as he sucked his large Coke through a straw. Doctors, oh they'd be duking it out over this one. It was about red wine, how someone had found something in it that looked damn close to a cure for cancer. Bonaduce could see the hypochondriacs arriving even now, sick line-ups at the liquor store, fists squeezing necks of plonk. Responses by other doctors would be a week away, articles about the dangers of guzzling, about how red wine *caused* cancer.

Doctors — he glanced at the young types slouched over their

fries and bookbags, as yet unstricken with any of this — doctors were our gods. Doctors certain of themselves and lord how we're glad they are. It's just these damned second and third opinions.

... Unfortunately for you it was a pyramidal attack ...

... Good news: the attack was pyramidal ...

... Now on the other hand, if you'd had a pyramidal episode ...

How, how could there be such basic contradictions?

Mr. Bonaduce, multiple sclerosis is genetic, is hereditary. Bob, may I call you Bob, MS is a matter of diet. Hello there, sir, pleased to meet you, multiple sclerosis is viral, something you caught as a child, and it flowers — I'm sorry, perhaps that's not a good word to use — twenty years later.

Well, doctors, I guess I don't really care how I got it as much as I want to know, how do I fix it?

Mr. Bonaduce, you don't. Your nerve roots are covered with a myelin sheath, which has been damaged, and blocked with this white crud, "plaque." It'll keep occurring, more and more. Bob? You fix it with diet, visualization and prayer. Sir, you can do any of the diets if you want, they probably won't hurt you, but mostly you rest, and take any number of drugs indicated by any number of symptoms.

Okay so I don't fix it. But if I have it — and I don't have it — give me the scenario. Tell me what would happen.

Bob, you will continue to experience deepening bouts of localized paralysis. Double vision or spot blindness. Fatigue. Fatigue is persistent. Pain. Later, aside from general immobility, of course incontinence must be provided for.

Incontinence? That's—

Yes. But, strangely, there's another, final thing.

What.

At this point euphoria is a common complaint. Well, since it's euphoria, "complaint" might not be the word to use in this—

That's funny.

But it suggests not only spinal and optic deterioration but also that somehow the actual brain tissue is—

He'd heard nothing more, frozen on the incontinence being provided for, on the image of diapers, unable to consider them and unable not to.

Sure, he probably shouldn't be drinking this Coke. Or having white bread, sugar, beer, Cheez Whiz, chips — right. Diet was one thing most of the gods agreed on, especially the alternative types. There was only one thing upon which all and everygod agreed: fatigue. *Don't, Mr. Bonaduce, Bob, sir, let yourself get overtired.*

Now how would a university student or hockey player ever get himself tired? Bonaduce rattled the cubes in his paper cup, sucking it dry, making the sound of a child finishing his milkshake. He savoured the dread possibility that Jason could come in here at any second. Bang, his son. His only blood family. Here's Dad hangin' in the SUB with a Coke, books scattered around. Hey Jace, how ya doin. Casual wave, like it hasn't been years, like Jason wasn't some unknown creature now, nothing remotely like the ten-year-old of their last handshake. Maybe nothing the same but the DNA.

Whoever Jason was now, he'd be thrown for the loop of his life. Off-balance and full of big questions. Frightened, in a word.

Well, better him than me.

Gail Smith's class was a secret hot room in hell Bonaduce hadn't known about. The intimate size of it, six, was extra-hell. Both black-mood Phil and glare-teeth Kirsten were in this one too.

Introductions were made for the latecomer. Bonaduce felt big and stupid already. In Winnipeg, because home room was French, if you were late you were *en retard*, and he hadn't dropped the association.

Gail Smith called everyone either Mister or Ms, and she herself was "Professor Smith." Bonaduce was about to witness her sitting up straight for three hours. He would not catch a smile, but to show she got a student's wry aside she did a thing where she turned down the corners of her mouth and jerked her head up and to the side, looking off into the sky with amusement and tolerance. It was like she saw herself as a seventy-year-old guy from Oxford. She could actually be kind of pretty except that she was so careful not to be.

Bonaduce would stay mum the whole time. The first hour was occupied by what looked like an argument, but probably wasn't, about what constituted "Britain." It seems that Professor Smith's inclusion of several South Asian writers on the list made Phil and Kirsten take offence on their behalf. Smith's point, that they were victims of British imperialism, and "forcibly adopted, as it were," seemed to rankle Kirsten in particular, in that she was certain the writers would be outraged at being thought victims. Smith countered that the only fact that mattered was that all these writers *had moved* — she almost shouted this. Which made Bonaduce wonder why she hadn't dropped the "British diaspora" thing and just called her course "Writers Who Have Moved." He also wondered if these writers — Vassanji, Ondaatje, Begamudré — would care what Smith or Kirsten thought. Luckily he didn't have to contribute this or any other musing, for these seminars were set up so that each week a different student did most of the talking, or "presented."

It wasn't as if Robert Bonaduce was afraid. Not overly. Humanly nervous in front of new humans. For all intents and purposes speaking a foreign language. People sat so alertly. Even Phil's dark slouch looked coiled and ready. Drawn blinds kept the sunlight outside where it belonged.

But all it was, really, was that these guys had worked up a decent act, all witty dash and brain-pizzazz. The ordinarys in the cheap seats could see this. But knowledge *was* power, and these types knew tons about that which the poor Bonaduce had no clue whereof nor whatsofuckingever. Phucking Phil, today's presenter, began his Malcolm Lowry spiel with shrugs and hand flaps as if to suggest he'd thrown some thoughts together out in the hall. Then launched into a sentence beginning, "Now of course the temptation is to foreground a reading of *Volcano* with a reading of Lowry's *life*, but those narrative contrivances in the text — linearity, closure, what have you — subsume in their very *artifice,* artifice by which the text, as 'novel,' derives, shall we say ..." Phil was especially good at belittling certain notions by pronouncing quotation marks around certain words and getting people to smile, and Smith to jerk her head back.

The sentence continued for quite some time, and at first Bonaduce was spellbound. Then worried that this was the way you talked in this room. Was he supposed to "present" in this language? Then he smiled, enjoying the notion of *This is Phil presenting.* He remembered hearing the word used like this before, as a verb with no object, in TV nature shows. When a goat stuck its chest out, or a salmon turned itself bright red, or an antelope lifted its ass to another's face, they were *presenting.* Ten minutes in, Bonaduce was stifling his laughter — at Professor Smith's stupidity for allowing such a sentence to continue, at his own stupidity for not having a clue what was being said, and at Phil's stupidity for caring about any of this in the first place. He grinned picturing himself when his turn came three weeks from now, him with his upper dentures out, *presenting* with a sloppy lisp, dumb-on-purpose, saying "Well I theen the movie on thith inthteada the book but," and he was wearing his hockey gear, and three days' beard, his posture *presenting* so to threaten violence if anyone fell from wide-eyed attention at anything he said. He grinned harder and shook his head with an insight into the essential difference between his last career and this new one: if in the other game you disagreed with someone, you physically attacked him. What made him laugh aloud and got him reprimanded by Smith, who asked him, as if he were six years old, to "Please share it," was the image of him understanding something Phil said enough to disagree with it, then lunging across the table and grabbing Phil's little arm and snapping it. Bonaduce decided against sharing this and mumbled an apology. Thinking himself understood, disagreed with and laughed at, Phil glared at him, and Bonaduce felt instantly overtired.

The ordeal was finally over. They gathered books and notes. Bonaduce had drawn a few decent pictures of his station wagon. He decided he could maybe do this course if he got serious and learned the rules, and the meaning of "postmodern," and next time read the book. Leaving the room, Bonaduce tried to be friendly to the other guy who'd just suffered through with him, a teammate if you will, a bespectacled Mr. Webster. Filing out, it was like the siren had gone, and they had lost but hadn't deserved to; they were bruised and weary and going for a shower together. Pointing to the slouched, exhausted Phil, Bonaduce threw an arm over Webster's little shoulders and whispered, "Guess we're gonna wanna buy our essays from *that* guy." Mr. Webster didn't look Bonaduce in the eye and his smile was nervous, but he did seem to know it was a joke.

In the department lounge, as usual, the glances at the Bonaduce body as he scanned the bulletin board or stole coffee, dropping two loud nickels into the can instead of quarters. Young or old, prof or student, library nerd or nose-ring artist — up came whisperings of *professional hockey player*. Looking at him harder by not looking, Bonaduce the walking car accident. He'd expected this, body-people being exotic to head-people. Models, athletes, embodied some kind of ideal, so said the Greeks, though the notion had lately fallen from favour. And him doubly exotic — accepted into grad school, a jock who presumably wasn't stupid. These types were magnanimous enough to enjoy the little thrill of a preconception broken. But, hey, he'd show them: he could be stupid in ways they'd never dreamed of.

They wanted to know about the fights. Especially those who thought they didn't want to know. Those who so quickly shrugged off the ludicrous subject in fact looked a bit like deer alert to a trouble-noise. Or they were hungry for the information, if only to have theories refuelled. It had not been a surprise to Bonaduce that half the fans at a New York boxing match were intellectuals, many of whom were women.

Stupid rough hayseed hockey players. Bonaduce wanted to explain things. He pictured the guys in the dressing room, on the bus, in the bar. The levels of wit he'd heard. But mostly it wasn't words, it was the way a guy being interviewed taped a stick while spouting bad clichés on purpose, or waggled his ass below the gaze of the camera. It was shared looks at the swelling colour of a teammate's knee. It was hotel and nightclub and taxi savvy. It was sound public management of pride and envy, something academics were famously inept at.

Language, simply, was a route not many of them took. Should he tell these loungers that in 1968 Eric Nesterenko scored thirty-two goals for Chicago and published his first book of poems? But that would be falling into their trap, accepting their definition of intelligence.

On the ice is where it really happened. The brilliance of some. All senses sparking, working at the widest periphery, aflame with danger and hope both, seeing the whole picture, the lightning-fast flux of friends and enemies, the blending of opportunity and threat. Words didn't stand a chance here. Words were candy wrappers, dead leaves.

Bonaduce took his two-nickel coffee over to the main table, ringed on three sides by couches, seven or eight people on them. Might as well get to know some of these guys. Especially since half of them were young women.

"Can I wedge on in here?"

All the bodies on all three couches flinched to make room. He sat in the largest gap, smiling and nodding at the stiff young woman on his left and the nervous young man on his right. He grabbed up a *New Yorker*, chuckling at its cover, its tight little in-joke, an urbane mocking of the urbane, in this case a bunch of businessmen hustling to work in a demented way.

True, sure, dressing rooms had their share of morons. Guys who would say *libary* if they ever had cause to say it. The stuff he'd heard come out of guys' mouths. *Twats, queers, hosebuckets*, and half the room laughing. But a dressing room was your basic cross-section, this seemed only reasonable. The fact remained that half the guys in any dressing room he'd ever sat in could have ended up here in this lounge, thumbing *New Yorker* cartoons and being wry. They had for various reasons taken a different route, the body-route. The logic and joy of having it work like that.

Out of the blue and apropos of nothing except their being inches apart, he stuck his hand out at the guy beside him, whose head was down in a book which smelled freshly purchased. *Lady Windermere's Fan*.

"Hiya. Bob Bonaduce."

French fries in the SUB and then a long evening bent up in a library carrel, reading Brian Moore, in his head pronouncing it "*Bree*an," which coloured everything. Home by midnight, and on the kitchen table, weighted down with a buttery knife, a scrawled note from Marg: "Friend of yours called long-distance. Fornay? Fornier? French accent. All excited. Said you MUST begin something called a yeast diet. Said to tell you it's a cure? He's sending you a book on it. I assume you know what he's talking about."

You wake up with vision so fuzzy it's like sleep's dreamscape has continued, and then you find the legs don't work too well. Couldn't even bloody walk, he was a big nightmare puppet with packed rag legs. It wasn't some awful new injury, because he'd been feeling so weak and weird lately he hadn't even been playing. Rolling and flopping himself across the floor, it was almost funny. There wasn't a lot of pain aside from some deep nervy stuff he recognized as having been there for a while. The hands didn't work either. Despite dumb eyes and sleeping fingers, he eventually got Fournier on the phone. *Fournier, Jesus, you're not going believe this*. Damn if he wasn't slurring his words as well. He made a joke about the mother of all hangovers. Fournier promised he wouldn't, but an ambulance came and the boys in dull green, all intent on his survival, in no mood to crack a smile at the Bonaduce jokes, packed him up and away he went. Halfway to the hospital he was halfway better; a few hours later he could walk, he could see okay and he was feeling foolish.

But tests, tests, tests. Sitting in the blood-sample room full of sick people, holding a number, waiting for his name to be called, exhausting the *Sports Illustrated*s, endless baseball and basketball, in your stomach a drone of worry doing a dance with your trust in a body that had never let you down.

Passed from doctor to doctor. (After so many high-tech gizmos and scans, the test of choice turned out to be the cartoonish popping him on the knee with the rubber hammer.) Have you ever experienced double vision? Bonaduce ping-ponging his eyes from the doctor to the curtain and back, asking, Which one of you asked that? The doctor deciding to smile, but continuing, How about blurred vision? To which Bonaduce answered, actually serious, Do you mean concussion-blurred vision, or the kind that's just sort of usually there?

Waiting for tests, feeling better, he half-enjoyed the image of him in the corniest of scenarios. He was lying in a hospital bed, adult-diapered, limbs mobile as breakfast sausage, a professionally flirtatious nurse spooning vanilla dessert into his yop, and he asked the doctor (who'd be checking things off on his clipboard, brow furrowed, when everyone knows there's nothing *on* the clipboard): Well, Doc, does this mean that's it for the NHL?

The doctor is a wise-ass hockey fan. He says, Hell no, Bobby — there's always the Leafs.

Answering the questions, he was made to recall his body-history, which in his work was more or less typical. Finger, two noses, cracked a footbone, a hairline in the right collarbone (the most painful), lots of sprains and cuts. About a hundred stitches in the face, all healing well and looking just fine except the rubbery scar-mess over the left eye, and those white lines criss-crossing his five o'clock shadow. Like Krieger, he'd had a job as a fencing mask in Heidelberg.

The only bad one had been the leg. In Rochester, which is a broken-bone kind of town, an innocent shove had conspired with a rut in the ice. Deep in the skull you hear and feel the snap. A beloved leg suddenly foreign, angling off into new territory. The senses falling in another direction, into a deep inner black, into fainting. Embarrassing, but no choice in the matter.

Then the strangest thing: coming to, what he felt was, what he even said to himself was, *I'm out of it.*

The war was over. Tonight's game, but also maybe the season, maybe hockey altogether, the career. Balled up there on the ice, Terry-the-Trainer's whisky breath asking if it was a knee, he felt the descent of a peace, he could even smile a bit in the wincing. He must have looked macho being helped off — smiling while the leg dangled so ugly. The tough Bonaduce. No one would see in the smile a little kid home from school sick, in pyjamas, TV all day, a warm bed, Mom's bustle in the next room.

The year-of-the-leg he was back for the playoffs and he played ten more seasons. All part of the job. Everyone played with pain. Injuries were unsurprising. In fact they felt nothing but appropriate. If you played the game right, you were in their arena, so to speak. You were sort of asking for them.

Waiting at home for test results, he began to see disease the same way. As life-injuries. We're alive, so we're in their arena, we're really just waiting. He thought about death and saw that being alive in the first place was sort of like asking for it. Waiting for test results you think all sorts of things.

But you can point your attitude one way or the other. He wrote everything off to a deep flu, to a stubborn virusy thing. The clumsiness was frightening, but viruses were getting weird, weren't they? He could still skate okay. Funny, he could skate better than he could walk.

It was like an injury that was taking time to happen. You could actually forget about it, forget it was still happening, until the dropped spoon, or the delay of the comb. Then you understood how big it was. You could feel how life itself had become a hovering that was nothing other than sick. The air around you an impending deadness. They said it was going to come back; relapse and remission were the poles of your new planet. The whole thing would, simply, get worse.

In hockey it was generally all nice and quick.

"Leah there by any chance?"

There. Done. Some things you have to just do.

"She is. I'll just go and locate her."

That would be Oscar. He sounded okay, kind of funny, mocking his use of "locate" as he said it. Oscar Devries. She was still Leah Miller, like she'd always been, eschewing the tuneful Bonaduce moniker on their wedding day, contemporary gal that she was. Phone to his ear, he could hear Oscar walk away, wooden floors it sounded like. Oscar was a lawyer with NB Hydro or something. Probably an elegant old house, reno'd from the rats to the rafters.

"Hello?"

"It's your best nightmare."

"Bobby?"

"So that was Oscar, eh? You still with Oscar?"

"That *was* you! You're in town!"

In her voice excitement and fear.

"I am."

"Marilyn called, said she saw someone she thought was you. Remember Marilyn Bauer? 'It *had* to be him, and he was *skating*, it *had* to be him.' So I guess it was! Is!"

"Here I am."

"You here playing?"

"No, hell no. Packed it in. Old age, eh? But don't tell Jason. That I'm here. Surprise."

"Sure. So — you here for a while?"

A definite note of concern behind the cheer.

"Could be. It's kind of a long story—"

"We really have to get together, but, look, I'm out the door.

I'm really late. We're having a party Friday night. Oscar will tell you about it. 'Bye."

And Leah was gone. Leah who would never for as long as she lived ever have to apologize to him, because he was the one who'd left. Leah who felt that the distance between them was now great enough for her to be excited over the phone in front of Oscar, with no fear of anyone misinterpreting. For her to invite him to her party, easy as could be.

But he'd heard what he knew he'd hear. Not in her voice, but in her silences, and the way she breathed. He knew she'd been holding the phone with both hands.

"Hello?" Oscar again. "Now you'll be wanting directions, is that it?"

You could hear him smiling, an ironic, friendly guy.

It was a decent little bed, and something conspired to keep him in it. His first single bed since he was a boy.

Maybe if you just stayed put, lying down, and eased your mind in the right direction, this pure and gentle going-in that almost erased you, a tender secret muscle the size of your body that turned you to air if you flexed it right — if you stayed here like this, you could be one of those people, and he knew they existed, one of those people who know only what matters, who can play life like the game it is, who know its movements — its tides and wind and forest smells — and understand all the efforts of the heart. You would know to keep in mind that everyone's lost and no one's to blame. You would be able to lie here in bed like this but be content with it, content to look out this window to see those birds leaving that branch, moving off one by one in a sprung rhythm that suggests music.

This morning he found his roomies at the kitchen table, puzzling over heating and phone bills and such. Rod was wondering what had maybe been paid and what could be "left again till next time."

It was raining outside, cars were *whooshing* loudly by, a tableful of roommates were talking house matters. Things had a homey, practical feel. Toby already had a beer going. Bonaduce rummaged through his assigned half-cupboard, looking for the can of smoked oysters he was sure he'd bought. He was politely invited to take part, so he shuffled over, and he listened to Toby's suggestion that he take his turn and pay the phone bill. He decided to hold off airing the logic that this particular bill, some of which was long distance, covered a time previous to him setting foot in this country, let alone this house. He wasn't sure how things here ran yet, so he wrote out a cheque. Doing so, he briefly eyed Toby, who openly eyed him back.

Then went to his "room" and searched his "closet" (six hangers hanging on a string strung between two nails) to "get ready" for tonight's party at "his wife's house." What did you wear to such a thing? Were they rich, casual, stiff-necked, hip, what? And did he want to fit in, or did he want to shine?

He went to the bathroom. Sitting, he looked toiletside and noticed dark, flame-shaped stains of wet rising from the floor up the wall. The drywall was permanently damp and thickened with it, whatever it was, a rank ecosystem of climbing swamp. Instead of paying a phone bill, he'd love to come in here with a sheet of drywall and can of paint. Point this house in a new direction. He would discuss it with them. In the meantime he had Leah to get ready for. He picked up a paperback *Hamlet* someone, probably Rod, had left lying upside down on the floor, beside the swamp.

He lay naked on his bed, looking out the window at the stars. The party wasn't until nine and he didn't want to be early. He was already tired. Hard to kill time this time of night.

Red, white and blue rubber balls in both hands, you squeeze

until it hurts, get the ligaments popping out in the wrists, and on the forearms blue veins almost the width of a cigarette. You do lose a step or two, but keep the wrist strength up and you always had your shot. He'd seen oldtimer games, and some of the old boys could still rip it pretty good. Forty feet out, a flick of the wrists and, bingo, the biscuit's in the basket.

These stars in this clean New Brunswick sky were a treat. The whole eastern seaboard of America had basically erased its stars. City lights and a bit of carbon burning was all it took. Fournier, who'd gone up hunting in Labrador, had a story of a Japanese girl visiting Goose Bay and pointing in amazement at the night sky and asking her host, What are those? The smiling host, about to explain the wonder of the aurora borealis, looked up and saw none. And then realized she was pointing at stars — she lived in Tokyo and had never seen stars.

Squeeze the balls. Look at the stars. Tyger Tyger. Looking at stars is a feeling that's probably identical to what a dog gets looking at the controls of a stereo. Twinkling stars. Feel them pull at your little mind in that gently eager way they have, let them remind you for the first time in years that what you are looking at you are incapable of truly seeing and that the only honest response to this is to drop to your dull and sorry knees.

Loud stars. Hungry stars. *Synaesthesia*, grad-student word for the day. This jazzy darkness. Your citrus heart. Sweet and sour Leah.

Montreal traded him to Toronto in the middle of the season, just after Christmas, so he'd had no time to get his affairs — such as moving, such as abandoning his wife and son — in order before reporting to the Rochester Americans.

His plan was agreed to by Leah. At least, that was his memory. He'd go check out the town of Rochester and ascertain his status there. Because everyone involved was fully confident he'd be getting called up to Toronto sooner rather than later. One little injury to one Leaf defenceman was all it would take. Why move Leah and Jason to Rochester when they'd only have to move again? Leah was still in school, third year, so she should stay put, stay in Fredericton.

There were lots of reasons why this plan was agreed to. No one dared raise the main question.

Sex was great, it was always great. But between sex and the next sex was that edgy lack of purpose, a waiting which seemed most of all to be a kind of vacancy. They did share some vital loves: the same food, the same luscious colours in a picture or a sunset, a French horn for the way it came lording in. Smells. And of course sex, its textures and pace. They shared the senses, the runes of body. He'd even understood her eating the dog food, understood her after she'd been caught so embarrassed with the can of it and she told him it was like eating meat from the centre of the earth. They were joined perfectly in bodies' routes of need and terminals of pleasure. But with most else — friends, politics, questions of whether happiness came more from a Cadillac or a hike — on little could they easily agree, and it was so loud a problem it never had to be discussed.

Jokes though, they could share jokes. They could always make each other laugh. At a party, eye contact to confirm something scandalous they'd laugh at later. Sometimes they even joked about real things, about which they had no business laughing. What's your name again? Smiling sadly at the truth after they asked, Do we even know each other? Have we been properly introduced? No, though I believe I've just been Bonaduced.

Their joking was probably something close to love. As she tucked into a steak he could gently bark and whine, even in company, though she'd quit the dog food by now, and she'd laugh. She understood; they both felt the loving comment on her carnality, and her deeper needs, which seemed funny in the midst of a boring chatty party and their bed waiting upstairs.

He made attempts. He did. He tried and tried to expand his love, and to harden it against the hard times to come. Now and then even falling to the corny — flowers, a necklace for no reason, once a poem set and sung to moody music. But finding himself stooped and corny, he could never follow through. Couldn't stay pure, had to screw it up — he'd mock his flowers while handing them over, and the poem he wrecked by tacking on a spontaneous raunchy verse. Or when he fertilized her lawn for her. He'd seen on a lawn across town how green a chemical fertilizer could make grass — careless spreading had left a dark green spaghetti-drawing on a field of yellow. He got a spreader and commenced to write a message in fertilizer on her rented lawn. But the bag was empty after the second word, and the *I LOVE* that appeared several days later was messy and lopsided, and read more like a saint's axiom than a corny guy's love note, and Leah laughed but wasn't roused in the larger way he'd intended.

Ten o'clock, Grey Street full of parked cars, a party. The cars mostly newer though nothing too luxurious. Their house was a pleasing old place not in overly tip-top shape. Something about it shaggy at the edges, though it was brick. Oscar, smiling and ironic at the door, said, "Big Bob Bonaduce!" Leah must have described him. What words would she have used, she who hadn't seen you in ten years, or loved you in twenty.

"You must be Oscar."

He seemed okay. He wore the constant smile-of-a-host, but his was gently wry, and he had a shagginess to him as well, a slight sloppiness that Bonaduce liked in friends, though he was never that way himself. Both of them were wearing jeans and a sweater, but Oscar's jeans were faded to weakness. He wore wire glasses, was getting bald, with the round face baldness gives. A deep, croaking voice for that small body.

And not an ounce of nerves. Apparently no fear of losing her back to the hockey guy.

"Your old wife's somewhere in that." Oscar hooked a thumb back toward the main crush of people. "Beer's in the fridge, everything else's on the counter. I fetch you your first one." He raised his eyebrows in question.

"I guess a beer. Thanks." Bonaduce was already looking in over Oscar's turning shoulder, and there she was.

Leah. Even the name. There she was. Even the word *she*, the way it divided the world in two. And then ripened and rose in the blood.

She was lifting a dipped mushroom to her mouth, tense in the shoulders, pretending not to have seen him yet. Her body as aware of his. Frightening how clearly his body remembered. Seeing her confirmed how exactly remembered. Her skin, its planes and hollows, both hidden and seen. The feathery hair on her neck. The way she held herself, even when relaxed every motion verging on the next, more than ready.

Panic in her shoulders told him she remembered as well. The only question was, would she hate him all over again for this?

Maybe this wasn't the only question.

She was wearing jeans too, and a fuzzy black sweater, mohair, the kind you'd get at a Used store, mildly campy and showy. A thin, almost invisible gold necklace draped her collarbone and then fell on into the sweater. A bit of makeup it looked like. Funny how they'd spent years and miles apart, but something of them had stayed front to front, talking loud and clear. The mushroom was in her mouth and she made as if to consider something as she began to chew. The choice of a mushroom wouldn't have been deliberate. She was staring off, composing herself, or revving up, one of those, because he could see that once she stopped chewing she was going to swing his way, lift her face and see him.

A teammate in Tulsa had a weird wife, weird in that she had written a book. Bonaduce learned it was self-published, but that didn't matter to anyone: Buddy Simon's wife had up and wrote a book. As Buddy described it, looking vaguely afraid, as if listening for something behind him, the book was about "ideas and philosophy and that." All the guys' wives or girlfriends received one at the Christmas skating party.

Maybe the weirdest thing about the book was that it was actually pretty good, pretty entertaining. Bonaduce relieved his jealously scoffing Julie of her copy and thumbed through it, a collection of homespun theories about this and that, most attributed to local farmers and off-kilter thinkers and old almanacs. Why cows lie down before a storm, a talking albino crow, Native prophecies about drought and pollution, home remedies — one of which, the inside of a banana peel rubbed vigorously on a bee sting, the author herself had seen save an allergic teenage boy's life.

One idea, a few pages long, its source "a naturopathic healer in our general vicinity," made Bonaduce see himself, the distant Leah and twelve-year-old Jason in a new light.

The idea was that ideal mates were brought together by a combination of looks and gestures, and to a large degree smell. The result was that, when two compatible people got together, it felt like good sex. (Bonaduce provided some adjectives of his own: *dirty* sex, *breakfast-lunch-and-dinner* sex.) What the two bodies communicated via their smells and such was genetic compatibility, which would lead to superior offspring, kids strong of limb and agile of brain. (Buddy Simon's weird wife noted that "one might see a mix of both Darwin and Hitler in this view.") But the gist was that if Nature's purpose was the best baby, its slick lure was the best sex. Two naïvely compatible parents led blindly grunting along the path to procreation.

Lying on his latest couch in his latest apartment, reading this sex theory in Buddy's wife's book, two hours before a game, Bonaduce thought of Leah. It was no effort to remember her. Her body, with its imperfections that were perfect to him. The little gut, showing that her body knew how to enjoy itself. The fingers on the stubby side, but strong and curious. Thick ankles and calves, to better hold that body up for more curiosity, more pleasure. And her soft skin — her skin was the best, it was the place where giving pleasure and taking pleasure were one and the same thing.

Her eyes, her bright eyes. You looked in and saw she was smarter than you but also that this wasn't a bad thing. You could also see how she felt her body to be not quite hers, or not quite her. She could hold her body at arm's length. You could see she respected her body, but also that she saw it to be a kind of playground.

Smell — said Buddy's weird wife's book — was the key. Here he was in Tulsa and he could still smell Leah. Her body's *root*. Even now it made him ache. I would climb the highest mountain, swim the widest sea. The smell was urgency itself. Mixed with heartblood, and with grace. They'd been helpless with each other. The very first night they did it three times and, not that kind of girl, she hated him for it, as early as that. He knew even while inside her that in his life he'd feel nothing else like this. It took them a year to catch their breath and begin to suspect that their bodies had duped them.

Lying on the couch, considering this woman he hadn't seen in years, Bonaduce might have masturbated had Julie not been there in the kitchen, plus he had a game. He closed his eyes and pictured Jason. Perfect Jason. Healthy, tall Jason, possessed of that symmetry Nature indeed seemed to favour. With the hard Bonaduce jaw, and noble nose; with Leah's light hairlessness, slightly feline eyes, wide smooth face.

The times he did come through Fredericton and saw Jason, one problem was what the mother and the father did for a living. How it defined them. Nothing was ever said but there it was: Leah the social worker, helping refugees settle in the Maritimes. Aiding victims of war and torture, far from family and home, their lives ripped from them like skin. Leah's days were filled with their stories and, in retelling them, her heart was so overfull she would sometimes have to cry. On a few occasions she told them to Bonaduce, a man who had dedicated his life to working violently hard at preventing people with different-coloured uniforms from putting a puck in his net.

He'd be in town a single night, now playing for the visiting team, and before or after the game he'd drop by. Jason would be off having a snack or something while Leah cried about someone she'd met that day through her work, and Bonaduce would see as if in a mirror the trivial ugliness he represented. Hockey. It wasn't as if Leah was asking him to consider who was the right or wrong role model (there being no question), but rather which one of them Jason might want to follow in the way he lived his life.

When he visited it wasn't always clear what she was crying about.

He visited when Jason turned six. He'd been looking forward to talking with his son, reasoning with his growing boy, his kid, and he came away surprised at how naïve he'd been. The whole bus trip up he'd dreamed of what they'd do together, visions of skating on the river, himself showing off a little. Maybe a movie, he'd ask the mother. But they would definitely talk and talk, two guys wild about seeing each other. *Jason, I love you. Jason, what's it like being alive and six? What does life look like stretched way out like that in front of you? Hey, what's it like being my son? I'm sorry that I cannot live with you. You see, life is a tragedy for some. But we are connected by our blood and so it doesn't matter where or when we ...*

Jason looked at ease in the shades of olive and mauve Leah had dressed him in. Bonaduce smiled, no yellow and purple for this kid. Jason was also at ease seeing him, more excited in the gift of the toy ambulance than in his dad, then quickly pouty because the toy didn't take batteries or "do anything." Clearly, Leah, who had after an assessing pause in the doorway left them alone, hadn't done enough to prepare the lad as to the significance of this visit.

Bonaduce couldn't help staring at his boy's body, couldn't help the out-and-out butterflies at seeing how the little arms turned in their shoulder sockets, how the lungs puffed in and out, and how fast the kid scrambled under the bed and back, how he *knew* the tarantula gun was under there in that mess. And how quickly Jason's moods went screwy and sought only the silliest things. How what at first seemed a respect for adult stuff — yes, for *fatherly wisdom* — was nothing of the kind.

"Is lightning the biggest thing?"

They were in Jason's little sky-blue bedroom, Bonaduce sitting thrilled on the boy-sized bed.

"Nope. It's not."

"Gareth says it is."

"Well it's not."

"What's bigger?"

"Well ... air."

"No way."

"Well, it is. Air is way bigger. It—"

"Lightning could *kill* air."

There was nothing to say to this, and Jason waved the eight-barrel gun in the father's helpless face.

"If this had real bullets it still couldn't kill you."

"Really?"

"No way way way."

"What's your favourite season? Do you like winter?"

"No ... But bullets fit. Do you think if the bullets will fit it could kill you?"

"You don't like winter? No way! Don't you like Christmas? Playing hockey?"

"Know what I'm getting for my birthday? *Laser bullets.*"

"Hey, good stuff. You know lasers, they're a kind of 'ray,' like a space— But your birthday's not for eight or nine mon—"

"Or night-vision goggles. Get me night-vision goggles for my birthday."

A mischievous laugh, looking the dad-man in the eye, aware of his own greed, doing exactly something Mom told him not to do.

"I'll send you a surprise, but it won't be night-vision goggles, so don't be dis—"

"I'm way stronger than you."

"You're probably right, big buddy. You — well — wait now — you probably shouldn't hit. You really — I mean it now—"

No doubt real fathers learned the key. But when did a kid start making sense? Bonaduce had no memories of being stupid himself.

But there were also times to cherish. It was never hard to find the good.

Jason was eight during one visit, and it must have at some point occurred to him that his father was a pro athlete, because he dearly wanted to impress Bonaduce with what his body could do. His friend Luke had a tramp and Jason could do a flip, *C'mon and see me do it.*

It was late fall and it had snowed and Bonaduce couldn't imagine who would have left a trampoline out, but he borrowed Leah's car and turned corners where Jason pointed. Jason described his flip and variations of it, and then it became a double flip, and he was the fastest skater on his hockey team, and he could do lifters that sent the puck right over the net, almost taking the goalie's head off.

"But if you shoot it over the net, you can't score a goal," wise father explained, then instantly regretted it, seeing he'd tossed some damp into Jason's fire. It wasn't about scoring goals.

Nor was it about trampoline flips. After too many wrong turns, always followed by what Bonaduce came to see was a too-theatrical puzzlement on Jason's face — "Gee, I thought it was over *there*" — he realized they wouldn't be finding Luke's trampoline. And though he remained curious about whether Jason could in fact do a flip, he saw it wasn't the point and never had been. He was only mildly saddened that he had been following a route of Jason's untruths, that the boy had thought it necessary to go this direction to impress the father when it hadn't been necessary to go anywhere at all.

But it would be great, Bonaduce decided, it would be fucking great to have the time and place to get out and play hockey with his boy. Skate fast, take a goalie's head off, whatever. Everything, even standing up all wobbly, would be great. Holding hands through mitts, Jason looking up at him, them gliding fast enough to scare him a bit, Jason's bright-eyed look full of body's pride and thrill. And it would be the one time they'd ever truly *share*, because what did kids really know — in fact what did people really know — other than the feelings in their bodies?

How many times, on a bus, with a guy, had the subject come up? How many countless quiet talks about getting married and having kids, wondering together about that kind of future? Most guys saw it as a given, and it turned out they were right. But how many times had Bonaduce sighed deeply and announced, "Well I've actually *got* a kid, up in Canada. He's seven now." Or eight now, or eleven now. The sigh before the announcement was a complex sigh, not just a sad one. There was even a bit of pride in it. Under its tone of melancholy at having fucked things up, there was also a hint of satisfaction that, because of this son's existence, life would never be empty. His son was no longer a little kid, he no longer had a kid's blind respect for feats of body so he no longer blindly respected Dad. He was being pummelled by adolescence, sussing out life's many green routes, alive to and aware of Bonaduce only in some unknown measure.

But how often had the *fact* of his son saved him from the depths. Thanks, Jason.

You understood it was the cheapest immortality any man had ever clung to. But there it was, a comfort.

· · ·

He'd survived Leah's party. It was time to see Jason.

He'd been antsy all day with the good butterflies, those of spirit rather than fear, those that helped a sharp performance. Only amateurs aren't nervous.

This morning, feeling the phone in his hand, the black plastic against his head, he'd called. Timing it right, nobody home. He left a simple message: "Hey, I'm in town. See you later today at the rink."

But funny how his nerves were as much about hitting the ice this afternoon and playing some hockey as they were about seeing Jason. It was just that these young guys were going to be in top shape and Bonaduce wasn't. He'd gone for ten runs now, and public-skated three times at the Lady Beaverbrook. One leg laboured a bit, but you wouldn't call it a limp. He was almost over whatever it was. Doctors were the first to admit theirs was an inexact science. Hey, he was going to play with his boy, he was going to play for the Varsity Reds, he'd be charging out from behind the net, he'd spot Jace circling to split the defence, he'd send him in alone with a perfect bullet on the tape and Jace would score a fucking beauty and then with the rest of the guys gather smiling in a huddle on the bright white ice and Jason would whack Bonaduce on the ass like a buddy.

All these years he'd made little of the fact that there'd never been a divorce. That on paper he was still married to her and her to him. He'd mentioned it once in an early letter, offering her any route she wanted to go. But she never mentioned it back, and in the meantime you couldn't help but wonder why not. Women were generally so keen on clarifying anything to do with relationship status. Perhaps not Leah.

But why were they still married? She was Catholic but, except for the wedding, she'd not gone to church in the time he was with her and he couldn't fathom her being bound by those laws. Was it instead that she cared so little for the piece of paper that she couldn't be bothered? Had she married him in the first place to satisfy her parents, and him? A shrugging traipse through a dead institution? Leah was contemporary and left-leaning and this might indeed be the case. Did she care, had she cared, so little for the marriage in the first place that divorce didn't even occur to her?

Strange to think that the marriage meant either too much or too little for her to end it, and that he didn't know which.

Skates in hand, he stood twenty-five rows up in the stands and watched. He told himself this wasn't hiding. There was Jason down there flying around. Good strides, low centre of gravity, fast. Professional speed. Not great with the puck. Shitty shot, actually. But good sense of position, a decent head for the game.

All this took Bonaduce about a minute to see in his son. What was sad, this was his son's chosen career he was seeing and any scout would see just as quickly that this youngster didn't have the goods for the big league, or even the next-to-big league, the one the father had made. Father watched son swoop past a check but then lose the puck for no reason other than wooden-handedness.

He continued watching, mesmerized. The way Jason leaned on the boards, catching his breath. The way he turned to hear a buddy say something, nodded curtly, said nothing back. Bonaduce found himself thinking the words "Scorpio. Bedroom eyes. Soar like an eagle or crawl like a lizard." Then saw himself and Leah standing over their magic little son, Leah reading aloud about Scorpios from a book some friend had given her. Neither of them believed, though Leah seemed for the moment open to it, her new-mother's hunger for information of any kind. Still it was fun thinking of a one-month-old having bedroom eyes, or that he would grow up either noble or flirting with the ditch.

Hard to read someone from the way he played hockey, but the young man out there on the ice seemed maybe kind of bland.

He and Fournier used to mock this goalie, René Leblanc. Over two seasons they'd noticed Leblanc going over the other teams' programmes before games. Tightening his skates, he'd shout to his defencemen — "Hey, watch Peca, eh? Watch Peca, Peca an' Smythe, they gonna have good game. Stay on 'em." And after the game, if Peca or Smythe had scored, he'd give the guys shit. It turned out he had the whole astrology thing memorized, and by looking at players' birthdays he knew how they were supposed to do that night. After being found out, Leblanc eased off because Bonaduce and Fournier had taken to warning everyone that Number 6 had Pluto in Aquarium and he'd be throwing elbows tonight. Leblanc, a believer, did not crack a smile.

Bonaduce pivoted away from the pillar. Time to strap on the blades. Say hi to his young eagle down there. Time to do his Gordie Howe thing. He found the stairwell. It wasn't exactly a limp he was suddenly into, but he had to use the handrail and he had to laugh at the timing of how our bodies hate us. Pimples the night of the date.

In the lower corridor he searched for the Reds' dressing room. He had a notion. If the planets and whatnots actually did stamp a code on us, it wouldn't be at birth but at conception. The baby that came out pissed off and howling had obviously been long stamped, it'd been in there hiccuping and with its own style of punching Mom in the gut from behind. If you got stamped at all it was when you were a quivering single cell, a tender jelly wild with newness. Leah's parents used to embarrass her with their story of a train berth somewhere between Ottawa and Montreal, this her start. Two cells meeting in the middle of a rocky night. Nature's biggest deal, the merger of chromosomes, the trading fire for fire. Bonaduce couldn't remember the precise time of Jason's coming, but it would've been in Leah's old room there on Charlotte Street. He could picture the sky-blue room, the morning light through its small window. It could have been any night of many when something stamped the ooze that came to be Jason.

He rapped once and pushed in the dressing-room door. Liniment and sweat, it smelled like most. A young guy packing rolls of medical tape into a metal cabinet stopped to look at him.

"I'm Bob Bonaduce. I talked to Coach ah ... I guess the assistant coach. Said he had some gear for me?"

"You talked to me. And I forgot."

The trainer went to a locker and started pulling gear out. He tossed it on the floor in front of an empty stall and pointed to it. Then he startled with a thought.

"You cleared all this with the coach, right?"

Looking down, Bonaduce gave him the thumbs up.

Just like at every training camp, the nameplates above the stalls had been removed. Make the team, your name went up. They'd need initials this time. J. Bonaduce. B. Bonaduce. Where in this room would they seat themselves? Bonaduce would enjoy it side by side, but it might be too embarrassing for the boy. J. Bonaduce.

Hey, obviously Leah stayed married so Jace could keep the good name. "Jason Bonaduce" was a good hockey name. Though it wasn't a great hockey name. "Bobby Bonaduce" was a great hockey name.

Was it an accident so many great players had the great names? Short muscly ones, gold on the tongue: Bobby Orr. Bobby Hull. Syl Apps. Others, despite their names, hadn't made it to greatness: Bronco Horvath. Morris Titanic. Merlin Malinowski. Others, like himself, who despite the great name hadn't made it out of the minors: Hal Cabana. Vic Pitt.

In this working-man's poetics there was the perception that a "Jason" was either spoiled or rich. A kid named "Jason" had grown up with brand-new hockey gear, had gone to summer hockey schools. "Jason" was almost grounds for other teams to run at you, or for your own coach to bench you at any hint of you being lazy, or selfish with the puck.

The gear was stiff with someone's old sweat. Blood swelled in his face when he bent to his skates. He couldn't quite work his right ankle, nor did the toes on that side have their power. Hey Jace, how ya doin there, thought I'd come out for a dangle.

He himself was a Leo. Leos can purr or they can roar, but they're best at shining quietly, knowing they are admired.

Leah, delicious Leah, there at the food table, nibbling. He joined her and it was the two of them chewing away, food to nourish their bodies, they'd always loved eating together. Damned if this wasn't also like seeing your best old friend. You hit a certain age and you find certain judgements have worn away or gone underground. Nibbling, happily pressed close together by the crowd, they talked about nothing serious. You're looking well. Nice house you have here, is that oak? Beside him her body. The small paunch. Her skin. He pictured her twenty years ago wearing his leather Express jacket, way overlarge, like wearing her big fella's own tough protective skin, in the manner of Fifties sports guys and their gals. Much more aware than him that it was the Seventies, she'd humoured him. He did like her in it. Maybe she'd liked it a little too, though he remembered her erect posture in it, her look of patience and independence.

For Oscar's sake he tried not to stare at her. Good pâté, he said, nodding as he chewed, though he'd never been wild about organ meat. She laughed and told him, Guess what? She was vegetarian now. And they both laughed perfectly, knowing without saying that it had gone from dog food to this. He'd never forget it, he'd known her all of two weeks, catching her spooning it right out of the can into that cute little face. Leah horrified at being caught, but Bonaduce had felt strangely touched, not because he'd found a weakness but because something in this ultra carnality was akin to her hunger in bed, a horniness which felt so good to be a party to. Plus, Leah being refined, and petite — well, dog food was a contradiction that deepened her immensely. During that evening twenty years ago she came to know him enough that she could laugh about it. A few months later she said that telling him — he was the only one she'd ever told — had helped her drop it, her weird craving. After a year she reported in all seriousness that she was down to the occasional Gainsburger, which she ate more or less out of nostalgia.

Vegetarian now. He shrugged and she shrugged back, as if saying to each other, *Of course* apples become oranges.

"A minor shift from the Alpo diet." He pointed at the carrot she turned in the dip.

"My history is *not* for public consumption." The hissed mock-panic, a nudge of the shoulder into his chest.

But it thrilled him that maybe Oscar didn't know.

"You know Jason is too?"

"What, vegetarian?"

"It was actually him who got me into it." She went ironic, sounding just like Oscar. "I mean, the kids these days."

"Jesus, why?" He wanted to say "how." How do you play vegetarian hockey? His body felt sure that no meat meant a lack of something powerful.

"I think there's something moral going on. But I don't know what came first. He just stopped eating it, around fifteen, said he couldn't stand the taste. Except for chicken in Chinese food, then that went too. So how long are you in town for?"

"You still drink? Can I get you a beer or something?"

Leah stayed put while he sidestepped and squeezed his way to the kitchen. Oscar was there, laughing and chatting, and it was weird drawing a beer out of his fridge for his girlfriend.

A woman friend was talking to Leah in low tones when Bonaduce arrived back. Eyes down, half-smile, she zipped away pretty quickly. He wondered what, exactly, the talking was about. Ex-hubby hockey guy. Leah's Jason's daddy back in town. There was a rich and tangy high-school taste to all of this.

"I've moved here."

"You—" Her face quickly shut off, became unreadable. "Did

you get traded again? Traded here?"

"No, hell. I've retired. Actually ..." He'd decided beforehand to be perfectly straight with her because she would find out in any case. And there was the chance she'd be an ally. "I'm going back to school, a master's degree. You know, English."

No response. Beautiful Leah, paused with celery stick. Unable to decide what dip, or wishing her celery was metal, sharpened.

He'd said "English" with a respectful weight he wanted her to hear. Sure, he wanted her to think of him in other than hockey terms, why not. But also he had changed his mind about English. Something good had happened in his bathroom that evening, him sitting there with *Hamlet*, the wet flames of swampwater crawling the wall beside his leg.

Arriving in Fredericton he'd been prepared to defend preconceptions of his violence and stupidity by mocking English literature itself. Hey, it's nothing special you're doing. In fact it's perverse. Your face in the blinders of a book, indulgently gorging on words despite this dying world, the starving masses. Someone you know is gasping in the terminal wing and you sit reading *Lady Windermere's* fucking *Fan*.

In the bathroom he'd thumbed the paperback *Hamlet*, remembering maybe liking it back in high school. Sitting on the toilet, free of any pressure, free of having to do something *with* the stuff — maybe that was why it clicked. How could you not be cowed? Here you were perfectly described, here you were crawling between heaven and earth, a dirt-bound angel. Caught helpless by the demands of heaven, yet helplessly mired in earth's crude gravities. Animal stink wafting up between your legs. Noble yet snuffling along for the next sandwich. Dull angel or special dog, take your pick.

This deepened the way he said "English." He wanted to free Leah of her celery and meet her eye and explain to her his new feelings about it. How our struggle can feel only tedious until someone like Shakespeare renders it worthwhile, and for their good words we must thank writers everywhere. English. You read *because* people are in the terminal wing and your turn is coming. Maybe you even read *Lady Windermere's Fan*.

"Why here, Bobby?"

"Well, the whole thing's wacky, but I'm going to play hockey here too, with UNB. With Jason."

This got her. Tucking back, giving herself a double chin, she began shaking her head. "Well that's ... that's ... I don't know ..."

"What don't you know?"

"What to think. For one." She managed a little smile.

"Jason doesn't know what to think yet either — I haven't told him." Tiniest of jokes. "So, could you maybe not, you know, if you see him ..."

"Hey."

Leah put both hands up as if warding off the food table. She wouldn't look at him. In the side of her eye he saw a flash hinting at what might be her reservoir of anger.

"He's an adult. You can both do whatever you want."

Funny, the last bit. Father and son as co-conspirators. Her uncontrollable boys. Bonaduce wasn't at all unhappy that she summed up the situation in this way.

Standing at centre ice with the coach, Bonaduce registered the instant Jason spotted him. It now became intensely difficult trying to talk some sense into this young fellow Whetter when you knew that, over your shoulder, catching his breath after a drill, the long-lost son was staring at you in bewilderment and who knows what else. He tried to listen to Whetter while sneaking sidelooks at Jason, whose plumes now gradually quieted. The lad was a plugger even in practice. Bonaduce shot him a wink he maybe didn't see.

"Thing is, our first game's in a week and a half." Whetter had his elbow cocked, whistle ready in his hand. He kept shaking his head, kept toeing a pylon with the point of his skate. He had on four-, five-hundred-dollar skates. Why did coaches need the best skates? Up top he wore glasses, and looked like a broad-shouldered accountant.

"You're not in shape and—"

"*Game* shape, no."

"—and the guys have been at it since August, dedicated from the start, and cuts were made a month ago ..."

Whetter let the last bit rest, content with bureaucratic cowardice.

"You gonna make the playoffs?"

You hated saying such an arrogant thing, but time was awasting. Almost smiling, Whetter gave him a *touché* look, point taken. Bonaduce shrugged. The shoulder pads were too small and the helmet rode up too high. He whapped at it with his glove, then threw his head to his left shoulder, popping the vertebra that had been getting stuck since he couldn't remember.

Jason wouldn't come over as long as he stood talking to the coach.

"Bob, the other thing, maybe the only thing, is the pro rule."

"The pro rule."

"The sitting out a year."

"The what?"

"A pro comes back to school — it does happen — they have to sit a year out, don't ask me why."

Bonaduce felt the cold sweat of foolishness break out. He didn't respond because he couldn't.

"So first we have to find out if Utica — East Coast League, right? — if Utica constitutes pro."

"Of course it fucking constitutes pro." Now feeling himself turn red.

"Well okay, and if that's the case, you sit. A year before eligibility."

Say something. Focus. Ineligible? It was a creeping, bureaucratic word, nothing to do with this game. The hockey he knew, the best guys played, the others sat.

"Actually I wasn't playing, I haven't played since last

December. I was injured. So — hey — maybe I'll be eligible in December."

"If you were still under contract I doubt it but—"

"Well actually the contract got all screwed up too. So maybe I'm free to play. The owner, this unbelievable sleaze, he just—"

"But anyway, hey, we'll get everything checked."

Whetter turned, bringing the whistle to his lips and saying, without looking at Bonaduce, "If you're ineligible you can't practise with us either, we'd get dinged. Get the gear off."

Whetter blew the whistle hard three times, skating away from him.

Hard not to move his body, dance around, as he waited in the concrete tunnel outside the dressing room. Hard not to plot hellos, hugs. It was all so—

Jason. Here he was, coming out through the door with a smile already set, breathless, flushed in the face. He stopped five feet away. Steam rising off his soggy longjohns in the slight cold.

"So what the hell," he said, almost yelling, much of Leah in his smile, "what the hell was *that*? A cameo? What you doing in town?"

It sounded rehearsed, but now they shook hands easily. Jason had become more slick in performing the rite than however many years ago it was Bonaduce had last had this pleasure, this hand in his.

The father smiled back. He should speak, but found himself taking in the son's lanky body, the shoulders not so wide, Leah's shoulders, they could take some added muscle and he'd still be mobile — he hadn't peaked, he could do more. Weight training, he'd make a decent power forward, bash the corners, crash the net, you don't need the good hands.

"Well, actually I thought I'd stay the year."

"Wow, no kidding!"

Bonaduce — as casually as he could, shrugging and smiling

with self-deprecation, leaving out all medical news — explained his plans.

At first Jason said, "Really?" Then in the clutch of nervous laughing his eyes pulled away and something bubbled up in his tight gut — you could see it — and buckled his spine. Jason's stuttering inbreath filled the hall with his confusion. The boy just standing there, yet moving so fast. Looking at his father he brought a clawed hand up as if cradling and juggling a ball, a very Italianate gesture. Bonaduce could see Jason's grandmother in this.

Trying to laugh the same laugh again, Jason couldn't look at him now. Nor could he speak. His face went a new red.

Speechless and in trouble himself, Bonaduce watched his son spin away for the dressing room, double-palming the door with more violence than he'd shown on the ice.

That night, for the first time in his new home, he broke out the guitar. Slow picking, with interludes of languid strumming, at his feet a case of beer. At some point into the room came Margaret, Rod, Toby, and some other guy whose name he did not catch. They heard some Bonaduce versions of blues standards, some Howlin' Wolf stuff. They were patient with and then mocking of his dip into country, which was fine with him because humour went well with the genre, and Toby knew a few and warbled mockingly along. They were briefly intrigued when, beer done and time to think about bed, he dug deeper into his time-bag for Muddy Waters, then way back to Woody Guthrie, the room falling quiet for the simple good politics. Or maybe everyone had left. When he looked up and saw that all but him and the roaring Maui surf trucks had found their way to bed, he started his secret string of tunes from that alltime hardcore ragtop heartbreaker, Roy Orbison. And damned if Bonaduce didn't lose a tear or two, there at the end, head down, the candle casting a light less sad than perfect in the way it put a glow on the front of the guitar.

II

Societies differ mostly in how each culls its herd.
—F.A. d'Amboise

Why kill yourself to win? Sure as fuck not for me. And not for the fuckin' money in *this* league. *It's the guys.* Look at each other. Look around. *That's* why we put the fuckin' biscuit in the basket. *Now get out there.*
—Coach Murray Murphy, Tulsa Oilers

MARGARET.

At the sink she repotted plants. Like so many other jobs in this house, this was hers by default. (She wondered, trying not to be too judgemental about her roommates, whether it was more a case of "not noticing" than "letting things die.") One plant (mother-in-law's tongue?) was all roots, pale clean roots woven tight, shaped exactly like a pot. Amazing how it survived, just on water, with maybe the decay of its own skin as nourishment, whatever. She should stick it, potless, back on the windowsill, see if anyone noticed. Or let it die again.

Her back was to him and, because of last night, as he brushed past she half-expected a pat on the rear or some sexual tease. He looked the sort but apparently wasn't. He was a kind she really hadn't known before, a boomer who hadn't done the hippy thing or the business thing but instead had played sports. He seemed the least Sixties of anyone in this house, which was ironic, him being the only one alive at that time. All the same there was a sort of restless *On the Road* feel to him — she'd read Kerouac in Hawaii — but you weren't talking Sixties now, you were talking Fifties. Beats, the boys' club of the day, bunch of dads gone wild. There was also something about Robert more basically Fifties: you could see him with slicked hair behind the wheel of a smooth rod with stuffed dice dangling from the mirror and deep purple hoor-lures framing the back window. It was effortless to see him so. His smile, a smoke or toothpick in the James Dean mouth.

The dreamcatcher, he'd thanked her but joked about it, how this fancy new air freshener didn't smell hardly at all. When he saw she took it a bit seriously, and after she explained the psychology of it — how knowing it's in the room can trigger lucid dreaming — he seemed to reconsider. He wanted to know if it could affect luck. In fact now he seemed a bit in awe of it. The man's been out of the picture for a while.

It wasn't like someone's father living here, but it was close. The creased pants and polite manners and constant corny announcement of his limit of two-drinks-a-night, though after dusk he sometimes slurred. His lame "Time to hit the books, eh?" and then you could hear him snoring through his closed door. The others were still a little mad at her for renting the room to him, unable to kick all the way back with a guy like that around. Until his helpful ways and that goofy guitar night showed his harmlessness. That and the fact that he spent so much time in his room. He seemed generally tired.

But he didn't belong. Where did a Robert Bonaduce belong? In this he was a mirror for her because she was hanging on in this house by a thread herself. This house out on the highway, the traffic roaring east or west without doubt, and her life lacking any direction. The bare halls and rooms felt like a stage upon which she was acting out her limbo-life: between men, between jobs, between journeys. It was unhealthy to be banking on memories of Hawaii, to be nostalgic at twenty-four. She was at the wrong university to service her fading passion for archaeology. Which was probably good because she'd been understanding that bones and such were maybe best left buried, and that to search backwards in time was exactly what she should not be doing. In that school of thought, the whole world was a crypt.

When he'd driven up looking to rent, Rod had huddled with her and laughed, No way, looks like some sort of mafia guy. She'd shrugged and said, So what? Her whim was to give the house some range. Bonaduce might be a spark, a bit of colour. And a practical joke, why not. Rod's I-can't-believe-you're-going-to-jump-his-bones look put exactly that idea in her head and made Robert doubly interesting. Maybe a bizarre romance, Christ, who knows. He was old but in a dented way cute, and a grad student in literature, so smarter than he looked. He would have stories to tell.

As it turned out he would keep his stories to himself. Behind the corny cheer he carried a weight. He'd sit staring in the living room, then grin hiyas and howdys when he saw you. He worked his face a lot when people were near. Good in public, bad alone. Her opposite.

Toby didn't like him, but at least there was some strange respect. *Grudging* would be the word. In a way they were similar, stuff going on underneath they tried to hide. Indirect. Toby was funny with his new description for Robert every morning. "He's Moose, Reggie, Archie and Jughead all in one." Or, "He's what I would have been were it not for drugs." Hilarious him straight-faced saying that, his tiny body a hundred pounds less, his withered arm. Robert could tuck him behind an ear like a pencil.

Robert must have had some fine injuries — he'd grab his feet or legs as if to check that they were there. She caught him punching himself in the foot and he made a madman joke of it, punching calf, knee, thigh, tongue hanging out. He could be funny. Some days he limped and bumped hallway walls. He didn't like to talk about hockey unless to run an anecdote by you for the novel he's planning.

Then last night he came to her. It was way after midnight. He asked softly at the door if she was awake. He sat on the end of the bed. It felt fine that he'd come. He was shy. They both dropped their joking and she welcomed this. She tucked up her legs to make room, but then slid a foot back to tickle his thigh through the covers, she didn't know why, didn't know if she wanted this from him yet, or ever. The physical part alone might be okay, because he didn't seem selfish, and he had a worldliness and humour. But it seemed very likely that he'd go gushy on her. Thinking she needed that. And thinking he meant it.

He seemed not to feel her toe's welcome. Then, destroying

all romance within a million miles, he asked, How close do you feel to your parents? At first she tried it out as a joke, a Groucho Marx sexual thing and a way to acknowledge their ages, but he didn't smile or waggle his eyebrows. Jughead Archie Reggie and Moose had asked her a serious question.

She thought a moment, then told him she couldn't put it into words. She apologized for being so lousy with words, thinking how he must always get that apology, being in English. He said she was great with words, and asked other questions: Did she think it was automatic for a child to love a parent even if the child didn't see the parent much. Did she love one parent more than the other. Animals were connected by smell and such — did she think humans had anything like that as well.

She spoke her thoughts to him for what they were worth. She didn't ask why he was asking. It was pretty obvious he had a kid somewhere. One thing she said made him stiffen and fall silent. What she said was, "There're plenty of assholes out there, and lots of them are parents," but she'd only been talking about her own situation. She worked her toe harder to get him out of his worry.

"You have a kid?"

"I do. Yes."

"You're not an asshole, Robert."

"Not to you." .

"I doubt it's even possible."

"Oh it is," he said, and in the dark she could hear him shift his shoulders, could hear his tired smile. "I contain multitudes."

An old hockey guy, quoting what was probably literature.

§

In the department lounge someone whose name he didn't know had invited him to Rye's Pub, see you there. So now Bonaduce

— get out of that sleepy little room for a change — found himself downtown in a bar, celebrating some guy named Murray's oral defence of his PhD being over and done with. Kirsten and Phil and others whose names he didn't know had claimed tables. Some surprise at seeing him. Sure, he didn't know Murray, or his "thesis area," or exactly what an "oral defence" was — if the subject came up he would resist his joke about spitting. Something in the air had told him that grad-student socializing was encouraged, which was not a bad thing at all, hang together. Maybe as the bar was closing they'd get in a brawl with those History bastards over there.

His mood was definitely better. He'd decided Jason didn't hate him, nor was it a snub. Jason was shocked. What else could you expect? He'd basically abandoned the boy. A beaming, *Hey! Great, Dad!* from a dumb-knob son would've been unnatural and disappointing. This setback showed Jason's dark depths. What parent wanted a child who was uncomplicated?

He was good at patience. Maybe there was nothing he was better at. Though let's not bring up the pathetic side of this, his twenty years in the minors waiting patiently by the phone.

Eventually Murray arrived, accompanied by Professor Daniel Kirk, who was Murray's thesis supervisor and who Bonaduce hoped wouldn't remember him, for he hadn't yet made it to class. People shouted and raised glasses to Murray. Murray was a homely tall-and-lanky, like a weed that towered over the garden. He looked myopic behind his glasses, perhaps partially blind, lenses thick as porcelain. He smirked cynically by way of general greeting. Bonaduce had the sense of Kirk trying not to look his way, which was good, let's both do that. And they both did, though when Kirk sat they had only Murray between them.

It proved a strange little time. A poor team party. Half of them left after a single beer. After the one bland toast there was a jerkiness to any conversation, a lack of tone or build. The table-talk broke into shadowy murmuring pockets, Murray not even in one. Bonaduce felt bad for him, though as the minutes crawled by and from Murray's few blurts he came to suspect that Murray was an unliked loner and the cause of this rhythmlessness to begin with.

It took Murray ages to get his first beer halfway down, at which point Bonaduce ordered him a second. When it came, instead of a thank you, Murray glanced at it with what looked like annoyance. He dutifully poured some into his glass, glugging the beer from straight over-top so the foam rose fast and some spilled.

"In Germany the mugs are tapered at the top. Which" — Murray demonstrated with his hands as God might squeeze a volcano top to contain the eruption — "quells the climbing head."

"Ah." Bonaduce smiled. "So you did the beerfest?"

His damaged recall of his own Munich visit didn't include tapered mugs. Maybe he hadn't made it to the classier tents. Murray turned his head to him but didn't look up from the table.

"I haven't been to Germany, but I collect."

"Ah."

"My father travels. He gifts me with steins."

This was pretty good, *gift* as a verb, one of the better ones in the new language he'd been learning here. Other verbs he didn't like so much. *Dialogue.* Let's dialogue. Hell, why not get Sally and trialogue. Eight of us at Murray's lousy party, octaloguing away.

He went to the bathroom, to urine. Coming out, wondering if he shouldn't just go home, a waitress gave him a stern look and asked if he'd washed his hands. She was good, her coy smile delayed just right. She was attractive enough to make the joke racy and it all a bit exciting. Late-twenties, countryish, maybe a little wild. "Coral," said her name tag. How to answer. Coral, no, I didn't, I thought you liked them dirty. Coral, could you come and show me how.

He looked witlessly down at his hands for her. "You mean these?"

She made to snap him on his ass with her tea towel. She'd made it all a little dance, already moving off and smiling at the next guy.

Another one or two had left. Murray was talking loudly, to Kirk.

"—no. It's not racial, it's cultural. The reason there are no philosophers from the equator is because they allow *desire*."

"Nonsense."

"They have sex at puberty! What more could you want? What's left! What's left to puzzle at after that! You net fish for the kids to eat! Think about it for God's sake."

Murray was actually fairly funny. Ballsy too. Here he was lecturing Kirk, professor. Now he turned to Bonaduce to lecture him as well, though Bonaduce could see from the eyes swimming in their lenses and staring past his ears that he could have been anybody.

"*We* sit up in the northern climes, *squeezed* with unfulfilled craving. Of all kinds. So what we do is sit and *think*."

"But education has its—" Kirk began.

"No. As long as we continue to privilege restraint, restraint over pleasure, we will remain, as it were, 'philosophical.' And they will remain childlike and happy, happily non-abstract. They do what they *want*, for God's sake."

What are you thinking, trying to fit in with these types. *Privilege* as a verb now.

Coral came by to empty ashtrays and wipe their table with her snapping-towel. Her manner was a bit theatrical, knowing she was being watched by the likes of Bonaduce and whoever else. Wiping in his direction, she leaned over so far that — hey, she was probably only doing her job but it was the kind of thing you can construe as an invitation.

Nothing was clear tonight. The heav'ns felt rotten, or something. When Murray left — big stein-expert man making it through almost two beers in one sitting — those who remained started jabbering about him like he was some sort of genius. Murray was squeezed all right, just like Kirsten and Phil and all these guys, thinking so hard and long they'd thought themselves into some fancy corners. From the sounds of it they were in awe of Murray (well then why weren't they nice to him?) because he'd "tossed off" his thesis while working harder on his real interest, which was a journal.

"I heard him refer to it as his" — Kirsten dropped her voice to a whisper — "his 'commentaries.'"

"He's been prolific as hell," said Phil, with the most respect Bonaduce had seen from him. "Three volumes." He shook his head in amazement. "Three volumes."

"How long has he been journaling?" Kirsten asked, her airy teeth for once looking more beaverish than judgemental.

"Since coming to Fredericton. Five years."

Journaling. This was getting good. *To journal. To beer.* Let's really beer tonight. Hey: *to verb.* Let's verb another noun.

The only question here was why did these supposedly smart folks admire a guy who wasn't thirty who'd never been to Germany or anywhere else, yet who was insane enough to have written three volumes of what was for all intents a fucking autobiography? "Prolific" just means you don't get out enough. Three books about himself. Sitting in a fevery hunch in the library, in love with his own brain and chewing at it like a worm. Egoing like crazy.

Coral swept by again, giving Bonaduce a look, knowing that at this dead table she had a good audience in one at least. She made as if to dab at her forehead with her little towel — Whoo ain't I hot an' workin' hard? — and giving it some sexiness to boot. Then gone, smiling at the next table, good at it and knowing how to have an okay time at a shitty job. Coral was a trueheart and a relief. He could handle a Coral.

He could Coral all night long.

．　．　．

Post Game
by R. Bonaduce

After violently winning that night, they went to the strip club. Canary Singh, a wiry little centerman not born in this country, but part of the Asian hockey diaspora, sat a row back of the action, while the other guys had their usual handhold on the beaver rail. Their hoots and hollers occasionally brought Singh's head up out of his newspaper and cup of tea.

"Hey buddy! Hey Canary!" a few guys eventually called out to him. "What ya think of *those*?" They hooted and pointed in glee at the bounteousness of Darling Doctor Gail, two parts of whom were looming over them.

"Well, I think that those would feed a great many people in my country," said Canary Singh, gently rolling his head like they do.

Those of the guys that heard this stopped smiling and instead looked slightly sickened.

"'Tis not a mysterious thing, these entertainments of yours," Canary continued, sitting up now and pointing at Gail. "The bull is but of course made stiff at the sight of the sacred, what, the sacred *oo*ders? ooders of the cow. And just as it is with the cobra, in its rising to—"

A fist knocks Canary Singh's face out of the picture, and another fist flashes through but you can only hear the smack. The guys turn back to Doctor Gail.

Rolling his head more slowly, fingering the stitches under his eye, which had been sewn in just that night but now were popped, Singh picks himself off the floor, spits some gore and a coupla teeth onto the butt-burned carpet, flips open his paper again, hoping his buddies haven't gotten any of his blood on the sports pages. His name is in the summaries tonight. Two assists. He always sends the summaries home to a cousin in Calcutta.

. . .

Marg had offered him the loan of her laptop, leaving it here in the living room. With a hundred books to read and family relations to repair, he'd opened the thing, shaking his head at the foolhardiness of deciding to begin his novel, a project he wasn't supposed to even think about for a year. And as if he'd still be here.

The beers from the PhD party had him a bit goofy, and any serious intention was gone by the time he got the machine figured out and the title tapped down. Years ago he'd played a few months with a guy named Singh, an arrogant bastard. Singh had been both a fighter and a lech, a cruel loudmouth in strip bars. It was fun to turn him into Canary. The rest of what he wrote made him smile, dumb as it was, the fault of another beer and the echoes of Gail Smith's class that morning.

The second class hadn't gone any better than the first and he verged on dropping the course. Or having it dropped for him, the more likely scenario. He had to find out if taking only two courses kept his student status full enough to let him play for the Reds. He also had to maintain a certain grade. He should find out what that grade might be.

His little quip this morning hadn't helped. They were hashing out the "diaspora" definition again, arguing whether certain names on the reading list deserved to be there. While it was gratifying that no one else appeared to like Gail Smith either (in the lounge he had heard Phil whisper acidly that "Smith's reading list is nothing but whimsical"), the day's discussion was another round of grand language and hooded spite.

Bonaduce made two contributions. Neither his first, "Well, a good book's a good book," nor his second, "Hey: we're all just mutts from away," seemed to secure his position as worthy participant.

It was really too bad about Smith's class because he did like

Canadian lit. During the long and scattered path to his BA he'd managed to find CanLit courses in, of all places, Kalamazoo, which from the sound of it you'd expect courses in Popeye, or Aztec Cooking, not books by Canadians. During the classes he'd decided not to pull rank by revealing his nationality. But he felt he had insights into the material that the others lacked. Reading her novel, he'd felt a shovel-the-snow kinship to Atwood, though her tough-shit sharpness made him nervous; and to Davies, though he was a stuffed shirt. But you could just tell they'd both shovelled driveways.

And Leonard Cohen, his CanLit favourite. You couldn't quite picture Lenny shovelling out a driveway, or even having a driveway, but here was someone who knew the body and its deepblood longing, and he wasn't afraid to sing it into sweet words, hard for a guy. He could have been Irish-Italian. He even looked Irish-Italian.

The first time he came "home" and walked in on their game he thought he'd lost it, thought he'd left his brain in class. Going about their domestic business — which for Toby meant lounging, for Rod reading, and for Marg and her sister cooking while washing enough dishes to eat off of — his housemates conducting a conversation that went like this:

"Lobster trap," Toby said, for some reason.

After a moment's hesitation, Marg said, "Handicapped parking."

"The concept," said Rod, focused on his book, "I'm struggling with."

"Hell," offered Marg's sister.

To which Toby shouted, "Nope!"

Marg's sister, slouching in thought, stirred spaghetti sauce, looking a bit nervous. "Heaven!" she said next.

"Better," said Toby, "but, nope. Heaven's still a concept. C'mon."

Marg's sister looked angry now. "Fuck!" she tossed at him. "Cunt!" she added in defiance, while Toby, supercilious, nodded at her.

Toby settled grandly back. "Some of the Flemish painters," he announced.

"Let's stop growling," said Marg.

Toby and Rod looked at Marg, then at each other, in some sort of agreement.

"His future varicose vein operation," said Rod, nodding toward Bonaduce.

"Hiya," said Bonaduce.

"Howdy," said Marg's sister.

"Nope, nope, nope," said Toby.

Not looking up, Rod asked Toby, "Nope, what? Nope 'Hiya'?"

"'Hiya' was fine. Nope 'Howdy'."

"I was saying hello," Marg's sister explained. "Don't insult me."

"*That's* better," deemed Toby.

"Brad Pitt's bum," said Marg's sister, to which Toby closed his eyes and subtly shook his head, for some reason not pleased but deciding to let it go. Toby had lately begun to make Bonaduce think of a hamster cage. The seedy hair and the way it fell, and the frayed collar, and the colour of his skin, gave you the combined feel of dank and dusty shavings.

Understanding now that this was a game which, at a minimum, involved coming up with something weird, Bonaduce decided he was up for some fun. He was decent at weird. He jumped in.

"Trained hamster you keep tied by a string around your neck that's trained to, whenever you start choking on a chunk of food, it goes down your throat and eats whatever's stuck."

The housemates looked at one another for a moment, then explained to Bonaduce the notion of "non sequitur," how you had to say something that absolutely didn't fit. There could be no connection at all. Even opposites didn't work, because they had the connection of being opposite.

"And make it short," added Toby.

"Toby? Was that your turn?" asked Marg's sister.

"Was that yours?" Toby answered back.

Bonaduce had another go, answering a pretty good "Kangaroo high-jump record" to Marg's "Is the Lord's Prayer punctuated?"

But then he sidled off to his room, to read. No wonder these guys were good at irony — they came home at night and *practised*. They worked out like pros. They had non sequitur relationships, lived non sequitur lives. They even had a non sequitur diet: doughnuts, tofu, fresh basil, moonshine. Bonaduce recognized now why he'd found them in some way smarter even than the grad-school types: not giving a shit about normal stuff, like conversation, gave you a sort of intimidating power.

In the days to come the game continued on and off, in spurts, and Bonaduce understood that he'd been witness to earlier versions of it but hadn't cottoned on. You never quite knew when it might start. The next morning, in fact, he was in the kitchen putting on his shoes to this scene:

"Any of that left?" Rod asked, gesturing to the frypan Toby held with his good hand while scooping out bacon with his bad. The room reeked of old oil and scrambled egg.

"Tuesday," Toby answered.

"Melanoma," said Rod.

"I wasn't doing it," said Toby.

"Clinton didn't resign eventually," offered Rod.

"I wasn't doing it. Tuesday. We have nothing. We shop tomorrow. Tomorrow is Tuesday. Today we eat shit. He" — Toby pointed at Bonaduce — *"ate the last egg."*

Quit your fooling around. Quit your moaning. Get off your ass.

One shoe on, pause, breathe, take a gander out the window — Mr. Neighbour should really paint that old trailer of his —

pull on the other shoe, work at getting that frayed lace licked and in and through that damned eyelet. Time's a'wastin'.

It all comes down to, what do you accomplish within the clumsy grab of the day. What do you do between the calloused hands of dawn and dusk. What do you need, and find, and use. The squeeze is on.

You could say it's a duty, either to others or to yourself. But a duty all the same.

Oscar Devries answered the door, waved him in, and as he ran upstairs shouted something about Leah being called out on an emergency, just make yourself at home.

Bonaduce removed his shoes and wandered into the living room. A Beatles song was on, but he noted an odd roughness to John's voice, then a harmony that shouldn't be there, then laughter — it was an outtake, this must be one of those anthologies. Great, let's hear it. The party here a few weeks back, he recalled the wafts of music, old British-invasion stuff: Animals, Who, some Kinks you didn't normally hear. Now some connoisseur Beatles. He liked Oscar even more. This was a friendly house, a sweater dropped in the very middle of the living-room floor, and three dirty cups and orange peels on the coffee table.

He sat deeply into the couch and took note of his old man's sigh. Man he was tired ... *Of course you will find that fatigue is the biggest day-to-day impediment* ... and this fight was not the good fight, because the enemies were big and shadowy and there were too many to see. He put his feet up on the coffee table, nudged a cup with a toe and wondered if he would fall asleep here in his wife's house.

He might have. Last he remembered he was really liking an *a capella* version of "Because," and now here was Oscar coming in with coffees, and the cups at his feet were gone.

Leah had been called away to a church in Sussex, where a Guatemalan family, facing deportation, had last week taken illegal refuge. The little daughter had developed a fever and earache, and they'd wanted Leah's help, only Leah's, in getting a prescription filled.

"It's after hours, it's Sussex." Oscar shook his head, blowing into his coffee. "We can assume our Leah's having a red-tape kind of day."

Our Leah.

"So I'll call her tonight, set up another time?"

"No, she called and said she'd be back soon. She wants you to wait. She apologized profusely." Oscar smiled. "Actually, she didn't apologize. Nothing comes between her and their suffering. Her priorities are clear."

"Guess you can't blame her."

"Oh, I manage to." Oscar keeping up the smile.

The coffee was the strongest Bonaduce had ever tasted. Why did it feel odd to find out that Leah had ended up with a nice guy? Kind, with pleasant wise-ass tendencies. Balding and shortish like an Oscar should be, but also not caring about this, an Oscar worth his salt. Bonaduce felt revved up in his presence, could easily fall into friendship with this guy. Jesus, what would Leah make of that?

"Actually, she was on the news last night. Did you see it?"

Bonaduce shook his head.

"They mostly interviewed the father, who was typically tearful and amazed at our Canadian hospitality, and then there was Leah, large as life. They let her have a few sentences. She came off quite well."

"Hey, did you tape it?"

"I should have."

Proud Oscar. Leah the celeb. Bonaduce recalled the times in Fredericton they'd watched him on local sports highlights and a couple of times interviewed after games, major five-o'clock shadow, sweaty hair plastered to his forehead. Him wincing to see and hear himself, Leah joking not to worry, last week Tony the goalie had sounded even stupider. And there was the time he'd propped up a football-sized baby to see the screen. *Look,*

Jace! Look, Jace! See Daddy's pass?

The Beatles finished and Oscar went to the CD rack. Bonaduce had come to talk to Leah about Jason, to see if the boy had said anything. To solicit Leah's help. At least advice.

"Any preferences?" Oscar asked, flicking plastic against plastic.

"Well, I'm definitely into the old stuff too. I liked what I heard at your party. Hey — so anything." He paused. "So how well you know Jason there, Oscar?"

Oscar was into a drawer of cassettes and he held up a hand for Bonaduce to wait. He popped one in, made some equalizer adjustments, and on came "Here Comes the Night."

"Hey. Early Van."

"You know it?"

"Sure, it's great. 'Them.'"

They sat and listened for a moment, attuned as much to the other man's listening as to Van Morrison's young throat hitting its raspy limits on the chorus.

"The Brit guys were pretty innocent, eh?" Bonaduce offered. "They all did the big attitude." Acknowledging Van's Irishness would only complicate things here.

"Sorry, I'm not following."

"It was all an act. Like the Stones. Everybody was five foot two and in art school."

Oscar smiled, his shoulders leaping in a silent laugh. He looked happy for this guy talk. Should have him out for a beer.

"Oh, now, well, I think the British have their fair share of tough guys, and psychotics."

"They love a stage is all I'm saying."

"You think" — Oscar pointed at the stereo, pausing then shaking a finger just as Van Morrison went into one of his wails — "you think that's an act?"

"I know it is." You could picture the wee guy in a booth, headphones on, holding the mike the exact proper distance for an undistorted howl, this his third take, he's warmed up now. "You don't scream like that for real unless, I don't know, you're watching your own blood pour out of you."

"Okay, I suppose." Oscar, enjoying this, searched for something to counter with. "But on TV, videos, you see these bands that look evil and I tend to believe it."

"They've had to think more, you know, visually. Can't just stand there and sing any more."

"Well, I guess, sure. Learned to act." He paused. "Okay. Have you seen Iggy Pop?"

"Hang on, I mean Brits. The *Brits* are the actors. All they did was put American R & B on stage. Iggy Pop's real."

"Oh, I see."

"No, it's true. Go ask any Brit superstar, go ask the Beatles who turned them on and it's always Chuck Berry, Elvis, Jerry Lee Lewis. Even Carl Perkins, for Christ sake."

"I suppose."

"Oscar? Americans couldn't fool anybody. They don't even try."

He was up with Oscar now, hunched shoulder to shoulder and peering into the music titles. Oscar was indeed an Anglophile. Stones, every Beatles you could think of, even Petula Clark, housewife with a ditty. Elton John, well of course, and Supertramp, the whiners. Lots of Moody Blues, who were The Lettermen on drugs.

"So you have it down to a kind of British-versus-American thing."

"Oscar? How many American bands can you recall who wore the matching, you know, 'outfits'?"

You had to admire the Brits for their imagination, but, well. If Jerry Lee Lewis was mad at you he'd shoot you in a second. If David Bowie was mad at you he'd put on a costume and stare.

Oscar had been thinking. "You got me."

"The Byrds did, for a while."

Bonaduce tried picturing Oscar and Leah together. They weren't a likely mix. He didn't feel jealous, in the way he sometimes did over sexy women he didn't even know, couples he passed in the street. He saw Leah being cheerful with Oscar, efficiently going about her day, threatened by nothing in the man at all.

"So the Brits only *look* like they suck blood from animals," Oscar mused, mildly imitating Bonaduce. "But they're in actual fact just — clarinet wusses." He grinned, pleased with himself.

"There you go."

"In all probability Ozzy Osbourne doesn't bite chickens' heads off at home, true."

"That was great coffee."

Bonaduce slumped back on the couch. Two regular guys sitting here talking music. Oscar was getting more comfortable. Good thing he hadn't thought of Paul Revere and the Raiders. Or Kiss, Alice Cooper. It would've been all over.

"This body piercing's pretty spectacular though." Oscar shook his head in a kind of admiration. "How far is *that* going to go?"

"It's a contest, isn't it."

"I saw a nose ring the other day, not the usual tiny little thing in the side, but a big, thick hoop" — he pinched thumb and forefinger into both nostrils — "like a bull. She couldn't have been fourteen. And man? I saw a bone once, in Toronto."

"Hey — guy in Wheeling has one. Or had one. I mean a hockey player. He—"

"Nose ring?"

"Nose ring. He attracted some attention. Guys trying to get at it with their sticks. Guy had balls, I guess. Hockey player with a nose ring ..."

Oscar smiled appreciatively.

"Earrings have been around," Bonaduce offered. "Guy can have an earring and still be a stud."

"The code." Oscar nodded to himself.

"That's right." Bonaduce lifted his cup, forgetting it was empty. "So. So how well do you know Jason?"

"Not well." He shook his head with self-judgement.

"Ah."

"Considering we lived together for three years. I mean, I can tell you what he doesn't like for breakfast."

"Right."

"I came in at a touchy age I think. Fifteen. I just made myself available if he needed me for something, but he never did. Well, the car, a summer job, that." Oscar pulled a bullied face and made as if to go for his wallet. "But emotionally, no. He's such a private kid. But you know that."

"Right."

No, you don't know that. You don't know that at all.

Hard sitting still at the highway house between classes, between *jogs*. Between the last thing and the next thing. Breaths.

The Maui trucks made it harder. Something adhesive in them, you could get dragged out of your thoughts by a big truck, get towed on down the road. Maybe it was just that he envied the driver his destination. Here he was, stopped, while so much of the last twenty years had been a road trip. Buses from Rochester to Muskegon, to Springfield, to Portland. Portland Oregon *and* Maine. On those endless purgatorial all-nighters he'd often be sitting up awake, eyes on the black window, generally unaware of but held anyway by the bus's constant muffled roar. No one else on the road except the big trucks, working the interstate. Catching up to one, buddy-buddy alongside for a while, the truck's whining, roaring insistence would blend in with and double that of the bus. You can see the driver lit up ghost-green behind his wheel, staring straight ahead, both of you rushing in the same direction. What's the guy nodding to, what beat? You try to guess the tape he's listening to, you almost hear it through the noise, hey it's Beefheart, no it's Johnny Cash, no the decades have flown by, it's Vince Gill now. You know in all likelihood it's Abba, or funk. Though a guy likes funk you don't automatically hate him, despite his obvious deficiency. At least it's not disco, or *Belafonte's Best*. It's probably Anthony Robbins, or Sri-somebody, the driver's probably nodding yes, inspired to be all the trucker he can be. Actually you can tell from his intent face that, like you, he's alone with nothing but his own rambling thoughts. Beside you on the road, in a sixty-mile-an-hour easy chair. The guy like a teammate you'd never meet.

Reaching across the table with his good arm, Toby poured the wine. He usually poured because the wine was usually his, homemade red bought from a friend for two bucks a bottle. The friend made a fifty-cent profit per bottle, so Toby didn't feel guilty.

Bonaduce lifted his jamjar for Toby to stop pouring.

"Studying tonight." He smiled but didn't know if he was joking or not. At night he'd been accepting the glass of wine Toby always offered. In training, he always stopped at two.

It was a decent domestic scene. Rod, never much of a talker, sat in a corner sipping and reading. Despite the slightly froggish set of his lips and eyes when he read, Bonaduce liked the look of Rod, the relaxed alertness as he sat, the graceful way his spine arced out of his collar. Tonight Rod was reading something by the Dalai Lama, and occasionally he would mutter a quote, some kind of gently wise truth you'd expect. Bonaduce and Marg had taken to keeping the Yahtzee game at permanent readiness on the coffee table and played it nightly, as they did now, a dime a game. Toby talked.

"It's not the best," Toby said, as usual, after topping up everyone's jar, "but it works. And it's cheap. Bloody booze tax. It's all taxes. Fucking, government, monopoly."

Bonaduce had lived with Fournier for much of the last decade — five, six years? — but otherwise alone. He'd forgotten that roommates weren't always a bowl of cherries. These young types were okay in general and Marg here was a jewel, but Toby — Toby was getting on his nerves. From the first he'd noticed that Toby had a certain nasty air about him. Then it dawned one night, listening to Toby speak, that every single thing Toby said was negative. Life was taxes, government monopolies, sleet. Even when he smiled it was hooked by a sneer. His chicken arm hard against his chest, blocking open laughter.

"Well, taxes, yeah." Bonaduce gave a little shrug. "But then we don't pay medical here."

"Yeah, right." Toby rolled his eyes and looked away, possessing information Bonaduce did not.

"Well you ol' *luck* bucket," Bonaduce exclaimed to Marg and her large straight. Marg liked his cowboy talk. He scooped the dice and rattled them loudly up at his ear. "Baby needs a new pair a feet."

You don't want to avoid the people you live with, skulking off to your room in the evenings like some kind of loner. You want to participate. But evenings, while drinking Toby's wine, you couldn't help but get his constant dark slant on things, his voice being the dominant one in the room. Some complainers you understand and forgive, others you don't. If Toby were to lean in and look you in the eye and say how God had given him a shitty arm and a shitty life, you could sympathize. But when a guy complains constantly, constantly, about the bad things we all shared — weather, politics, good food too expensive or cheap food tasting bad — it got a little tiring. Thank you, Toby, for always reminding us, for always making clear the lowest shitty denominator.

"Free medical? The drug companies charging sixty bucks for a bottle of pills it costs two bucks to make?"

"Yeah" — Bonaduce made himself nod — "I guess it is pretty bad that way."

"AIDS medicine costing thousands a month?"

"Right. That's wrong."

"Wrong, man, it's criminal. We're afraid to die and people cash in on that. No one should make more money than anyone else. It's immoral. With health it's criminal."

Bonaduce nodded absently, thinking about the drugstore today, where he'd gone for vitamin C, devil of a cold or something coming. He'd found himself in the geriatric row — walkers, trusses, canes, all beige and ugly-practical, easy to hose off.

He'd had to force himself to walk the aisle, pretending he wasn't noticing the twenty feet of adult diapers, a whole fucking section for them.

"And everyone *knows* it's criminal," Toby said.

They'd had an argument once, almost a fight (Bonaduce had actually been able to picture them fighting, Toby attacking him with both arms, an ugly image). Toby, who was on unemployment insurance, had been ranting that the government changing just the name, from "unemployment" to "employment" insurance, was typical in that their solution to any problem they couldn't fix was to euphemize it. Toby was right, but Bonaduce made the mistake of joking that the government would soon be calling death "Afterlife Canada," and to this Toby said, "It isn't funny, man," and glared at him until he was forced to get up and go to his room.

Toby was uncorking another bottle of wine, as usual making a display of it. Bonaduce didn't like thinking it, but he suspected these one-handed shows of non-disability were why Toby had gotten into his wine habit to begin with. Toby was opening wine and staring accusingly, and it felt like gritty déjà vu. Bonaduce sighed and looked away.

"That's how it is, I guess."

He hardly heard himself. He'd been halfway into a sip of wine when his own ditty, "We don't pay for medical here," came back to him, echoing. He stopped his sip at the possibility that on some deeper level he hadn't chosen Canada so much as he'd fled the medical bills of the United States.

"Your roll, there, Robert," Marg drawled. "Howse about a quarter a game? My ol' *luck bucket*'s gettin' full of your dimes."

OSCAR DEVRIES.

When, out of the blue, Bob Bonaduce called on a Friday night near the end of November and said in his way, Hey Buddy, let's do a pub crawl, Oscar was surprised and impressed with himself, first that he agreed and second that he felt glad for it. And when Bonaduce pulled up in his wreck and honked, he was actually doing it, he was pulling on his coat, smiling and shrugging to Leah, waving, going, incredible. Doing the male thing. Poor Leah, she no doubt had some complicated feelings about all of this. His "Honey, I have a date with your ex" seemed to get to her somehow and hardly let her smile. This outing apparently wasn't quite what she had in mind on those occasions when she suggested he go out and find himself some friends.

The idea was to hear some music. Over the phone they'd agreed on a bar called Chevys, which Bob had heard played nothing but oldies.

Considering they were middle-aged men who didn't know each other, in the car it was surprisingly smooth. Just two fellows venturing forth with what looked to be adolescent drinking intentions. He'd been made aware, during sessions with the counsellor he and Leah had seen, that with men his own age he was at ease only when the roles were clear, when the sign "Client" or "Employer" or "Sales," or what have you, was shined up and pinned to a chest. Oscar had nodded politely at the woman's exaggeration, but he did take her essential point home with him.

Declaring just how fine a beer sounded, Bob Bonaduce grinned, nodding at the windshield, and Oscar understood that he was going to a dance club with someone who was "ruggedly handsome."

So, this was the man Leah had married. And this was the father of Leah's son. Most of all, though, in the air was the fact of Bonaduce having slept with her. Twenty years ago or not. Leah had described it as "adolescent passion," as if these words dismissed it. On the contrary it made him consider this thing called animal magnetism, it made him remember how at the party Bonaduce had looked at Leah, the simple but profound gravity in his eyes, and it made him consider his own lovemaking, which was infrequent these days and which — under the glare of true animal magnetism — might amount to little more than feeble.

He glanced down at their two pairs of blue-jeaned knees. To his knowledge he had never been alone with someone who had slept with the same woman. It was a vague and queasy thrill, the proximity and palpable sense of their two laps side by side here in the car.

"Decent night," said Bonaduce, head tilting back in meditative satisfaction. "Decent fall."

Oscar agreed.

He had feared a heart-to-heart, some confession or plea from this man who couldn't help but have unrealistically romantic notions about Jason. The cheap pathos of absence. According to Leah, Bonaduce was orphaned at some young age, the father leaving, the mother dying. In any case Leah said she feared unresolved father stuff surfacing here in Fredericton in some kind of overblown way. What words had she used? "Walt Disney way." Play catch with me Dad, golly jeepers, atta boy Son.

But once in the car Oscar saw that Bonaduce would neither blurt nor plead. No, the man had slicked-back hair and he opened his window in preparation for lighting a small, thin cigar with a comic flourish. Bonaduce kept smiling. He exhaled luxuriously and announced with corny pleasure, "Only on special occasions." Which made Oscar feel good, to be called a special occasion. The fellow had some social grace. No doubt in his career he met people all the time. The smile appeared genuine. He could have been a successful minor politician, that small-town charisma. The clothes, the relaxed athlete at the wheel, the casual vanity of the man. Looking over at you for no reason, smiling and meeting your eye as if something were transpiring.

Other than ask directions to Chevys, Bob Bonaduce was happy to go on about nothing remotely serious. As with his blather about British musicians and nose rings. Tonight it was questions about Fredericton, about nightspots, about when Oscar thought the first snow would hit. He asked about "your lawyer job," nodding politely to the litiginous intrigues while not listening. He really did need to talk but the need had nothing to do with content.

Chevys revealed a side of Fredericton Oscar hadn't seen up close. Everyone was between forty and sixty, which was a nice surprise, and which made sense given the music. In the first ten minutes they played Young Rascals, Elvis and Dusty Springfield. But he'd be damned if this wasn't a singles bar. Tables of ladies sitting wide-eyed and available. Men standing posed in shadow with arm crooked, their beer bottles held pointed in comically suggestive angles. Quick, serious swigs as if suddenly considering something. Swallow, as an afterthought. Ripple your jaw muscles.

He couldn't help but smile — he had never felt so stared at. Women in their forties, even fifties, made up to the hilt but in tight jeans like it was 1975, giving him a hungry unblinking come-on. Oscar Devries, piece of meat. Great stuff. Bonaduce didn't seem to be noticing, though he was getting double the eyes. Well, the man must be used to it, scenes like this. What else does a man do? In Kalamazoo.

The volume went up for an old Doobie Brothers, and if it was hard to talk before, now it was impossible. He and Bob had more or less guzzled their first beer (it seemed to Oscar that they'd each been trying to keep pace with the other) and now Bonaduce appeared with four bottles, two for each of them. Oh-oh and oh well. The DJ behind smoked glass spun a slow platter next, "Ruby," that Kenny Rogers cowpat about a good old boy home from 'Nam sexually disabled, him watchin' his Ruby goin' out to git herself laid, poor him waitin' up, drinkin' the wine. With this song the mood changed as if the DJ had pulled a switch, some kind of perverse romance suddenly in the air, everybody's face taking on the cartoon loneliness and tragedy. The guys swigged with inner torture now, and the gals were stricken in their chairs, eyes wider than ever. And Bob Bonaduce — oh goodness, look at this — there was Bob Bonaduce, eyes downcast, disabled, suffering the same.

Oscar tilted a beer and decided to climb off his arrogant perch. This blue-collar watering hole had lain hidden somewhere in his oddly polar world of executive suits, on the one hand, and

Leah's impoverished refugees, on the other. Despite the manipulative music it was elitist and hypocritical to stand here in disdain
of the tabloid loneliness of Middle America. For apparently
Middle America crossed the border. And you couldn't help but
visualize the wanton middle-age sex. By the looks of things this
bar would lead to a lot of it, all these divorced old—

"This is great, eh?" Bonaduce shouting in his ear.

"Yeah."

"Good music."

"Yeah."

Except for the ubiquitous "Satisfaction" and the Hollies' "He
Ain't Heavy," there'd been precious few good tunes. All Top
Forty, the expected Motown, Creedence, nothing remotely obscure. Bob seemed bored too, eventually. He didn't seem interested in the women, of which, from the looks of them looking at
him, he could've plucked his choice and taken home with the
effort of one waggled finger. He'd already refused two women
asking him to dance, but now accepted a third, she a rotund
sixty-year-old who made her request a self-deprecating joke.

Weird being here. Leah's early husband. Weird watching him
down there dancing. The grace of an athlete, the stiffness of
having muscles like that. Somewhat flinging his arms around in
humour and confidence, and also implied threat, though that
would not be deliberate. How much of any dancer's dance was
deliberate, exactly? There were questions he wanted to ask Bob
now, because Bob was quite possibly not as uncomplicated as he
seemed. Living across the river in a house of twenty-five-year-
olds. Middle-aged grad student in English but who spoke and
looked like a fellow who — what, owned a gun shop? ran a gas
station? Apparently he was serious about the hockey with Jason.
Jason had reacted negatively to the idea. How was that developing? Leah had not returned from Sussex the day Bob had come
over to discuss it. Maybe they'd spoken since on the phone. Who
knows? He was staying out of it. He thought the father/son
hockey a sweet idea, but so completely innocent. Let's play catch,
son. A given that Jason would find it awkward. "Lame" is the

word he'd use.

"*Wanna head out?*" Bonaduce, puffing, limped up. Lame.

"*Sure.*"

Bonaduce led him out of Chevys. In the car he said he knew another good bar, Rockin Rodeo, which he then disparaged as "kind of hick." Oscar, who had just experienced the hickest scene of his life, wondered what was in store.

"I've had four beer, probably have the same there, we cab it after that," Bob announced, clicking on his seat belt.

"Taxi's on me." Oscar smiled because both of them were still almost shouting.

"Sounds good." He flashed the Bonaduce smile. "I'm on a student's salary these days. This is my big night out."

What salary would this man attract when school ended? An English MA, in his forties, God help him. Oscar had done an English BA, but only as a route to Law, and perhaps one shouldn't mention this. Bob Bonaduce had basic problems he wasn't dealing with. This constant good mood of his clearly strode on rickety stilts. And if any serious conversation was going to ensue tonight, now was the time, and maybe it was his job to start it.

"I've wanted your side of this and now I can ask you: how come you and Leah never did get divorced?" It wasn't that he didn't believe Leah's version. And he hoped this didn't sound in any way jealous, because it wasn't. Leah wasn't speaking fondly of the man.

Another Bonaduce smile. "I guess we weren't on good enough speaking terms to get one."

Oscar chuckled appreciatively.

"Yes, well. It goes with the territory. We've had some problems ourselves. An early affair ..." He shrugged, content to leave ambiguous an affair that had only been Leah's.

"Ooo, hey, it happens."

"But — I love her, Bob."

Now, hell, what was this about? He'd shrugged as if casual but hadn't it come out like a plea? Four bottles of beer and he'd turned to pathetic mush, telling about affairs — he'd never told *anyone* else — and now confessing his love.

"That's good to hear, Oscar."

He and Leah did have a good one, a good relationship. They'd healed and worked through. They had an unspoken understanding of where they were headed, of what was *utmost* in a relationship.

"That's really good to hear."

Oscar looked over to him and smiled, though Bonaduce was staring straight ahead, driving carefully. His poise at the wheel. Big carnivore in graceful repose. He could picture Bob Bonaduce with Leah. To picture this was also to understand that, when sex was mindless, when sex was inevitable as gravity, *utmost* had no chance.

He waited a half-mile before asking the next one.

"So is this hockey thing with Jason important to you?"

Bob either shrugged quickly or suffered a neck spasm of some sort, it was hard to tell in the dark of the car. The man who had been an orphaned adolescent didn't otherwise answer the question, though the car was going faster.

Oscar regretted his question for what he now saw might be its latent cruelty. But Bob's silence was so turned in on himself that Oscar wasn't made to feel awkward. In fact he felt freed of any involvement. Outside, it had begun to sleet. Mixed with road grease and bugs already there, the windshield turned the colour of mud. Bonaduce didn't appear to notice.

"Can you — can you see? Do you have any wiper fluid?"

§

Bonaduce remembered the washer fluid running dry about an hour out of Fredericton on the long haul here, seemed like ages ago now. You always try the wipers anyway, make that same greasy mistake. He found a wad of paper on the floor, pulled over, got out, spit, wiped a face-size hole in the mess. Old Oscar could ride blind. I love her, Bob.

Too bad they didn't have a couple of road beers.

"Bob, can you see?"

"No. Why?"

"Good. Excellent."

Windshields were one of those things you don't think about until they make themselves known like this. He'd completely forgotten, but recalled now when this windshield had last entertained him, and the reason he'd run out of fluid: the firefly. An hour out of Fredericton, middle of the night, he'd seen off the highway what looked to be a cloud, a swarm, of fireflies. He'd never seen a cloud of them before. Hundreds at least. Marvelling at the auspicious luck of seeing a cloud of fireflies just as he was embarking on a new life, a sudden *splot* woke him up, a double-take wake-up because the fresh-dead bug was a firefly, its guts phosphorescent green on the windshield, eye level, right there.

The bug was dead but its guts were alive. Bright, bright as a tiny flashlight. Green fire undiminished. Again, and though not a nice event for the bug, he saw it as his luck. A neat little story to tell, and some science to boot, a firefly's light outlived its life. The fire came first, and it was bigger. So what was the human equivalent?

All kinds of thoughts swirled as he drove at speed. He'd quit the bungee music for now and had rolled up the window. You could stare at the little green sun and at the same time see beyond it to the road. He was awfully tired, road-delirious, and his thoughts about luck took a turn. Because when the bug's light finally did start to fade, he saw this as the true image of his luck. So swirly and dream-caught was he, that it being a green light cemented the bad-omen deal, green being not only Irish but also part of the Italian flag. He watched it fade, he watched it fade, using the wipers to get it away, his luck draining, running out, bad choice coming here, bad sign this setting-sun fly, just go away. And there was no human equivalent.

Oscar silent beside him, he drove peering through his faced-sized hole. He knew he was superstitious. Firefly, dead air freshener, dreamcatcher. The luck of the Irish. Italian. In voodoo, scientists say, it's your own superstition that kills you. If that was true, what a truth it was. Because, if you could kill yourself with belief, it meant you could also fix things — anything. Well. Of course it was foolish to ponder these big questions, even when what might be an evil disease was shouldering you in that direction. Life throwing its gloves off, staring you down. It was even more foolish not to ponder them, even if you know there are no answers. You let twenty years slide by without considering the big questions, you obviously haven't been doing enough wrong, or right.

He drove, enjoying Oscar's nervousness. He'd thought he might get into this stuff with Oscar tonight, but wouldn't. A good guy, but Oscar was simply too cynical about too much. Marg had the better ear for it and, incredibly, the better words. Lapsed Christians had a good take on things. In fact, watching her, it had dawned on him that, since there are no big answers available to the big questions, maybe the key was to go smaller. Ask questions less huge, questions not aimed *directly* at the big stuff. Not what is *the* meaning of life, but where is *meaning* found. Not *what* is the answer, but *how* should I ask it. Where to locate yourself.

Love, of course, was a place to start. Which was sort of why he was here.

At the instant Bonaduce thought this, Oscar asked a question about Jason, which startled him. Coincidence packs a jolt. Coincidence felt like religion's messenger-boy. Startling as well was the next insight supplied by his beer-fuelled reverie: Superstition was the only religion he'd ever had.

Another beer would be nice. Expose Oscar to a bit of country twang. He seemed to have a decent sense of humour.

• • •

OSCAR.

When they pulled up in front of Rockin Rodeo and studied its neon sign replete with lassos and boots, Bob broke into the most superb westernisms. "Thar she be, Randy-buck. Settin' thar all purty as a rivershell." It seemed that in his years south his ear had absorbed some of the essential American tongue.

Bob found a parking spot a block distant. It was a beautiful night now. Decent indeed. A hard white moon had come out. Overnight would be cold enough to start ice on the puddles. He had not in a million years thought he'd end up in this country-and-western joint he passed with no curiosity each day on his way to work. What was disturbing was that after only four beer Bob — big beer-drinking Bobby Bonaduce — staggered walking the block to the bar. He actually didn't seem drunk; but Oscar felt offput, and then a little custodial. As they neared the bar, once again his friend launched the lunatic drawl, a cowboy rant that mixed cheek and nonsense.

"Why, this'n here hombre's dirt-mad enough" — Bob was pointing into the face of a scowling woman leaving the bar — "to take and kick the ass-tanks off'n a bull in a toad storm. An she'all knows it, too."

The blonde hombre decided to smile as she climbed into her taxi. Bob kept up the showoff as he pushed in the double glass doors, then the fake saloon doors, talking louder and louder over the music. He stood surveying the place. He pointed at various women.

"*She* was so purty that, wellsir, ever' bigbone weevil from all hunnert counties took and went on a stomp for her benefit, and her benefit too, and hers'n — spree the likes a which six yaller dang bitch coyotes couldn't howl 'nuff to keep *tam*."

Everyone was in jeans, half wore cowboy boots. Even a scatter of cowboy hats. One fellow in a shiny aquamarine cowboy shirt, thumbs hooked in his belt loops, stomped the floor with his big heels, quite serious. Oscar told himself that this was not unlike walking into a meeting place of the Klan, then he understood he only wanted to see it this way for the thrill of it, because he was already bored. This was loyalist New Brunswick and it was dress-up. Though there might likely be fights.

Bob Bonaduce was loud enough that a few heads were turning, and while Oscar smiled broadly to show everyone it was all a joke, he really wanted Bob to stop.

"Well thar, mister, watcha thank of this'n har line-dancin' dude-pit?"

"If you shut up I'll buy you-all a beer, Big Bob."

Rockin Rodeo was fine from the point of view of studying exotic culture and its music, but two beers later it was very much time to go. Then it was later still and he'd had too much to drink, having stupidly agreed to the cowboy-macho thing of two tequila shooters back to back. Coupla manly men. It was fun drinking in this bar with this man but not worth sitting hung over in tomorrow morning's light. If anything it made him realize his love of Saturday mornings. Him alone with his coffee and paper in the sunroom, Leah sleeping in. The click of his cup, the smell of the coffee, and newsprint.

Outside, impatient with the task of getting a cab for each of them, what with these womenfolk flirtin' their way in front, he was foolishly manly again and drove Bob's wreck to Bob's house way out on the northside highway. He was afraid Bob would've driven himself if he hadn't. Bob's legs weren't working right, and his tongue was thick and slow. *Helll. Owwe. Ahhh-fisss-errr.*

Stupid. Cops did love to catch a lawyer. Why was he doing this?

Bob snapped on the radio and sought music, music being the string through this night's beads.

At Bob's house a clutch of kids dressed in black stood in the gravel parking area, staring into the sky. They yelled at Oscar to turn the car lights off, they were looking for the Hale-Bopp. Bob launched into a string of puns about Halley's comet and bebop music and Bill Haley and the Comets, none of which the kids seemed to understand or want to.

Oscar somewhat self-consciously stepped through their midst and into the house to phone a cab. But Bob Bonaduce took the phone from him and mannishly replaced it with a beer, screw Saturday. Some of Bob's tapes were truly classic, the fellow did know music. He had a big cardboard box packed with tapes. In his funny little room. Bob was enacting some sort of student-hell parody, living with these vampire kids, but he seemed to be enjoying himself. The box had Musswell Hillbillies, early Who, Fairport Convention, these the only good Brit stuff, for Bonaduce was indeed married to the early American white boys. Jerry Lee, some uncommon Elvis, Gene Pitney, Del Shannon, and anything pre-Dylan. Pre-complexity? The Brits had always been into complexity perhaps because, well, to give Bob his due, they were already at a remove, copying the Americans.

The gang of glowering youth came in from their comet and sat in the living room drinking tea and talking softly, more than likely stoned, definitely not wanting two drunken old men in their face. There was a small laughing argument about what went on the stereo, Bob laughing that he'd sue, and then goddamn renovate this place and everyone in it, he had his own lawyer along too. Oscar for one would have been more than happy just to stay in Bob's room and flick through the tape indexes, sit on the bed and talk about whatever, but Bob had a guitar by the neck and insisted Oscar stay in the living room and sing. Bob bragged that he knew how to play every song off the first album of some band called Los Lobos. It was unclear whether or not they were about to hear every one of these songs.

This wasn't to be the case, but it was still largely awful because Oscar was forced to sing. This only after the young people had drifted off, and only after much ridicule and another beer, and another beer. Some of it wasn't bad funny-singing, Bob "doing Oscar Devries doing Mick Jagger," and then a spontaneous ode to the Hale-Bopp comet, except that some housemate asleep above started pounding on his floor, and Bonaduce, hissing how he didn't fucking like that one-armed gimp, pounded the ceiling with the head of his guitar. Oscar was drunk enough that it was more amusing than scary to see Bonaduce's anger fire his muscles like that, the speed of it and the teeth-clenched smile, a rage that may have served his profession but rage nonetheless. Bonaduce left dents in the ceiling, and the guitar was sprung out of tune.

§

His eyes blinked, stayed open. Sure, this morning had to come. He realized he'd been expecting it. A morning when the truth dawned clear and hard and woke him before the sun did: There was nothing to do with his life than the thing he was doing now, and no one wanted him here doing it.

All he could manage under the weight of this truth was to go up on an elbow and look out his window. Scan the stage. It was grey, windy, shitty out. Nothing else. The comet had left for now. Right, he'd seen it last night, his first comet, and it had surprised him. Paler than starlight. It was fuzzy and playful, like a child's crayoned happy-thing. He'd read in the paper the previous day how comets were regarded as harbingers of doom, and standing with Oscar beside the car he'd had doom in mind as he searched the sky for the comet. Toby had impatiently grunted, There, and Bonaduce got behind him to sight along his good arm. His eyes found this softly glowing fuzzy-bunny thing. Now instantly doubly sinister. You are shown the face of death and it is Shirley Temple's.

Up on his elbow, Bonaduce could feel the entirety of himself gaining, by the moment, a dark and precarious weight. He knew he was one step away from going down and staying down. He willed the eyes to stay open. He looked through the rainbow threads of the dreamcatcher. Marg had called it this, explained its reason for being.

He looked through, seeing what he could, eyes zooming through blurring threads to focus on the distant treeline, the empty stage. Dreamcatcher in reverse. Hey, out there. Catch this one.

Well, with any luck you can find something specific to blame a lousy mood on. And he was a bit hung over. Quite a bit hung over ... *and of course fatigue* ... Lucky him, he could blame a variety.

Last night had been all right though, his date with Oscar, ending up back here for some tunes and a nightcap. The guitar, right. Toby's stereo had been eating and ruining his tapes for a month and Toby refused to demagnetize. His young roomies had nothing but CDs themselves and unfortunately it wasn't the right kind of music. In this he and Oscar had been in agreement.

But now how in anyone's hell could a successful lawyer in his forties be shy about singing the good oldies in front of a bunch of kids? They wear black and nod their snarky little heads to Nine Inch Nails but so what? Even Marg he didn't like last night. Young types who give no credit to anyone but themselves for anything. You laugh at the purity of Del Shannon, it's your loss. Live your lives in a snarkier-than-thou postmodern house of mirrors, go ahead.

Despite what it was speeding toward, there was something okay about age, there really was. Last night, him and Oscar like buds here in this romper-room house. At the writing workshop he and Big Jan sometimes caught each other's eye and almost smiled after a blurted youngism. In the halls at school, nineteen-year-olds ambling smug with all the latest trendy torn cool junk on their bodies and on their minds — it was stuff you knew nothing about, but you couldn't help feel sorry for them, looking down from your perch of age. Because you knew, and they didn't, that what they so absolutely believed in right now, what stiffened their spine and curled their smirk, would in twenty years be gone. You knew, and they didn't, that in twenty years

they wouldn't know anything at all, and feel just like you.
Imagine telling this to Jason. Imagine the look.

He opened the fridge. Toast, toast would be good. With jam. Or maybe meat, this looked like meat, liverwurst. It didn't smell off, too much.

"There's a giant hole in the bathroom wall."

Here was Marg, standing in her big white terrycloth robe. The whole idea of her was hard to look at.

"Was that all that noise last night?"

Shit. That's right, the bathroom wall.

"Well, Marg, it was all rotten there. I decided to fix it."

"Looks like you kicked the wall in."

It came back now. He'd fallen hard against it for no reason and dented it with an elbow. Then he'd lost it a bit and started kicking, starting with the swamp-wall beside the toilet.

"It was all rotten." It was. Some of it the fist had gone through easy.

"But I mean we're renting. That's like, the landlord's job."

"So where is he? It was all piss-soaked."

"Well, now we have this totally screwed-up wall."

Marg's face was slack, her voice was monotone. She wasn't into reasoning.

"I'll fix it. I just couldn't stand it. I hated it. Can't see how anyone could sit down beside that and take a—"

"*He* might hate it, you kicked in his wall. It wasn't rotten all the way to the bathtub like that." Marg turned her back on him and started doing something fast at the counter with her hands, grabbing up papers or something. "I just cleaned it all up, so I know."

"Marg? I'll fix it."

. . .

THE HOCKEY NOVEL
by
R. BONADUCE

It is not only species of animals that die
out, but whole species of feeling. And if
you are wise you will never pity the past
for what it did not know, but pity yourself
for what it did.
—John Fowles, probably talking about
old-time hockey

Oscar Devries, immigrant baby, was given his first pair
of skates at age four weeks. Outside their sod hovel the
prairie winter wind howled like a she-devil as Father
laced Baby Oscar's skates up tight. So tight that blood
began beading up at the lace-holes. But little Oscar didn't
cry. He cried only when they removed the skates and he
kept crying until they laced them back on, tighter. They
taped popsicle sticks on for shin pads and stuffed his
little rig into a thimble. Helmet? No helmet, Oscar
thrashed his head until they gave up trying to put one
on him, he wouldn't be a fancylad. And fuck the
mouthguard too: he already had no teeth. They noticed
he had come into the world with several facial scars.

Oscar's first game he played naked, save for his bleeding skates. His foul temper kept him warm and red and
his skin unfrozen. He went goalless but, using his adult-
size stick, he sent six players to the Winnipeg Regional
Hospital.

• • •

Bonaduce poured himself his second glass. Red wine, hey, I feel a tumour coming on, pass the red. He wondered if Toby would miss this bottle, if he kept count. Downstairs, Toby kept his bottles stacked dusty on their sides as if it was a fucking wine cellar, not a rat cellar.

He was having nothing but trouble coming up with anything for Big Jan's workshop. He'd whined to her and she'd simply said, Write what you know. So he'd joked, Hard to write about nothing for very long. And she'd said, Nonsense. And he'd said, Nonsense it will be!

So, sure, he could write about hockey. But what? A pack of anecdotes? The exotic stuff? He'd seen a goalie's artery slashed. He'd seen teammates shit their pants during a game, one guy — who was that, O'Dowd? — forcibly trading the dirtied pants with a frightened Russian rookie, O'Dowd the satanic joker. (Here ya go, Jan and Phil and Kirsten, good stuff, eh?) Or Donny Carter, his nervous breakdown between periods. That nervous little look, the glancing around like a timid baby, not talking, took a few days for anyone to catch on, then a year on the sixth floor for Carter. Or should he just write a stupid Rocky story about a guy who overcomes the odds? Everyone liked that crap, maybe even Jan. Bill Spunska, clumsy immigrant, barely makes the team but scores the winning *yadda* with *yadda* left on the clock in the *yadda yadda* finals. Do you do the social comment? team-as-microcosm thing? Modern gladiators, boxed vicarious bloodwar, testosteronic bugs in a bell jar. Do you write for an audience at all? Or do you just scribble for yourself and hope someone else gloms onto your heartbeat? But how to convey the subtleties of a thing, how do you hold the good mirror up to the rink's old wet-cigar smell, or the sound of tape tearing off the roll as distinct from ripping off an ankle, or the kaleidoscopic personality of a dressing room? Or the game itself, the fresh ballsy chugging, the deepgut serenity of a solid hit and the guy going down. Or the danger of it all — you have the puck and you're lugging a bag of gold to market surrounded by fast bandits.

How do you know if anyone will care?

Tonight at the laptop, once again he'd begun with a legitimate beginning, the Fowles quote, then fouled it up going right into the Oscar joke. Well, Jan's other advice had been, just start writing, no goal, freeform. Maybe he'd try again tomorrow. Maybe he'd shove this in Oscar's mailbox in the meantime, why not. Too bad it wasn't this fun writing essays. Humour — humour was the antidote for all that wasn't humorous.

His first piece of mail. In the student general mailbox a message from Professor Daniel Kirk regarding the "New Traditions in the Carnivalesque" seminar he'd registered in but so far had not attended. Hard to say how old the note was because he hadn't been checking the box. Come to think of it, he'd passed Kirk in the hall a few times and the guy's stick-up-the-ass response to a friendly hello Bonaduce had written off to personality rather than circumstance. Sorry, professor, my mistake.

A word in the last sentence was underlined:

What are your intentions?

Nice, a catchphrase for him to go to sleep to and wake up with, a jingle for life. Come on, *what* are they?

His second piece of mail was old news. His grant had been turned down. He was to subsist on the assistantship alone. Once a week he met thirty students, Engineering types mostly, to work on writing skills. It was strange. The course was called "Aspects of the Novel." A Professor MacAphee, whom he hadn't met, gave twice-weekly lectures on novels the class was supposed to have read, then on Fridays the lectured-to students broke into groups for a session with a grad student, to work on essays about these novels. Bonaduce had questions about this. If they wanted these guys to learn how to write essays, give them subjects that mattered to them: movies, computers, sex, whatever. They lacked the tools to say the right things about the novels even had they read them. They wrote MacAphee's lecture insights down as best they could, and it was Bonaduce's job to help them hammer these notes into essays. He encountered poor slobs trying to work in "Apocalypse now was of course but the bastard celluloid son of heart of darkness the masterpiece," not knowing if this meant it was good or bad.

Bonaduce figured he was a decent teacher, because in their tongue-chewing labours he saw himself mirrored in Gail Smith's. He got on their good side, even the back-row sneer-doctors in the ball caps, by clapping his hands and saying, "Gotta do it so let's do it, let's fuckin' go get 'er, ya wanna be as dumb as ya look?" It at least got their attention. The only reason they bothered to stoop to try to put fancy sentences together was to pass the course, get the degree, the job, make as much money as possible. Bonaduce had chased rubber for twenty years, but compared with these guys he was a philosopher and bohemian. If teaching this course was depressing, its social forecast was scary. What had happened to the liberal fucking education?

Regarding his first piece of mail, Bonaduce decided his intentions hadn't changed — that is, he had no clue *what* they were — and he left Kirk no note.

That night, there it was, in the centre of his window, the comet. The Hale-Bopp happy face, all plague-spewing innocence. It had an intensity you could almost hear. Having it in your window was funny and not-so-funny. It was hard not to feel singled out. Apparently for the next month this comet would be exactly right there.

What can you make of a ball of nasty dirty ice millions of

miles away framed perfectly in your very own bedroom window? Monster pulling a gaudy dirt-tail longer than lifetimes. Hanging there in your window utterly still — yet moving at a speed your mind can't take.

Absolutely no sound out there, ever.

What were its intentions?

THE (HO)KKY NOVEL
by R. L. Bonaduce

The history of hockey is actually herstory. Not many persons know this.

In 1846, on the outskirts of Halifax, little Gail Smith picked her nose out of her book and cast her steady regard through the window at the mess of boys playing out on the pond. Slipping and sliding in their boots, they chased a frozen turd around, batting at it with their bent sticks in hope that it might careen betwixt two wooden pails. "Score!" they would shout with glee, as if it mattered, whenever this occurred.

They had rebuffed her again. Not that she wanted to play. But they'd made a point, when going their smelly way out-of-doors, to make sure she knew she wasn't allowed. Their taunts, directed at her size, her gender, her appreciation of books, only privileged her steely resolve. To the sounds of their faint, wolfish shouts of "Score!" she went to the cellar for the knives.

It had taken her a week of evenings, working away with file, with hacksaw, with Whitmans auger. Her one pair of boots were ruined — but sacrifices were necessary.

When she appeared on the pond, bent stick in hand, there were the expected hoots of derision, but these were now laced with anger at her daring to challenge. Those that weren't engaged in red-faced yelling might have noticed that she was newly taller; those with the keenest eyes may have had to squint at the glint of sun off something excellent and unimagined beneath her feet. But all noticed, and were struck dumb, when little Gail Smith swooped in amongst them, confiscated and held onto their turd, performing defensive twirls and offensive thrusts, dancing the turd back into their mass and out again, just to taunt them. And in the end, all the boys and girls — many of them were girls after all — all lying in pain on the ice, dismembered, impotent, deconstructed, she casually nudged the turd 'tween the buckets with her shiny toe, and shouted not the crude word the others had used, but stated her own, fairly and without closure: Hello

MARGARET.
It was morning when Robert's French friend from the States called again, waking her up. Referring to himself only as Fournier, asking for "Bobby," then all sorts of guy jokes. How's the big Bonaduce doin'?

She went downstairs to get Robert. The call had become mixed with the dream she'd been having, just as the phone rang. She re-pictured it, a dream so obvious it was silly. She had seen a shirtless Robert coming toward her, crawling toward her. He was emerging from some sort of hay loft, he was above her and grinning as he crawled out of the hay, his muscles glistening and defined by shadow, bits of straw clinging to them like beauty marks. He needed a shave, which was fine, which was even better, and as he grinned at her, crawling closer, his black hairiness turned blond and then longer, now great curling locks cascaded in rivulets in the valleys of his wet muscles, which got even bigger, and his smile grew even more perfect, and suddenly it was one of those strange ones where the dream is obviously goofing around on you, almost mocking, and the dream knows this before the dreamer does.

Robert wasn't in his room, and his coat was gone. Fournier, when told this, kept joking around. "Hey, so where is the guy, you hidin' 'im? You his wife? How many wives he have now? All with a flirting edge, just in case. The kind of guy who knows no other way with a woman.

Fournier calmed down when she had no answers to any of this. His questions turned general and sober. So how was he really? His health. Was he walking okay?

"Well, he'll like, bump into the fridge if he doesn't see it coming."

"Jesus H."

She'd meant it as a joke, exaggerating Robert's clumsiness, his occasional shoulder hitting a door, which might send him into a little stagger. His friend's concern surprised her.

"I just want to know, did he get the book I sent up. The yeast book."

"I don't know."

"Maybe it got stopped at the border. The herbs and pills and stuff, eh? Jesus H, I told this to Kim. He didn't get it then?"

"I don't know. I mean, I didn't see it."

"He didn't get it then."

"He keeps to himself. He might have gotten it."

"You gotta tell him to do it when he gets it."

"Sorry? Do what."

"What the book says. When he gets it, you make him to follow it to a tee. He's a proud sucker but it's important, eh? For sure he can get better. Kim's instructions for the herbs and pills are in there too, eh?"

"I'll tell him." And make him do the herbs and yeast and pills. Okee-dokee.

"Bobby'll laugh — my girlfriend Kim, she's into the alternative stuff, right? — Bobby'll laugh, but she says you can snip it in the bud if you get on it early."

"Robert has like a disease or something?"

Silence on the other end, Fournier finally sussing.

"He has, he has MS, eh?"

"MS. That's ..."

"Jesus H. Didn't tell you, eh? He's got multiple sclerosis. Can kill the stupid bugger."

"He didn't say a word to me. Wow, that's awful."

"Hey, it's the shits. He's pretty depressed about it."

"Well, yeah," Marg agreed. Picturing Robert in his room, aware of his presence in this house as if for the first time, she added, softly, "He is."

"He didn't tell anyone?"

"I don't know."

"Didn't he tell his wife?"

This was getting good. Marg couldn't help smiling.

"Which one?"

Fournier laughed.

§

HOCKEY NIGHT IN THE KREMLIN

What has the game become? Money. In a brief time we have seen the game change to its corporate, crumbling state. The way owners buy winning teams, the way the players change teams ...

It will get as bad as baseball, the money hunt. What are young kids making of this, seeing their heroes' sights are set on anything but loyalty?

To win, a team has to work as one body. Gone are the days you would kill and die for a teammate. Guys hardly know each other now. All the Europeans, even in the minors. Foreign guys sitting lost in the dressing room, no much eenglish, touching fingertips to their freshly stitched wound, wondering what they've gotten into.

Nor can we understand them. Look at the those Detroit Russians, who our game privileged with the Stanley Cup this past year. Them taking the cup to Russia and right into Lenin's Tomb. How can you understand people like that? If it's humor, it's different from ours. What it looks suspiciously like is loyalty and tradition, and of a sort we no longer have, if we ever had it at all. Father, Comrade Father, we have successfully deluded them, they think we are like them, we now have their money and their cars. Father, look at this trophy, we will touch it to your face. Wake up, Father, we've won.

He didn't try to conceal the Salvation Army store bag. He laid it on the kitchen counter, took out the can opener and put it in the utensil drawer, which was otherwise filled with broken spatulas, crumpled bills, gummy screws, widgets. A month had gone by and these guys were still opening cans with a hammer and rusty hunting knife, no doubt another ploy of Toby's to force everyone to watch how dextrous he was.

In his room, it was time to lie down. But first he took out and once more tried on the leather coat. A classic: wool-lined, ass-length, a little beaten up. Buffed at the elbows and lapel, where you could see past the dye into the old cow herself. Forty bucks, but winter was coming, and it was a coat that would last many more years. He hung it on the biggest nail.

His favourite book growing up had been *Robinson Crusoe*, and his hands-down favourite movie had been *Swiss Family Robinson*. As an adult, the main positive in getting traded (aside from sometimes getting a raise, or escaping a brainless coach) was the fresh start, with nothing. Survival of the freshly marooned. Later trades especially, he'd taken this idea completely to heart and jettisoned everything — furniture, car, dishes, even the bulk of his clothes.

More often than not, a trade involved a player coming your way from the other direction; a pissed-off or elated phone call from the guy often came the same day you got your news. But Bonaduce would politely decline the offer of the ready-made, furnished, dish-stocked apartment. Instead he hoteled it for a while, then on a free day found himself something small, clean. The first week he might buy a couple of pots, maybe a solid chair. Goodwill and Used stores were fine if the stuff was well built. Adding to your nest bit by bit, this was the Crusoe feeling. Locating the best little grocery was Crusoe finding the bread-fruit tree beyond the hill. The dented pewter mug was the half coconut shell, the yardsale carving knife was the fish hook fashioned out of a bent ship's nail. Comforts growing. Bonaduce would sometimes even think *coconut*, and *survival*, as he drank his milk out of the mug in the morning.

He would picture women in his new place. And eventually one would come, and him with curtains, with dishes for four, with a rack of spices Bonaduce would have no clue when to use. Women seemed to like shopping for him in this way, maybe it was his dumb-dog trust. More than once he had a woman help him with his Crusoe-shopping before they'd even slept together and, generally speaking, this little burst of shared domesticity would lead her into the sack. Not that that had been his plan from the start, not exactly.

The Crusoe routine shifted when he was bought by Tulsa, and he met and roomed with the goalie Fournier. The arrangement was expedient and stop-gap. Here he was in Okie, the middle of nowhere, truly. Road trips were so long you were never home. In Tulsa it was common for four or five guys to room together, foamies and cots in the living room, save some bucks waiting for the next road trip or trade or call-up. Bonaduce saw how the guys here banded together more than usual. Oklahoma was a deeply strange place for a Canadian to be. Dust, heat, Okie-talk, pickup trucks downtown. Strange to be the home team here, trying to beat the shit out of a busload of fellow Canadians while all the cowboys in the audience hollered. They didn't shout here, they hollered, and sometimes they yipped. On the scoreboard the word *HOME* could tear your heart out. Within days of arriving in Tulsa, Bonaduce had all the lore about guns pulled out in bars, about places not to go. Safe in the dressing room, they enjoyed constant mock cowboy talk. *Well-sir, I reckon it's 'bout tam we should take and work up a lather out thar on the frozen ceement pond ...*

It was common knowledge that all goalies were weird, no matter where they may be trying to fit in. But with his accent and Montreal suave, Fournier fit this place not one bit. His English wasn't great, but the glint in his eye leapt easily over language. He had a way of smiling at your subtle question, looking at you with understanding but saying nothing. If you persisted, he might wave it away and say happily, "No matter!" But he was the kind of guy you gave the benefit of the doubt to, both because you wanted to and because he may have in fact understood. He read so much. He and Bonaduce had more books scattered about their place than the rest of the team put together. Maybe, they joked, the league put together. Fournier was a little hippyish, and had "two professional-hippy brothers" in Vancouver who sent him flattened hashish in letters, which he used in moderation. Fournier frowned on cocaine or drunkenness.

A three-year veteran of Tulsa when Bonaduce met him, Fournier was desperate to get out, had been from day one. Immediately he'd bought furniture, car, and all the rest of it, riding the common superstition that as soon as you plant roots you get traded. When this didn't work he went the other extreme, making almost a religion out of his bare fridge, cupboards, apartment. Once he'd gotten to know Bonaduce enough, he stated shyly that his lifestyle was in keeping with the tradition of Zen. He shopped "only for the food of one meal." He had two sets of clothes, one clean, the other on. If he needed a car or a tennis racket, he borrowed. No TV. He was usually the best-looking guy on the team, and French to boot, but he avoided the bars and tended to meet his women in the grocery or library. These women tended to be Zen or health-food types themselves. They talked that talk in any case, though in those unlikely cowgirl accents.

But Fournier was a good guy and Bonaduce went along. It felt okay to go out in the morning to buy that day's food. (Not unlike a hunting-and-gathering Crusoe.) Made you feel focused, life so simplified. He kept his closet lean. (The ship would be coming soon, take him home.) No stereo, so he bought an old guitar, learned the basic chords, started making up his own ditties. Where the rest of the guys went into debt for a muscle car, he walked or took taxis. For all this he felt lighter, more ready for the game, party, movie, or call-up to the bigs. He felt this leanness gave him speed. It was Tulsa where he began playing naked under his gear — longjohns in the heat made no sense, they soaked up your sweat and you carried these extra sopping pounds by game's end. Naked, skating blew you dry.

Here in his highwayside house in freshstart Fredericton — which in the minors was called Freddie Beach! — he had two shirts, two T-shirts, jeans, cords, sneakers, dress shoes. Underwear, socks. Guitar, box of tapes. Skates. He'd bought a towel, now a leather coat and can opener. He'd been given a dreamcatcher.

A Mirror

We're a rack with meat hanging off it. Sometimes you get banged up or sick and the meat separates from the rack a bit. Things puff up or flap and dangle. Sharp hurt or bruise hurt or weird hanging-nerve hurt. Sometimes in the crammed dressing room after a road game you look at the other guys over thirty, those few that are left, and they look like you feel. You sit there actually laughing at what you have become, at how you feel, how at this very moment a shoulder and a lip, and a few ribs, and a foot, and maybe a deep organ somewhere to the left, are smashed numb or throbbing. Shaking your head in amazement, you sit there dripping sweat. You can smell yourself, the naked body there below your nose. You have a herpes flare-up and a cold. You are being yelled at to hurry to climb onto a bus, which you will ride all night sitting up.

Beside you a younger guy stands whistling, still eyeing the NHL, and one foot from your face he's flicking talcum powder onto his balls.

It's all more funny than not.

He woke in an instant. Brain abuzz. It was definitely the middle of the night. The room was dark but somehow vibrant. Effervescent, but beneath sight. He could hear that the highway was still. He wondered if it was this pregnant silence that had woken him. No, he sensed something alive outside. He went up on an elbow to see it.

There. Fierce, bigger than the sun, the full moon rising over the treeline. Huge, loud as kettledrums you couldn't hear. Its light stolen, and more powerful for it. You could feel all this, important, in the blood.

When he arrived, Leah and Oscar were in the living room together. The curtains were closed. She was on the couch drinking coffee, feet tucked up under, the Saturday *Globe and Mail* spread around her. Hard to say, because he'd never seen them together before, but the room felt stern, jagged, as if they'd been fighting. Though maybe this sternness was their comfort zone, the kind of air they breathed. He had no inkling of how they got on. Or who Leah had become.

He'd called a few times, and Leah could never manage a

time to do it, to get together to talk about Jason. Today, crossing the bridge into town, he'd decided to just drop by. The friendly Maritime way. It was Saturday and sunny so he stopped en route at the farmers market and spent the last of the month's money on a block of Emmenthal cheese.

Along with his leather coat, he handed the cheese gift to Oscar, whose thanks was a surprised raising of eyebrows. It actually even looked like a gift — a square wrapped in butcher's paper, tied neatly with string.

"Thanks," Oscar said. He hesitated, then smiled cautiously, not looking up. "And thanks for that little — I don't know what exactly you'd call it — that 'hockey story' about me. It was ... strange."

"Fiddling around, thought you'd get a kick out of it. Hope it was okay I sent it to where you—"

"My secretary found it *extremely* strange. She opens my mail. She might want danger pay from here on in."

"Hey. Wait'll she reads about Oscar-the-Teenager."

"I had no idea I had such, ah, *robust* beginnings."

"You smaller guys are the meanest. There was this little guy, Amis? You wouldn't—"

But, laughing, Oscar had already turned and walked.

With Oscar fetching a coffee in the kitchen, Bonaduce turned to Leah and got to it. She'd been pretending to read the paper, but looked up as soon as his question was ready.

"I was wondering about Jason, if he's talked to you."

Leah actually seemed serious when she said, "Bobby, if you want to play hockey with him, why don't you just play outside? One of the rinks, they flood the tennis courts, always by Christmas. Take your sticks, you see lots of fathers and—"

"No. Jesus. That's not—"

"You'd really have as much fun just—"

"No, it has to be—" She really had no idea at all. "That's kids. That's just fun. It has to be way more, you know, I don't know, 'serious.'"

He shook his head, surprised at her. It had to matter. Danger.

A team. Together, rushing the prize pig to market, bashing through deadly bandits, loving these guys who ran the gauntlet with you. Glory, laughter, sloshing tankards of ale at the inn.

Leah was quiet for too long. With no further word she uncurled off the couch and left the room. Oscar, who had returned, who had been wearing his ironic smile all along, shrugged and said, "It's a tricky one!" Then he fell to silence as well, staring at the floor, looking glad to be free of having to have an opinion.

The hall toilet flushed and, while Oscar didn't appear to hear, Bonaduce felt a little shy of it, of what it meant. He pictured Leah pulling up and zipping her jeans.

She returned and sat. In her stern silence the mother's love clearly reflected the son's troubles. Well, Bonaduce was here today to try to fix those. First he had to find out what they were.

"I came on too strong with him I guess. It was a little much."

"A little."

"Old Gordie," he said, smiling, "probably had a family powwow first, see how they all felt about the old guy coming to play." He looked up. Not even an indulgent smile from her. "Gordie Howe?"

"I know."

"I guess me coming here to live would have been heavy enough."

"Coming here to *visit* would have been heavy enough."

"Sure. I guess."

"And Gordie Howe was totally different."

"Well, yeah." Though what did she mean? "The principals raking in big money, the sentimental thing for the fans, sure, that really adds—"

"*No. Shit.*" Leah clapped her hands, once. He remembered seeing her do this to get Jason to listen. "He had the *right.* He was a goddamn *father.*"

Oscar, rising and trying to flee gracefully, dropped the CD case he'd been handling and it clacked on the coffee table, another rude clap.

A goddamn father. What could you say to such a thing?

Nothing that wasn't feeble. I want to try to be. I have to start somewhere. Maybe we could all just.

"Well, Leah, I'll think about that." Think about what, exactly. Maybe she wasn't wrong, but she certainly wasn't right.

"I mean, Bob, do you have any clue at all?"

About fatherhood? In Tulsa there was Cynthia, with Lisa, her seven-year-old, and the three of them did almost a year together. He knew Lisa's homework, what she ate for lunch. Lisa had let him hold her after she'd fought with her mother. He had never exactly lived with the two of them but—

"Do you have any clue what Jason wants, or what I want?"

Ah, that's what you meant. No, I guess I don't.

"No, Leah, I guess I don't." Do you have any clue what I want from Jason, or from you? Yes, you probably do. "I guess you got me there."

He shrugged softly from his chair. He waited, then aimed a little smile at her, like a wedge into her hardness, an invitation to the intimacy she was working like hell to avoid. But she wasn't looking his way.

He got up to go. Leah did nothing to stop him. In fact she pinched up a section of newspaper to get on with her morning. She was that mad. Jason was that mad.

The sun came out from behind a cloud and flooded the window behind her, backing her in bright light, turning her black. He could no longer see her clearly without squinting.

He left then in thudding awkwardness, not letting her see his eyes. He was aware of his legs in their long walk to the door, and then the sound of its opening and clicking closed.

He stepped out into the sun and the draining knowledge that, of the two people he had journeyed back so far to see, he was now on speaking terms with neither.

MARGARET.
It was a week after talking at length to Robert's French friend.

She still hadn't mentioned anything about it to Robert, finding neither the opportunity nor the nerve. Nor the feeling, not really, that it was hers to do.

Though maybe tonight. They were alone in the house together. In the spirit of devil-may-care they had declared all the food in the house fair game and were preparing something good. There was her own angel-hair pasta, plus some nice hot Italian sausage from what looked like Rod's spot in the freezer, and the rest of her over-dry sundried tomatoes. Robert found some half-good garlic at the bottom of the vegetable tray along with a romaine with enough crispy leaves in the middle.

Standing with him at the sink, washing and ripping, almost touching shoulders. Here she was, making dinner with a man who was deeply sad of late but who did a pretty smooth job covering it up with cheerfulness, a man Fournier had called *one of the world's greatest guys*.

It was ridiculous that Robert made her think of her father, they were so unalike. Maybe that was why! Her father had never stood at the sink with her like this, she couldn't remember once. Or if he had, he would have made a big deal out of it: Let's everybody smile, here I am at the sink with my daughter, what do you all think of that? His spotlight for a moment including her. Her father had taught her in the end that there were many styles of insanity, many of them acceptable. One style let you have a business, a family, respect, and then let you disappear — well, San Diego — with a cliché secretary. He had no conscience, none. She was unclear in herself if she ever wanted him to call, say, at Christmas.

And here was Robert, appearing, from the States. Let's not take the equation any further please.

Fournier had been amazed at a few of the things she'd been able to tell him about his friend — He goin' back to *school? No!* — which told her how private Robert had been with Fournier too.

He'd found a jar of beets, which he held out to her in question, and which she suggested might not be appropriate for the

meal. Her adding that they were Toby's mother's seemed to decide it for him. He winced and bent his knees opening it.

"Can't beat Harvard beets," he said. She couldn't tell if the
stupid pun was intentional. "We can crank the stereo, play some
Yahtzee later," he said, hands in the sink, jerking his head in the
direction of the living room.

But he's a bit of a loner, eh?

Yes and no. Last night, again just the two of them, he'd
brought out his guitar. She was ready to be embarrassed for both
of them, but he wasn't a bit shy as he sang. Occasionally he'd
look up and smile at her. One song he said was from Lovin'
Spoonful, "You Didn't Have to Be So Nice." This one he sang
right to her, smiling coyly, holding her eye, meaning the words.
It was all so ordinary and simple she thought her heart would
break. She realized then that he was the best she'd ever seen at
looking at you, and almost meaning it. He finished, saying how
that song had made him buy an autoharp, which sounded like
"an angel's guitar," and that it was too bad John Sebastian had
turned out to be "creepy and a sheep."

She tested the sundried tomatoes and they still wouldn't bend.
The water they soaked in had turned to thin brown blood. Robert
hummed as he melted butter and found the sugar and scooped
in a "guesstimate" — she was starting to like his corny words —
with his cupped hand. She tried not to be obvious as she watched
him move. He looked practised in the kitchen, no stumbling,
almost graceful. Mincing the garlic, the way he set down a plate.
She didn't add to her beet-criticism when he brought out the
Louisiana hot sauce, which was all vinegar too and wouldn't fit
Italian either.

*He really should not eat certain things, eh? And the main thing
— don't let him get stressed, or tired.*

Okay, Fournier, I won't let him.

Marg had been staring straight into but now noticed the frost
pattern on the window in front of her. It was truly spectacular,
backlit as it was by the kitchen porch light. A thousand prisms,
shifting if you did. Framed in the window, it was a display, a

happenstance gallery. If you had the time, you could watch it grow. Intricate patterns, hundreds of geometric storylines. No artist could do that, Marg didn't think. An artist would miss the precision or else go overboard into foliage and elves, something human. But how could beauty be so obvious and so painfully subtle, both at the same time? Some saw beauty like this as proof of God. That was too simple, though calling it an accident was too simple too. Not that that window display was proof of an intelligence, but more that it was what created expectations. And what made us try. That window display was what made us think there was something better. In store.

"Robert. Look at the window." She pointed, shaking her head, the prisms shifting colours as she did so. "I mean, *look* at that."

"That's pretty cool."

"Remember when you had the time to like, look at stuff like this? Magic Jack Frost?"

He nodded but didn't look convinced. She could see him take her comment and go within. Memories, worries, what. He smiled and looked at her. He had his hands up in front of him, dripping and limp at the wrist, fingers turned toward his face.

"I do have the time. I call it 'time to kill.'"

No dishcloth in sight, he wiped his hands on his pants. Then went to the fridge and, drawing out two bottles of Heineken beer, fell into his cowboy talk.

"Some especial-occasion-type beer, little lady?"

"Great."

"Crack the heads off'n a couple foreign weasels?" He waggled the Heinekens at her.

"Go to it."

He looked suddenly speedy and impatient. *And, hey, you really don' wanna make him mad.*

She hadn't liked hearing that one. The build of the man. His blocky hands ripping salad like it was air. Though Fournier had said it in an admiring way, and added, *Oooweee.* When she asked what he meant exactly, he said, "Ask the people of Kalamazoo, they tell you, eh?" and laughed. To her silence he'd actually laughed and added, "Don't worry, you're safe."

The bathroom hadn't been safe.

How mad would he be getting? The day after Fournier's call — and it wasn't like she'd hurried to find out, she was in the library already — she looked up the disease. And read about it, horrible. What must be going through Robert's mind? The thing was, anything could happen to the man now. Including nothing.

As she began to serve up, Robert told her to wait, mumbling "Hang on, hang on." First he fussed two tea towels into napkins. Then he cleaned off the table with his hands, one hand brushing crumbs carefully over the edge into the other. Disappearing to the living room, he returned with a Christmas candle, a foot-high Santa with only a half-inch of his red toque melted down. She decided against telling him this was Toby's special candle. She watched him light it.

"*Mah* Oklahoma," said Robert, sitting down finally and jigging hot sauce on everything, including the salad, "includes fancy eatin'."

The accent was totally believable, and went with the way he tucked in.

§

WHAT IT TAKES
—By BoBo Bonaduce

There are three kinds of toughness.

The second kind is the famous kind American fans like, the toughness of the big guy who can fight. Each team has at least one guy like this. If he's won enough fights early on, he can skate through the rest of his career with his head high, face calm, sometimes even that cultivated look of boredom. Cocksure as a dog who gets paid to piss. Even the guys on his team fear him, sometimes hate him a little, because his job is to punch a guy's lights out with no provocation and if you get traded he'd do the same to you. Still, it is sad watching these tough guys topple, when the younger tough guys start beating them up on a consistent basis. The father bested by the child. It means the end of a career, at thirty, and these guys aren't going to any Hall of Fame.

The third kind of toughness depends on everyone's fear of the unknown. The game of hockey is license for some truly crazy men to inflict pain. These men can't be summed up or described. They're all different, because one aspect of crazy-toughness is that it's a kind of genius and it doesn't repeat itself.

He stopped typing. Picturing the guy's face, what it felt like to go into a game against him. Even thinking about him, the feather of fear tickled the gut. Shorty Amis. Bonaduce had seen no better practitioner of this toughness than Shorty Amis. He'd been on the receiving end of the rodent's abuse more than a few times himself.

The thing was, Amis and his kind were beyond tough. As in Amis's case, it often had to do with the shoulder-chip venom of being a little guy, but it was more a general condition of having an eagerly sick spirit. Amis had no teeth, and his assaults were two-voiced — a piercing shriek overtop a deeper, honking, ragged attempt at words. Guys fifty pounds heavier were unnerved by his voice. Before, during and after a tussle, Amis yelled at you and continued from the penalty box, shrieking until he lost his voice. Bonaduce had seen him shriek till he retched.

Amis had once been called up by Philly to play the Bruins in tough old Boston Garden, a kind of experiment probably, a let'sunleash-it-and-see-what-it-does. Amis knew why he was there, and his NHL career lasted less than a minute, during which time he speared one guy (sending him to the hospital for a spleen), started a fight with the guy who avenged the spear (Amis getting beaten up), finished two more fights (getting beaten up twice more), shoved the linesman (getting tossed for this), spit at a fan on his way off the ice, and spanked the hat off the head of a cop for gawking in disbelief.

Amis would cut your face for no reason other than the colour of your jersey. He'd cut Bonaduce twice. The first time, Bonaduce fought him and, literally adding insult to injury, lost to the wiry prick. The second time, Amis's stick missed his eye by a hair, and Bonaduce was bleeding badly and too protective of his eye to fight. Other times they'd gone into corners together and ended up gloving each other's face and whatnot, and in the box the weasel-faced shit wouldn't stop shrieking. "Fuckin' stick your fuckin' eyes out, fuckin' chop your head off, fuckin' *shit* down your fuckin' *neck*, fuckin' *kill ya, I'll fuckin' kill ya, I'll fuckin' FUCK ya.*" Retch.

Once, Bonaduce realized the shrieking had stopped. Feeling like an air-raid siren had ceased, he chanced a look over. And he caught in Amis's glaring back something like humour. Bonaduce met his eye. When he saw Amis's quick wink, the hair actually rose tingling on his neck. He sat back and caught his breath, and later looked over at Amis and studied his calm profile. He looked quite bright. If Amis hadn't been born in Timmins but, say, in New York City, he might've been a poet.

He cradled the green plastic pot in the drive-way wind, the spindly plant brushing his chest and tickling him under the chin. He hustled it to his room. There are plenty of substitutes for blood kin. Anyone who forms bonds with pets, plants or inanimate objects knows this. The crone and her cat, the boy and his dog. The guy and his car. Even the *engine* of his car. Even a new engine *part* can be your special buddy.

Sure, it was a pathetic gesture to try to add anything to this little room, to try to make it more like a home. And a weakling plant like this one — a drooping pine-thing that lay somewhere between a bonsai and Charlie Brown's Christmas tree — a weak-sister plant like this could go the dangerous other direction and confirm a tawdry, lonely life, and cause fits of uncontrollable weeping, tears coursing the beard.

There was nowhere to place it but on the floor. He put it in the far corner, though nothing here was far, wedged it in tighter with his foot, and wished it well. It had been inevitable; at some point he always bought his house a plant.

His favourite, in Tulsa, he'd brought in under Fournier's wary gaze the day after teammate Lonny Miles went up on the rape charge. The rape charge had upset him, he wasn't sure why. The girl — Jennifer — was in fact a girl, or looked it and acted it at least, being only seventeen. He'd met her at a party the night before the alleged crime and liked her, perhaps because in certain ways she reminded him of Leah. It wasn't the clear skin and large-eyed cuteness they shared, it was more the brain-package, the depth and brightness and humour in the eyes, the basic read on the situation that made you wonder what she was doing with a bunch of hockey players, himself included, and Lonny Miles in particular. A crunchy little detail, one Bonaduce would be willing to offer up if he was called as a witness at the trial, was that, from the look of them sitting there on the couch, Jennifer didn't seem to like Lonny much. It looked like she wanted to be at the party but not stuck with Lonny, thin-lipped, brash, loud laugher Lonny.

Bonaduce sensed some connection between yesterday's rape news and today's walking down the sidewalk with a new plant. He'd liked Jennifer, however briefly, and he'd never liked Lonny Miles. What made him like Lonny Miles even less was the way he'd smiled when he'd said this morning at practice, "She got into it." He'd spent the night in jail, been bailed by the owners, came to practice almost gloatingly. When asked by the guys what the hell happened, he picked up his head and superciliously scanned the room, which fell quiet, uncharismatic Lonny Miles from Sydney Mines getting maybe his first spotlight ever. The little smile was an arrogant smile and, when mixed with the Clint Eastwood–like "She got into it," worked to suggest a whole slime-bucket full of things: he was irresistible, she couldn't help liking it, the bitch was deranged and the rape charge was absurd and wouldn't stick, he was so hot-damn he didn't care anyway because all that mattered was that she "got into it."

The piece of slime that stuck to Bonaduce was the literal meaning of those words. For the words did admit to rape, or something close. Because they said this: at the beginning, she wasn't into it. How not-into-it she was was anyone's guess — and Bonaduce couldn't help remembering her looking at Miles with something between tolerance and disgust — as was the degree and kind of seduction, more like coercion, probably physical force, used by Lonny Miles.

Bonaduce realized that this — even *wanting* sex with a woman who wasn't into it with you, who was very not into it and didn't fucking even *like* you — was foreign territory to him. Jesus, who'd enjoy that sex? Why not go stick your dick into some gravel?

Thoughts such as these walked with him down the sidewalk with his new plant. It was almost three feet tall and rustled beside his ear. Her age wasn't an issue apparently, perhaps this being the South. But in the newspaper were blatantly disparaging remarks about hockey players and Canadians, and the fact that hardly anyone went to see these games anyway, as if the converse would somehow have excused the rape, as if the star quarterback from Oklahoma State would be above such charges.

He brought in the plant, and Fournier, man of material simplicity, looked up like a lean wolf, instantly alert to excess. Bonaduce had recently joined his religion and yet here he was carting in this extraordinary bauble. It may as well have been a neon sculpture or ornamental barber's chair. Fournier watched him place it on the floor under the living-room window.

"Who will water this when we're gone?"

"I'll get someone."

This is all they ever said about it, Fournier being as sensitive as Bonaduce had always suspected.

It was called an umbrella plant. It was bushy and looked nothing like an umbrella, and he had no idea where it got that name. He looked down on it, fiddling a leaf between thumb and forefinger and on the verge of meditation, Fournier holding his tongue.

Here, this little Charlie Brown fern — Bonaduce had decided it was a fern — would not likely grant him the depth of friendly relationship the umbrella plant had. He'd kept it alive over the remaining Tulsa years, and bundled it off to his next stop back east, violating his own rule about starting fresh. It had uneven patches and rust spots now, but it stayed his buddy until, in his new place, a girlfriend poisoned it with tequila. He knew it was her and he knew it was deliberate. She secretly wanted control of his decor and didn't like that plant, or maybe it was his pure and simple affection for it.

WHAT YOU NEED, CONTINUED

The first kind of toughness — it's what you need just to play the game. More a state of mind than body, you learn it as a kid or not at all — though you can see its birth in some Europeans over the course of a few seasons. It lets you play with a broken foot bone and not complain; it gives you dignity as you walk your chin to the dressing room to get it stitched, no freezing, so you miss no more than one shift. It lets you see pain as just another pebble in your shoe.

That's the key: it lets you see pain rather than feel it.

It's not as macho as it seems. In fact it's a trick. In the clash and speed of a game, things hardly hurt anyway. (I once took a skate on the forearm and didn't even know it until a guy smiling on the bench pointed at my blood-soaked sleeve.) But it's more than that. Like in war, where it's said a soldier's biggest fear is fear of cowardice, so it is on the bench surrounded by the guys: it's harder to show pain than it is to just sit on it.

In this way your pain is absorbed by the team. It's not a bad little trick.

And this first kind of toughness: when you walk into a bar, say, even if you aren't particularly witty, or sexy, or tough even, it lets you believe you're all of those. This belief shows in your face and in the way you speak, and makes people think you are those things too. Not all people, but enough so you get the rewards. You see this in guys again and again. You see complete schmoes almost become what they believe they are. It's not a bad trick, actually. It's one more thing you can do.

A hard and hurtful sun cut through the narrow ice-house windows, its rays deflecting off the saliva of Kirsten's bucking teeth into Big Jan's poetic goddamn hair, which baffled and trapped it.

God he was angry. He couldn't blame his mood on his little two-wine hangover. Nor could he blame it on this writing class. At least he wasn't afraid in it. People spoke English, he could hold his own. Though the day was coming when he would have to bring in a smash of work for them to tear apart. So far all he had were snippets, nonsense attempts at a novel that wasn't looking like a novel at all.

He even liked where the class was held, this old renovated ice house. It had thick stone walls you could lean your chair back against. It had *rafters* — how often could you use that word any more? The best part was this ancient oak table, must be fifteen feet long, for all to gather around, the kind of table you could imagine royalty supping at and tossing bones to dogs from.

He'd even almost enjoyed what they'd done this morning,

spontaneous drills to sharpen their "artful incongruity." The more twisty and stupid-on-purpose he got with his stuff, the more Jan seemed to approve of it. This morning he'd come up with lines that went nowhere and fit into nothing:

My nose points to what isn't me

It was a shit-climb to the mountaintop, upon which sat a shit-shaped rock, which could well have been shit's temple

Life is a Cyst in Death's Immortal Flesh

Who put the Hale in the Bopp-shoo-Bopp-shoo-Bopp?

But this morning, because he suddenly liked Jan less, he liked his lines less, and the class less too. He'd thought her an ally, all her talk in class about getting at real stuff, the heart, and fuck everything else. Quote unquote. You trusted her saying this. She would've made a decent coach.

Before class they'd congregated in the lounge for coffee. Despite the hostile potential of Phil and Kirsten, something like camaraderie had been tempting the spirit of this group lately, maybe due to their "creative" as opposed to "academic" status. They'd begun referring to their academic counterparts as "inmates," this evolving from Bonaduce's joke that you didn't see those types much because they'd had themselves committed to the library. He'd said "libary," and they seemed to get it, appreciating self-deprecation though never going near it themselves.

The little creative team had huddled at the lounge bulletin board, sipping, reading a fresh notice of a PhD thesis having its oral defence. Bonaduce crowded in — some of these things were amazing, the language in them. This one you could understand. It was on Shakespeare. But it wasn't about themes, or poetic language, or characters. It was *speculation* about *possible* uses of the *trapdoor* in *early versions* of *some* plays Shakespeare *might* have written. The thesis was more than three hundred pages long, and Bonaduce suggested while hunched there that they should find this inmate and rescue him before he wasted the rest of his life. Phil supported Bonaduce with a snort, but otherwise no one said a thing.

Sure, maybe he'd been arrogant in saying it, and maybe you shouldn't make jokes in a public place about wasted lives, since the inmate in question turned out to be Kirsten's boyfriend. He couldn't blame her; in fact he admired her balls when she turned to him, the scabbard of her lip lifting to reveal her sword of teeth. She said simply, "Shakespeare's a waste of time. Hockey isn't. Oh." Her eyes were already dull, having dismissed him in advance.

He was ready to do sheepish and admit he was a pot caught calling her kettle-boy black, but before he could, Jan jumped in to lead Kirsten away by the shoulder, leaning into her like a friend, with a stage whisper for everyone's benefit that "our Robert has given up chasing his silly pucks, though perhaps a little late."

Well, now stop. *He* could belittle his life and his game, and it was only fair that Kirsten had her little whack at him, but Jan was not allowed. So, in class, still pissed off, ignoring most of the creativity drills, he wrote and reworked this:

> Not that they ever will, but if anyone ever asked me which was more important, playing hockey or reading Shakespeare, I will declare free from doubt:
>
> When you read a book you are nothing but a fan. And fans of books have nothing — nothing — over fans of hockey. That a puck is an utterly meaningless thing to chase is exactly the point. They might never think of it this way, but hockey fans are drawn to the spectacle of men who are the best in the land at using their bodies to fulfil *pure desire*. Pure, because these are guys who will basically kill to get at a puck, this chunk of dumb rubber

the perfect symbol of worthlessness. It is so abstract, so pure in its meaninglessness, it is almost Japanese.

It got him thinking about them — fans. Generally, players didn't like them and didn't think about them much. But they didn't like to think about that either, about not liking the people who paid your salary, admired you, in some cases adored you. It was pretty simple, really. How can you respect anyone who likes you and doesn't even know you? If people hate you for your skin or uniform colour, it's of course more painful than if they *love* you for the same reason, but the scenario is similarly stupid.

There were lots of decent fans of course. Appreciators of the game. Guys who used to play themselves. Mums and dads who took their kids. The row of folks in their wheelchairs, some with heads resting over on their shoulders, others done up with team jackets, waving pennants. There were memorable, funny fans as well. Here, in Freddie Beach, twenty years ago, he'd forgotten about her — she was maybe sixty, floppy homemade hat in team colours, cowbell, tartan blanket on the lap, and most of all the big whisky-voice. She would pick quiet spots, ring her bell twice, and the fans would fall quieter still to hear her yell her weird stuff. *Hey, Seven. Yer mother still stink?* Another one he remembered, *Hey, Ref, that a banana?* Years later in a bar in Dayton the subject of this fan had come up and Bonaduce was surprised that other guys had all assumed that she was a weird old *he*. Anyway, lots of fans used the game to get their ya-yas out. Ripping shirts off and jumping up against the glass, leading cheers, picking fights, grenading the visitors' bench with cups of beer, whatever. In the Des Moines penalty box, Bonaduce had taken an empty mickey bottle off the helmet. His team went into the stands after the guy while he rested for a bit with his head between his knees.

In the lounge Bonaduce had nodded to Jan after her traitorous quip and said, "Yeah, me grow up." Then refilled his coffee and started down to the ice house. It was as close to a fight as he was going to get. He would be only nice. To Jan, to Kirsten, to

Phil. To Toby and Leah and everybody. You get too tired for anything else.

He drove home with a kink in his neck after an awkward snooze in the library reading room. The chairs there were designed for sitting up; a guy should complain. Downtown at an intersection he found himself staring at a pack of kids. It took him five seconds to register that they were dressed as a witch, a Darth Vader, a what might have been Robin Hood. Jesus, Hallowe'en.

He pulled into a convenience store and spent far too much money on their whole stock of Mars bars. Screw the bags of little Hallowe'en-size bars, it was one night you could be a hero for not a lot of money. A real bar falling heavy from your hand, surprised muffled shout through the monster mask: *Wow, thanks.*

Marg and her sister and Toby were home, Marg and her sister on their way to a costume party. It was also a Friday night. In her white robe and pants, black belt and headband, Marg was a karate person, while her sister was a Bad Santa — your basic Santa outfit but with stitches on the face, toting a machine gun, bottle of whisky sticking out the pocket. Toby, slumped in the living room starting a bottle of wine, and who Bonaduce realized was a sort of natural Bad Santa, wasn't going anywhere.

"Wanna come, Robert?" Marg asked, martial artist forcing down a quick beer at the kitchen counter.

"Don't think so, thanks. I don't have a costume."

At this Toby snorted, and Marg shot him a look, the exchange making Bonaduce see his creased pants and tight haircut. Not bad, Toby lad.

The invitation was tempting, especially as he'd be here alone with Toby otherwise. But he wouldn't know anyone, and Marg's voice in asking hadn't been enthusiastic. He found an old salad bowl in a kitchen cupboard, dumped the bars in it and came back to the living room with that and an empty glass. Because Toby would offer him some wine, he would accept, and Toby would say, Well, go get yourself a glass then. Bringing the glass in advance risked looking presumptuous and might lose him his offer of wine, which would be fine. He set the bowl of bars on the floor by the front door and switched on the porch light. He found the Yahtzee score sheet and the dice, one still lost. He hated playing with four, you had to reroll one die and remember too much. He did like solo Yahtzee, however. It gave you a feel for averages, and the duration of luck, which felt less like stamina than grace.

"No kids'll come," said Toby matter-of-factly, in the act of rising to fill Bonaduce's glass.

"Why not?"

A car crunched into the drive, Marg and her sister banged beer bottles on the counter and rushed out the back door, calling goodbyes.

Toby answered as though Bonaduce were a kid himself.

"It's the Trans-Canada Highway, there's no streetlights, there's a house only every hundred yards. The people around here are poor and they drive their kids to the rich suburbs."

Well shit. Bonaduce eyed the bowl of Mars bars. As he did so the doorbell rang. He opened the door onto a two-and-a-half foot devil, a three-foot grim reaper and their Satanic mom. Ooo, Toby would hate him for this. He dropped a chocolate bar in their bags, empty so far, and in a childlike voice their mother sang a thank-you on her children's behalf.

"Maybe if," Bonaduce said, closing the door, "you know, maybe if the porch light's on, they'll come."

"Well there's going to be a *few*."

In the ensuing hour he was ready to concede this round to Toby, because only one more kid had come, and he was alone, tall enough to be fourteen, and under the tossed-on costume you could see quick hot eyes that looked less intent on candy than on vandalism.

Bonaduce picked up the empty wine bottle to take to the kitchen to rinse while Toby went down for another. Some CD of Toby's by a band called Dead Can Dance was on in honour of the night, though the music sounded basically Middle Eastern, a quarter-tone-wailing female singer backed by spacey ambient organ. As he washed out the bottle, he noticed the homemade label said "Mountain Frog '99," and he got a chuckle from it.

In the bathroom he found a garish red lipstick Marg's sister had used for her face blood. He smiled as he applied it to his nose. He liked Hallowe'en. He almost never got to enjoy one, there always seemed to be a game scheduled, the arena full of clowns and witches and team-colour harlequins, an extra buzz in the air. The nose began with just a small dot on the tip and then, what the hell, the whole schnozz, bright red. What was he? Maybe a wino.

He used to like those houses back in Winnipeg where instead of just dumping some candy in your bag they'd make you come inside and do something: sing, or a joke. Often they were European, or foreign-sounding at least, and they'd be dressed up too. Ten-year-old Bonaduce stumbling to get a song or a joke out, his buddies nervous or pissed off beside him. At one of these houses in his neighbourhood lived a boy — maybe he was twelve, maybe much older — in a wheelchair, and he'd sit there smiling like crazy, his head sort of flopped over and his fat hands palm up and unmoving on his thighs. Hallowe'en was the only time in the year you'd see him. Rumour had it his name was Jordy. Then one year Jordy wasn't there. In any case — Bonaduce finished the nose, even going up into the nostrils a tad — these people who invited the ghosts and goblins inside and made them come alive for their candy seemed to know something more about Hallowe'en than the rest did. Because, otherwise, these big-eyed four-year-olds upon whose heads parents had slammed a hat and mask, these little first-timers must be thinking, Holy, alls I do is go up there with this bag and they throw candy in it, why haven't we been doing this every night?

Toby snorted a kind of approval at Bonaduce's nose when he looked up from his display of bottle uncorking. Bonaduce lumbered over to read the label and this one was an Earth Spit '53. He laughed aloud at this and commented to Toby that his friend was pretty funny, to which Toby shrugged, noncommittal. The music got cranked up so that conversation was made difficult, and Toby wasn't pleased when the doorbell rang again and Bonaduce invited a Zorro (a Zorro! They must have a big ol' attic) and a princess inside. With a pretty good Irish wino accent, he demanded a joke or song of them, their teenaged sister or babysitter looking on nervously. They sang a quavering Row, Row, Row Your Boat, got three full-sized Mars bars each, and that was it for trick-or-treaters that night. Though Bonaduce himself hung in there till one a.m., the radio turned to what twenty-year-olds might be listening to at this moment, eating bars and sipping intermittently from a bottle of "Tidal Flats '02." No, he wasn't sipping, he caught himself gulping.

He put his hand over his mug, as if it was someone else offering to pour, then laughed, took his hand off.

This morning he'd been reading a book by Ven Begamudré, a male Asian Canadian writer writing, about being a female soldier/gourmet in Scotland. It was decent writing, but for some reason he'd grown cold and he couldn't get warm. He had been cold a lot lately. He saw how the bit of wine at night had helped warm him and smooth things. Beer was good after games with the boys, get the grin on, but wine was good alone, in the night. Mornings he felt gritty and more tired for it, even after two glasses. Last night he'd had a bucket-full. How soothing was alcohol, how thick the bandage, but then the bandage gets ripped off in the morning, how clear and hurtful this part was. His body felt beaten and shocked. So, no more drinking. It was just boredom. He shouldn't be drinking at all, he was in training, and he was, he was possibly — it just wasn't good for him right now. But no worry about making it a habit, he was too poor. Nor could he afford to keep stealing Toby's.

Nor was he all that worried he'd tossed last night's last swallow of wine against his wall.

This room, this bed, had become his place. His nasty little niche. Jesus, look at it. My, how he'd come down in the world. You get used to anything. Tired all the time, of company in general and Toby in particular, he read here, strummed here, lap-topped here, sipped wine here.

Paced here. He stopped himself. A three-step pace is ridiculous anyway. And it was a sham, an act — you can pretend all you want that you're a martyr and a prisoner but you're not and you know it.

He lay on his bed. Eyes can pace too. He pictured himself as a wolf in his forest den, a wolf who has eaten and is lying on his stomach, head on his paws. His eyes are open and looking, and his ears twitch at this sound or another, but the wolf is otherwise quite calm. Apparently waiting for something. But, being a dumb animal, he doesn't have a clue what it is.

He remembered last night deciding that his room was green. Years faded, it was one of those industrial almost-colours. Depending on the light, it was grey, or yellow, or even blue. But it was green, barely green. Last night he'd added the splash of red wine, a sudden impulse to see if wine would sink in, or drip down. It did both, a blob sinking in and the rest running down, an octopus body with skinny legs dangling to the floor.

If the ways of your own damn heart are hard to know, what dumb grin of red-lipped stupidity leads you to think you can know the heartways of anybody else?

How much of their anger is just anger at the past?

He ached picturing Jason's face. In the concrete corridor, in wet underwear, the steaming body. He'd seen clear as life that something of the father had created the boy and swelled in the boy's flesh ...

Arrogant to assume this, and infantile to need it.

He lay back on his bed and closed his eyes. With the light off, his room was so dim that closing his eyes gave him perfect darkness. Which, if you cared to see things a certain way, could be a desirable and perfect thing. No comet, dreamcatcher, wine octopus. No stage.

. . .

Oscar.

Leah rose and quickly stepped into her clothes. Mornings it was her wont to linger here, choosing blouses, hair clasps, trying things in the mirror. Turning away from him — modestly? unconsciously? coyly? — when she removed underwear. Either not caring that he watched — because she did know he liked to watch — or perhaps understanding that a committed relationship legitimized his brand of voyeurism, if that is what it was called. Then she would stand at her writing desk and consult her day planner, review the human disasters on her schedule this week. After which she liked to lean on the windowsill, take in their view of the river over to the north side, gazing out, perhaps contemplating human suffering and the potential for freedom from it. It occurred to him this morning that maybe it was because Bob Bonaduce was over there on the north side that lately she hadn't been doing this.

This was simply not good. She was so knotted about Bob's being here and she could not talk about it. It was not good keeping such things inside. With prodding, Leah usually opened up. It didn't appear that Bob Bonaduce was going to take a hint and leave town. Or even well enough alone. Jason was knotted as well. Though it was harder to tell with him, due to Jason's knottiness in general. That was a horrible pun. It was like something a Bobby Bonaduce would say.

Wafts of coffee drifted up the stairs, his wake-up call. The timed coffee-maker one of the century's underappreciated inventions. Leah descended to pour herself her half-cup, which she would top with hot water, the coward.

He leapt up and peeked at her day planner, saw she likely wouldn't be heading out for an hour. She sometimes came back up with her coffee, so he quickly put on his robe and sweat pants. He no longer liked to be caught undressed. He realized he had become content to just cover up the ten pounds he seemed incapable of losing. Maybe it was fifteen pounds now. Maybe this year he would dust off the NordicTrack ski machine, or the stairstepper.

Leah arrived back in their room. He felt the slightest hurt that she hadn't brought him up a cup of coffee. Not that she wouldn't happily do so if he was to ask. Would she just as happily doff her clothes if he were to ask?

"Leah?"

She raised her eyebrows for him while continuing to jot notes in her planner.

"I really think you should make amends with him."

Leah put her pen down flat and lifted her gaze out the window, across the river.

"What exactly does that mean? 'Make amends.'"

"Well, air it out. Talk. Make peace." He came upon a smart idea. "You know, instead of popping his balloon, you could help him pop it himself."

"He makes me see what a teenager I was."

What?

"Well, maybe that's not a bad thing."

Leah didn't respond. Uneasy, he was tempted to make a joke about Bobby Bonaduce the fountain of youth, but humour didn't seem right, didn't seem to enter into her current relationship with her ex. Her mood also prevented him from telling her what he'd planned to tell her, which was what an odd duck he'd decided Bob was during his last visit. After putting the strange gift of Dutch cheese in the fridge, he'd returned as she and Bob were blurting at each other about Gordie Howe. What he'd seen was Bonaduce as an Eighties man, being out of touch with everything dire about the Nineties. But then he seemed more Seventies, because he was so impractically naïve. On third thought, make that Sixties — the fellow was absurdly idealistic. No, wrong again, he was Fifties, just look at him. Okay, let's keep this going: the post-war simplicity of the Forties supplied the best description yet. Simplicity, or simplistic? He envisioned the pictures of sailors docking, getting off their ship, the certain looks on their faces, soon to be genuinely happy with wife and job and new barbecue.

Watching Leah and Bob hard at their argument, he'd still considered Bonaduce a good man, and maybe in the right, but he'd also understood that, twenty years ago, Leah had been intellectually slumming.

"Leah, I think you should call him."

"Why."

"For Jason. Even though he's twenty" — Oscar found himself voicing what he'd formulated — "and even though he never did have the man around as his father, the psychology of broken homes is complex, and gluey, and so maybe for Jason's sake you might consider, I don't know, normalizing diplomatic relations."

Leah stood gazing at the north side of the river.

"I will act as your ambassador if you like."

Leah staring across.

"Call the man. I can't stand your, your *mood* any more."

§

Sitting cross-legged on the bed, he glanced out his window, at the leafless trees through to the river. Knees sticking stiffly way up, he cradled a notepad over his crotch. Time to write something serious. Beside the bed a first cup of coffee steamed on a table he'd banged together out of two-by-fours and a serving tray he'd plucked from roadside garbage two houses down.

After a couple of sips and some staring into space, he wrote:

The leafless trees looking black against the morning's frost.

He reached for his coffee, took a sip. It was a decent observation. Where it would go, who could tell, but those trees looked extremely black this morning even though you knew they were brown. Leafless? He crossed out "leafless." Jan's rule number one said that every word had to count. If there was frost, readers would assume leafless, wouldn't they? Unless they were evergreens. Hey, that-there frost was so white, even the *evar*greens looked black.

He changed it to:

The treetrunks looked black against the snow.

Because the idea, the effect, was snow, rather than frost. Then he crossed out "looked." Why did you need it? They *were* black against the snow. Though without the "looked" you might think the trees were in fact black, whereas "looked" suggested the optical illusion. Well, but, so what was the sentence about — the blackness, or the illusion of blackness? What *should* the sentence be about? Well, what should *any* fucking sentence be about. Settle down. Maybe once the paragraph got going he'd know. Maybe you shouldn't dwell too long on any particular—

"*Hey Marg.*" He heard Marg stop walking up the staircase.

"Yes?"

"*Get in here.*"

She came in smiling at his yell, she was a buddy. He had no shirt on, but he sensed this was okay, though some women weren't enamoured of body hair. And his, from the belt to the tops of his cheeks, didn't give your eye much of a break.

"What colour are those trees out there?"

"*Wow* this room is small."

"Welcome to my coffin."

"You hardly fit."

"Tell me what colour those trees are."

"That's a nice place for it." Margaret was looking at the dreamcatcher hanging low in the window. "Though if you hung it higher it'd, you know, be more up in the sky. Framed by the sky."

"No, there I can look right through it from bed."

"Why do you look through it?"

"So what colour are the trees?"

"Those?"

"What colour."

"I dunno. Brown?"

"No, I mean right now. Sitting against that white frost like that."

"Grey? The frost is almost gone."

"Shit. No, c'mon."

"How should *I* know. Charcoal? Charçoal. No, don't cross out what you had. What are you writing?"

"My novel. Until you ruined it."

"I just—"

"Marg. I'm kidding you."

Some people, when they go serious, it's like all their skin suddenly falls off and everything hurts. And they aren't so great to be with. He would've liked to tell Marg this, but she was serious at the moment.

BOBO DOES THE TREES

BoBo Bombsaway was right tuckered after cuttin seven cord a hardwood usin only a ax. Choppin all them trees into finnicky eighteen inch chunks. But the wife Marg liked hers eighteen inches, heh heh. Though she yelled at him, why'd ya fuckin cut all them trees down? Cause they was too fuckin BLACK! he yelled back. An buy me a new chainsaw, woman! BoBo kicked at the old one, lyin there on the bed. These saws, once their teeth are mostly broke off, all they're good for is fixin cars.

. . .

MARGARET.

Robert opened her door and poked his head in like he knew she was awake. It was past midnight, maybe close to one. She'd heard him downstairs playing Yahtzee by himself, which he did a lot lately, head down and immersed sometimes for a couple of hours. Like he said, killing time. But she hadn't heard him climb the stairs, maybe she'd fallen asleep after all. She'd been lying in bed trying to decide whether or not to move out. Lately she'd gotten very tired of the general slovenliness of the place. Her sister was not around much, and Joyce was not around ever, and these bastards were trying to leave the cleaning to her, screw them. Jesus H, there was still deepcorner grunge from the tenants before them. And the aura of depression here lately, or was it just aimlessness? It had changed from what she first took to be a cool, healthy open quality, a letting things fall as they may. A "don't worry be happy" house mood. No TV, and that uniquely open gesture of Toby's when he unpinned his bedroom door and stashed it in the basement. But gradually this good house *mañana* had fallen to a lazy and wheedling "So I wonder what's to eat and who might get around to cooking it?" The guys, Robert too, would too easily tip into dinosaur ways and let themselves get waited on hand and foot and not even notice it was happening. Robert you might expect this of, and you might forgive it. Robert was kind, he would make it up in little ways he had. He would get all concerned, for instance, about how you talked — gently joking about how you, like, talked — and he would sincerely try to help you. Corny bugger.

Food smells too. She suspected she was allergic to the food smells of this house, they actually seemed to plug her up. When one of them did cook, it was all onions and grease smell for hours after. It went into the curtains, it smelled like years of grease in those curtains. Lately Robert had gotten into a habit of midnight popcorn. She could smell it again tonight.

And tension. Toby and Robert at each other, who knows why. They were quite a pair. Boys, play nice.

Toby was the last straw. She had slept with him three times now, and he was beginning to make demands and have expectations, though they'd promised well before the clothes were off that this would not happen. Rejection was such a hideous monster to him. Which was to be expected. But it would be impossible ever to tell him the truth, that his arm bothered her less than his drinking, or his being two inches shorter than her. He would still blame it on his arm. You could see how he used it as a magnifying glass, all hurts coming through it and burning him. Life was probably simpler that way.

As life would be simpler if she moved.

But then Robert's knock on the door, Robert poking his head into her plans. Her first thought was that he was going to read some of his novel to her. The second was that he'd discovered she'd slept with Toby and felt a little lonely because of it. The third was that they were going to talk about his illness.

He sat not at the foot of the bed this time but in the middle, and when she sat up, his arms opened and he was hugging her. All heavy and serious, his heart and body both. He felt even bigger than he looked. She had never felt a man like this. Hard as wood. Solid as ground. But denser, the moving blood in him somehow making him seem denser still.

Her breasts moulded to his shape, and she could feel his awareness of them. She pulled back a little and kissed him on the neck, small and soft, not at all clear what she wanted. There was something so passive about him and, despite the heaviness, so ready to change. To be led away like a dog.

He answered with his own identical little kiss on her neck. He removed his hand from her shoulder. What was he going to do with it? So softly she could hardly feel it, the hand was on her hair. Then it was pressing, huge and sad and gentle, spanning the back of her head, cupping it ear to ear. She resisted falling against the hand, trusting it fully, the way it cupped her head, holding all the thoughts she might ever have.

Then he sighed, long and low. The release of something deep. At its sound she knew nothing more would come of this night, nothing physical. But neither did he speak. He squeezed her head again, and once more kissed her neck. She pecked his neck back, identically, almost as a joke, but one he didn't get, because he sighed again sadly. It was all quite dramatic, really, as he got up in a hurry then and stood watching her in the darkness, and then went to the door and watched her some more, then left. Alone once more, she felt herself glad it had happened, whatever it was.

Still she thought of moving. Where to go. Jesus H, after this house, where. Alone?

The image of Robert and her sharing a place scared her. Not because it was a naturally bad idea, but because of how the image grew, and flipped. First it was them at home, a phantom living room, smiling together over a glass of wine that wasn't Toby's, the Yahtzee dice on an elegant table. Then it was her standing behind him, able to see only the back of his head, which wobbled with the movement. She was pushing his wheelchair.

§

Bespectacled Patrick talking, talking. After these couple of months, Bonaduce understood half of it. Bits and pieces he caught himself actually enjoying. Getting the hang of it was no small source of pride. You spend time with this stuff, you witness yourself falling into word-mode too. In class on occasion he even caught himself clucking and taking ironic offence, a regulation grad student.

Normally shy Patrick had worked himself into a fever of confidence. Speaking, he looked over people's heads lest errant eye contact dam his stream of words.

"Ideologically embodied in object." That mean "symbolic," Patrick? A Marxist hidden inside every shovel? A dope in every hockey stick?

"Sub-meta-fictional." Patrick, c'mon Patrick, that translates as "under above the story."

Presentation finished, fielding questions, Patrick fell to nervous defence. He stuttered into sentences that began "I didn't mean to imply," which was like tossing blood bags to sharks. Phil slouched diagonally in his chair, radiating boredom, eyes taking in the shape of the room, as in: This discussion occupies not a lot of my brain. The posture worked. The others, Patrick too, were as hungry for Phil's approval as they were for Gail Smith's. In hockey as well you saw the one or two guys who worked the attitude and got to be daddy, backing it up not with words, but with goals or violence.

It was still mostly bullshit. The circle of wristwatches ticked, and Bonaduce sat occasionally in awe, generally asleep, other times nodding as if he agreed, but hating these long dips into fakery. He was intimate with everyone's jewellery, hair-habits, moles. (Phil had a hefty wart on his temple, at which he pictured himself pointing and laughing if things ever got rough between them.) He let himself x-ray Kirsten's limp sweater, arriving at a likely sense of her pair, and shame when this image stirred the nether zone. Sometimes he winced with the wasted time — What was Jason doing right now? Where was, where was his fucking Utica *money?* — but stayed willing to encounter language at its best, hearing new groups of words and feeling little wafts of oxygen coming off his understandings. He'd begun jotting down phrases, and words to look up. You never knew what you might use writing a novel, even one about hockey. But mostly he suffered a drifting mind, one which was repeatedly elbowed in the snout by fear. Once he woke hearing someone quote, "as he waited for his cataracts to develop so he could have the operation," and he decided that this described the sensation of sitting in this room with these people.

"Disfunction of the male–female." This from Doctor Gail, summing up. Disfunction at Gender Junction. Almost an old blues line there, What's the function, of the junction? Hey, what's better, Gail, "Disfunction of the male–female" or "Smash-up at the hairy-ugly"? C'mon, Gail.

Look up:

    nascent
    concomitant (sp?)
    self-reflexive (sounds kinky)
    quotidian

Neat Phrases:

    delicate with parody
    gently hyperbolized diction
    rife with serious play

It was UNB's third or fourth home game. Dalhousie in town to do battle. Bonaduce lined up like a loner to buy a single ticket. Not looking right or left. Checking out his shoe tops.

He sat surrounded by empty seats in the thirtieth row, feeling foolish, collar turned up, flinching into himself whenever Jason skated back to the bench. Averting his own eyes as if this would hide him from his son's.

He still hadn't tried calling him, not since outside the dressing room. The longer he left it, the more foolish he felt and the harder it got — it was one of those.

Doubtful that in the heat of the game the boy would catch

sight of him. And Jason's back was almost always turned — he wasn't getting off the bench much. Jesus, the fourth line. Number 19. *BONADUCE* in red letters.

This arena could seat four thousand, and tonight there were maybe three hundred, clustered at ice level behind the benches. A few scattered, like Bonaduce. He knew the players could feel it too: like a lone rider on a bus, like a BB in a boxcar. Sounds echoed, haunted. Most of the crowd were students who wanted to cheer and party, but what should have been a crowd's roar was thin and tinny and worse than nothing, a reminder of what it wasn't. It made everything you did on the ice feel a little apologetic.

Fourth line and killed penalties. Here was a guy with pro ambitions, a nobody in a league not bothered much by scouts to begin with. Though you never knew. He did have the size and speed. And guys did suddenly "get good," as if their bodies found some dormant source grace or oomph that clicks like it had been there all along. But for now Jason was likely on the fourth line for a reason.

There was Whetter, pacing behind the bench in his cheap suit and tie, as nervous and frustrated as any coach anywhere. Bonaduce hadn't called him either. Had Whetter bothered to pursue the matter of his eligibility, or had his disappearance been a relief? Maybe he would saunter down after the game, have a chat. Maybe he wouldn't. Some avenues of life here were embarrassing to walk.

By the third period he understood. Jason was a right-winger, and the three right-wingers ahead of him were maybe the three best guys on the team. Jesus, luck of the draw. All Jason needed was somebody to get injured. Then step in, pop a few goals, make the newly healed guy work to dislodge you. It could happen. The first-line right-winger, guy named Harrington, Bonaduce hated from the getgo. A bony, haughty guy, wouldn't go near a corner, and both times after both his goals he cruised to centre ice doing a white man's try at a touchdown dance before letting the other guys high-five with him. Harrington was the kind of guy who could break an arm and no one on the team would mind.

The Reds won six-four. For a close game it was boring. Dalhousie was a bunch of small skill-guys in yellow uniforms. The refs let the bigger Reds get away with lots of clutch-and-grab. Jason would have been effective in a game like this. If he focused on defence he could be a small Bob Gainey, a guy so unflashy yet so bothersome he was noticed only by the other team.

Bonaduce rose from his seat ready for a beer. But, wait, he hadn't earned it, he hadn't played. Smiling, he saw he was nothing but a dog, salivating at a buzzer at the end of a game.

OSCAR.

Bonaduce called just as Peter Mansbridge announced the top stories on the ten o'clock News. Bob had a knack for putting a wedge in a man's routine, which, while theoretically not a bad thing, could be irritating. Phone to his ear, Oscar tried to watch the News as well.

"So how're things there, Oscar old man?"

"... Great ..." Kosovo had proved a shameful mess. Another mass grave with all fingers pointing to—

"Sorry for that bit of kerfuffle with Leah the other day. Last week, whenever."

"Not a problem ..." He should tell him it was Leah who had felt badly about it. Leah should be apologizing to you. The look on her face, the staring-at-nothing for ten minutes. It had given him a jealous pang.

"How was the cheese?"

"Absolutely fantastic. Thank you."

"Oscar, I was wondering. I really have to get in shape here before playing with UNB and I was wondering if you knew of any oldtimers' teams. I need a contact. You know, our age, guys who play, friends of yours—"

Oscar sighed and muted the TV.

"—someone I could call to see if I could get on a team. My eligibility's still up in the air, but if I don't get on the ice soon, well ..."

There was loud laughing and banging in the background, and he noticed now that Bonaduce had been close to shouting all of this.

"Where are you?"

"At the arena. Aitken Centre. Jason just had a game."

"Oh! Right, right!" He probably should be going to these games but he was fairly certain Jason didn't want him to. And Leah wouldn't go near the place. He could go with Bonaduce, of course. Join the mess.

"Did he win?"

"You know it."

His attempt, last week, to talk with Jason about this mess had been a parody of concerned parent interrogating mute youth. "So your father's in town!" "Yeah." "Quite a surprise?" "I guess." "And I understand he's going to be playing on your team?" "I dunno." "Well, how do you feel about that?" Jason at the fridge gulping milk from the carton and, to complete the sitcom scene, shrugging. Impatient, Oscar had repeated himself. "No, how do you *feel* about it?" Equally impatient, Jason met his eye and said, "I don't *know*." And Oscar felt stupid. As if knowing how you felt was a simple thing, and Jason hadn't been accurate the first time.

"And Jace had a few good shifts. They're playing him on sort of a checking line. And penalty-killing. I guess he's your basic digger."

Oscar could tell from the man's voice that he and Jason still hadn't spoken. Bonaduce was slurring, it sounded like. Not good. You could imagine the fellow in the bleachers sipping rum from a flask. He had the compassionate urge to tell Bob he shouldn't take Jason's silences personally because his son was as a rule quiet and, on top of that, simply shy, emotion not being one of the lad's skills. But Oscar couldn't locate the delicate way to tell a father something so elementary about his own child.

"Well, that's right, he's certainly always been eager about the game." He felt awkward having nothing more technical to offer. He also would've liked to add that Jason was especially shy around other men. But this might imply the equation of Jason having grown up with the role model *in absentia*. There was so much you couldn't say.

Jason had smiled and shrugged again for him as he put back the milk, shut the fridge and left the kitchen. There'd been something of the father in this and other gestures — Oscar could see this now. Traces of Bonaduce in the latent power of Jason's legs and arms, and in his almost musical striding away. Jason "carried himself well." As in Bonaduce dancing. In such synchronization one could sense invisible, internal juggling, bowling pins kept effortlessly in the air. There are those who can walk and chew gum at the same time.

In any case, in the kitchen, watching Jason move, Oscar had suddenly felt a more solid presence of Bob Bonaduce in town.

"I do know a couple of oldtimers players. Not friends exactly. I don't know if their teams are filled up or whatever, or how that might work, but there's this fellow at the office, Andrew Frenette. Andy Frenette."

"Great."

"You want his number?"

"Please." A pause. "Actually, I don't have a pen or anything."

Oscar suggested that he'd get Andy to call him. Bob sounded doubtful, indeed he pulled away to ask passersby for pens, but in the end he let himself be assured that Frenette would call.

"From the sounds of it" — Oscar heard himself chuckle raucously into the phone — "they have quite a colourful crew. Andy tells me a good many of them are rural lads, as he calls them, and the little trips they take for tournaments and what have you tend to the, shall we say, wild-and-crazy."

"Sounds good."

"One fellow, in fact, according to Andy, one fellow, a tough character, was convicted, along with his uncle — this was some

years back, but — convicted for raising fighting dogs. Outside
of Moncton. Dogs for dogfights, gambling. Can you imagine?"

"Well you probably wouldn't want to tangle with a lad like
that."

"I should say you wouldn't." Not that "tangle" was something Oscar imagined doing with any lad at all.

"Oscar? I should go. But hey, we should do it again some
night soon. Whatever it was we did the last time. Rockin Rodeo."

"Some night soon, Bob." Actually, why not? Beer, music,
discussions never remotely crucial. Though why was it that talking to this man made him feel lonelier, more friendless, than
ever?

"Oscar? Sounds good."

§

Everyone was asleep when Bonaduce got home. In the arena
parking lot, his car hadn't started and he'd fiddled under the
hood with it and ended up wearing down the battery. He'd had
to collar someone for a jump. He'd cut his finger on the cable.
He was tired, gritty and cold.

He washed his hands at the kitchen sink, eyeing the bottle of
wine on the counter. White wine, a rare thing, labelled "Beard
Filtered '72." He left the wine and took the half-bowl of cold
popcorn into the living room. Marg's laptop was there.

> story about a guy, in the kitchen cuts his finger to the
> bone and washing it sees his bone is made of what turns
> out to be pure diamond. After some thought he ampu-
> tates it, sells the diamond-bone, gets enough to buy a
> house, etc. Gets used to the house of course, cuts off

and sells another finger. Lives high for a year, nice car, sea cruise. Sells off a little toe, another finger, etc., gets to the point where he weighs lifestyle against healthy body, ends up with one arm and legless in a motorized wheelchair, but has private jet, tropical island, servants, women. Maybe end it with him waggling his lower jaw in the mirror, wondering if he needs it. Use gently hyperbolized diction.

He woke earlier than usual, senses already attuned to — what? Maybe it was the muffled highway traffic. Maybe it was the soft light coming through the window frost, the grey prism-shadows on the ceiling.

No, it was out his window. He got up to an elbow and looked. It was snow. The first real snow. Wonderful, a wonderful sight. As always. Didn't matter where you were, what your life was like. Look at that. Winter wonderland, get the toboggan, the skates, the hot chocolate.

Pause first, settle the kid-in-you. Look at the world turned white. It felt like everyone's good fortune. You could almost smell it through the window.

This wasn't much more than an inch or two. It was only early November. You could still see the spikes of cut hay. But nice all the same. He wanted to wake somebody up, get Marg up and tell her. It was still snowing lightly, they might get a proper dump after all.

What was that red blotch? Who'd spilled paint in the middle of— There was blood out there in the field. Blood is what it had to be. He dressed quickly, plugged in the kettle on his way through the kitchen, pulled on his leather coat. He had no gloves or scarf or boots yet. He went round back, past the pile of beer cases, now with snow on it, the cardboard would shmush when it melted, a nightmare taking them back — he'd get on that today. He'd claim the money for gas for all the trips to town.

Through sneakers you could feel the snow's cold. He approached the red, a two-foot splotch that faded to pink at the edges. It was some animal's smeared meal. He stood over it. He wouldn't have seen it without the background of snow. Canvas for an intense little painting. Bits of fur, anonymous brown. One thin clean bone, curved, a rib. Just beyond the smear a furry foot. He found a twig and stooped to prod what might be the foot of a rabbit? gopher? cat? He decided rabbit. It must have happened recently, no more than an hour ago, judging from the way this lightly falling snow was covering it up. Bonaduce thought he could remember hearing, in his dawn dreaming, the faint ragged growls, the piping screams. It had happened under the fuzzy cartoon comet.

He stood and surveyed the surrounding fields. For what, he didn't know. Cold, he tucked himself deeper into his coat and walked back for his coffee. Maybe this happened all the time, you just needed snow to see the blood, it was a battlefield out here, a charnel ground. Almost funny: this was the first wildlife he'd seen from his window.

He considered going back with a baggie for the foot. Let it dry, hang it from his rearview all stained and beaten up, and kind of intense for that. Though what would such a thing have to do with luck?

Ideas:

she looked at him with eyes that were two
tunnels to the sun. (tunnels to hell?) (tunnels to
nothing?)

A man stroking a rabbit's foot with a vigour unknown to the sane

You're safe only when you're in the middle. Because when you're inside it, it's not inside you.

. . .

The night of the big grad party he started out shaky but got calmer with time. The shakiness came from two phone calls. The second call, right before the party, was Oscar's buddy Andy Frenette calling about oldtimer hockey. According to Frenette, not only his team but all the oldtimer teams in town were to his knowledge full, too full in fact. Guys paid to play and were protective of their icetime. Bonaduce asking, You sure? and finally as a last resort sliding in how he'd played pro, so maybe some team would ... But this guy Frenette says, No, no, I heard about ya, Oscar told me, thing is we got some pretty good fellas too, and winning ain't all that important in this league here, just a good time. Bonaduce is now gutfrozen with shame. Hanging up, he heard his Tiny Tim words to himself: Nobody, not even old hackers, wants me on their team.

He shrugged that call off and showered, and got Marg going, and the party turned out well enough. Nice just to relax in wealthy digs for an evening. The solid comfy chairs, the sinky cream carpet. Grad students' eyes going big at such finger food: shrimp, fancy cheese, the see-through ham with the Italian name, toothpicked to green melon. Everything tasteful. On the stereo a medium jazz no one could argue with.

Marg didn't say much, maybe she was intimidated. Maybe in their midst she could hear herself and how often she said "like" and "I mean." Marg working on that wouldn't be a bad thing. She'd earn more respect, people would see past the valley girl to someone most likely smarter than they were. In any case, despite her looking at him a bit too close for his comfort these days, she seemed okay being left pretty much on her own while he nibbled, and sipped his limit of two beers, and listened in on conversations more than added to them. He had nothing much to say. And he couldn't quite get over the morning's phone call, Leah.

She had called him, finally. Her voice warm, soft. It followed him now to the fridge as he hunted more shrimp. It followed him to the bathroom, her voice was in the mirror behind his face as he washed his hands. Leah apologizing. Admitting to her confusion about him being here in general. Suggesting they meet. Somewhere where they wouldn't be seen and interrupted and nudged off the matter at hand. She named a motel restaurant off the highway, twenty minutes out of town.

The party rolled along fine, any nastiness being confined to the professors, of which there were eight. The main participants of one duke-up were none other than his own Gail Smith and Big Jan Dionne. The spat — all smiles and edge — was about creative writing versus literary criticism, which Bonaduce considered apples and bananas but didn't say so, and good old Jan stated the obvious, that without the creative there'd be nothing to crit, but she said it in the properly deluxe way. Apropos of something else, Jan got off another one, something that made him reconsider the books he was up to his eyeballs not reading. She said, "If what you read doesn't change you for the better, why read it?" Bonaduce and a few gathered others gave this rhetorical grape some silence and a nod. But Gail Smith turned it into a raisin by asking how one could possibly know what might change one until one's read it? She looked Jan Dionne in the eye and shook her head. Eager nods now, a snicker. For the *coup de grâce* Smith turned to the nut dish and said, "Plato died, get over it," and walked away.

Bonaduce found other sparring matches worth attending. He almost liked this world. They had guts and a willingness to scuffle. The party was at Doctor Professor Daniel Kirk's house, and another prof — a Professor Tillmann, Classics — arrived wearing no less than a black cape. He entered, took in the furnishings and then host Kirk, and announced in a fey, ballsy way, "A retentive, at play!" You could see Kirk's tight humour had no room for this, or maybe they knew each other's secrets and the remark was a get-back. Kirk mumbled something about the phantom of the opera, but it was clear that Tillmann was the type who loved anyone saying anything about him.

Other than Smith, no professors talked to Big Jan, or maybe it was the other way around. In any case she was surrounded by students, and seemed part and parcel with them, though cerebrally taller perhaps, something of Socrates-in-the-grove about her, except that she laughed too much, too eager with the young jokes. Once, on her way to the bathroom, Bonaduce grabbed her and pulled her into the dining room to dance to a dumb old Dr. Hook song. She was game enough, though disturbed by the question of sex — them so close in age, of course it's going to be in the air. He had no way of reassuring her that his intentions were only fun, that she was nice but — but she could in no way compete with Leah, whose soft voice wasn't leaving him tonight, whose body he—

Where was his head, what was he thinking? It had only been a phone call. As if it meant anything. Someone treats you like a human and you respond like a dog. And what about Oscar?

But a decent party. He even had a word with Phuckphace Phil, Bonaduce first humbling himself by plunking down on the couch and asking him outright, "What the hell does *deconstruction* mean, Phil?" In this world such a gesture was the animal equivalent of approaching with underbelly exposed. Bonaduce sort of knew the answer, but Phil enjoyed the chance to say, "If we liken any given piece of text to a sphere, around which one visits its context, historical and current, as well as the reader's pre- and misconceptions," and so on. When Bonaduce, friendly hockey guy, asked near the end if this meant keeping an eye peeled to just who's doing the reading and the writing, Phil paused and thought and nodded in tentative agreement. When Bonaduce asked if Phil'd mind getting him a Moosehead, because his leg had for some reason gone all wobbly, Phil did so in good humour, and Bonaduce knew he had maybe an odd friend in the making, one who would in any case laugh when asked if he'd sell him an essay.

Otherwise he enjoyed his second beer and came downstairs with the guitar he found. It surprised everyone all to hell, like they'd never seen a guitar or heard Jerry Lee Lewis before. He had a way of doing a guitar like Jerry Lee did a piano, the machine-gun thing and, despite each of them having an old dusty book up their ass, since this was the Maritimes they eventually did get into it.

MARGARET.

He was boyish asking her and had to joke about it. Pointing to where it said "Mr. Bonaduce and Friend" on the xerox sheet, he said if he went Friendless it would be a waste of free booze and food, and she was looking frail these days, which they both knew was so not true. He said she didn't have to see it as "a date" if she didn't want to, him using that word at all showing their ages again. She told him, "Robert, I am definitely seeing this as a *date*." He seemed embarrassed enough, asking at all. She wondered what it meant, though, the difference between date and non. A corsage? A smooch goodnight at her bedroom door? He was acting as though the other night in her bedroom had never happened.

Robert explained that this was a yearly event, the profs hosting the students. A prof supplied a house, the English Department supplied supplies. On the drive over, more than once he asked himself aloud why he was even going. He liked no one, he didn't fit in. He did want her to meet his creative writing prof, Jan, who he described as "a regular guy." He looked serious saying this. Knowing she still played with the idea of grad school, he added that this was a chance to see for herself how boring that world was, how amazingly neurotically boring. A real spectacle, the rest of the world wouldn't believe it, especially how they talked, it was like a Monty Python parody. Archaeology might be different — it was bones, not words — but he bet it was the same. This rant seemed to get Robert excited about going.

She'd planned to use the drive over to get into the illness

question. And the wife question. And their long and serious hugging too. But watching him jolly at the wheel, joking himself out of his nervousness about this bad-party and their non-date, she decided to wait till the drive back. She hadn't told him about his friend Fournier's call, it had been weeks now and she'd left it too long. But she'd been watching him closely, how he moved and spoke. When she'd proposed to Fournier that maybe he was getting better, Fournier had paused and at least considered this. He told her his girlfriend, Kim, said MS could go into remission but it never went away. Mostly Fournier emphasized, actually raising his voice at her, that "if you're a friend, Bonaduce has to fucking look after himself, okay?"

These words had stayed with her as she watched Robert and his late nights, his obvious bouts with Toby's wine, and now through the party. Late in the evening she heard him drop a beer bottle in the kitchen — Was that him drunk or sick or an honest mistake? He was never not holding a beer. He laughed, he was confident, he'd either drunk away his nervousness with these people or he knew how to hide it. He and his professor, Jan, were the only ones who had the guts to dance, and he was stumbling as he twirled her. He had to be pretty drunk to go right into a bedroom upstairs and come down with a guitar. He started to sing, and everyone was embarrassed for him, and then a guy named Phil started to sing along mockingly and now she hated these people. She started to sing too, but seriously. She wasn't good at it, but hell she was on a *date* here and this was her fella, and ten minutes later everyone but the most shy were bellowing away and it got uncool *not* to sing. Good for him.

The last to leave, they drove home at three, trying to see Hale-Bopp through the dirty windshield. Robert was funny, declaring astronomers had the best jobs in the world, "teams of mountaintop nerds and throb-heads" up in their observatories, where they invented liqueurs and named things Dog Star and Hale-Bopp and Johnson's Worm Hole, which they claimed *sucks in everything, including light and time*; giggling, their eyes swimming behind lenses like plums in milk, they put out press releases saying that that comet out there, let's see, what should we tell them? yeah, it's made of *dirt and ice*, yeah, but that's only what we can *see* — inside, we suspect there's this giant magic *surprise*, something that should, if our predictions are right, make cults in California castrate then shoot themselves.

When they finally clattered into the kitchen she was an inch away from joking to him that he partied pretty hard for a *married man*. Or even venturing, Care to come up for another *hug*? But Robert's velocity through the door kept him going down the hall and lurching off to bed. He did look suddenly exhausted, as if all evening he'd kept his body propped up to perform, and at last he could relax. He slurred a goodnight, and when he slowed up to look back over his shoulder and smile at her, he was staggering.

§

Saturday night, UNB versus St. Mary's. Jason had one shift in the first period and none in the second, after which the game was tied at three. Close games you don't play your weaker players.

If UNB lost, he'd go down and talk to Whetter. If they won, he wouldn't.

The Reds lost six to three. Jason got on near the end, only to take a cheap shot in the face and leave the game with a towel pressed to his mouth. At the buzzer the guys clomped mad down the tunnel to the dressing room while Whetter lingered at the bench to argue a bad call with the ref, who listened patiently, eyeing his tunnel across the ice, looking like he wanted a beer. Whetter finished with a friendly enough "I dunno, Dave." He turned away and found Bonaduce there waiting with his hand out.

"Hiya. Too bad there's a third period sometimes."

"God, yes." Whetter shook his hand and stared angrily at the wet rubber floor. "But it'll come. It'll come."

"It will. I was wondering if you looked into that matter of my—"

"Only two games left."

Bonaduce nodded as if he knew what this meant.

"February fourteen, you're free. We phoned around. You left a sinking ship there in Utica, eh?"

"Sure did."

"Since you didn't play from mid-February, it seems by then you'll have sat out your year in effect. You were still under contract of sorts, but it's a technicality I think we'd survive."

"Hey. Good stuff." Only by feeling good news flood his body did he realize how rare good news had been.

"Not that it'll be an issue."

"No?"

"Because by then we only have two games left in the season."

"But, and the playoffs."

"We need more your kind of optimism." Whetter smiled and looked up at him for the first time.

"I'll be there."

"Well, hang on. Thing is, you still can't practise. Not officially. So no way you'll be in game shape. Two games won't give you that either."

"I'll get on with an oldtimers team, skate my butt off."

"Maybe. Sure." Whetter hesitated. "What I really wanted to ask is a favour. After we talked, it hit me. But no one had your phone number. Not even Jason." A brief but questioning look from the younger man. "He said you were here incognito."

"I've been hittin' the books, eh?" Bonaduce smiled so as to let Whetter know he'd also been having himself some fun. It was suddenly strange, the two of them talking here, tiny in the bottom of this immense building shaped like a funnel, surrounded on all sides by empty seats. Two men in blue uniforms with brooms were way up top, beginning with the highest row. When they knocked over an empty Coke cup, you could hear it.

Jason could have got his number from all sorts of places.

"Anyway, the obvious thing was to ask you to be an assistant coach. The defence coach. Ever thought of coaching?"

They turned and started through the mouth of the tunnel. Bonaduce lagging behind, wanting to hear this but not wanting to go all the way to the dressing-room door.

"Thought of it." Thought he'd hate it. Telling the guys what to do, shoved you right out of the loop. Guys, management. "Sounds good."

"And that way you could get some ice. Practise without really practising. Scrimmage even, who's gonna know."

"Sounds good."

"So maybe you get in shape and maybe we use you."

"Sounds great."

"Puts Jason in a position, the boys might poke a bit of fun, but he wouldn't mind that, I don't think."

"No problem there."

"He's a good lad."

"Hey."

"Took a good one on the mouth tonight."

"Happens."

"And he'll get his chance to play."

"Good stuff."

"Whoops, gotcha—" Whetter had him by the arm.

"Tripped on piece of mat there."

Bonaduce stamped his foot on the culprit. He'd tripped, sending Jason in alone with the perfect pass, Jace tucks it upstairs to win the game and send them into the playoffs, he circles back to whack Assistant Playing Coach Dad on the ass like a buddy.

Set a guy up, no matter how much he hates you he has to come and whack you on the ass.

. . .

Ideas:

Castrated men shed their containers to chase the
holy comet. We see them as the silly-dead.

Ball of ice, keeping its distance from the sun. Snowball in hell.

these words become a line
that turns into a poem I need
for Big J to give me an A
so I will be allowed to stay
and play
wiff the boy I wuv

"Whatever happened to subtlety?" Toby says, chewing, the blank
face of the professional passive-aggressive.

Sometimes you know you've been insulted. Toby, man. He
could get to you.

You cash your little teaching cheque, you make a choice between the used snow tires you're going to need any day now and
a Mexican take-out spree for the house. To celebrate your new,
secret, unpaid job of assistant coach — and also Frenette calling
you last night after all and you going out with his team, a weird
experience despite scoring your first official oldtimer goal. To
celebrate all this you arrive with a double box of beer and four
bags of Mexican, spiced extra hot. The start of a good night for
the house: Marg, Beth, Rod, even Joyce was home to sit down
for this. A hissing of beer tops and clinking of bottles, and everyone's just fine, except Toby, who suddenly hates spicy. He in-
forms his housemates that its only purpose is to hide the taste of
bad meat in poor hot countries and bullshit like this, pure
Tobyness to knock in one fell swoop not only you for buying his
dinner, but also any country, from Thailand to Togo, for enjoying

a bit of pepper in the mouth and sweat on the brow. Then, Whatever happened to subtlety? Looking right at you as you shovel the rellenos in. You can now not brag, as you'd been gearing up to, about how in Tulsa you would chop jalapeños right into your scrambled eggs and could even gobble one of the buggers straight. Sure, macho sneer at boredom perhaps is all it was, but why not give the mouth a little hip-hop.

You had to hand it to Toby. It's a rare spice-wimp with the pills to turn the tables on everyone else. Almost made you stop chewing and feel your numb tongue, almost made you feel like a tasteless beast because it was true, you could in fact no longer taste the refried beans. Which almost made you say something very unsubtle to the one-armed bastard. But there he was, opening up another of his bottles of wine for everyone. Then going to his cupboard and coming back with a big bag of ketchup potato chips to eat.

He watched Toby eat his junk, his two-buck bag of treasure wedged in his lap, not offering any. Greasy shitty red-coloured crispies. You could see the link between food and body. It wasn't hard to connect Toby's shit-food with his shit-spirit. It wasn't farfetched. You are what you stuff down the hatch.

In Rochester, briefly, there'd been Yoshi, that Japanese winger. Purportedly a huge star in Japan, the best there ever. He had NHL speed, for sure, but aside from speed he had nothing. Too scared to relax into the flow, too used to stardom to recognize his new status as average guy, and therefore unable to adapt and learn. But the main thing was his undeniable foreignness — which Bonaduce put down to food. You could see it. The way he skated wasn't meat, it was fish. You could see seaweed in the way he sat inscrutably in the dressing room. Noodles in the attitude, tofu in the shyness. You knew you couldn't really see anything so exact as that, but Yoshi was definitely marked by a general dietary weirdness. Same with the Russians. Wooden bread, tough bad meat. The spoke like they ate.

Toby sitting here with his rancid, pinched, cellophane thoughts.

• • •

Fuel
—by Robert Bonafide

Whether dogfood or spice, food is a window on the soul, so on roadtrips, in restaurant after restaurant, it's impossible not to get to know your teammates in this way. Tommy, your defense partner, with his taboo about any vegetable — amazing he stayed alive let alone so nimble and bashing. There was Ray, who loved pizza, but only without the tomato sauce, said he couldn't stomach it (no matter how many times he got yelled at for contradicting himself by *eating the tomatoes in his fucking salad*). A lot of pizza goes down in motels after games, but with Ray around you couldn't just say "large works" into the phone, you had to explain twice to some guy with a heavy accent. Or you'd be in a real city and want to hit a sushi place and two thirds of the guys won't even bother responding to the suggestion, won't even try the word out in their brain, even after you explain how they can get teriyaki there, which they'll love, it's barbecue. But the unstated thing looms about hanging together as a team, and once more you have to forgo sushi for the steak joint, all dark and done up like a gold chain in black chest hair.

Guys who never eat breakfast, guys who only eat breakfast. Some guys, enormous cheapskates, banking their per diem while they order nothing and eat the table's basket of buns and breadsticks and butter, and then half your fries. Some guys with what might be actual allergies, JD with a bad one for anything wheat, maybe it was even Crohn's, he did eventually have an operation after getting traded to Phoenix — no matter, he was hated for being a pain to find a restaurant with. Some guys eating ugly with their mouths open. Some prim with little knives and forks in big hammy hands. Some eating at private tables — coaches, management. Some dumping ketchup without caring what it landed on. Some don't talk while they eat, some can't shut up. A few have a butt going in the ashtray while they stab at six a.m. eggs — though you don't see this much any more. Nor do you see as much carefree guzzling after games.

It seems the younger guys have learned about food, what it does. You hear words like "amino acids." "Complex carbohydrates." Last year, last road trip in my playing career perhaps, enough guys expressed interest in hitting a health-food store on the way out of Wheeling that they actually got the bus driver to stop. I watched the old coach sitting waiting for them, brow knit and staring, like his guys were in there looking at porno or astrophysics or something equally out of his league.

He was exhausted, he should sleep. Leah tomorrow. Leah, roadside motel.

He closed the laptop, thinking: Recipes. He should put in some recipes, these days every novel had them. So put some in, put in some genuine hockey player recipes: Mac 'n' Cheese With Big Chunks of Meat. Spagetty With Tomato Sauce On It. Potatoes Cut in the Middle With Butter In There. Ham Samwidge With Two Slices of Ham.

Probably shouldn't have stolen the bottle. Why steal wine that costs two bucks? Because you spent all your money on the guy's dinner and he took you down, that's why. And because it was impossible to out-and-out ask him for it. Better to steal the guy's wine than say something truly hurtful, like challenging him to an arm wrestle. He'd sipped his two glasses of it, then had to pour the rest out, hide the evidence.

He could hear Toby upstairs now, bumping around the bathroom. It was maybe three. You could somehow tell it was Toby. And Toby was probably aware of him down here typing. Toby didn't seem to sleep much either.

Leah. It really was not the best time for this. He'd hardly slept. He didn't feel good about much. Tired, gritty in the eyes, unsteady top to bottom. Thoughts didn't come clear. His inner ugliness showed. Whenever he'd pictured today, he'd looked his best.

But why? *What* are your intentions?

He showered and shaved. Somehow he was late. It was cold, the coldest day yet, the bleak time of year, with the leaves long down but no snow. He felt thankful for his leather coat.

One of the chest buttons popped when he got into his car, and this made him sit and stare out the window, shaking his head. He cupped the big black button in his hand, examining it. He checked where it had come off, the circle of darker, shinier leather, the four pinholes and ragged broken thread.

And he had been somehow prepared for his car not to start. He ran his battery down trying, then faced the choice of hitching or calling a taxi. He'd be late either way. Maybe he shouldn't go. He shouldn't go.

And felt cheap as hell taking his sixty cents change from the ten. Sixty cents is sixty cents. He said, Sorry, I need it, but the taxi driver said nothing and wouldn't look at him, a mopey martyr for sixty cents, something to gripe about with the boys at the stand.

Bonaduce stood in the parking lot. This was like out of a movie. It certainly wasn't real, in any case. Roadside motel, and fronting the row of rooms her red car, its little ass pointing up. There in the big window of the café, Leah sat alone in a black-leatherette booth. Thinking hard at something as she sipped through a straw. Seeing him approach, looking quickly down, then looking up again and smiling.

The booths even had those private chrome jukeboxes on the wall, and when he sat across from her he had to resist the urge to search the titles, maybe find something corny for them to hear, something she'd recognize and they'd laugh.

"You're limping."

"No I'm not."

"I thought you were."

"Well I've been working out a bit."

Her lips, you couldn't tell if she had something on them or not. Wasn't that exactly the point, the art— But what was he thinking here? And what about Oscar.

He'd promised himself he wouldn't read anything into her idea of meeting at, well, at a motel. But here they were, together at a motel. Her suggestion. Back in those days, their days, when beds *meant* sex, motels meant beds. Look at her. Shy? Sad? Her silence thick with what? Jeans and a fuzzy sweater again, like at her party, his favourite, he might have told her this once and she might have remembered.

Was Oscar a buddy?

"So. Hi, Bobby."

Apology in her smile. A sad summing-up.

"Hiya." Look at her. "So, how's work? How're those guys down in that church?" He felt twenty again with her, inarticulate. He didn't mind this.

"They're still 'down in that church.' They might be there a year. But they're safe. Donations have been good and they have a nice little apartment set up. We even had to turn down a new living-room suite from Wal-Mart."

"Hey, I'll take it."

Leah smiled. "It gets so complicated. Wal-Mart is American, and its investment portfolio includes, you know, 'the usual.'"

His look prompted her to say more.

"Well, Juan admits to his involvement in a group that pamphlets against the monoculture — bananas — that's destroying all other agriculture there, and the whole pesticide health issue, and it's all American-owned, all Chiquita and a couple of others, so his real fight was against the U.S. So, Wal-Mart? Sorry."

"Maybe Wal-Mart's trying to make it up to him?"

"Right." Leah smiled with him.

She'd used *pamphlets* as a verb. She was a professional, and he no longer was. He shook his head at twenty years.

"What?"

"I dunno. A year in a basement. Holy."

A waitress came for their order. Leah ordered a sandwich and tea. He asked for a glass of icewater. He was desperate for a coffee because the cupboard had been bare and he'd done without, but coffee was eighty cents plus tax. You couldn't borrow a quarter from her. If you want a relationship with her son, you could not be a destitute bum.

And maybe you want more than a relationship with the son.

"Half a year easily. Ottawa's sitting on it. If they get in, the rednecks argue everyone'll get in. As if we can't tell the heroin smugglers from the— Juan has *scars* on his back. The kids saw their *uncle* killed."

"Who put the scars on his back?" He resisted a Wal-Mart joke.

"It's complicated."

The last thing you want to do is blow this. She hates you enough already, even if for a while there back in history she was your home. The last thing you want to do is misread the situation, come on to her just when she's got herself ready to talk and treat you like a human. You could blow it by looking at her wrong, by raising one cool sexy eyebrow, don't forget how well she knows you. Blow it when you don't even know what you want yourself, you can't put your finger on your intentions long enough to see whether your need is to get the mother in your camp so she'll get the son to come too, or whether this mixed-up welling of sadness and tears and breathing at the sight of her has to do with her alone or with you not being with a woman in God knows how long and needing, Christ, maybe just needing to be touched like this on the arm by someone.

"What's wrong?" Leah leaning in with tilted head. "Bobby? You crying?"

"Ah, hey, you know. No." He felt her eyes still on him, though no one spoke.

"Well, Bob. Jason ... he lost a tooth. The other night."

"Really?" He looked up. She didn't look like she was blaming him for it.

"Did you know? A front tooth?"

"I didn't know. He okay?"

"At least it wasn't from a fight."

Didn't *look* like she blamed him. Fighting. The subject had been heavy in her silences, her distant look when it was celebrated in the bar with the guys and their wives after the game. If he'd studied her more closely that first season, he would have learned sooner that the few times she was not in the mood coincided with the few times she'd seen him fight. And here he'd been feeling jealous whenever Jim Murphy got into one and from behind the bench his Cindy would yell *C'mon, Murph, C'mon, Murph*, the good warrior's-wife. He imagined a Cindy more eager that night in bed, her black-and-blue knight gallant on top of her. He'd joked once to Leah something about how you'd figure a gal who fanged into the Alpo wouldn't be opposed to a small display of brute force from her man. But Leah had no use for it, and it was not one of her secrets. She smiled politely when he dismissed fighting as two tempers in a teapot. Or when he shrugged and said simply, "Consenting adults." Sure there were loose screws out there, guys who might try for an eye. In general, fighting was a war-in-a-box where no one got hurt. Black eyes, the odd nose or helmet-broken finger. And how many times did you see guys who'd fought that night clink glasses later in the bar?

It wasn't until he'd left Fredericton that he realized she may have been afraid. Not for him. Of him.

Well, hell. He wanted so much to tell her how that just wasn't in his makeup. Also how he suspected that hockey players in general were less likely to get violent with their women. It only made sense. At home on the couch the guy had no reason to be anything but a pacifist: hockey his outlet for whatever violent streak he had. He was happy to be home and at rest, a gentle sigh at the wife's ministrations.

Bonaduce had since dropped this theory, and not just because of all the athletes in the news for domestic stuff. Things had changed. The pressure. The frustrations at not making it. These days, to play in the minors was seen as nothing but failure. Fighting was more calculated now, a career tool, a spectacle, no real honour left in it. And steroids. He could imagine women in the awful privacy of their homes getting whacked because of that shit. Jesus, but he'd seen some young guys on the 'roid rage, flailing away, 220-pound tantrum, anger unheld as a child's, all teeth and paranoia, guy's face with its spread of telltale pimples oozing bad hormones and grease.

"Shit, a front tooth. But he's okay?"

"If he wasn't okay, he wouldn't have told me."

"Well, are *you* okay?"

Leah looked down, nodded. When she looked up again he could tell the subject had changed. She had dismissed their son, she had not invited him here just to talk about Jason. Her eyes were deep and clear, and rich with what she had become in the last twenty years. She was checking his eyes for what he had become during that time too, and it was hard not to look away.

Now it seemed that she might cry.

"Bobby, let's — let's not be in a hurry."

The words gave him an instant erection, though her eyes showed nothing but openness and sincerity. Her sandwich came, and his water. When her coffee arrived he said it smelled so good, could he have a sip? and he drank some, and when she took it back and drank some too, he saw how her lips touched the same spot.

He stood in his driveway, her car getting smaller, his hand still up in a wave. When he'd gotten out, neither of them had smiled.

His dead car with its hood open. In his hurry to the cab he'd forgotten to put the damn thing down. What did Leah think, seeing this yard, this house, this car with its hood up. White trash. In class Kirsten had given Phil shit for using that term, saying it implied that expected trash was black.

The keys were still in the ignition. Another picture of Bonaduce in a hurry. He decided against trying to start it, and closed the hood. None of what happened would have, had this car not died. Should he thank it or pound on it with a hammer? He would go in and have a bath, let it all percolate.

They'd ended up in her little car, Leah about to give him a simple ride home. They had talked and talked, Bonaduce ordering his fill of coffee, having decided to play the dufuss who'd forgotten his wallet. He'd come expecting a business-like discussion about Jason and for that alone he would have been grateful. But she had met him this morning to make a connection. They talked like ordinary people, they talked more about her work and he talked about his school, and she laughed at the stories of his fumblings. They talked about Oscar and Jason, but not in the sense that there was anything to *do* about either of them, and Bonaduce had only the slightest pang at the news that Jason's sights were set on Law. It was them simply catching up, enjoying each other's company, though of course they both knew that underneath it all was the *bloodbeast* that erupted in Leah's car. It was a tiny car and he was a clumsy hulk climbing in. He couldn't remember whose fault it was that their knees touched, and then he simply patted it, her knee, safe there in her jeans, and he thanked her.

"Leah? Thanks for this," he'd said, and meant it. Both for the ride, but also more. And it worked because she looked up at him and he down at her and their faces were so close that the kiss was both their faults. At first neither of them betrayed anything other than a friendly kiss, a smack with the eyes open. But the kiss continued, and deepened, and got gently wild and down to business. Leah pulled away and, alone with herself for a moment, swore and slapped the steering wheel. Then she laughed, they both laughed. They kissed small again, then got right into it this time, and they were almost out of control there in the parking lot.

He did feel the dumb dufuss while she paid for the room. When they walked in, he wondered if she'd envisioned — maybe even planned for — this moment, too, this thrill, the delicious doom of the door locking shut behind them, then the brief relapse into shyness, their eyes falling on anything but the bed.

It was the best possible time. Right now. With his fingers on her neck and cheeks, the skin so soft he could hardly feel it through his own roughness. With her breasts and her legs teasing him with its clothing. With her head falling back under the full weight of this moment, with her fingers finding his belt loops, gently taking hold and drawing him to her.

III

At first light, the old men upright and drooling.
—Cormac McCarthy, *Suttree*

He was consumed by doubts as to his own identity, as to the
nature of his body and the cast of his countenance.
In what manner did he relieve these doubts?
By the sensory perception of his ten fingers.
—Flann O'Brien, *At Swim-Two-Birds*

December 1, Bonaduce bought a Christmas tree. It was early, he knew he was pushing things, but there they were as he drove by. You could smell the shaggy stack from the street through his open window, reek of pine after-life. If he wasn't supposed to buy one, they wouldn't be there. That it was the same gas station where he'd bought his only other Fredericton tree twenty years ago clinched it.

He interrupted an old guy who was just finishing the job of unloading the trees from the flatbed. He was skinny, unshaven, and permanently asquint from the smoke of the cigarette dangling in his mouth, surprising he could move one tree, let alone a stack. Anywhere but a jobsite he'd be taken for a derelict.

"You're the first." He gave Bonaduce a congratulatory nod and pocketed the twenty. He may have chuckled as he watched Bonaduce wrestle the tree onto his station wagon.

"Got some rust, eh?" the man added, indicating with his chin and cigarette the bottom of the driver's door.

"I guess."

Bonaduce groped in the back-seat mess for the bungees. What do you say to such things? You're wearing clothes, eh? You have yellow eyebrows, eh?

"Well, get 'er in some water quick."

It took a moment to realize he meant the tree, not the rust. He tried to picture what kind of tree stand might be scroungeable back at the house. A big bucket, full of stones, bricks. Maybe he'd have to buy a proper rig.

But the car wouldn't start. He tried and tried, then got out. He didn't open the hood, because it wasn't flooded. The old guy standing beside him, he stared at his station wagon sitting there mulishly stubborn, as if it didn't like its burden of the tree.

"There's a good one right in there." The old man jerked his head back toward the garage. A sign read: Mechanic On Duty.

What money he might have had for tree rigs was now gone. Only because he was at a gas station to begin with did he decide to spring for a proper job. The old guy helped him and the mechanic push his car into the bay. If it was something major, kiss the car goodbye, he'd have to walk away from it. And the tree.

Well, but. He'd been trying not to think about it, the American Express card in the back of his wallet. He'd maxed it out before coming north. What sort of trouble could you get in for just trying it? Oops, silly me, wrong card, jeez I thought I'd lost that. And what about these guys you read about who, in debt to six maxed-out cards, declare bankruptcy and in a month receive invites for new cards? What if his card worked, what if he had three thousand U.S. to spend? Hey and while you're at it, throw in all those doughnuts, and that case of pop. And that bin of ice scrapers, please, I go through them.

It was a strange sight, his wagon rising on the hoist, Christmas tree on top. Two worlds strapped together, one fresh and green, the other stinking of oil and rust. Both in their way half-alive. Or half-dead, depending on your mood.

He walked and ran all the way home, adjusting his pace to the waves of fatigue as they rose. You could get on them, surf them. It was not unpleasant to slow life down, letting the cars *whoosh* on past. The noises, the smells. This was fine. It all depended on your mood. Moods were upon you, no choice in the matter. Sometimes you could stick-handle your way out of a bad one, sometimes you couldn't.

That Christmas in Tulsa, with Fournier. Christmas, never a good time for Bonaduce, was this year awful for Fournier, whose mother was sick. How sick, Fournier didn't know, and this was the crux. He hadn't made it back the previous year, and once again their game schedule was rotten. A travel agent helped him calculate that, with Christmas congestion and changing planes, he'd have a total of minus five hours to spend in Chicoutimi with his mother. So Fournier was down in the dumps. Sitting in a chair in the middle of the kitchen, he told Bonaduce with great gravity that Christmas in Tulsa was hell on earth.

Misery secretly loving company, Bonaduce went out and bought four bottles of champagne. Well, bubbly white. He'd once seen Fournier get near silly on the stuff. He also bought a funny Christmas card. In the background was the lower part of the tree and spread of presents. In the foreground, a guy's feet dangled in the air. It took you a second to see he'd hanged himself.

The card worked and Fournier got near silly on the wine. They gathered at a teammate's with eight or ten others who were suffering Christmas in Tulsa. A couple of them snickered but, unlike Fournier, they thought the card was sick.

A mile to go, along the Trans-Canada. Freezing rain was falling now and Bonaduce had to stop and turn his face away when a semi roared by. Some guys just didn't get black humour, had no talent for fire-with-fire. They didn't understand that sometimes you could slap a mood in the face and win.

The Birth of Hockey

Because it is dark and smoky inside. Because Granddad drinks and after he wakes from his sour moanings his mood is prickly and his eyes follow you, looking for reasons to shout. Because outside it is bright and clean, and the pond gives you magical speed, and the faster you go the bigger the thrill, till it scares you. Because inside, the smell of a cooked onion takes all day to leave the house. Because Grandma gets sour herself when Granddad doesn't talk all through supper. Because it's only December and already she's hanging on for spring. Outside, your friends escape their hot houses and drift by with plans. Because you are too young to hunt and there's no money for bullets in any case, but there is the pond. Because inside, you can't read the Bible any more for it reminds you of inside and winter, of where you were, yet there is no other book. The catalogue is five years old and ripped, and the dreams it gives are tired. Because outside the rules are clear, to the point that if McIlhargy busts your shins again with the club he calls a stick you will fight him. Because inside, you cannot play another game of cards beside the flickering candle, tobacco smoke smarting your eyes and stinking so bad your nose can no longer smell it. Because outside you make sure your little sister played, and that the teams are even because it's more fun that way. Because sometimes, as the sun goes down, you find yourself hugging each other and cheering: McIlhargy falls, but not before the puck slides between his legs and through the holy posts, to nudge up against the backing snow.

On the phone. Out of the blue.
"Hello?"
"Hi. I was just wondering—"
Jason.
"Jason, hi."
"—if you wanted to go see Bob Dylan."
"Bob Dylan?"
"He's on the fifteenth. I've got these—"
"Bob Dylan's coming to Fredericton?"

"It's in two weeks, so—"

"That's incredible. Bob Dylan. This is the real Bob Dylan?"

"Yeah, do you want to go?" A trace of impatience. Things to do, fast twenty-year-old life.

"Hey, well yeah! Sure I do. Thanks. And I'll grab the tickets — so where do I—"

"Well, I sort of already got them."

"Hey. Okay. Great. Wow. Bob Dylan." Jason, Jason taking him to Bob Dylan, in Fredericton.

"Okay, see ya."

His boy hung up. No small talk, no further arrangements. No apology for the time in the corridor. All of which was fine. What Jason had just done had been hard for him, what he had just done was a great thing. From his voice you know it had been hard. Good lad.

And Bob Dylan. He sort of liked him, certainly had never loved him. The folky extraordinaire. The kind of guy if you went to high school with would be too arty and distant to like. But you couldn't deny he'd changed the world. He'd been reduced to Fredericton? A superstar demoted to the minors. But it would be great. Bob Dylan. It would be like seeing the *Mona Lisa*. The mummified body of Lenin. He'd get Jason over for a beer before the show and tell him what Bob Dylan meant to the world.

A world full of messages today. He'd just put the phone down, his ear full of Jason's echoes, hungry to replay them, when Marg was handing him a box, its surface colourful with U.S. stamps and Customs stickers.

"There was like a note for you from the post office that something was, you know, there for you. But, I mean, I was in town anyway so I just picked it up."

Why the nervous concern?

"No, I'm glad! Thank you. Great. Thanks."

He plucked the rusty hunting knife from the junk drawer

and took it and the box to his room.

On his bed, looking at the window, he tried to hear and feel Jason's voice, but felt nothing more than a jittery stomach. He'd see him on the ice tomorrow night in any case. It was great the boy had called, the timing perfect. Fearing another disaster, Coach Bonaduce had been thinking of not showing up.

He hacked carefully at the parcel, half its top covered in stars-and-stripes stampage. Like he was opening a box containing his past twenty years. Amarica. His fellow Amaricans. Three months here had shown him how he'd become used to them. Their way of talking, proclaiming. Even their hesitations had a showy certainty. They were brave, it was true. Bashers on the biggest rink. Cradling this box, he realized in a mostly physical way that the America he'd left behind contained a neat two decades, a career, a game.

Why dwell on it? What was there to figure out? Over. Finished. Buzzer's gone. What of those past twenty years was even useful to think about? That this box was small seemed appropriate. You could pop it into a closet. You could flick it, *flick* it, out the window.

He put the knife to it. Inside was a health book about yeast infections, a letter from Fournier and a stern note of instructions from the girlfriend. Six bottles, vitamins looking like foliage crushed and capsuled. The two-page typed instructions said first you did the kidney cleanse, then the liver cleanse, then you started the main— You drank this at eight, that at noon, then you took— After the two-week juice fast you started the brown rice, introducing one different steamed vegetable every—

Fournier's note made no mention of their possible last paycheque except to say, "Wharton he's fucking unbelievable." Referring no doubt to continuing dirty legal manoeuvres. Fournier had finished his real-estate course and was about to start his new profession. "I wonder if buyers will trust a handsome Frenchman." Bonaduce pictured Fournier in a suit trying to sell something. Fournier would look good in a suit. If he relaxed and didn't smile all the time. Fournier could do the little

charismatic eye-glint if he slowed down and didn't want something out of a situation.

Bonaduce restuffed the box. He placed it on the floor and,
without looking, heeled it under his bed. What sounded like a
vitamin bottle fell out and rolled to a stop somewhere. He didn't
have a yeast infection. In fact he was feeling pretty damn good.
Yesterday from the garage he'd more or less trotted all the way
back here. It had to be four miles. He'd walked maybe only a
mile of it and today his legs felt okay. Appropriately stiff and
achy. In his general soul it did feel something like a flu rising,
but he hadn't had a cold in a while so he was due. He was fine.
Tomorrow was the start of his playing-coach career. Things were
picking up, the towering gears of the universe were clunking
more harmoniously of late. Though you couldn't deny the logic
of it all: You sleep with the mother and, bang, the son calls, asking, Hey Dad, wanna go to a show? Had Leah spoken to him,
put in a good word? Well, why the hell wouldn't she. She sleeps
with you it means she at least likes you. Something about you.

Hey Dad, wanna go to a show? Hear some music? Just like it
should be. He smiled, shaking his head. Life was a running stumble in the dark forest, truly wild. Bear pits, trip roots, cannibals.
Sometimes you got a berry patch, a surprise waterfall, a sunlit
clearing.

Bonaduce had to laugh, taking in his tiny bed and tiny room.
He reached out like Jesus on the cross, and his hands almost
touched both walls at once. Fournier had ended his letter saying
that he and his girlfriend were thinking of driving up, pay a visit,
could he put them up at his place, was there room?

Did Fournier think that when he'd left Utica he'd been called
up to the bigs or something?

God he was tired. Time for a long nap, stay in bed all day,
happy enough, but hope for no more boxes or messages.

The time he played in the NHL. "The Show" the kids called it

now, copying baseball. His third season he was called up from
Rochester to join Toronto on the road, meeting them in Phila-
delphia to play the Flyers that night. He would always remember the limo from the airport. Him with skates and overnight
bag. That it was a plane at all was a taste of the bigs. He would
always remember walking into the Leaf dressing room, the scattered greetings from guys who remembered him from training
camp. There were three trainers, instead of one, taping ankles,
giving rubdowns. Everything a bit newer, the gear better, lighter,
cleaner, no thought of budget. Towels thicker, everything laid
out, a choice of shampoos. There was Sittler; there was Lanny,
who, when he said hi through that moustache, you couldn't see
his lips move; and there was Tiger Williams, not as dumb as he
came across on TV. They were as pale and bruised and mortal as
the guys you left in Rochester. Same habits, same morals or lack
thereof. As funny, and as limited in their speech. But there was
something different in their eyes — a loftiness, a genuine knowing. Which posed a question you needed to answer for your
own professional future: Was this confidence their reward, or
was it what got them here in the first place?

From the bench Bonaduce watched his teammates get beaten
by Philly, six-one. Clarke was fierce, and television didn't show
how fast Leach could fly. But Bonaduce saw he could play in this
league, these guys weren't all great, there were grinders like him.
He was put on for the hell of it with two minutes to go. His shift
lasted forty, fifty seconds and he didn't touch the puck. After the
game he was informed of more travel arrangements. He had to
hustle in and out of the shower and leave the dressing room just
as the guys, sitting in their steaming gear, started to shake off
the loss and joke around a bit. He was put on a smoky overnight
train to rejoin his real team. And in the years that followed, whenever anyone asked if he'd ever played in the NHL, if he'd ever
been called up, he simply said not yet. Because it hadn't really
happened, not in the way it was going to.

He wouldn't know whether to remember it as life's treat or
life's tease, this feast he'd been allowed only to smell. It was, as

they say, a learning experience. The curt impersonality taught him that no one cared. Getting traded that second time — rupturing whatever family feel the team had given him — taught him he was alone.

Last night a dream about going with Jason to Dylan. Though in the dream it became the Harlem Globetrotters, as Dylan's warm-up act. Jason was thirty and paunchy, unshaven and surly. He smoked. And, damn, Bonaduce realized it was the kind of event you brought far younger sons to. The girl took their tickets. Father and son navigated the crowd, checking their stubs against the numbers over the tunnels. They passed a group of midgets, and Jason laughed at them cruelly and openly. This father–son thing, who said it would be easy? Bonaduce asked, "Ever seen these guys?" and Jason's answer, "Can't remember," irritated him. To say the Globetrotters could make so little impression that maybe he'd seen them, maybe he hadn't, was rude. He'd said it with a slackness of face that was ruder still. But he was being honest, they were beyond fake politeness at least. And they had the great seats. Couldn't help but love the Globetrotters, look at them warm up, shooting casual hoops, God they were loose, all high-five and whoop-up. How could you not love a seven-foot guy leaving the floor at full speed, faking a shot and cruising mid-air beneath the basket to come out from under and spin in a no-looker? You didn't see big guys like this in Canada. Sitting beside them suddenly, a tiny black man, the team clown, birthed a full-sized wet basketball from his hinged, snake-like mouth and Bonaduce knew this was a dream. He turned to Jason to tell him, and Jason was a huge fat older guy, stuffing a hotdog in his frowning maw, his belly resting on his thighs, one big repulsive bad mood. It was all funny now, just a dream, none of it true.

. . .

In the morning he arrived humming in the kitchen. It was incredible but his lack of a car and a ride to give seemed to be sparking resentment in his housemates. Toby's deadpan, Well, what the hell else ya good for? was dangerous but funny, and Bonaduce shot him an approving wink. They leafed through the junk-drawer paper for a bus schedule they doubted they'd ever had. They grumbled about pooling their dimes for a taxi. No one was at all enthused by his smiling invitation to join him in his jog-and-walk to campus. He knew they found him idiotic in his sweatpants as he bolted his coffee and did his stretches hanging on to the counter edge. Even Marg was disturbed with him. Her asking, So what was in the box from the States? arose with a clunk out of some strained need to make conversation, and his reply, "One big yeast infection," didn't put the kind of smirk on her face it normally would have. Maybe she took it as sexist sass, and not a decent non sequitur. Maybe he shouldn't have had that tender moment with her up in her room.

He sometimes shortcut through fields and leapt ditches, feet crashing in brittle leaves, their crisp and perfect December sound. His steady breathing was the sound of health itself. The smell of smoke and pleasant garden-rot wafted over from what looked like a cauliflower farm, lots of unpicked white–brown bodies. Pungent smell of gravel kicked up by his feet. Soon all would go into the deepfreeze, this could be the last day of the sun warm on the face. Crows yelled at him from nearby trees and chickadees made him smile with their mournful, *geee*zer. If you're going to go schiz and let the world start talking to you, let's hope at least some of the voices are funny.

Things were coming together. The son. The son's mother. Even the hockey. Maybe even the school, why not. Next week, the last week of classes before the Christmas break, his stuff was being done in Big Jan's workshop, and then he would present *The English Patient* at Gail Smith's. He'd whined successfully to

get both delayed and now time was up. He'd done only peripheral work on either, but pressure was his middle name, in the
playoffs just drop the puck and turn the Bonaduce loose.

He was jogging first to the garage to pick up his car. If it
wasn't ready today he'd jog in again tomorrow. It could only be
good to fight through this tiredness. Put some teenage back in
the legs. Things were moving and things were okay, everything
pretty much as he'd wished, pretty much as he'd foreseen.

Luck, often you don't know you've had it till it's gone, but
sometimes, like today, you can feel the blossoming, and you can
feel that it's way bigger than you. That time, a solid month in
'Mazoo, when the goals just started coming, first a bunch of
flukes and deflections, and then he actually started trying to score,
turned into a bit of a rushing defenceman, and they kept coming. Basher turned offensive threat. He anticipated a call from
on high. Call they did, but only to suggest that he stick to his
game, not try to do too much. At which point he started to doubt
himself, just enough to knock him off his edge and put a stop to
the goals. Doubt can kill luck all by itself.

Jogging, he discovered he was whistling. It was a phony whistle. Trying to distract himself.

He made a quick trespass over the highway, to the river-
edge where a stand of cattails promised entertainment. Holding
his hands up like a boxer, he took left-handed swipes at the brown
cigars, *whap*, he'd read the Natives used to eat these things, *whap*,
made a kind of flour, *whap*. There were frogs down there in the
muddy roots, *whap*, didn't they freeze, *whap*, solid?

Shit, why is it, *whap*, in middle age, *whap*, even the good
times, *whap-whap*, are only iffy?

Right, damn, so let's have a look. Why the doubt. I'm jogging along, happy as a fast clam, yet here's doubt and here it had
been all along. Doubt making the breath sound only hopeful.
Doubt rising up deep from muscle and bone. Here was the sun
full on the face — why the dark and the chill?

Because of the look on Leah's face.

Because of the sound in Jason's voice.

Because doubt has brought up the one and only question: Why jog, why do anything, when you're only going to die.

It's like there comes a time when, if you haven't been honest with yourself about certain questions, they get fed up and stand and shout at you all by themselves.

At Leah's insistence, communicated only through her hands, which moved as though caught in a graceful trance, the clothes had come off slowly. They did each other's, tugging at foreign buttons and clasps. In the delicious pace and clumsiness of this, he could feel all the more the hunger of twenty years. Slower, her hands said. I want to remember this — her mouth explained slowly into his ear — because it's going to be the only time.

While her saying this didn't dent his ardour, if there was darkness about their coming together, her words darkened things further. It was her right. She had the partner. Bonaduce was only free.

They stood in their underwear lightly embracing, pulling back a little in the semi-dark to take each other in, coming together to kiss and squeeze and almost lose control again because it was too much. If time had drained and scuffed their bodies, it wasn't noticeable in this light, and time hadn't hurt their urge at all. Leah was shaking. As for him, he was almost there from just the hard hugging, which would be a shame, a waste of this. She was smiling down at his underwear and what it could hardly contain. The straining thing in its ridiculous push, Leah looking a bit proud of herself.

She took further control, which again was fine and for the same reason. Shakily she whispered that if they didn't "literally" make love she could maybe live with herself. She had them retreat to separate beds. She pulled off her underwear, he pulled off his. Looking at him from across the two-foot chasm she played with herself. He did the same, though carefully, intermittently, because it was still almost over. He forced his thoughts to wander.

He'd noticed that above both beds hung what appeared to be identical pictures of lake-and-distant-snowy-mountains. He checked now and they were in fact identical. What was the thinking.

"What's that?"

"What?" He stopped his hand and looked at her. Leah was pointing at his inner thigh.

"That."

"Oh. Bruise." From the oldtimer game. It was purple as a birthmark, fresh as a stamp, the size of a saucer and growing. Maybe it was age but he'd never had one quite like it, its centre almost black. He wished she hadn't seen it. Hockey was so much of the reason they had stopped—

But Leah could no longer stand it. She pulled her hair, she screamed, she laughed, and then she was in his bed. She had him promise that they wouldn't actually, *actually*— He said "fuck" for her but felt tainted for it, though it was a word they'd once used in play. Oh but now the deep taste of her, her soft and helpless moans, he could feel both in the pit of himself. The rules of their touch were further circumscribed when he lifted back his head and warned her not to, not to do *that*, stop, he was too close. It's been a while since the last time, he said, which she took as a joke, meaning since them.

In sweet frustration they continued what they allowed each other and neither could stand it for long. After a look from her and a look from him, in a blur of greased decision and a groaning roll they were on the floor between beds, furiously coupled, rocking now in the heartblood root of each other, and even as they both came she was already hissing, *Oh shit, shit.*

She was quick dressing. She had to meet a lawyer and with him drive a Chilean woman to Nackawic. The woman had all her belongings, there was a question of whether they could do it in just one trip. Leah tried to be cheerful, but couldn't quite pull it off, couldn't look at him squarely. The guilt on her face was plain and, Chilean woman or not, her hurry had more to do with getting away from him and what they had just done.

. . .

"... for this reason one can see the text as an interrogation of the *pretence* of romantic ritual rather than as a interrogation of the ritual *per se*."

Kirsten's sneer dropped like a theatre curtain as she ended her introductory sentence. Bonaduce had read the novel and liked it but had seen no interrogation of romantic rituals, never mind their pretence. It was basically about some East Indian guy in Canada landing only grub work and walking around moony-eyed but too shy to get laid, too shy for the rituals to ever happen. Kirsten's sneer opened on her second sentence and the words "If we consider that" and the next two hours loomed large. The sun was bright outside the window and Bonaduce felt close to panic that life was racing by with him stuck here, a bug pinned writhing, impaled by words so empty they felt evil. Leah was out there cruising highways, alone, passing churches and motels, her ass restless on a car seat.

What was real was his headache. He never got headaches, but now he had a doozy. It was maybe the result of his run to the garage, sometimes a good workout will hock up the toxins. Of which no doubt he had plenty. Toby's wine. He hadn't been eating well. He felt akin to a sink strainer after the week's dishes were done, a carrier of oily rinds and pallid blasted fat.

"... clearly the point is that the rites of matrimony in the old country had become, here in Canada, mere farce. But he believed in the farce and she didn't ..."

Or the headache came from the American Express card. He'd been helpless. The car was ready. Sitting out there in the lot, Christmas tree on top, in fine running order. The mechanic smiling at a job well done, praising the vehicle and all the miles left on her. Bonaduce staring at his car, still seriously puffing from the run. Apparently by signing the work order he'd okayed any necessary work. So they'd planed his warped head, changed the gasket, flushed the rad and replaced all fluids. Sure, he nodded, reading the smudged work order, Sure, I guess it had to be done. When the mechanic said, "I'm surprised it was still running," Bonaduce had to peer at him to see if this was a joke, because, well, the reason the car was there was because it hadn't been. The mechanic assured him that five hundred was a deal and looked ready to get angry if Bonaduce had a question about this.

He slid the credit card from his wallet with what he hoped resembled bored efficiency, handed it over between two fingers like a habit, like a cigarette, jeez I've used this thing five times today. He signed his name with delicate pressure, hoping a too-faint carbon imprint might save him. His stomach went empty and his sweating felt colder, less healthy than it had jogging. The mechanic punched some buttons and inserted the card. The intolerable wait — Bonaduce pictured a severe woman in Washington, D.C., scowling at a beeping computer screen — ended with his card being handed back along with a receipt. Both were smudged with grease, it was that ordinary. The mechanic had already turned away when Bonaduce called him back, holding his card out again and saying, I forgot to ask you how much those snow tires are. And could you fill it up?

"... what could possibly be wrong with her expectation of equal and consensual sex? Well, as we see at this point in the text, *both* cultures find plenty wrong with it, and though her crime was, at most, *naïveté*, the world will extract from her the penalties ritual demands ..."

Leaving the garage lot, car shod for winter, he waved to the old Christmas-tree guy, who stabbed a finger at his roof rack and yelled, parental concern in his raspy voice, Get 'er in some water! Late for his seminar, he risked a ticket by parking in the professors' lot, right up against the building. Who cared about a parking ticket when you were on the Most Wanted list? That's his car, sheriff, the rusty one tied to that Christmas tree.

He'd gotten good at checking his watch without moving either wrist or head. Ten minutes had passed. Next week was his turn, and he would begin it with this: *"The English Patient* is a masterful, poetic work about the tragedies of war and love, and it poses this difficult moral question: Does love excuse a traitor?" After that he had no idea. Other than to say, Well, of *course* love excuses a traitor. Somewhere along the line he would slide in a coy "All's fair in love and war, eh?" But could he talk about nothing real for two hours? He began to sweat again, for the third time today. He realized he could smell himself. This smell was real too. Moronic to dress in track gear and run five miles before sitting shoulder-to-shoulder in a cramped room with this bunch of lily-whites. Some of whom probably wore a nosegay while pooping. Maybe next week if he smelled this bad nobody would notice what he was saying. He'd eat garlic wings and drink heavily the night before, sleep in his clothes, then run five miles and sit right next to Doctor Gail. And oh shit, there she is now, glaring, thinking yet again that he was smirking at today's presenter, not at the presenter to come.

Do you call her? He lolled like a big old morose teenager on his bed, the new phone on the floor beside him by virtue of the thirty-foot extension cord, both of which he'd charged at Radio Shack. His face felt puffy from lying around so much. Might as well lie around in here as slump around out there.

He'd also bought a little cassette player, and *Simon and Garfunkel's Greatest* was on softly, good old-fashioned candy.

Do you call? The signs — not eating, not sleeping too well — probably meant a teenager was supposed to do something.

She'd whispered, *This is the only time*. Nothing more had been said about the possible shape of their future together.

He pictured her after their beautiful fury was done, piecing herself back together, the static crackling of clothes hurriedly pulled on, Leah all too soon a social worker again. Him reclined on the bed, far from sated, but shy now like Adam, the sheet pulled over. He could still smell her in the bed, which was both a balm and a stimulant, and she was getting away. At the door, drawing on her long coat, rifling her purse for keys, about to leave the room's darkness. Then — like she didn't want to but felt she should — she looked back at him and smiled. The smile was worried and therefore false, and you could see her eyes were already focused on problems to come. The door closed behind her. Then opened again.

"How you getting home?"

Looking after him like he was a boy. He'd tried waving her away but she sternly told him to hurry, don't be silly, and so she drove him home. Sitting quietly beside her as she worked her car out of the parking lot onto the highway, he could feel how his letting her drive him cancelled whatever power he may have gained, and that she knew this too. They drove in silence, except for a few small jokes, as when they passed the bright pink car, and when nearing his house he stuck out his hand and introduced himself as Ray and she introduced herself back as Suzy Wong. They'd always had the little jokes.

So do you call her? Bonaduce flopped onto his stomach, his chin deep into the pillow and its strong smell of his hair. He really should start washing things, really shouldn't live like this, the student life should not mean disintegration. Do you risk ruining her trust that you understand her need for distance right now? Or is that just your imagination, the paranoid sore of lying bug-eyed in bed for too long. Look out the window at the flaccidly falling snow. Could easily be she wants you to call. Even if she doesn't know she wants it. Oscar's "There was an early affair." Maybe it was all no big deal, maybe she screwed around all the time. Could even be she feels fucked and forgotten, she's waiting by the phone like the other half of this teenage cartoon, staring off, curling a finger in her greasy neglected hair, which she will wash, grinning, after you two speak, after you get off your ass and call her.

No, she doesn't want you to call. Some things you know.

He cocked his left leg, touching his knee to his ear, and bent his head forward to his groin as far as his grabby old spine would allow, not so far these years, to check out the Bruise. There it was, its rainbow of bruise-hues, but blacker, and yellower, and still growing. He'd started thinking of the Bruise as having a capital B, because he'd never had one quite like it. And he'd had bruises everywhere. He'd had bruises *on* bruises. He'd never had a week during the season without one. Simple impact crushing and killing a tiny chunk of your body. Dead blood gone black, days to flush. He'd had bruises you couldn't see — the kidney, an eyeball, esophagus. Testicle. Never his penis though. Maybe his unit was his only virgin bit left, all safe there behind the tinny. Dumb little contraption, the balls hanging a bit below it, dangling this huge pain potential. The time, it was first-, second-year junior, when he took a shot full on the rig and it caught an edge of unprotected balls. There was the second or two of delayed hell, during which time he fell off the ice onto the aisle beside the bench and spent the next minute trying not to vomit, the pain simply ridiculous, no reason for it at all, but the funny part was the erection. Instant, surprising. Why sprout a hard-on at such a time? What was the possible point? Was it linked to whatever sick biology it was that caused hanged guys to spring one as they drop through the trapdoor and ejaculate at the stop? What was *that*? Either an extremely positive preview they may have just had of the afterlife, or maybe more likely their body's pathetically feeble last attempt to replant itself. Jesus.

Enough to make you shudder in the warmth of your teenage bed. Body's attempts to replant itself and what it makes you do.

Absently fondling his Bruise, now Bonaduce pushed it, pushed two fingers hard into the deepness of dead blood until he gasped with the hurt and shot into a wakefulness. He pictured a blood clot dislodged and rushing to his brain. He waited.

C'mon Leah, you did feel it. Pretty little angel eyes. Angel eyes, what a perfect two-word description of love, love that went both ways.

There were only two people, two friends, he could ask advice of. The first, Marg, still carried this apparent torch and her advice would be bent wonky. The second friend was Oscar, which was even funnier.

That evening at practice he began his career as a coach. The on-ice part was fine, almost fun. The players showed him friendly respect, though whether it was due to a pro background or a position of power was hard to say. The defencemen in particular acted like a word from Bonaduce might get them on the powerplay or benched, though he himself didn't know if this was the case. He and Whetter hadn't really talked. But it was fun taking shots on the goalies and laying down passes during drills, great to get some puck-work in a non-pressure situation, get the timing going, the small muscles tuned. Fun even to pick up the pylons and crack the odd joke and generally be useful.

He wore nylon warm-ups instead of full gear. Helmetless and unburdened, he felt the wind in his hair, and on a few glides he got the baggy pants to snapping behind the knees, could imagine little pennants trailing. He felt faster than he likely was, because he had no real oomph and one leg was playing a little dumb. Jason he treated like one of the guys, and Jason treated him like one of the coaches, a distance which in this situation was perfectly right.

His favourite time was giving the defencemen pointers about nullifying the enemy in front of the net. He said, "Okay, I've watched you in games and some of you don't know this stuff, or if you do know it you don't do it," to get them listening. He showed them the skate-nudge, then the back-of-the-pants thing, where a two-inch down-thrust with your stick buckles their knees without toppling them, resulting in them fighting to keep their feet but not in you getting a penalty. The guys seemed to appreciate it and laughed when, demonstrating, he went quickly guy-to-guy and sent each of them into helpless little flails.

In the dressing room it was harder. Protocol. Did a "playing coach" dress in the coach's room or out here with the players?

He hadn't done the full workout, so did he shower or not? The more frightening protocol was the father–son kind, of course, though Jason was pretty adept at ignoring him. Which was fine, probably the way of any coach's son in any dressing room. When Bonaduce had first arrived he and Jason had acknowledged each other with a nod and Bonaduce offered a quick "So, the fifteenth, huh?" and Jason had looked richly blank. He supplied the missing information, mouthing "Dylan," and Jason tossed his head back and said, "Right, right." At which point Bonaduce thought it best to leave well enough alone.

Maybe, Bonaduce decided — unlacing his skates in the players' room but on the bench closest to the coach's room, in this way straddling worlds — maybe it was all any parent could expect from any child, this sort of minimal attention. Why should the young pay attention to the older? Much more exciting were lives yet unlived. The young instinctively knew this. As a parent there was much for him to learn. Another utterly basic idea he had to keep in mind was something Marg had told him just last night — that all children are different. Bonaduce had been amazed that such an obvious truth could catch him off guard. At some level, sure, he knew all kids were different, but he hadn't been operating like he did. No, he'd been asking himself what nineteen-year-old boys did at ten o'clock Tuesdays nights instead of asking what it is Jason might do. "I mean," Marg had added, adding obvious onto obvious and making him feel stupider still, "they're, like, just like you and me." She pointed back and forth at each of their chests, their basic differences, and Bonaduce sat smiling and shaking his head, at his own stupidity but also at the proximity of her two "likes," and wondering if she'd ever stick two right together. I really, like, like you.

He decided he would shower, show these punks a body twice their age, expose them to the hideous consequences of playing this game. His groin bruise had flowered in grand new directions, its basic colour settling down to mauve while taking on an encircling yellow aura that wrapped his entire thigh. Naked, he thought he could feel his son's furtive eyes on him, checking him out, it was only natural. He was trying not to do the same with Jason. Lined up waiting for a free nozzle, he chatted with Tommy, a centreman, and Mike, the spare goalie, about their chances of making the playoffs. Playing it straight, he asked Mike what was each player's share of playoff money if they went all the way.

He heard Jason's low chuckle. He turned and saw his son naked, in line, laughing not at the Bonaduce quip but at something unrelated, some jibe from around a corner.

Maybe it was Bonaduce feeling only average in this roomful of sizable men and muscles, bodies you might in another situation take time to admire; maybe it was the being naked, everyone simply naked. Because the catchphrase he'd for two hours been breathing to himself, "We're both pretending I'm no one special," now transmuted to the thought *He's not pretending.*

Mike the spare goalie chattering in his ear, sucking up a bit, Bonaduce stared past his son's shoulder into the room's centre, into the pile of sticks and pooled meltwater. Why, how, was he in any way special to Jason? How was he any different from any other rutting deer or porcupine or slug who'd done the deed then empty-headed wandered away? Maybe Jason harboured none of the delusions Dad did. "Dad." Yes. Let's put that one in quotes.

Or maybe Jason, who owned a fine scowl and whose expertise at ignoring "Dad" was starting to bug "Dad" a little, maybe since Jason's relationship with Father was still so young, maybe he was only now going through the Freudian phase, the wanting to kill the him and sleep with the her ... It would be so great to be able to joke with the kid about this stuff, run back out to the shower line, grab that naked shoulder and look him in the eye and plead, deadpan, Do what you have to do to me but *please* don't sleep with your mother, son.

You couldn't help suspecting by now that this kind of joking might never happen.

Whetter there watching him, smiling at him staring off.

"You look a little tired."

"Took a beating out there, those pylons, I dunno."

"So you want to work the bench against Acadia Friday night?"

"Sounds good."

This morning he woke out of a truly wild bad dream, heart pounding, hot sweat, everything. He'd been in the campus bookstore, browsing. Suddenly the whole row of novels was by Kirsten, her face on the cover jackets, a different sneer for each. Now there were books by Gail Smith, and everyone he knew, Marg and Toby and Jason, and even a trainer from Dayton he hadn't thought of for ten years. Everyone had written books except him. He sidestepped to the next rack, it was health books. One title was *MS and You*. Another was *Multiple Sclerosis*. The whole rack was on nothing but. One, *SCLEROSIS!*, had letters embossed, backlit and flashing like a cheap marquee. He picked up one, *YOUR SYMPTOMS!*, and tried to open it but — ha ha, very funny — his hands no longer worked. They didn't work and didn't work and still didn't work, flop flop thud, two slabs of dead baloney, he couldn't scream and couldn't scream and couldn't scream.

Marg's fucking dreamcatcher was turning out to be some kind of comedy machine.

"Your dreamcatcher's turning out to be some kind of comedy machine."

He said this to her big behind as she stooped to sweep under the kitchen table. As soon as he said it, he realized he'd have to avoid some details. Though he had his suspicions now about what Fournier may have blabbed to her. He was just basically trying to engage her in conversation, for it felt like they hadn't been talking much lately. He'd been in his room a lot. He hated the feeling of fading friendship.

"How so." Marg was breathing hard, arms working away. Toby, at the table finishing his scrambled eggs, lifted his legs for her to sweep there. A rustle and scrape of wrappers and beer-bottle caps.

"I had a wild dream. You were in it."

"What was I doing."

"You were an author."

"That's comedy? Thanks."

"No — everyone I knew was a famous author, except me."

Marg was putting the broom away in the closet. She turned her head and smiled for him.

"'S not funny," Toby said, leaning back, mouth full of egg and toast, "'s pathetic."

It is funny *because* I am aware just how pathetic it *is*, you mean and gimpy twerp. Marg was wrapping a lunch sandwich in wax paper. Bonaduce, hungrily aware that his cupboard was bare, said in singsong: Make me a samwidge an' I'll drive you to school?

In the car she stared out at the riverside underbrush. Looking for winter birds. Some time ago she'd told him how birds bored her except in winter, when she loved seeing those that stayed.

Whatever she saw out that window was keeping her quiet. She commented neither when he slapped his forehead for always forgetting to take the damned tree off the roof, nor when he complained about how noisy his new snow tires were.

"But I guess they'll plough through anything winter can throw at them."

She turned to him with a no-nonsense look.

"Are you bothered by me and Toby?"

"Sorry?"

"No, please just say if you are. Are you bothered by me and Toby."

"Well, I'm sure as hell bothered by Toby."

Not missing a beat, Marg said in identical tones, "Well he's sure as hell bothered by you stealing his wine."

Ooo. Yikes. Damn. An embarrassment best left alone. How

did he know? He didn't seem the type to keep count. Bonaduce leaned down to snap the radio on and fiddle for a station.

"You know Toby has lupus, and he had a stroke when he was sixteen? Can you please maybe see why he's a little bit bitter?"

"Well hell. I didn't know that." He was prepared to feel like an asshole, and indeed sat prepared for the feeling to dawn. But he felt fine. He saw that, at the mere mention of lupus, he had instantly decided there were others with lupus who weren't mean.

"So it doesn't bug you that he and I sleep together."

Then snapped the radio off. Marg and Toby? Was he supposed to know this? *Did* he know this? He didn't think so.

"You're both adults. No, it doesn't bug me." Did it? He didn't think it did.

"That's good. I'm glad."

She didn't seem it.

"Well, sure, yes it does bug me — that it's Toby. I mean, it's only natural for me to want you to be with someone I liked. Someone who's good for you."

Marg met this, his decent declaration of friendship, with more of the same severity. Only when he bent forward to threaten turning on the radio again did she speak.

"I mean like, you've been awfully distant lately."

"I guess."

"Sitting there in that room."

"How do you know I've just been, you know, 'sitting'?" He winked, but no humour in the lady today.

"Marg, I'm in a phase. It's a strange time of life for me." Try her again. "I like to think of my room as, you know, a cocoon. And out of cocoons come, you know ..." She wasn't budging.

"I want you to talk to me, okay?" It was as if she hadn't heard him. Her voice descended into warmth as she said this, and her hand slid across the fabric of the seat and took his right hand, which had been at rest on his thigh.

"Hey. What ya wanna know?" He smirked for her but his hand and senses were afire, the hair on the back of his neck bristling. Young people could scare the hell out of you with their directness. Your own words could get stunned in the surprise and glare.

"Your friend Fournier says you're really sick."

"*Oh* hell. Hey. Fournier's all over the map. Don't listen to Fournier. He's French. He's a goalie."

"He thinks you're not taking care of yourself. And, Robert, *I* think—"

"You can't play university varsity fucking hockey if you have a serious fucking disease."

"I didn't know you were playing."

"I'm about to start."

"Maybe if you just looked after yourself a tiny bit better, and waited to—"

"There's nothing wrong with me."

"There is and I worry about you. Fatigue? Fatigue and depression are two first big symptoms, and all the time you spend in your room?"

"I've been writing."

It felt like punishment the way she withdrew her hand.

"Even if I did have it, which I don't, there's nothing you can do. So I'm not going to get myself in a knot about it."

"Well, I mean, that's not true. There is stuff you can do."

"Think positively. Swing a rooster over your head."

"All your joking," she said softly, making him sit up a little straighter, "all your humour is gallows humour."

Oh, she wanted morbid, did she? Well, he could help her there. In his sweaty little cocoon with the octopus-stained walls, he'd become a grad student of morbid.

"Marg? Where we're all going? *All* humour is gallows humour."

It was his turn to shut her out, some of her own medicine. They were at a red light. A gust of wind hit the back of the car, and a scatter of Christmas tree needles rained on the windshield.

"You know, like, I'm moving out?"

Marg all softness again. Bonaduce nodded for her.

"Well, and sometimes I've wanted to ask you if you want to

get a place together."

Bonaduce became very aware of his driving.

"And sometimes I don't. I mean we've become good friends but I guess if we lived together I'd want to be able to talk about stuff that matters."

"That only makes sense."

He didn't enjoy Marg like this. Like she had completely lost control of herself. Her seriousness bugging out all over the place, staring at him. Nor did he like what was expected of him in this conversation. They were nearing the campus. He would either drive her to her building first, or she would tell him to go park and she would walk in with him.

"Living together might, you know, be 'dangerous,'" he said, giving in. "Just the two of us?"

"I know. I don't care." Her voice husky and fatalistic and unsurprising.

"There's all sorts of stuff you don't know about me."

"I know. I don't care." Repeating this, she smiled, more a smirk, the Marg he liked. She started chewing some gum they both knew wasn't there. "Like what?"

He almost said, Like I'm in love with someone.

Stopped at a crosswalk while a string of students Marg's age filed in front, he played with the sound of this soap-opera sentence. He checked out the feel of its main word. He couldn't tell if it was true. He hadn't used the word in a while. What a word it had turned out to be, it, too, growing so complicated with age. All the guys and their wives who'd had counselling to help them find it or get it back, who learned the words for love's fool's gold: obsession, dependency, habit. These days, on bus trips you could actually hear such words murmured through the drone, guys with fat lips, black eyes, earrings.

Marg nervous beside him as he pretended to be frustrated by all these pedestrians. He would love to ask Marg where good old lust fit in. He would love to describe to her what he could still clearly picture, he and Leah lying in the motel bed not knowing what to do with their eyes. Each time they met eyes, twenty years was giddily flown right over, gaining a version of each other that was up-to-date and surprising and too too full, a potency forcing them to look away, except for a brief few times when they made themselves hold it. One time he told her it felt like looking in a mirror. However corny it sounded, he felt it was true, and her angel eyes staring deeply back he took to be her agreement.

"Wanna just park? I'll walk in with you."

They walked through the lots, past student housing, and damned if he wasn't limping again but worse, like the hip joint had lost its little brain. Marg seemed lighter in mood, but she still wanted to hear about how dangerous living together would be. Bonaduce didn't announce his soap-opera sentence less out of fear of hurting her than of having to talk about it. Best talk to himself about it first.

As to living with Marg, the notion felt undeniably cozy. He could see, as though it were already happening, the pots of spicy pasta, the games of Yahtzee, the endless talk. Bohemian friends dropping by. He liked the idea of looking for used furniture with her, joking about each other's bad taste. He could be buddies with her, with a woman. Why not? He could be a Nineties guy. Apparently all the kids were doing it. Boys and girls playing together. Who needs sex, we're friends. If you believed what you saw on TV, it was like the war was over.

He pictured Jason coming by, checking out his place and thinking Dad a pretty cool dude.

"But like, definitely we'd get a two-bedroom place."

"—Whoops! Ouch. Fuck *off*."

He shouted at the foot that was still on the other side of the snowbank, it having refused to take part in his little leap over. He'd caught his fall with his hands, scraping his palms on the sanded sidewalk ice; it looked like he was doing a spread-eagle push-up. When they got going again, good old Marg took his arm in a nursy way, as if supporting him. They both smirked at this, but she left her hand there, and he went on the alert again, feeling through her mitt and its soft squeeze the expectations that must be smoothed away before moving in together could be an option. It wouldn't be fair for anybody.

"Well, hey, let's definitely talk about it."

Nurse Marg squeezed his arm.

"But do me a favour and leave Toby where he is. We don't want to be living with Toby again."

Damn, it had been a joke, a simple "I don't like the guy." Not at all a "I want you to break up with him." But through her mitt you could feel all the way up to her head, thoughts shifting into high rev over it.

ROMANCE
—by Lady Bonaduce

You might not think it, but what a soap opera the minors are. Consider the mix: you have a pack of young men whose only goal is to be somewhere else and who, if in their third or fourth year in the minors, are staring a life's failure full in the face. You have women who, while not exactly groupies, are attracted to these men mostly for their bodies and the fact that you have to pay to watch them. You have road trips and bars and more not-exactly-groupies, and young, tireless men-in-motels glad for the team's code of secrecy. You wouldn't say that many minor-league romances begin on a firm foundation, unless you're talking about the quality of the bed.

Soap opera. You see some good scenes before road trips outside the arena as the bus idles impatient diesel fumes, its cargo doors open. Shouting matches, public demands, mascara-blasted eyes. A guy stowing his gear in silence, the girlfriend conspicuously not there, the whispered rumors. There are the usual couples who milk a crisis to get things up, but most of the displays are painfully real. But the bus has to leave, and as it reaches the outskirts of town, you can look back at the rows of guys in their seats, a whole smack of them just staring into space, maybe shaking their heads in awe of what soap operas their lives had become. Jesus H, they were just down here to play till they got called, hadn't planned on meeting *her*, hadn't wanted these questions of loyalty. But soon enough the cards come out, or if it looked like a guy was ready for a laugh Bombsaway might haul out the guitar and do a hurtin' song. Soon begins the quiet talk about tonight's team, which asshole to watch for in the corners, and the new nightclub two blocks from the hotel where you can get two, three quick ones in before curfew, and hey isn't Toledo where they have that little place with the lasagna? Mother Tucker's? with that waitress? she still there? what, traded to a Pizza Hut in Des Moines? Bullshit a relief from the jagged sourness left behind. Later that night on the ice, sometimes you find a good heartache fuels your game, and sometimes you find it drains you.

Someone up cooking bacon. Out his window, a frigid morning like so many back on the prairies, sunny, windy and hard-assed. The term "freeze-dried" came to mind.

He considered his wardrobe hanging on its hooks, the choices available to him. He recalled Whetter behind the bench in the standard sports coat and tie. Okay, did an assistant coach wear a tie. Or did he go casual like a trainer. Would the guys respect him more, or less. Would they even notice. Would Jason. Did any of this in the slightest way matter.

Clothes. He used to like clothes, what they did.

Noon he paid a visit to the English Department office to drop off the stuff to be xeroxed for the writing workshop — a manila folder of his collected observations and aborted beginnings to novels, most of them silly. In the mailbox he found a memo from the registrar informing him of his revised status, from full-time to part-time student. It showed him listed only in Gail Smith's and Big Jan's, meaning Kirk had officially pulled the plug. The note asked him to confirm this status or inform them if an error had been made. If he was in fact part-time, said the note, "overpayment of tuition monies might be owed and subsequently reimbursed."

Wearing a dress shirt under his leather coat, and a tie rolled tight in his pocket, Bonaduce frowned at the piece of paper in his hand, seeing right through it to the clear horns of his dilemma. He would love to be owed and subsequently reimbursed. Otherwise, unless he tried his credit card again, he would not eat today or all weekend. This horn was already goring his stomach. The second horn was more fuzzy: if he confirmed his part-time status, he would officially not be allowed to play for the Varsity Reds.

He ripped, balled and tossed the memo. Deny he'd seen it. He'd knock around in academic limbo a while longer. Limbo could last a long time, being the one thing bureaucracy excelled at.

There's no thrill in coaching. You stand behind the defencemen. They're yours, you oversee their changes and pairings. You can feel what a masochist's game coaching is. If the team won, who takes credit? It's the guys out there with the blades who take the hit, feather the pass. If the team lost — well, why didn't the coach have a system that worked?

It was a tight game, they were up two-one early in the third period, hanging on. Acadia was small, fast, gutsy. Anything could happen. Coach Bonaduce did catch himself growing excited. But it was nothing like being out there working your guts out to be the hero, working even harder not to be the goat.

When the guys were filing through the corridor on their way to begin the game, Coach Bonaduce had shouted, "Lean and mean, guys, lean and mean!" and he hadn't felt out of place doing it. (He hadn't eaten and it was how he felt.) But he saw he wasn't one of them. At the edge of the tunnel he stopped and let them pass by, into the arena light and scant cheers. Red and white warriors, tall and anonymous in their helmets and face cages, clomping the rubber with their contrived steel feet. They yipped, hollered and punched each other's shoulders, a nervous herd urging itself to become something carnivorous.

The few shifts Jason got, Bonaduce found himself so intent on the boy he forgot his coaching duties, but so what. At ice level you got a better feel for the play, and Jason was fast, very fast, he could play in this league, maybe a bit beyond, who knows. What he needed was a break. The asshole right-winger Harrington stood in his way. You tried not to hope for an injury to anyone, but. Your heart lifts when the Reds score to make it three-one, then you understand it was Harrington who tipped it in and you wish it was still two-one. Jason just needed a chance. And — Bonaduce's gut sank for an instant — Whetter might be the kind of coach who feared showing favouritism to the point that he might play Jason *less* now that Dad was coaching. Jesus, maybe Jason saw this too.

During the game he spoke to Jason once — a simple "Go hard, Jace" as he jumped on for a shift. And touched him once. His general yell, "*C'mon guys!*," followed by his cupped palm — *whop, whop* — onto the shoulder pad of someone who just happened to be Jason, though Bonaduce had sort of known this out of the corner of his eye. Jason answered with the half-fierce nod of a player who hasn't been on for a while and might not get on again and whose disappointment is battling his team spirit. Had he known whose hand it was on his shoulder? Of course.

What struck Bonaduce a second later — he couldn't tell if it was pathetic or funny, where was Toby when you needed him — what struck him was how, while clopping his son on the shoulder, he'd had his nose wide open wanting a smell of the boy.

Hanging alone by the red line, Harrington picked up a loose puck and scored an empty-netter to clinch the deal.

. . .

He got home late, having gone for beers with three of the Reds, who apparently didn't hang together as a team. This was a known and significant liability and he'd have a cautionary word with Whetter about it. He'd heard Jason beg off in the shower, a cold coming on, gotta watch it, exams coming. (Coach Bonaduce raised his eyebrows at the boy's priorities: the worry about exams, not next week's games.)

On his arrival home, as soon as his tired body landed on the bed, too swirly in the head to account for two draft beer, a fight broke out upstairs, Marg and Toby going at it. Marg yelled a few times and you could hear Toby's monotone scorn. You couldn't quite make out the words, though he did think he heard his name. Beth's softer voice began moderating. Eventually Marg's door slammed, right overhead.

You couldn't hear her crying but you knew she was.

Coming suddenly out of all that noise, silence. The absence of noise had its own weird force, a rising steadiness. Bonaduce perked up. Out his window the night felt wide and deep. He looked and the stars were brighter because there was no moon at all. Having fun, aiming his gaze through the dreamcatcher, he studied the sky long enough to make sure the comet was gone. Taken its cold warm-and-fuzziness elsewhere.

There's a feeling you get for disintegration, how it sometimes feels right. Or at least inevitable, which was maybe the same thing. The house felt that way now. Though no one knew it at the time, they'd enjoyed a modest golden age, then a falling, now a falling apart.

Someday soon they'd all be in different bedrooms and circumstances, new loyalties, feeling all right. It all had a rhythm to it, as predictable as a song.

. . .

Leah, I want to do it again. I just want to do it again. There's nothing I want to do more. I can now admit this to myself.

And maybe I want more than just it. And maybe Oscar should be told. And maybe Jason should be told. Leah should definitely be told.

He found himself punching her phone number, hearing its coyly flat music. Don't think. Take the puck and go with it.

Oscar answered, a friendly singing hello.

"Oscar, buddy. It's Bonaduce. How's it goin'?"

"Great! How are things with you?"

"Great! Leah around by any chance?"

"Well I'll just go and locate her."

The teasing airiness again, but could you not hear something nervous in it, maybe an anger? Had she dropped the bomb on him?

"Bobby?"

Oh, there's the proof, when her voice alone can get you halfway there.

"Leah — why are we still married?"

She was long to answer. He couldn't hear if she was smiling or not.

"Well, Bobby, you tell me."

"Maybe I will, another time. I have my version. Maybe we, maybe we should talk about it." His chest swelling with romance.

"When I didn't get them back, I just figured, I don't know, I figured that—"

"What back?"

Silence, and then slow, incredulous laughter, not completely friendly.

"Didn't you get them?"

"Get what?"

Leah explained. Her business-like manner no doubt had to

do with Oscar being in earshot. She explained how she'd mailed divorce papers long ago. She'd assumed, when her lawyer didn't get Bonaduce's signature back, that he didn't want to.

"Leah, I didn't get any papers. So I thought the same thing. That you didn't want to." He forced a little chuckle.

Leah laughed lightly. "Imagine. All these years."

"Imagine." How, how lightly entertaining.

"So, well, I'm getting dinner ready here, but what do you want to do?"

"I want to sleep with you as soon as possible."

Her silence was dense and unreadable, but as five seconds became six he could hear a direction in it.

"Don't hang up, Leah."

"It's — not really the best time to get into these sorts of details," she said, instantly relieving and arousing him. Oscar, within earshot, wasn't the one getting the truth here.

"When's a good time? To get into every detail we can."

More silence, through which Bonaduce didn't breathe.

"No, I really don't see it coming to that. I don't think, I don't think they would be that ridiculous."

He could hear Oscar's muffled enquiry. Leah pulled away from the phone and said, "Bob never did get the divorce papers, and now someone's, they seem to be after him about marital status or some such at the university, something about tuition." More muffled Oscar words, and then Leah's "Here, you talk to him."

Leah, you bastard. He had to stop himself from hanging up. This wasn't fun. The phone being passed to Oscar. I love her, Bob.

"Bob? Legal difficulties? Here, I'll just turn my meter on."

"Oscar, yeah. But not really. Just, well, there's this form, when I signed up here, registered, it said 'marital status,' and I left it, you know, left it blank" — several coils of phone cord had at some point gotten wrapped tightly around his elbow and he saw his forearm was swelling up — "not knowing *what* the hell status I was, right? And they sent it back, and there's, there's—"

"Why would they send it back?"

"Well, who knows."

"That kind of thing doesn't matter much these days. None of their business. Legally or otherwise. Unless it's for benefits, or taxes. Spousal deductions. Curious."

Oh, Oscar knows. The sly dog knows.

"Well I did apply for a loan. And stuff. Good old bureaucracy, eh? Go figure."

"I'll look into the divorce status if you want."

"Nah — like you say, it doesn't matter."

"It's no problem, really. I'm having a half-price sale."

"Right. No, it's okay."

"It probably is. Well, hey. I hear you're going with Jason to see Bob Dylan."

"Sure are."

"Well, let's get together some time soon. You and me."

"Sounds good."

"No. I mean it."

Dylan was upon them and he'd heard nothing from Jason about arrangements. Where, when to meet, at what bohemian café, I'll be the one wearing the beret. He had a tape for him too, a *Dylan's Greatest Hits* he'd bought new and in the meantime scuffed up the cover, as with new running shoes, no sense embarrassing the boy with expensive gifts.

He forced himself to call.

"Jason. Hi. It's—"

"Hi."

Interrupting quick, hearing the father's wondering how exactly to identify himself. He'd been toying with "It's your dad," but feared Jason's possible anger there. "It's me" assumed intimacy. "Hi, it's Bob" made him queasy.

"It's your assistant coach here."

"Yeah. Hi."

"Anyway, couple of, couple of things." He stumbled, he was a teenager asking someone to a dance. "I was wondering if you wanted to borrow some Dylan music. You know, before going to hear him. I've got this tape you can have."

"Nah, thanks. I don't have a player."

His son's voice was deep, deep as his. Children did not have voices so deep. So resonant through the plastic, vibrating the bone of your head.

"No stereo at all? I mean, I could lend you the same thing in a CD."

"Nope. I'm music-less. Doesn't matter. Thanks."

"Okay." He'd told himself to not be instructive, yet here he was, launching in. "Maybe it's better that way, you won't be disappointed if he isn't as good as on record."

Jason agreed with his logic. They arranged to meet at eight, outside the main doors.

"You gonna wear full gear, or just your helmet?"

Bonaduce had had his two glasses of Toby-wine, and this had just come out. Jason chuckled, politely or not. Maybe their senses of humour weren't that far off.

"Another thing, Jace. A hockey thing."

"Yeah?"

"Now, *as your coach*," he said in a good deep comic voice, though there was no answering chuckle this time. "No, but really, I've been wondering about how much ice time you're getting, and it's the shits, eh?"

"Well, sure. But that's the way—"

"No. Bullshit. You deserve more. And I'm not saying this just because I'm, you know, on your side."

Nothing from Jason.

"Anyway, so I was thinking of saying something to Whetter about how if you're moved up to the third line, even the second, it would add your punch in the corners, you could dish it out to the fancy guys in front and in no way would it—"

"Jesus, no. Don't."

"No?"

"No way. C'mon. Thanks, but no."

"Yeah, you're probably right."

Why, why had he gone with a ploy he'd all along known was pathetic, the worst?

"Okay then. I guess I'll see you, you know, when I see you."

"Okay."

"See ya buddy."

"Yup."

See ya buddy. He felt barely tolerated, indulged. Some things you know you'll be cringing about in darker moments to come.

He rifled the medicine cabinet for aspirin. Nothing but a bottle of Midol, which he'd heard of guys using.

The hole in the wall beside the toilet was even more embarrassing on these frigid days when the exposed boards grew a white sheet of frost and you could feel the cold as you sat on the throne. He could imagine the girls cursing him, feeling like white trash as they suffered their icy morning pee.

He rattled under the sink, knocking Marg's and Beth's bottles this way and that. A clue to love here, him under this sink. How you felt about a female's cache of stuff was definitely linked to how you felt about her. The creams the scents the soaps the brushes — was it vain clutter or was it sexy mystery?

If you're in love, it doesn't even matter if she's clean.

He hadn't lived with anyone before Leah, and her discreet lotions and bath oils (pre-Bonaduce gifts, from who knows) and makeup; even her styling combs and hair dryer and, God, even her tampons, had been a surprising source of shy joy and horniness. That he was living with someone who used this stuff was proof of their difference, the difference that fuelled the fire. Under the sink this junky palette of Marg's and Beth's and maybe earlier tenants' was only irritating. There was nothing for him except the Midol, two tablets of which he pocketed in case the pounding got worse. Dylan tonight, but before that the workshop of his stuff, his "novel," no two pages of which fit together. Three hours of Bonaduce roasted. His brain's balls kicked and forked apart.

He closed the cabinet with a foot. What he really needed was some amphetamine. He was starving, and about to go into the kitchen to steal someone else's food. He'd lost weight and his lousy diet had been making him tired, he could feel it. *Jesus* it would be nice to bring home a few bags of groceries. He eyed the gaping wall, the frost, the roll of toilet paper sitting stuck in the ice on a two-by-four.

Had he ever gone grocery shopping with Leah? He couldn't remember ever doing that together. There was always practice, or road trips. It would have been nice. Choosing a lettuce, cuts of meat, aren't we out of dish soap? How would you know? she'd quip. He'd be coy in the pet-food aisle. Bring a huge load of food home and over the days put it all in their mouths. How basic and sexy can you get?

He realized that he would love nothing better, save having sex with her, than to go with Leah to a drugstore and watch her buy lipstick, watch her try it on, wipe it off, another colour, that one, choosing the colour of his lust.

"Marg. G'mornin'." He spoke to her baby-blue-bath-robed back, elbows going up as she lifted bacon out of the pan.

"Morning."

"Any spare crusts of bread for a fella to catch the drippings?"

Before the workshop Big Jan found him in the lounge, having a nervous coffee. A bunch of writers were about to discuss his writing. He knew it wasn't spectacular. It sure could have been better. But he did care about it so he should have sat down and put way more effort in.

He looked up, Jan standing right over him. He grimaced for her and made as if biting his nails. Jan didn't crack a smile back. Which wasn't like her. Maybe on the day you were being roasted you got treated with nothing but professional—

"Come out in the hall. We need a word." Unsmiling, in fact shaking her head, she turned and left the lounge. He took another sip of coffee and glanced at Phil, who shrugged.

Out in the hall, a glaring Jan Dionne met him. She shook her head again, this time baring her teeth. Before she spoke she stopped to glare again.

"I was going through Manuel Diaz's new collection yesterday, Robert." She stared him in the eye, waiting.

Nothing occurred to him, save the tiniest seed of panic at the guy's name, Diaz. Diaz.

"A poem called 'Eye of the Cross.'"

His memory churned, caught, then blasted apart in panic. He'd forgotten it, all those poems he'd borrowed to get in here.

"I mean listen, fuck you, Robert, you didn't even spell the title right."

"Well, I think I was trying to fix it. '*On* the Cross' gave it two mean—"

"I don't need this. I could easily, *easily*, have you kicked out. Out of the whole program."

"Jan? What it was, was me having no time to get enough of my own stuff together."

"Last night I felt betrayed, Robert. But right now I don't feel anything."

How clear his own feeling was. He cared less about getting kicked out than he did about being hated by the one person in school he liked. And yet in the back of his mind a childish voice was telling him, Doesn't matter, I'm going to Dylan with Jason tonight.

"Jan, I know saying sorry won't do it, I know that. Do what you have to do."

"Don't worry. I will."

"I guess, I guess if I could ask a favour, it would be that you look at my real work, the work I've done for the class, and let it rest on that. I swear *that's* my work."

"Robert? I know *that's* your work because it's not very good.

If I do you this favour your chances aren't much better."

He didn't say touché. He knew she liked his work better than that. She was a hard one, staring at him not out of teacherly anger but something worse, an emotionless, clear-eyed dismissal, the kind that rings so true you take it home with you on your skin. And avoid mirrors for a while.

This was the shits, because he still liked her. He could probably still talk to her.

"Hey, buy you a dinner some night?"

He'd meant it as a joke, he was pretty sure of this, though things were blurring. Jan wasn't up to humour right then and, after her disbelieving look, she turned and walked.

The arena, where a few nights previous he'd helped coach the Reds to a sloppy victory under bright lights amidst scattered fans, was now crammed full, dark, and rowdy with expectations. Jason's tickets were great. They were sitting off to the side a few rows up, overlooking the ice surface, which had been tarped and floored. On it sat perhaps a thousand. Up and down the aisles people moved, a bemused ambling. Lots of little kids running and pushing through. It was a hidden side of Fredericton, all these old Jerry Garcia, Gandalf, Che Guevara guys, their kids or maybe even grandkids wearing similar gear. And womenfolk in ankle-length gingham, unbelievable. Lots of ten-year-old girls with hippy bandanas around their heads. Probably lots of these older guys had come from the woods, back-to-the-landers trucking here in amazement that the Man had chosen Fredericton.

But there were also lots of regular sorts, even hockey-jacket types like him and Jason. Holy moly, him and Jason at Dylan. Who would've—

"See anybody selling Cokes?"

Bonaduce craned around, searching the aisles.

"Doesn't look like the vendors are out tonight. Probably have to hit the concessions."

Jason got up without a word and squeezed past people's knees.

The pressure off for a moment, Bonaduce sighed and stretched and looked around. This was fun, Jason or not. The steady deep buzz, the happy rumble, you could actually hear the smile in it, it was the noise of several thousand people who thought themselves lucky. You could smell marijuana — it wasn't hard to spot people passing joints. He hadn't seen this since Pink Floyd in Boston about a hundred years ago. He tapped his inner pocket, feeling the outline of the lighter and Rod's two joints in there, and the nauseating tickle of illegality. The stuff did make music stand out more brightly. Those times after a toke with Fournier, Fournier would go off and read and he'd lay back with the headphones and welcome a new take on songs he'd heard plenty of times before. He remembered one time listening stoned to Los Lobos and thinking he was able to distinguish, just through the way they played, not only their personalities, but also who were best friends and why. But dope could sure take the ambition out of a fellah. And playing your own guitar while high was too, somehow, complicated, a brain busy watching itself watch how fast those fingers—

"Coke?" Jason was handing him down a drink. Jason, decent, respectful son.

They sat sipping for a while, taking in the scene.

"Hey, aren't these great seats?" Off to the side like this they were actually too near the stage for good sound. But they'd be able to see faces, and who played what. They'd see Dylan squinting, they'd see his cheeks hollow to suck his harmonica.

Jason nodded and said, "Yeah, not bad," and seemed to look around for the first time. He even glanced up at the ceiling.

"And thanks again, eh? It must have cost a bit. You sure?" He started going for his wallet, the twenty in it he'd borrowed from Marg.

"No. Oscar bought them."

"Ah. Good man. Oscar."

This was fine. Of course it was. They were together, who cares how. Oscar, good man.

"So how's the school going?"

"Okay."

"You switched to Forestry, right?"

"Second-year Forestry."

"So, so is it mostly about the business? Or, you know, the biology. The way they teach Forestry. What they prepare you for."

Jason tilted his head and appeared to consider something he hadn't before.

"Well, it's lots of stuff. You have to have Chemistry, and Statistics, lots of different stuff."

"So it's not just bigger guys with bigger axes."

"I just hope there's jobs still out in B.C. when I'm out," Jason said, shaking his head wistfully, not hearing the little joke.

Jobs, foremost in Jason's mind. Well, you did have to think about jobs. Though what about that last letter, Jason communicating some kind of desire to play pro? Maybe his time on the bench this year had snuffed that. Which wasn't fair. That asshole right-winger Harrington. A selfish one-way game, scores a few goals. Fans don't see through that, and apparently some coaches don't either.

Because they'd started talking, this pause was painful. They shouldn't be sitting in this clumsy hell.

"B.C.?"

"I guess."

"Why B.C.? Seems to me they have quite a tree infestation right here."

Jason was studying a hash pipe as it moved right below them, cloying in the nose. He didn't seem at all shocked. The smell, for some reason, made Bonaduce think of Jethro Tull, Montreal, the prancing Brit with the codpiece and flute. A decent show, though.

He reached into his pocket not knowing if there was a good way to broach this. It definitely straddled parent and buddy territory. You didn't want to come off like you were just trying to be cool.

He nudged his son and pointed down to the guys passing the peace pipe.

"Ever smoke any of that stuff?"

Jason shrugged. "Nah. Parties maybe."

"Yeah, me neither. But, hell, I figured, Hey, it's Mr. Dylan. Spirit of the occasion. I brought some."

Jason frowned and nodded in a way that could have meant yes, so Bonaduce slid the joint out of his leather like a sliver out of a wound. In the little ritual of lighting it and inhaling semifiercely he realized he looked too practised. My dad, he didn't make the NHL probably because of his drug problem.

It tasted strong and went right to his head. He held it out to Jason.

"Tokahontas?"

Jason considered the smouldering thing for a second before shrugging and saying "Nah."

Well, hell, bad idea, and what to do with it now. He took another drag, then sat with it. The guy to his left was his age and had a ponytail, so he nudged him and offered it. The guy took it but didn't smoke any. Instead he passed it further along, and Bonaduce watched Rod's joint go hand-to-hand a few more times before anyone took a puff. And then it kept right on going.

"So I wonder when they're going to start this party."

"Dunno," mumbled Jason, staring straight ahead.

"So, you very familiar with, with, you know, his music?"

"A little. Not much."

"Well, what do you think, do you *like* it?"

"It's okay."

Laconic little bastard. If there was one word that perfectly didn't describe Bob Dylan's music, it was "okay." This boy of his had taken bad lessons in Clint Eastwood. The one question was, was Jason always like this? Was this Jason, or was this Jason being angry? Was this his normal cool, or was this him punishing a wayward father? More to the crux of the matter, was this shitty silence a call for the same distance from him, or a demand that amends be made?

Bonaduce was on the verge, but felt that a gushing apology, here and now, would be ridiculous. But maybe not. Maybe one good sentence. One perfect phrase. Jason, let's. Jason, why don't we. This silence was ripe, was torture. God this dope was strong.

"Jason—"

His son turned to him, they met eyes. But the lights fell, and the crowd roared. Bonaduce felt the relief whoosh forth in his huge exhaled breath. Those *eyes*. He'd never seen into them before, and why was it that he was so surprised to see himself? And Leah, but mostly himself. But the boredom in them, the aggressive neutrality, it felt— It ripped your—

The band walked on, a bunch of young guys in T-shirts. Then on stepped the Man. No warm-up act, no announcer even, just him. Casual, classy. You want Dylan, you get Dylan. His band could have been his children, age-wise. Two were black. Bonaduce had forgotten how he'd wanted to joke with Jason about what he'd read in the paper that morning, the description of Dylan's voice as sounding like a bee in a jam jar, which was pretty good. Then the gossip about how the band members were under instructions never to look Dylan in the eye. Yikes, what did that say about him? Either major paranoia or some kind of insane regal—

They started playing: bass riff, drum walking itself in, organ noodling over top, rhythm guitar comes chunking along in back, ooo this was nice. Bonaduce leaned over, whapped Jason's shoulder and yelled.

"*This is nice, eh?*"

Woops. The music stopped. It was only a tune-up.

"Only a tune-up I guess. But it sounded good, eh? I think this is going to be good."

"Sounded good."

"Isn't it funny how music, how music can, you know, 're-solve itself'? You know, how sounds can sort of ask a kind of question, and then come up with an answer? and we can *hear* that? I mean, in *noise*? The art of noise."

Jason nodding, staring at the stage, a little smile. Don't get paranoid yourself. But slow down.

What might have been the stub of Rod's joint was being passed hand-to-hand in the aisle below him.

Finally they did start, a song he didn't recognize. You couldn't hear the lyrics, the sound system was not great. Which was, c'mon, this was awful, the guy was basically a poet, his words his strength, and you couldn't make them out. Why hadn't they— Or maybe it was his voice itself, that nasal whining, it was hardly human, maybe no microphone could translate it, maybe with Dylan distortion was automatic. Man this dope was strong, but man this man was bad. Bee in a jam jar — guy who wrote that was the best poet in the English language.

Whoops, was that a little stagger? Dylan addled, to boot. Who knows what the guy's done to himself, booze and drugs fit for a king. Probably a travelling good doctor with him, keep him alive and tuned. Quick, yells the doc, get me my bag, the drummer just looked at Bobby, he needs a sedative, he has a booboo on his spirit.

After two songs Dylan took a short break, it looked like to replace a guitar string and fiddle with the sound mix. It was a laid-back show, no sense of hurry or trying to keep the crowd happy. Well, with the Man no one was going anywhere. People looked as attentive to how he sipped from his cup as they were to his music.

Bonaduce made a loud gush noise sucking his own cup dry. It sounded better than Dylan. This was fun, he was definitely having fun. Not even Big Jan could steal his fun right now. Though why was he on her case, it wasn't her fault. But it wasn't his fault either, Jesus Christ. He wouldn't be here having fun if he hadn't lied his way in. The workshop had gone okay, considering. He hadn't been keen on continuing after what had come to pass with Jan, but you sign on the line, you pay the fine. As expected, Jan was not too praising, and the others picked up on this and followed like the righteous lemmings they were; though Phil, good old Phil, had laughed and liked his stuff, liked that it wasn't connected, called it a "revealing pastiche." Next term, if there was a next term, he would prove to them that he could write up a big fine piece of—

A woman, a wild-bodied Asian beauty, was bouncing up the steps, all eyes on her. He nudged Jason with an elbow, feeling instantly foolish for it. Well, will you look at her. She was in stylish rather than idealistic hippy gear and in full body-stocking flaunt. He turned to Jason and Jason smiled and nodded and facetiously waggled his eyebrows, and Bonaduce had to tell himself not to feel insulted and stupid. God this kid of his was a quiet bugger. The thought that he might be gay struck him. It felt suddenly possible. He'd never heard mention of a girlfriend, and come to think of it he hadn't been part of any dressing-room sex banter Bonaduce had heard. Well. He knew he was entering a stoned tangent now as he interpreted all of Jason's silences to be akin to shame. Don't get close to Father because then Father will find out. This was all nonsense, of course. Jason was too — what? — too boring to be gay, gays had a spark. Though what if he was? It would be fine with him. You wouldn't *choose* it for your son, but hell he wouldn't hesitate marching in a Pride parade with him, why not? hell, he'd wear his team sweater to bug the guys — maybe a goalie mask too, stay hidden, ha ha — but you wouldn't choose it, I mean why subject your kid to the roll of the dice when it comes to AIDS, and you don't want him to suffer the social thing, the life of paranoia about what people think. Then that switching over to snark and hate, you couldn't blame gay guys for hating everything that wasn't gay. Come to think of it, maybe life was easier that way, something to focus on, and anger for fuel. This dope is extremely strong. It's fun. And the *main* reason you don't want Jason to be gay is because — there she's heading back down the stairs and the horny little bugger is stealing glances at her — is because then Jason wouldn't grow up and have children and have *this same joy inside, this joy of having a son of his very own!*

"What's so funny?" Jason staring, smiling at the dad's endless laughter.

Bonaduce was about to try to explain, that is, lie, when the band began again. A huge relief, moving the load from inside the head to outside. And it sounded beautiful, it truly did, until the Man stopped sipping whatever was in that cup and got up off a chair and began to play along. Bonaduce noticed something else when Dylan began to play. The band had been having a great time, but as soon as Dylan wanged out a couple of bars they went sober and rigid and watched him — actually turned as a group to face him so they could see his guitar work, and not because it was good. It was bad and unpredictable and they were on the lookout for accidents. Bonaduce saw it actually happen, Dylan springing out of sequence and the guys having to stutter with their fingers to compensate. A few times Dylan was simply unfollowable and the song had streaks of chaos. Luckily the speakers were cranked up to fuzzy. You had music more polished than this at any bar in town.

Between songs Jason leaned over. "That one was one of his radio hits wasn't it?"

"Yeah."

He'd been unsure what song he'd been listening to. But— Jason, asking. It might be a first. Cherish this. It's beginning. He sat back in his seat and watched Jason from the side of his face. Watched him nodding to the beat, took in the bobbing nose, the blinking, the parted lips, the jaw working the gum. Jason knew he was being watched and seemed to accept it, naturally the long-lost dad's going to check him out. Maybe he liked being checked out. Maybe he had the Bonaduce ego. What's in a DNAme? This was great, this concert was great. Thanks, Oscar. What was the question? Radio hit.

"I think it was one of those he had right around his stupid Christian—"

The song erupted in what became an embarrassing barrage of what turned into the Man playing a five-minute lead. Acting out senile old dreams of Clapton grandeur. *This* was Spinal Tap. The guy had been playing guitar for decades and hadn't learned how. He'd love to get Jason back to the house and play for him, a few tricky ones, maybe even sing a bit — could he sing to

Jason? Might be a bit queasy for both of them. A crooning dad, yuck. Dylan was blowing notes now and, c'mon, even his harmonica-playing — it was his trademark and his trademark was bad playing. The guy was maybe a great songwriter but that was all. People had mistaken eccentric delivery for great performance. This was also the guy who put deep meaning into rock and roll and in doing so took out the humour. After Dylan everyone had to be a philosopher, you couldn't rock around the clock any more. Guy takes some nice old Woody Guthrie stuff and lays the oblique snark to it and sings it like a hornet in a bean can and gets studied in English classes across the land. People forget this was a guy who had himself baptised in Pat Boone's white-shoe swimming pool. Not that you wanted consistency, and maybe Dylan did it as a huge tipsy wisecrack, but here he was playing lead guitar like an emperor wearing not one stitch of—

Jason was leaning into him, yelling.

"*Guy rocks, eh?*"

He dropped Jason off after Jason declined the offer of a beer back at his place, which was fine, it was late, the boy had a cold and had to study.

"See ya later. Thanks for the ride."

"See ya Jace. See ya on the ice."

Jason wanged the door shut, and a dump of needles hit the windshield, the strong bugger.

He watched Jason's lope on the snowy walk, pleased with the notion that after Christmas he'd be playing an actual game with the boy, let's not forget why he was here. Jason turned and waved in the glass door of the shabby three-storey building, not unlike the place Leah and himself had occupied when they first met, where Jason had been planted.

He had had enough family for one night, truth be told. However nice it had been, however nice a start.

Back home, no way he could sleep. He walked the house

lightly, aimlessly, ears still droning full. He checked Marg's room and she was out. Lots to tell her, where was she?

Well, damn, the dad also had to study. Time to put some major thought into Friday morning's presentation. In two days he'd have his ass up in the air in Doctor Gail's class. Here he was all dope-addled and tomorrow he'd be mud. In the living room — no more little coffin bedroom for him — he set up his Ondaatje notes and opened the special-occasion Heineken, one of the six he'd picked up in case Jason had come back. A beer to counteract the high, hopefully downshift to the pace of words on a page. It would've been so much more fun Friday to be a Bob Dylan critic than an Ondaatje critic. If Jason were here he could have practised, lobbing grenades into the Dylan myth, converting Jason with precision, rigour, the new academic Bonaduce tongue. Sad the boy didn't have a feel for music, but then neither did Leah, there'd been a sense of her putting up with rather than enjoying his record collection.

Another Heineken in Jason's honour. Then a third — take the night off — in honour of not worrying about Ondaatje. He'd read the book twice, how prepared can you get. He had the notes, the major points to make. He would have to fill in blanks, wing the bulk of it, but that was the nature of discourse, it wasn't a speech. He even had a way to get in the word *postmodern*: this book is not postmodern, but good old-fashioned storytelling. So there.

In the spirit of winging it, he lit up the other joint, because it helped words fly in his head. He'd stick a butterfly net up there and bring some down, get some insights pinned to the page. Friday he'd have a fighting chance.

He put on some of their snark music, not too loud, and stole another of Toby's bottles too, but came to his senses and cut himself off after one glass, remembering that not only was he not in shape, but that Christmas layoff would put a further dent in what shape he had. Tomorrow night was the last practice until the New Year. Actually it was a game, something called the annual Red–White Fight, where they divvied the guys in two, and the losers bought the winners pizza and beer. A little tradition, sounded good.

After tomorrow night, and Friday's presentation, it was two weeks off, no hockey no school. Then he'd have plenty of time for. He could do whatever he damn well.

He slouched deeply into the couch. His foot accidentally nudged Ondaatje off the coffee table. A Fredericton band, Modabo, was on. Nice harmonies. You could tell they were good guys. A clue about Fredericton, what it engendered in its sons, what kind of spirit. Despite his many sins, he'd left Jason in a decent nest.

He was glad he'd come back.

He caught himself sitting motionless, smiling, staring slightly up at nothing. A gleaming swirl in the gut was flooding up the neck, taking leaps into his face. Sometimes you cannot deny your happiness, there's a big happy fish looping in your stomach, you're on the verge of an idiot guffaw.

He had to move his body, something. He dove to the floor for push-ups. He counted. He did either fifty-six or sixty-five.

Still high, still happy, he brought his box of tapes from his room. He settled back with a homemade compilation of oldies. "Little Latin Lupe Lu" made him laugh, did these guys know how funny they were? Demanding sex, *shouting* for it, wailing, then a wheedling plea, pure pure jungle need. All in five-bar simple. Then "Stay," another pleading classic, hard-penis falsetto, some black Italian guy from New York City. Next a Woody Guthrie, his ultimate get-back song, "Little Black Train," about death, all of us being in the same boat, the train's a-comin' fer ya. Here, rich folks, you kin fight mah politics but you cain't argue this'n. Next was something Fournier had insisted he throw on the tape, some hot new poet type, Beck. One of these guys, like Cher, had only the one name, really cheap parents. Beck proved pretty negative, a Toby with a song to sing. But decent lyrics, "toxins won't kill your day job." Maybe a double negative makes a positive, who knows. But at my funeral, play "Pretty Little Angel Eyes" please.

No sleep yet. In deference to Oscar he tried some *Best of Pink Floyd*. It was okay; sure, they were good at ominous. But their druggy calculations told him they weren't playing from their balls, they really weren't. This thing Oscar had for Brits was a fundamental wall between them, it was worth calling the guy on, it would be a good argument over a beer. British was head, American was heart. You can't get much more apart than that. Earth and sky. Though Lennon's "Well Well Well" could scrape your guts out and cure your indigestion.

Coming out of a dream of what would've been the world's greatest song, Slim Whitman singing a cameo on Pink Floyd's "Money," he realized he was head-lollingly tired. He tilted the wine bottle for more but it was empty. He remembered having lots of insights, some about Ondaatje, but he couldn't remember what they were. He hadn't liked Dylan and Jason had. Unless he was being polite, wanting the both of them to be having a good time, a thought which took Bonaduce back up to glad.

This — Jason wanting them both to have a good time — was the closest he'd come to what Jason's love might be like. A fearsome thought, and enough for tonight.

He whistled — he never whistled — on his way to the bathroom. He almost went down, grabbed at a wall without looking. He liked it here, he knew this house's bones and didn't really want to leave it. Marg was bailing early. Kick Toby out, it'd be a decent place to live.

Howling, now he was howling. He heard Rod or someone yell *Shut-up* but he couldn't stop laughing. Because he'd found himself standing at the toilet, pointing the wrong way. Busy thinking of Marg moving, of life without Marg, he'd unzipped and taken his dick out, then half-asleep wondered if maybe he didn't have to do the other, so he'd pivoted, but still with his pants up and dick out, but now pointed at the bathtub, then he awoke to the situation and howled.

He turned to successfully pee. He'd once had a girlfriend who he'd *twice* found sitting backwards on the toilet, peeing. Elbows on the porcelain reservoir, hands in her hair, calmly deranged. He suspected a serious drug or alcohol problem and gently ditched her.

Still whistling, but sincerely bound for his room, he found himself stopping at the phone. It couldn't be all that far past midnight, maybe it was one or two. The idea was to thank Oscar for the tickets, for the idea to begin with, maybe give him shit about Pink Floyd. Good man like Oscar wouldn't be asleep yet. He pressed the buttons which his hands knew by heart, and wouldn't you know it but at the other end after some fumbling with the receiver it was her who picked up the phone tonight.

"Hello?"

"Hi, it's me."

That's all he said and all he planned to say, but her voice, all cozy and warm in the way she said hi back, the lovely sleepiness and the sweet concern, made Bonaduce simply lose his mind.

"I have to be with you."

Silence, a shuffling, then, "Hello?" From Oscar.

Bonaduce hung up, heart racing. Had Oscar heard? Had she passed the phone? Had Oscar grabbed it? What had just happened? Did Oscar know?

Did he want Oscar to know?

Why, damn, why did he have to call? What kind of guy are you, anyway? You don't do that to people.

Why do you want it *all*?

Right now, as he was finding a kitchen chair with his hand and Oscar was going upstairs to her, to ask about the call, who would she be truthful to? Neither answer made him feel good. What had he done?

The happy fish looping in the gut was gone. So was sleep.

. . .

Lat e

What am I good for, what am I good at, what's the point of m.

Can't help but wondering. Been wondering twenty years. The thing with playing in the minors, youre always wreslting mediocrity. As a description of yoursel. Worse because when a kid you were the best on your team etc. You grow up assuming youll always be that. Suddenly you arent, and there's a whole other league up there that wont even look at you.

To make it, you have to be the best, the very best, at one thing. Just one. In the minors its guys like me, jack of all, master of nothign.

Famous people are all like that, they have the one big thing. Can Bob Dylan skate? Who cares — he had the best words to put the tunes to. Could Ghandhi do anything else? Could he cook? Tell a decent joke? No but he was the best at taking punches without ever punching back.

Could the Buddha drive a jeep.

For a couple of years in Kalamazooo I was the best at being an asshole in front of the net. Was called The Zookeeper. I was a master. It was an act. Almsot worked though. Almsot got me called up. I was almsot a famous asshole.

So whats Jackofalltrades Bonaduce the best at. It isnt hockey. It isnt literature or writing. It isnt women. It definitely isnt fatherhood. Friendship has come under serious doubt, too.

No — how could I have missed it? Its right in front of my face. It made me phone her. Im the best in the world at staying up all night feeling sorry for myself. So, quit it. And typing is getttting

. . .

Panic.

It had taken him hours of steady breathing, of hard focus, to get this far. The meanest work he'd ever done, meaner than push-ups this getting out of bed, getting enough clothes on, getting to the bathroom after asking God to let you please just not piss on your floor. Fighting panic the whole while. Finally making it to the kitchen table. Easy to flip back into panic at any moment here. Pick up that fork.

Steady breaths. Normal life. Hold your fork. Dead hand on the lap under the table. Marg is watching.

"Tomorrow night, Regent Mall, eight-thirty?" she asked from the door. Wearing a big absurd beaver hat, the RCMP kind he hadn't seen since Winnipeg. It was apparently freezing outside. She had the earflaps down and the ribbon tied under her chin.

"Regent Mall. Eight-thirty," he repeated, softly, because even his tongue was gone this morning and eight-thirty was *ay-thiry*. He was trying to eat the eggs she had made him, hoping she wouldn't notice he was using his left hand.

It was almost noon. He had stayed in bed as long as possible, wishing it wasn't true. So deadbody tired that even lying down felt like a strain, so tired that staying alive took effort.

"I think it'll be four, five places at most. We can do it in an hour." She was talking louder with her earflaps down. "And I mean, thanks, eh?"

"Hey. For nothing." She'd lined up appointments to view apartments, and he was driving her around to them.

"Taxi's here. 'Bye."

It was her first day of a Christmas-rush job in the mall book-store, the same bookstore he'd had his bad dream about. Here he was with a floppy right hand, what a humorous meshing of worlds.

"Two of them aren't two-bedrooms," she was saying, pausing

in the open kitchen door, frosty air billowing in. Her eyes were impish, fun-filled, at her best. "Just in case you wanna, you know, tie the knot."

He worked up a smile. Said something approximating "We'll bring along the preacherman."

It was the kind of deeply frozen world he hadn't walked into in many years. It was a childhood morning, a prairie morning, arctic. Your face burned and, in a minute, ached. Well, today only half the face: ha ha, the hidden rewards. He saw the tree on his car roof and looked away because it seemed only dead. Too scant of needle to consider any more. Last night, Jason hadn't mentioned the tree on his roof.

The mucous in his nose had instantly frozen and his eyes were tearing and blinding him. He went back in, found someone's mauve scarf, came out again with it awkward and ugly around his face and head, a bad wrapping job, done with more awareness of a dangling right arm than of the left clumsily working, self-pity rising out of panic to erupt in a sob. He sobbed just the once and stopped it. Poor me. Feeling sorry for yourself — it felt like warm soup, you saw guys fall into it and never get out, you could see them wearing it on the face for all to see.

The idea was to walk it off.

Limping mummy, a slit in the thick bandage for his ancient sick eyes. Muted grunting at every right footfall. Why not drool through the scarf, scare some kids.

He worked his way along the highway, bypassing the snow for a while, heading for a distant field he'd seen all along from his window but had never visited. In this cold even the truck noise was thinner, muffled. Tires sounding hard as plastic on the cold concrete, you could feel the crisp sound right in your nerves. Jesus, what did the truckers think of him, hobbling maniac out on the road, heading east. He thought of his occasionally entertaining bus window, its flashing frame of car wrecks, grass fires, chicken yards, barefoot kids and gawking trashy idiots, roadside tragedies like himself.

There wasn't much traffic. The quiet was nearly peace if he could keep from thinking. He lurched up onto the snow. You could see the tree and its cluster.

As he approached, it sounded electric. It crackled, rice crispies freshly in milk. It soon grew louder than his crunching steps, louder even than his fear. When a pause and tremor appeared to rifle through them *en masse*, he stopped. He was a hundred feet away. The tree's branches were full and heavy with them, weighted down. He could see now what he'd suspected, that they were all one species of bird. All noisily eating, clusters of orange berries. The words *mountain ash* came to mind. You made hockey sticks from ash.

He took smaller steps, trying for a harmless-looking rhythm. His right mitt he tried to keep from smushing dumbly against his thigh. Hundreds of birds eating, frenzy in the extreme cold. Massed crackle of their plucking, beaking, biting. Closer, looking hard, he saw he didn't know what they were. Crested head like a cardinal, with what looked like yellow over the eye, and their bodies were a nice, a subtle, an almost unnatural kind of tan.

Like a child's view of things. In one black tree identical birds eat orange berries. On the snow a man with a scarf around his face watches, arms out because it's so cold.

He'd probably gotten as close as he could anyway, but at his faltering half-step they all leapt away, making him jump. A sudden flapping *whoosh*, the whole instantly apart in so many pieces, birds exploding away in all directions.

The full moon up there, frozen pearl bouncing at his shoulder.

He stabbed three times before hitting the doorbell, with his right hand. All day it had improved to the point where now a doorbell was possible.

From the street he'd seen their Christmas tree in the window, all lit up and heartbreaking. Wonderful, now he was invading their home. He could see in the door window many coats hung, boots on cardboard stretching well into the hallway. A gathering of some sort. Maybe an office party. Great, he was bashing and crashing a party on top of things. He just wanted to take her aside and— He didn't know what he wanted.

"Bob! Just in time."

"Oscar buddy." His tongue was back. He slowly unwrapped his scarf.

"Our little festival-of-nations party. Come right on in."

Oscar was good at not showing surprise, at showing nothing at all. Maybe he greeted criminal clients like this. Polite to murderers, thieves, adulterers.

"I just came by to—"

"Come on, come in, it's cold. Everyone's here. Jason's here. I hear it was a fantastic concert."

"Sure was. The Man. Thanks for that."

Oscar waved away the thanks and took his leather coat, didn't seem to notice that it was a while coming off. There was no friendliness, no eye-to-eye before he rushed away toward the kitchen, yelling behind his back to make yourself at home.

He stood in the entranceway. Everyone's here. He hadn't wanted Jason in on this. Whatever this was. But maybe it was okay. Maybe Jason was a buddy now. Maybe it was best, in fact. Had to happen sometime.

About twenty men, women and children sat around, the majority of them Latino. Many had gifts unwrapped and sitting in their laps. Cutlery sets looked like the popular item, that and ceramic teapots. Board games for the children. They kept their gifts cradled in the wrapping paper. They looked too tropical for either the gifts or the Christmas tree, which swelled in the corner with bright ornaments and smell, that essence sharp in the nose always reminding Bonaduce of snow.

You thought "Mexican," but of course, being refugees, they

were probably anything but. The women tended to favour lots of makeup, like TV women from the Fifties. Soon enough you could see the range of nationality, or race. Long faces, round faces, darker, lighter, some looked Indian, some almost Chinese. A few of the young men looked solo, and sad for it. A fair number looked like they felt themselves above this quaint gathering, their eyes bored and condescending. It may have been his nerves but some seemed to be watching him with suspicion. Well, he was the biggest guy in the room. Big tough hairy face. He didn't have the energy to think about this.

He felt like a huge fool and wished he hadn't come. This had nothing to do with him. There would be no talking with Leah here, if that is what he had come for. But how could he just run? At least say hi, Merry Christmas.

He took a seat on a couch beside a plump woman who looked his age. Though when he smiled at her and she smiled back, she looked younger. He noticed a scar on her head, on her temple, that looked like it had once been a hole. You don't come to Canada after a bullet to the temple. It was probably a pox scar, a vaccination scar. Though they don't vaccinate you in the head.

"Bob," he said, nodding. He'd almost put out his right hand, offering the limpest handshake in history. Here in Canada, we are very gentle.

The woman smiled and nodded back.

"Where are you from?"

"I from Chile." *Chee-lay*. Big professional immigrant smile.

"Ah," he said, tilting back his head as if she had explained something.

She added nothing more. He saw how much he didn't know this person, let alone these people. And people are not alike. He'd gotten to know Finns, and they were nothing like Swedes, who were nothing like Russians.

"How long have you been in Canada?"

"I here two day." Her non-stop smile, unfelt.

"That must— You must be in shock. Have you found— Have they found you a place to—"

"I just visiting." She smiled for real now, something of the imp in her, knowing his presumptions.

"Ah."

He should really get going. That clatter in the kitchen might be Leah. He could go in, say his hello, make his apology, go. That's why he was here, to apologize.

"My brother." The woman pointed to a man helping himself at the punch bowl. Oscar was suddenly at the man's side, holding a bottle of vodka. Oscar laughed and made some kind of moaning noise, glugged some into the punch.

Jason appeared bearing a tray of glasses. Was he wearing an ascot? The boy didn't look up, though by now of course he knew his father was here. Instead he went back to the kitchen and reappeared with a plate of something, some pastry Bonaduce didn't recognize. Jason said something to a woman who stood surveying the food, and they both laughed.

Jason had grown up with this, with these people. His son went back to the kitchen.

"He come ten years. Now he wife. Now he kids." She pointed to a Caucasian woman delicately fingering tree ornaments, many of which looked handmade.

"Now he help others come. With the worker Leah."

"Ah." He pictured himself shouting to her, a dumb American tourist, *Leah my wife!*, stabbing his chest with a finger.

Now here was Jason, approaching him with a beer, striding the room self-consciously. He looked nervous. Jason, take your father a beer, will you? Bonaduce gave him a little left-hand wave of greeting. Voices, what sounded like Oscar and Leah, arguing in the kitchen.

"Jace."

"Hi."

"What's with the neck?" He saw it wasn't an ascot but a towel, and Jason's watery eyes.

"I got this lousy cold."

"Looks like some kind of giant weird poultice." The image of ascots as poultices was amusing for some reason, ascots giant

poultices for intellectuals, absorb any unworthy, common notions trying to rise to the head.

"No. Just a shitty cold." He either didn't know the word
poultice or didn't find it funny.

"Jeez. And the Red–White game tonight."

"I'll probably be there."

"Jace, you sign the name, you play the game, eh?"

Hey, Jason, want to see your father try to sign his name?

From the kitchen, Leah definitely said "Bob." Something
loud about "Bob."

"But hey, you gotta watch your health, nobody's gonna watch
it for you."

"I guess."

"Though I *am* looking forward to you buying me my pizza
and beer."

"No way." Jason finally cracking a sleepy smile.

"Way." This was good, this was all right. "Just keep your
head up."

"Yeah, right. As if."

This was really okay. Jason, eyes down, but smiling and joking back. Hard not feeling like a loud fool around him but maybe
that would be their way, these the roles they would play. It felt
good just to have a role.

"Helpin' Mum a bit. Gotta go do some stuff."

"Okay. Go for it. See ya later."

Go for it. Loud fool.

Jason went for it, went to help the mum you could no longer
hear arguing. Not a trace of cynicism about helping mum in the
kitchen. Jason was a good kid. And if he was a momma's boy,
what the hell else could you expect after—

What came next was fast and furious. Jason had no sooner
left when Leah was loud again and he was at the party table
again with another platter of food. Oscar was at Jason's side with
the vodka, pouring. Neither smiled or talked. Bonaduce was startled to see Leah in the hallway, pointing a finger right at him.
She turned on her heel, looking nothing but angry. Apparently

he was to follow. She looked so pretty, heavily made up like these women she was hosting.

He followed her into the laundry room, limping stupidly past her with his beer as she stood in the door with her hand on the doorknob. She closed the door, locked it. Absurdly, the faintest notion of sex stirred below his belt. Who knows what she and Oscar do, allow, pursue. Ridiculous, because her face was set. She bent down, scooped up two sneakers and a plastic cat-food dish, wrenched open the dryer door, threw them in, slammed the door and hit some buttons on the control panel. The dryer roared into thuds and clatters that shook the walls.

"*What the hell are you trying to do?*"

"I just, *I just wanted to—*"

"*What was last night all about?*"

"*I'm sorry I—*"

"*Are you a complete moron?*"

"Did you, did you tell him?"

"No, thanks, *you* told him."

Ah, man, hated by Oscar. Didn't want that.

"*And now here you are at my party!*"

If sarcasm could kill, he'd be dust. He'd forgotten how good she was at mean. Her eyes cut away the two decades easily, and he saw it again, in her glare the knife that had severed and kept them apart in the first place. He'd forgotten but now could feel it, the truth of her, the truth of him and her. The truth he'd known while leaving Fredericton for Rochester, that this knife had finished off their hearts.

"*I just wanted to thank Oscar for the tickets. For Dylan.*"

Leah's eyes wide and incredulous, her head tilted to deal with a moron.

"You mean for *paying Jason to go with you?*"

"Well—"

"*He had to pay Jason fifty dollars before he'd go with you.*"

Ah shit.

"*Oh, good, you're drunk.*"

Stooping in the foaming beer to pick up the shards of brown

glass, he cut himself, then had to lean back against the washing machine.

"*Don't step in it. Jesus.*"

She moved past him to an open closet where the household brooms and mops were kept, good proper convenient household. He leaned against the washer and breathed. He thought he could smell burning plastic. Burning plastic cat-food dish.

"Okay. I'm sorry. *I'm sorry. I'm sorry for what we did, and I'm—*"

"*Don't worry. So am I.*"

"*—sorry for Oscar. I just want to get to know Jason. I won't bug you any—*"

"*Bobby?*" Smiling, shaking her head, not looking at the drunken moron as she swept up his broken bottle. "*Why do you even think Jason's yours?*"

Falling to all fours, he helped himself up to standing. He didn't look at her. One sock was wet with beer and he limped it past, to the door. He fumbled at the knob, swatting her hand when she shouted *Jesus* and made to help him. Burning plastic making them both cough.

Wet sock on the linoleum, a little counter-slap to the beat of his limping, you could almost smile walking past, in view of the living room. Concerned rising murmurs, they had heard the yelling and now they smelled strange smoke as you smacked by with your beer-sock. From a peg in the entranceway he plucked his coat, didn't want to, but while struggling with it one-handed he looked up and nodded to the swirl of Mexicans, Incas, Mayans. He went for his boots. What do you know. All this time, a cat he couldn't feel had been rubbing up against the leg.

The next morning, sitting in his car outside the building supply store, waiting for it to open, he thumped the wallet on his thigh and wondered what a chunk of drywall might cost these days. He also reviewed last night's Red–White game, how it had gone, how the Zookeeper had appeared out of nowhere. Though maybe he'd always known the Zookeeper would arrive, maybe that's why he'd come north to begin with. Can't build bridges, you might as well burn them.

It was storming pretty hard and traffic was slow on the way to campus. Despite the snow he walked quickly in from the parking lot. He could feel the flakes hooking onto the whiskers, he hadn't shaved in a while. The limp was glaring at this pace, no avoiding it, but you didn't want to be late. Didn't want to give them the chance to start talking without you. They'd all read the book, they'd probably read all Ondaatje's books. Someone like Phil would grab the reins and take over, and you don't want to walk in on that. You want to get in the first punches.

Moving through such benevolent big-flaked snow, you could almost feel that things were normal and good. Up all night, he'd slept no more than a fretful two or three hours. The fatigue and the worry that kept him awake was gone now, he was ready for the game. This kind of snow, like the sky is softly falling on your head. Its silence so deep it is a sound, *hush*. An awareness to it all. Snow like this made him think of the words *the baby Jesus*, and — he could see it clearly — a white embossed Christmas card he'd touched with his fingertips as a child. He could remember the card's pasty smell.

Up all night with Ondaatje, he could riff off whole paragraphs if called upon. To back up his points. Take, for instance, when Kip says. Well, this kind of metaphor can also be found in the passage where Hana imagines that.

He can even quote a critic on the book. Last night in the shaky two hours between Leah's delightful Christmas party and his spectacular Red–White game he'd found himself in the library, at the keyboard, searching. *The English Patient* was new enough that there wasn't much on it. Apparently it takes years for academics to work stuff up. But he found a few articles. One by a guy named Bird suited him perfectly, having to do with Ondaatje's good old-fashioned storytelling techniques of withholding information. In the stacks he located the journal and tore Bird out of it, and now in his bookbag on his shoulder Bird felt like the Bible. With Bird as ammo you could start the presentation with something like "It's all very ordinary. Behind the poetry *The English Patient* is a spy story, and a love story, only the whole time James Bond is lying mortally wounded in bed."

He could feel the melting snow as cold ointment against his old dead skin.

It was two minutes before class time when he got to Carleton Hall. As usual they'd all be early. They'd be up there in their strategic chairs, sipping coffee, firing up their synapses, whacking their wit on the ass, flexing their little shoulders. But no one will have gotten started on a good sentence quite yet.

So here you were at the annual Red–White game. Here in a room with a bunch of guys, throwing jokes about winning the beer and pizza. You're taking a while with the gear, the trainer tightening your skates for you after your story about dislocating a knuckle shovelling snow, bizarre how these things happen. The guy kneeling at your feet, grunting. Hey, I like this, says the Bonaduce, what else can you do while you're down there? He tells you to fuck off, guys laugh. You look and notice Harrington isn't laughing, in fact he's rolled his eyes and maybe that's what cements it for you. He's wearing red and you ask for a white jersey. You have fuel to burn.

Jason wasn't here. No surprise, and so what.

You step on. Whetter's suited up too, and they've got some guy dressed as Santa to ref. Girlfriends and scattered others in the stands. Though it's fun bullshit it's the closest thing to a game you've played in a year and the butterflies are going a little, despite everything else. Which makes the game of hockey such a wonderful thing.

You warm up, take a few shots. You can move okay, maybe you can hold your own. In any case here you are starting at right defence. A local TV station has sent a camera guy and he softsteps to centre ice to catch the ceremonial face-off. A Moosehead rep, whose company has funded the beer, stands ready to drop the puck. He actually looks a little nervous. In the penalty box is a three-foot dented mock-up Moosehead beer can, the trophy. One centreman is the team captain, a red-haired pepperpot named Sullivan but called Maniac, and the other is Harrington, who's an assistant captain and has no nickname. The puck gets dropped. Sullivan smiles and doesn't budge, while Harrington, whose teeth are gritted, actually slashes for the stupid thing.

No hitting to speak of, an unwritten code. So lots of goals. Bonaduce himself picked up an assist on his second shift, nice little pass over the Red guy's stick, laying down flat for your streaking White buddy to send him in alone. On the bench then, breathing hard, respite from a world where there's no time to think. A world you're a million times more familiar with, though it's always swiftly brand new. Catch your breath, feel your age, heart pounding, sweating freely, watch the game go by, involuntary groan when your guy hits the post. This is great, take a deep catch-up breath. Look down at your white jersey, look at the shiny lights coming off the black helmet beside you, look at the row of guys identically slumped. Just look around.

Third shift, Harrington put it through his legs trying to go around him, trying to suck him out, make a fool of the stumbly old guy enjoying his first game in a year. Wonky as he was it wasn't hard to fall into a curl and get his ass out to submarine the guy, catch his knee just right, you could feel it bend in the wrong direction, hear the second or two of surprise before the scream.

They carried Harrington off. Bonaduce, Whetter kicked off. Little Christmas present for you there Jace. Whoever you are. Gets fifty bucks, buys me a fucking Coke. Which I accepted with the dumb smile and big eyes of a dog. A Coke.

They'd already put Harrington into a car. In the dressing room there was no one to make Tonya Harding jokes to, except for the silent trainer, who actually smirked a bit — this Harrington was simply not well liked — and who was kind enough to help Bonaduce off with his skates. His skates which, after the good hot shower, after dressing and climbing into the heavy leather coat for the storm out there, after a moment's empty-handed consideration in the hall, he went back for. He picked the blades up out of their pool of water on the dressing-room floor, tucked them under his arm and, out in the parking lot, threw them in the back of the wagon.

This morning, inside Carleton Hall, he could feel snow melting on one side of his face, though you had to assume it was melting on both. Between classes the hallway was crowded. Out of the blue he was bone-deep exhausted, and dizzy in the sudden thudding heat. He paused a moment. Now he was moving sideways, now a wall thankfully against his shoulder. He took a few deep breaths. Something vital was sinking inside. He blinked, closed his eyes, and when he opened them, one eye was almost blind. As if one lid hadn't come up. He touched, and felt eyeball. Blindness was that fast, it was almost as if blinking had done it. Maybe it had.

Grab a little rest here, against the wall. He looked around, pretending to search for some notice announcing some event, a poster on these walls, the ceiling, trying to will his dead eye back. There was the sense of vision close under the surface, not unlike the sense of something huge but somehow forgotten, memory at the tip of the tongue. With the good eye he noted the bland colours, the grey, the beige, the ceiling the colour of nothing but shadow. He shouldn't be standing staring like this. Unshaven Bonaduce, studying walls. Security please, I'd like to report a staring mess loose in the halls of academe.

He'd caught his breath. The eye hadn't come back, but it would. There'd be no more hockey after Harrington, so why was he even doing this, going to talk for three hours about a book? It wasn't the first time he'd asked this question of himself. Well, you sign the name you dah the dah. As you stare into the grey shadows, on the constant verge of teetering because half of you can't see, whispered phrases sweep in and out, grey *English Patient* insights insistent as jingles. Of *course* Caravaggio had claws for hands, the guy *wanted* everything so much ... One vial of morphine equals one chapter of memory ... You can see why writing is appreciated in a grey place like this. Literature wouldn't have a chance anywhere else. You need boredom, you need quiet. Poetry wouldn't survive an arcade. You'd put Ondaatje down, you'd dump your quarters in the slot. The world had turned arcade. He was searching for a silent, beige classroom to talk about something that was rich and sinewy but could only be born in quiet.

The hall was crammed with hurrying bodies, and loud with everyone saying excuse me and brushing his shoulder, which for no reason had come away from the wall. He was late, and Gail Smith would be up there shaking her head, making a display of looking at her watch, and maybe she had already made her head go back, while here he was comically flailing mid-aisle. Before he went down he grabbed a water fountain, managing a graceful dip to take a drink. Keep moving kids, I just wanted a sip here.

There was just no way for those stairs. There might be an elevator somewhere in the building, but could he get to it? And he was already so late, so late, and damn but it felt like the good eye could be dead in another blink. Time to turn back and get gone.

But ah, damn, he had some good stuff to say.

IV

There is something in this more than natural,
if philosophy could find it out.
—*Hamlet*

Maybe we're going a bit too hard on him, he warned. You
can easily give a man a bigger hiding than he can hold.
We're only starting, man, said Shanahan.
—Flann O'Brien, *At Swim-Two-Birds*

OSCAR.
This Margaret had been in the bathroom a long time. It was strange being on a trip with an unknown young woman. Here at the café of a roadside motel barely a half-hour outside of Fredericton. Would anyone see him with her? As if it mattered now, as if it were anything but a bitter joke that such news might get back to Leah.

Why was he doing this?

He only vaguely recalled her as one of the scruffy kids in Bob's driveway looking for the comet, that night he'd driven him home. The sing-along with Bob, the mock-along with Bob.

Maybe she was in the bathroom doing some kind of drug, something for the nerves. If anything, theirs was a nervous mission.

It was a relief to be free of her talking. When he picked her up she'd been shy, but after a few minutes she'd settled down to talk and talk, about Bob of course, Mr. Bonaduce their one thing in common. But how kids communicated these days — I mean, like, y'know, cool. For each word of substance, five fillers, hesitators. Apparently she was in university. Perhaps Jason talked like that with his friends, but one wouldn't imagine so. Though when he'd asked Jason how the Dylan concert went he'd said, "*It ruled*," bobbing his head, genuinely happy about it. Seeing this rare effusiveness, Oscar had been surprised and felt happy for Bonaduce. At the time.

"Sorry."

Margaret slid into the leatherette booth, facing him. Still in the momentum of the slide, she clasped her coffee and brought it to her mouth, slopping some over the rim.

"Not to worry. In fact I ordered us each some apple pie. That okay?"

Margaret shrugged but appeared irritated by something in this. Maybe she was on a diet. Well then, it was good he hadn't ordered the clubhouse sandwiches. She had small eyes in a wide, unreadable face. One of her ears suffered a wild scatter of earrings that was uncomfortable to look at and resisted counting.

"I just thought, who knows when we'll be eating next?"

"Right, so I guess there's no, like, giant hurry."

"No." Woodstock was an hour and half from Fredericton and they were halfway. It wouldn't take a minute to find the hospital, and as hospitals go it would be extremely—

"I mean like, it's not like he's going anywhere without his toes."

She was sort of smiling, a first. And, like a teenager, chewing away on some gum.

"Doesn't sound like he is, no."

"No but I'm just, I mean, I feel like I'm in a hurry because I have this feeling he's afraid."

This hadn't occurred to him, Bob Bonaduce afraid. Well, there would be the general fear of mortality, certainly, and fear of what sounded like a diabolical disease. But not the kind of fear that was assuaged by two friends showing up. One friend showing up.

"Like, he wakes up in a ditch almost dead, and by now he's been alone for two days."

He realized that this Margaret was giving him subtle shit. His one sign of a dip from reverential concern for Mr. Bonaduce — in the form of a man simply wanting some pie — and her voice takes on the tone of, What kind of friend are you? (Would you like me to explain, Margaret?) Clearly she loved Bonaduce. What other entanglements had Mr. Bonaduce wrought here?

Perchance tupping the white youth. Whom hadn't he tupped?

Hard to know how to feel about this. His guts were, in fact, churning.

It was like his own ambivalence was being held out to him on a platter. The sequence of events had, by turns, found him angry, cruel, impatient. Then selfish, then sad. How could you wish such a thing on anyone? He had at last, and at least, been forced to admit what he and Leah both knew — that it was nothing personal, that Bonaduce could have been anyone, and that his and Leah's problems were their own.

"How well do you know Bob?"

This got her. She stopped and thought, then smiled.

"I don't know."

"I think it's exactly the same with me." He nodded instructively for her.

"No, we were like, thinking of getting a place together." Looking him in the eye. Pie was placed in front of her. "Thank you. But I don't know if it was going to be a platonic place or a non-platonic place."

"Ah, I see."

"That's why I phoned your wife. We were going house-hunting, he was supposed to pick me up, and he didn't."

"I see."

"I mean, when he didn't, I knew something was up." She held a forkful of pie under her mouth, which kept itself open between words, just in case pie was forthcoming. "So, I mean, I know Robert *that* well, anyway. That you can trust him."

"Okay. I see." *Robert*, right.

"Sorry." Margaret put her forkful down and pushed the pie away. "I really don't think I can eat. Can we just go?"

Certainly. Oscar wished he could just give her the car. (And what was this almost superior air about those who hadn't learned to drive?)

Why was he doing this at all? Whatever made him nervous about people in general was further exacerbated by sickness and hospitals.

When he'd first asked Leah, challenged her about the affair, she'd denied it. Only after Bonaduce called her in the middle of the night a week later had she confessed. His rage was simple and he'd threatened to leave. She'd parried with marriage counselling. Oscar, it's happened before, let's fix it so it won't happen again. Him incredulous. *Let's* fix it? As in *us* fix it, as in plural? What was his part in this fixing, go to Canadian Tire and fix her up a chastity belt? But, after some time he came to see that, though hurtful, it was not unwise of her to delegate some blame. These failures did take two.

But he was in no mood for the continuing story, including Jason's worried news of Bonaduce stumbling around drunk at some intersquad game and breaking a player's leg, apparently on purpose. Then Jason smiling and shaking his head in amazement, almost admiration. "Dad's a madman," he'd concluded, shrugging, as uncomplicated a gesture as one of Bonaduce's own.

How does one break a leg on purpose? He'd reached down and felt the dense weight of his own leg bone. Good lord. He imagined Bonaduce attacking that too.

Then the big news. At first he'd been only mad when Leah called to him to the kitchen, where she stood hunched over the phone, wide-eyed and mouth open, her hand covering the receiver. She told him that this was someone named Margaret, a friend of Bob's — Oscar was already enraged at the tears rising in Leah's eyes — and Bobby was in a hospital up in Woodstock, his car had gone off the road. Oscar felt his anger drain as her other words spilled out, multiple sclerosis, hypothermia, coma, amputated toes. He'd been found near the U.S. border in his car, in a ditch, he was there overnight. He's, they think he might be paralyzed.

"I see."

"Margaret wants to know if one of us can go to Woodstock with her. She needs a ride. She'll take a taxi if she has to. But she wants to go now. And I — I shouldn't, Oscar. Not yet. I think he's angry that ..."

She was crying and couldn't finish, and he saw that Leah was already deeply involved in a simple new equation that included him: their relationship was less important than Bonaduce's life.

To his surprise, he'd said, "I'll go."

Jittery with too much coffee, he paid the bill. It was his turn to go to the bathroom. Why he was doing this, he still didn't know. Did he want an apology? Maybe. Or maybe his animal side just didn't want Leah near the man again, though the man was very seriously on his back, and though Leah was going to see him in any case, tomorrow or the next day, depending on Oscar's report. Amazing, though, the jealous animal. Could there be something in him that wanted to see his rival lying there crushed and defeated? One could see now how one could be jealous even of the dead. For he'd been jealous anew even after hearing Bob's condition, when he'd asked Leah how it was that this Margaret knew to call her at all and Leah had told him about her calling Margaret first, the day before, to apologize to Bonaduce for things said at the Christmas party. Leah apologizing to Bonaduce? If there was anyone in morality's jurisdiction who should be apologizing it was Bonaduce and Bonaduce alone. From the sounds of it Bonaduce should be apologizing to everyone with whom he'd come within ten feet.

His question led to other questions.

"You mean Jason isn't even his?"

"Jason's his." Leah couldn't look at him. "I was angry."

"Ah. I see. I think you probably got him with that one."

He snorted derisively — he still had enough upper hand for that. It wasn't until he was alone later that he realized she blamed herself for putting him in that ditch, and that this entanglement wouldn't go away but was about to get deeper in ways no one could predict.

He and Margaret climbed back into Leah's little red Neon. His Jeep was in for a starter transplant. It was freezing today, it was unbelievable, this cold snap. He and Margaret huffed and puffed in the bucket seats while the thing warmed up, their breath frosting the windows, Margaret with a pie-shaped styrofoam doggie bag on her lap. She was actually too big for this car. She was a fair bit bigger than he was. Backing out, he twisted around to look and their shoulders pressed, his shoulder and a twenty-year-old young woman's, and he thought of Bonaduce touching her. Had Bonaduce touched her? Of course he had.

"Can we, like, stop at a store?"

"Sure. Of course." The gas station where they'd just eaten had had a store. He tried not to sound impatient. "Do you want to go back?"

"No I mean a sort of big one. One that might sell dice."

"Dice."

"He likes Yahtzee, and I could only find four at home."

"Sure. Okay. A dice store."

It's not like we're like in a giant hurry, Margaret. With his mitt he scraped frost off the inside of the windshield. Hard to imagine anyone surviving this kind of cold. Apparently Bob's old car had kept running till the gas ran out, sometime in the night. The tailpipe was in snow and enough carbon monoxide had floated in to do some damage, Margaret wasn't sure which kind or how much. You couldn't help but think brain damage.

"Were you on the phone with him yourself?"

"No. Like, he wasn't quite there yet."

"He wasn't ... quite there?"

"He wasn't able to. Wasn't up to it."

"Right."

Oscar tried to picture how it was going to be, seeing him. What he'd look like, what he'd do. He reviewed the MS symptoms Margaret had listed for him. Curious, the last one, the euphoria, at end stage. Euphoria, perhaps mind shielding itself from its dying body. Clever, the alternative being horror and agony. Euphoria was curious also because at the beginning there was apparently much depression. Margaret claimed Bonaduce had been here in Fredericton depressed for months and no one had known it. Oscar certainly hadn't. The man had seemed happy enough.

"I wonder if he's talking now?"

Margaret shrugged, staring straight ahead. As though to

suggest, why would talking matter?

Oscar's gloved hands shifted on the steering wheel. The way Bob smiled, looked at you. In his first anger he'd decided Bob Bonaduce had befriended him only as a way to get to Leah. But he knew now that wasn't the case. He'd always known it wasn't. One look at the man and you could see he wasn't like that.

He supposed he was driving to Woodstock because maybe something about him and Bob Bonaduce had survived, something that had nothing to do with Leah.

§

MARGARET.

Woodstock was tiny, and the mall wasn't far from the hospital. On her way from the Shoppers over to the Zellers, she had to double back past the car, where Oscar sat reading the paper. She waved as she crossed in front, but he didn't see her. Maybe it was just his mood. Robert had called him a good guy, but the man was almost a parody of uptight. He'd actually gotten out and fed the parking meter so that he could sit there in the space. When she'd bought him the gift of the newspaper, he'd thanked her, but slowly, like he was worried she might want something in return.

How hard could it be to buy dice in Woodstock? That Robert would want to play was certain, though whether he could play was not, so maybe this was foolishness. She could roll for both of them, he'd like owning one of her arms as his dice slave, he'd like that joke.

Don't worry about Oscar, let the fellow wait. And yet she'd liked Leah, she'd liked the wife. "The wife." Leah had sounded concerned, decent. Apologetic. "If I had only known he was sick ..." "Why did he feel he had to ...?" "I wouldn't have been so ..." Leah felt more like Robert's friend than Oscar did.

Oscar's nervousness at seeing Robert. He who Robert called the best buddy he had here. What kind of friend was that? She pictured Oscar reading his *Globe* in the car, severe little lawyer with the croaking deep voice. Did he stand up in court and accuse people? She had in her pocket Robert's little essay, which at first she wanted to read to Oscar but then decided he wouldn't care, so screw him, great friend. She found it in her laptop and printed it out to bring, on the chance Robert hadn't left it behind on purpose, his painful little thing about Mahatma Gandhi and Bob Dylan and whether they also knew how to skate. Buddha and the jeep, Robert as usual being funny and sad at impossibly the same time. But to suggest he wasn't good at anything. A professional hockey player! And who played an instrument like that, and sang like a tough angel. Though she knew what Robert meant. And that he was talking for her, too.

She groaned at the image of him not being able to roll dice. She walked, angry, wiping away a tear. Between Oscar and Toby, and the hockey team kicking him off, no wonder Robert was fleeing back to the States.

She'd almost cried seeing the bathroom. At first she was angry when he didn't arrive for the apartment-hunting, fuming while she paced, but that soon changed to worry. Robert wouldn't simply forget. She taxied home and saw his clothes gone, the dreamcatcher taken from the window. And new bathroom drywall put up, a clumsy but thorough job that brought tears to her eyes. No letter, not surprising. Robert wouldn't be one for goodbyes.

Here. Chess, Scrabble, cheap little plastic travel games. Eureka, dice. They were small, four of them in a package. They looked weighty though, well made. Good dice. It was absurd to think of some dice being more lucky than any others, but these did. She bounced them in her hand and found herself wondering if Robert was religious.

Only four to the pack. She plucked a second. If Robert was religious it was in a non-conceptual way, like her. Lately when she wondered whether she was still religious or not, the image of a spade pushing into soft fragrant earth came to mind, a memory from the dig in Hawaii. The good smell of God in that earth, wet, dark, as much rot as growth. Robert would agree. On his deathbed if you asked him if he wanted a priest or a really good sandwich, there's no doubt he'd go for the sandwich. Or a bowl of steaming soft ravioli with three kinds of cheese. Drizzle of spiced olive oil. Shit, she hadn't meant *deathbed*, not literally, not aside from the joke.

She realized she hadn't eaten in far too long. She didn't want Oscar's pie. She could go back to the sub place she'd passed. Was Robert feeling religious now? If he was, she wouldn't try to discourage it. She had some books he might like, ecumenical forays from hard dogma, which old friends had given to her, hoping to keep her with them in spirit, intelligent books that had almost worked their way on her but no. In any case her only plan for Robert, her only strategy, was to try to make him feel good. That was the bare religion she followed now: seeing your way to anything good, in spite of the facts.

If it looked and felt right, even if only to make him feel good she'd offer him the second bedroom in the place she'd just—

The man who grabbed her arm wasn't big, but his fingers dug in and you could feel his anger in them. She had just gone through the glass doors and had stood looking around for the car.

"Come with me, please." He was leading her back into the store.

She had walked out with the two packs of dice. They were so small and cost so little and she'd forgotten them with Robert waiting for her a few blocks away in a hospital bed. She didn't know what to say, how to begin. You couldn't explain things to people. She resisted the man's pull, turned around and waved and yelled *"Help!"* to Oscar's car. Oscar was looking at her, rolling down the window. She laughed while shouting *"Sorry."*

§

It doesn't take a lot of body to drive. One eye worked, one arm was pretty good. He sat back and tried to relax. As long as he didn't have to brake for a moose, the left heel pressing dumbly down on the gas was all the foot he would be needing. Around Woodstock, with the border a half-hour away, he began to practise clearly saying "Utica, New York" and "visiting relatives." This he changed to "on business," which came out less floppy. After you passed the breathalyser, what would a cop do when he discovered a slurring man hadn't had a beer?

He was freezing, and even in the depths of his leather coat he couldn't get warm. He pushed at the heater controls incessantly, maybe that was why he went into the spin. Or maybe it was the search for music. Each time he lost another station to static he wedged his knee up under the wheel to free his hand for the dial. Whatever caused the spin, when he woke in the ditch classical music was on, and he would spend the rest of the night with the CBC.

He'd lost consciousness but came to remembering the feel of the black ice, the sick angling-off, the vertigo, the windshield framing all the wrong things, the car pointing backwards, neither steering wheel nor brakes touching the slide one bit. Big helpless hunk of fast metal loose in the night. Had he actually thought, "If only the tires were skates," or was he just thinking it now?

The car was on its side. The bump on his head showed him how the driver's side window had been broken. Not much blood. His good shoulder was wrenched from its socket. The seat belt held him in position still. He could not feel his legs.

The windshield was in place but fissured along a thousand lines, a Jack Frost pattern, opaque. The passenger window, his lone view out, pointed straight up. Through it he could see shadowy tree branches and, beyond them, stars.

It took a while to understand that the car was still running. Old slant-six just idling away. Then his hand was on the key, thinking *explosion*. Then thinking *freezing to death* if he turned it off. If it hadn't caught fire yet maybe it wouldn't. He could smell no gas. If he turned it off, would it turn back on when it got cold? He took his hand off the key. He had maybe a quarter-tank, at most. He'd been waiting to fill up more cheaply over the border.

He did turn off the radio. He quieted his breathing, and listened. He'd left the road on ice, so no skid marks pointing the way. He couldn't remember hitting any trees. Had he ploughed a visible path? Not a lot of people would be making the journey, at midnight, into northern Maine. Maybe some drunks from Woodstock going to Houlton for the strippers. He imagined an oldtimer hockey team, a string of three or four rowdy cars, we'd all be lucky if they noticed the road, let alone the ditch beside it.

It was maybe half an hour before he heard a car and it was faint. It sounded like he was well off the highway, and maybe down an embankment. If that was a truck he was hearing, he was even further away. In the branches overhead there was no hint of headlights as it passed, its noise fading into the fucking quiet of the idling car. His eye moved to the steering wheel, the rubber panel you pushed to honk at a car in front of you, to honk at a passing car as you lay freezing in a ditch. He couldn't even remember what his horn sounded like, some wire rusting through ten years ago.

He began renewed attempts to get himself out of his belt. Even if he succeeded in this, with no decent arms or legs what were the chances of him climbing up, pushing open that door against gravity, hauling himself out?

He knuckled the radio back on, it was a classical piece he knew, a famous Christmas one, something from the *Nutcracker*? He was halfway into seeing sugarplum fairies, into making the best of this bad time, when the smell kicked him in the nose.

He had shit himself. There was no mistaking it. It hadn't happened during the skid, it hadn't happened during the crash, it hadn't happened when he'd been out cold. It had just happened now. It was still happening, the acrid stench building. His body emptying itself, muscles he couldn't feel.

Only one thing in the car was moving. He could see it, lit by the newly risen moon. The defrost fan was blowing on it, tickling it — the old good-luck charm air freshener. The cardboard tree shape was doing a little dance.

When the car died, the sound of its absence was awful, God it really was awful, and partly for this reason he groaned and groaned to fill it.

He didn't know if he'd been asleep. Terror and panic, if it went on and on, was a sort of huge sleep, so wild and full it was like bad, bad, dreaming. You could control it or not control it like you could or couldn't a nightmare. If you can see your own panic, who is it panicking? You can get bored with panic. Exhausted with it in any case. Too tired to be afraid. Too tired to be or do anything. Except die, the one thing that takes no effort at all.

His brain could still babble to itself like an idiot. Monkey-mind, in and out of sleep, chattering, even making lists, too stupid to know it should be nothing but afraid. He found his brain wondering if it should buy a Christmas present for Fournier's girlfriend or not, and what was her name again? He watched his brain fall into a dark, wet crater with Kip, defusing a bomb, over and over. He woke once in the middle of seeing himself writing in Marg's computer, he was writing something that he may have in fact written or maybe was composing only now, about all the guys and their superstitions. The famous ones you saw on TV, Patrick Roy jumping over the blue line on his way off, step on a crack break your mother's. That pitcher who throws an inning then races to the dugout and brushes his teeth at the water cooler, not caring who sees, superstition bigger than shame. The good zone you seek is delicate and there's nothing of it to hold on to, which is why guys have their little thing, they have to be first out or last out of the dressing room, hoping some other guy won't push in, being on the same charm. Shamrock, Buddha, girlfriend's bandana, lucky rock. Trinket in the pocket a trick to keep luck close to your body. Eat a salad, spaghetti, a peach, exactly four hours before the whistle. Have sex don't have sex, drive a car take a taxi. In the d-room some interesting ones, most of them camouflaged in the hubbub getting ready. A guy whose job grants him daily laundered underwear dons a stinking undershirt that's nothing but stringy rags, more dead skin and dirt than fibre, last washed in 1986. A guy always slaps his face hard, twice, or it's his skates laced up then taken off then laced up again, and he'll be late on the ice rather than interrupt this. Number 12 whacks the goalie's pads twelve times. In the road-restaurant at the pre-game meal no one's surprised to see a teammate freak out over his baked potato when he's told, Sorry, we're out of chives. Bonaduce reflecting a moment, then typing that it's like you're with a bunch of fishermen all dangling lures to entice the big luck trout. You've been doing your thing for so long you no longer see it. Your left skate is always first. You can't not start with the left. Sometimes you catch yourself, and ask what would happen if I just went ahead and put on my stupid right skate? You don't even risk it. It feels like doom. You don't want to play around with this stuff. You're typing in her laptop that you understand nothing about luck, meaning you know nothing about anything.

Except that you're so tired you're on the other side of everything you've known. You're cold and living off something vital, draining it. You want advice, you want magic, you want your luck back, any luck you've ever had, especially now that terror has arisen, terror that isn't crazy and has brought you through the crust of dreams into clear time, terror that claws this present moment as though it were the inside of a coffin.

. . .

They were apparently real. Or as real as sight was real. They were lit up from within and impossible, because he knew that it was night and that real life was sideways in a car.

Maybe his screams had brought them, maybe he had screamed, and screamed himself backwards into dreams. They were lit up and sometimes alone, sometimes together, appearing out of nowhere and through no effort on his part that he knew of.

At first he thought they were here to help him get out of the car, thought they had real bodies and could help. He could hear them as they approached, one by one, he could hear them and he probably yelled, *Who's here! Who's here!* and then here they were, right in the car but not looking at him, not helping at all, knowing he was there and even his situation but doing nothing. Guys he hadn't thought of in years. His grandmother. An aunt whose name he couldn't for the life of him. Jan Dionne, Gail Smith, Whetter. Toby. Fournier. They all came, each in their time, or perhaps all at once, none of them looking at him. Here was Leah, and here was Jason with her, but they were just faces in the line of teachers, friends and teammates, and they ignored him in no way more special.

He woke out of his own gibberish into a melting roomscape, into fragments that began and ended in dream-swirl. Once, the content of wakefulness was nothing more than the prodding weight of a headache. Another time it was knowing that he was finally warm. If he opened his eyes, seeing with only the one, what he saw was good because it was less frantic than his dreams.

Waking meant a different kind of seeing. The sun hard through the orange curtains was best, the light making the fabric more orange than orange, you could taste it, it quenched the hunger for all the sights he had ever been denied.

Sometimes vision leapfrogged a dark tangled hump and landed him in sudden clarity, where he understood not only the mechanics of seeing, but also the profound friendship between the seer and the seen. The radiator under the curtain was white, unless curtain went brighter orange and radiator turned grey. The change took place as much in his eye as it did outside of it. The one eye made this a simpler certainty, though these understandings, and clarity itself, may have been drug-induced. In any case the lucid times were but pinholes in the swirl, respites from endless slogging through mud.

Drugs were a dam, and pain a swelling reservoir behind it, deep and vast and ready to drown him if the dam gave way. Sometimes pain did push through a crack and overcome him with such ease it was terrifying. Body's terror. Quick nod to the nurse's offer of morphine. Christine wouldn't look at him, she would administer the IV injection with sober efficiency and an air of withholding. Marie though, Marie was with him eye to eye, and she would joke how some guys just wanted to keep partying.

Drugs could do anything. They could make you content with diapers and stupidity. Oh yes the unbearable lightness of peeing, whenever and wherever. Drugs could roll you over and sponge your fouled nether zone and your dead unit, so dead it ignored all nursely attention. Drugs would not allow the tiniest bit of shame to stick.

He woke, one eye staring up at the little TV set, hanging from its mechanical arm. In one of his home towns he'd watched such a thing from a dentist chair. Waking up this way irritated him — without his consent they'd turned it on and plugged him in — plastic earphone was jammed in his right ear — them assuming he preferred the jokes of *Frasier* to the less-staged ones unfolding out the window, or in his body, which was maybe or maybe not coming back to him, a finger or a foot too long hidden from sense but now uncurling, unwrapping itself like a gift. Who knows, though — perhaps he had consented to the TV. Perhaps *Frasier*, these jokes, perhaps distraction was part of the cure. The most irritating thing about this TV was that the noise was so close, wedged into his headbone in fact, while the action it was supposedly connected to hovered up there near the ceiling. In the tinny earphone the acting sounded like barking. Punctuating each joke, the canned laughter was so loud it was only static. It sounded exactly like surf. Each time the distant Frasier pulled a face, in your head the surf roared.

He woke to Marg and Oscar at the foot of the bed, whispering about whether or not to leave.

He smiled, but didn't know if it showed.

They were quiet and nervous at first, afraid of looking at him. He managed to meet Marg's eye and they held it for a second, and when she understood he was okay she loosened up and could laugh a little. Oscar, poor Oscar, had to begin with a speech about Leah wanting him to say how sorry she was and such, and that she would visit soon. Infected by Oscar's formal tone, Marg added that Fournier was also on his way, and that he had a cheque for him, from his old hockey-team owner, and that it was a lot of money.

It was good to see his friends. Though odd to see these two together. Two worlds. And Fournier coming, a third. Leah would make it four. It would be too much. All the smiling.

Silence fell as they sussed he wasn't too good at speaking. Marg elbowed Oscar and said that, well, the important news here was that she'd just been arrested for shoplifting.

"I was so out of it I totally forgot the thing about *paying* for things." She dropped two rattling Baggies onto his chest. "These'll be ready when you are."

"Bones," he said, in a voice of inventory. Though it sounded more like "bo's."

"Yeah, and here" — Marg dug into her book bag — "Toby brings you this. We should probably hide it." She placed a bottle of home-made wine on his side table.

"Less see." He tilted his head at it. Marg understood, and spun the bottle by the neck so he could read the label. It read, "Gift Horse '98."

"I brought something too," said Oscar, again taking his cue from Marg. He rifled through a Zellers' bag.

Bonaduce tried for "Merry Christmas" but said, "May Chriss," which they didn't hear over Oscar's rustling.

"He decides to like, 'do some shopping' while I'm being interrogated." Marg snapped her gum.

"I realized," Oscar said, bringing out a new walkman, encased in its package, "that here you were, stuck up here in nowhere with no music. Leah had these two in her car. She stole them from me, I stole them back." He took two cassettes from his coat pocket and put them on his side table, then began tugging at the walkman's vacuum-formed packaging.

Bonaduce made his head fall to the side. He read Oscar's printing. One tape was "Van Morrison," the other "Early Bowie."

"Suck here, wih, briss."

"Sorry? What?"

"Stuck, here, wih, *Brits*."

"Bob, when I come back up I'll bring—" Oscar visibly stilled his panic by taking a breath. He looked up at Bonaduce, meeting his eye for the first time. He smiled ironically. "Next time, I'll bring you your damn Everly Brothers or whatever it is you like."

"Than's, Ah'car."

Bonaduce managed what might be a smile too, and a little waving finger of demand. Bring me something pure. Roy Orbison. Gene Pitney. Something that doesn't make your thoughts for you.

"Well, so where'd they, like, put your stuff?" Marg suddenly getting all stern with an idea. "Your tapes. Your guitar."

He shook his head and raised his brow just enough for her to see.

Marg walked off on her mission. Right, indeed, where was the car, where was his stuff. He remembered getting hauled up, out of the passenger door, the pain of this, the pain forcing him beyond relief into bad clarity, it was almost like leaping right out of his damn body into the bitter night. But, yes, he'd seen the strewn back seat. Leaving town he'd pretty much just thrown it all in, but now it looked liked someone had hit the blender switch. When they lifted him out of his own mess he'd been embarrassed by his smell, but then also by the brown skeleton of a Christmas tree bungeed to the roof.

"Bob?"

Oscar hovered nearer and hunched in, his deep voice hushed to a conspiratorial croak. He was going to get serious now, which was fine.

"Bob?"

Bonaduce lifted his eyebrows for him. You don't want to talk too much.

"Leah, she wanted me to tell you—"

"No. Ah'car? *Oss*-car."

"Yes? What?"

"Sorry."

He tried to show with his eyes that people, friends, don't do to each other what I did to you. You just don't.

"It's — it's not your fault. You had — you two had unfinished business."

Right. So we did. But that brand of business is never finished.

"Leah said, she wanted me to say, about the fight you two had, that Jason, well hell man, Jason *is* yours. Is your son." Oscar shook his head, smiling at the lunacy he hadn't witnessed. "And that she's sorry. She was pretty angry, I guess."

Bonaduce had known, of course. How could he have ever not known? Just look at the boy's body.

"No he'sh not." He tried to smile wisely. Oscar didn't know

what to make of this.

"And, and also that, Leah said to say also that Jason wasn't paid to go to see Bob Dylan with you."

Bonaduce smiled. His muscles felt it to be a grin.

"In fact, he loved it, he loved the concert, he raved about it, and he loved going with you, I'm not just—"

"Ah'sar? Does' mahher."

"Sorry? Does ...?"

"Doesn't. Matter."

He tried to show with his eye all he'd learned trapped in his car. How phantoms had arisen before his face, and how, when they dissolved, he was free of them and had always been free of them, for they were just phantoms all along, and isn't it funny how you have to keep learning what you already know. He tried to show with his face, too, that what mattered here was not Jason but you, Oscar, *you*, because it is you leaning over the bed, blinking, tender. Just like you don't matter when it's Marie sitting here on her stool, skipping the grey peas for the decent dessert, attuned to him, knowing when he's geared up ready for another spoonful, whereas doing the same duty Christine's mind would be elsewhere and so in fact she wasn't here at all. What matters is this light streaming glory through the orange curtain, lighting up half your face, Oscar, dramatic, noble blood-colour, the rest of your face in shadow, it's—

"Ah'sar, you ..."

"What? Bob?"

"You look *grea'*."

Poor Oscar, on the verge now. Sometimes you really shouldn't say anything.

He may have dozed because the light was different and Marg was clomping back in, and Oscar seemed to have moved his chair further back. Marg put a sack of his cassette tapes on his bedside table, beside Oscar's two. She stood over him, shaking her head.

"You broke your guitar."

Twank. He remembered, yes. The sound. First the spinning. Tumbling. Then hitting a final something, the ground probably, with a pow and a *twank* of a snapping string.

He nodded for her. He'd heard its death song.

Oscar was grateful to go through the tapes and organize them for him while Marg disappeared into the little bathroom.

He cocked his head to the sound of the water running, its rush interrupted by something moving under it, being washed. Marg was hugely entertaining. Now paper towels ripped from the dispenser. Sounds of Marg drying, dabbing, then periods of no noise, of some kind of care.

She used the stool to hang the wet dreamcatcher, fastening its cord to the curtain rod, tying it tightly and well, setting up house, betraying that she had talked to someone and had learned he would be in this room for a while.

She clambered down, saw he had been watching her and smiled, pointing back to the dreamcatcher. She sighed, looked around, sat happily on the foot of his bed. When she realized she was sitting an inch from his feet, from his fresh wounds, she gasped, leaped up.

"Sorry! Sorry! Did I—?"

"Did' feel a thing. S'okay." He paused. "Si' a'ywhere on me y' wan'."

No one laughed at what was a decent joke. They were more numb than he was. He laughed at this, laughed again, then coughed, and started coughing, he hated the coughing because at the base of the deepest ones you could taste exhaust, and the taste filled his head with the memory and the fact of poison.

He tried to sleep. Fournier coming with lots of money. Pack his bags with money, buy a new car, drive Marg to Maui, she could show him Maui. This he would love, because so would she, wild about me. Lie on the hot sand, he was wearing a big huge wacky bathing suit, cover his delicate condition, his diapered nether bulk. He'd listen to the surf. The canned laughter, the Maui trucks. Marg is soothing his burned face, her vials of morphine lined up in the sand. He's still thinking of Leah. Frasier's funny little brother is everywhere. Marg content pointing out parrots flitting tree to tree, God aren't they big, perched shoulder-to-shoulder. In trees black against the sand.

"Robert? Did— What? 'Parrots'?"

He could hear himself laughing.

But poor Marg was crying, he'd made her cry, she was grabbing her face, trying to stop.

"Mar'? 'S okay. Cry."

"I'm not." She smiled, her face wet, her body lurching with sobs.

He could feel his laugh. He could also feel his tears, not on the side of his face but when they landed in his ear.

"Mar'? Me either."

ACKNOWLEDGEMENTS

For their insight, heart, and humour, I'd like to thank
Rita Donovan, Dede Gaston, Carolyn Swayze,
Beverley Endersby, and Jan Geddes. All lapses in form,
coherence, taste, and good sense — remain mine.